A Handbook of Pharmaceutical Sales

A Handbook of Pharmaceutical Sales

Dr. Subrata Ray
Ph.D. in Marketing, University of North Bengal,
MBA (Marketing & HR), IGNOU, New Delhi,
PG Diploma in Pharmaceutical Sales,
PG Diploma in Journalism & Mass Communication,
PG Diploma in Tea Management,
MA in Rural Development, IGNOU, New Delhi.
Former Field Sales Officer, Glenmark Pharmaceuticals Ltd, Mumbai, India.
Corporate Trainer – NHPC, India Post, EPCH, and MSME (Govt. of India)
Academic Expert & Industry Consultant in Pharmaceutical Marketing
Trainer & Mentor for Entrepreneurs and Sales Professionals.

Arindam Bhowmick
B.Sc. (Hons.) in Physics, IIM Calcutta (EPBM)
Former General Manager – Sales & Marketing (India), Exeltis India, Mumbai
Former Head – Marketing (India), Cadila Pharmaceuticals Ltd.
Former Marketing Manager, Sandoz (India)
Former Brand Manager, Ranbaxy Ltd
Industry Consultant in Pharmaceutical Marketing,
Academic Advisor and Curriculum Developer in various Management Institutes.

PharmaMed Press™
An imprint of BSP Books Pvt. Ltd.
4-4-309/316, Giriraj Lane,
Sultan Bazar, Hyderabad - 500 001.

A Handbook of Pharmaceutical Sales
***by* Subrata Ray and Arindam Bhowmick**

Published by

™ **PharmaMed Press**
An imprint of BSP Books Pvt. Ltd.
4-4-309/316, Giriraj Lane, Sultan Bazar, Hyderabad - 500 001.
Phone: 040-23445688
E-mail: info@pharmamedpress.net
www.bspbooks.net/www.pharmamedpress.net

ISBN: 978-93-49562-10-3 (Hardback)

This Book is dedicated to
my wife Dola Ray Som and my son Gooblu.

\- **Dr. Subrata Ray**

This Book is dedicated to
my father Late Shri Pabitra Kumar Bhowmick,
my mother Smt. Maya Bhowmick,
my wife Sumana, daughter Lisa and my sisters.

\- **Arindam Bhowmick**

Preface

The complex world of pharmaceutical sales, situated in the bustling corridors of India's healthcare ecosystem, the life-saving medications stand between hope and healing, remains largely unexplored. This universe, teeming with scientific accuracy, strategic foresight, and human compassion, forms the foundation for how millions of people obtain essential pharmaceuticals across various regions, from urban hospitals to isolated village clinics.

Written by two eminent experts with over 40 years of combined experience in India's pharmaceutical industry, the "Handbook of Pharmaceutical Sales" is a ground-breaking synthesis of academic rigour and practical knowledge. This thorough manual, which was written by Dr. Subrata Ray and Mr. Arindam Bhowmick, is not just another textbook; rather, it is a live document that embodies pharmaceutical marketing in its purest form.

Beginning in the pharmaceutical sales trenches at Glenmark Pharmaceuticals Ltd., one of India's most impressive pharmaceutical success stories, Dr. Ray's journey developed from a 1970s start-up to a global powerhouse that ranks among the top 15 generic businesses globally. From the busy markets of Siliguri to the tranquil hills of Kalimpong, Mirik and Kurseong, from the tea gardens of the Dooars to the pristine valleys of Sikkim, from the under developed markets of Uttar Dinajpur district to the uninformed markets of Jalpaiguri district, his three-year journey through the difficult terrain of North Bengal gave him unmatched insights into the difficulties of pharmaceutical distribution in India's varied geographical and cultural landscape. He is in a unique position to integrate the frequently separated fields of theory and practice because of this grassroots experience, his subsequent academic endeavours with an MBA and a Ph.D in Marketing, and his 17-year stint as an Assistant Professor at the Department of Management, University of North Bengal.

The remarkable career path of Mr. Arindam Bhowmick, who rose from a Medical Representative of Emcure Pharmaceuticals Ltd. in Siliguri headquarters to the General Manager – Sales & Marketing at Exeltis (India) in Mumbai, is a testament to this foundation and one of the most inspirational journeys in Indian pharmaceutical marketing. Mr. Bhowmick, a graduate in

Physics and an alumnus of the esteemed IIM, Calcutta, has held executive positions at several of India's largest pharmaceutical companies, including Exeltis India, Emcure, Ranbaxy, Sandoz, Cadila Pharmaceuticals, and Lupin. This handbook becomes a strategic compilation rather than just an instructive manual thanks to his experience in managing important pharmaceutical portfolios, planning pan-India product launches, and creating ROI-driven brand strategies.

The pharmaceutical sector in India is currently undergoing a significant transformation. India's pharmaceutical industry offers tremendous potential and previously unheard-of complexity as the world's largest supplier of generic medications and vaccines, accounting for more than 50% of the demand for vaccinations worldwide and 40% of the demand for generics in the US. The industry's transition from a mostly domestic concentration to a worldwide manufacturing hub has drastically changed the dynamics of pharmaceutical sales and marketing. A new generation of professionals is needed to drive corporate growth while navigating legal frameworks, understanding varied consumer segments, using digital technology, and upholding ethical standards.

Through thirteen painstakingly written chapters that cover every aspect of pharmaceutical sales, from comprehending the global industry landscape to mastering future trends and breakthroughs, this handbook responds to these changing expectations. Beginning with industry foundations and gradually moving to specialised areas like product lifecycle management, regulatory compliance, and emerging technology, the writers have cleverly structured the content to reflect the real-world journey of pharmaceutical professionals.

This textbook stands out for its constant dedication to academic depth while maintaining practical usefulness. Every chapter skilfully combines the theoretical frameworks with real-world case studies to guarantee that readers—whether they are academics researching industry dynamics, seasoned professionals looking to expand their knowledge, or students starting their pharmaceutical careers—find immediate relevance and useful insights.

The authors' profound admiration for these frontline warriors who manage difficult territories, negotiate complex friendships with healthcare professionals, and act as vital conduits between pharmaceutical innovation and patient care is evident in their special attention to the investigation of medical representatives as the cornerstone of pharmaceutical sales. The handbook's discussion of this topic extends beyond traditional sales tactics to look at the relationship-building abilities, ethical considerations, and emotional intelligence that set great medical salespeople apart in the current competitive environment.

The thorough examination of distribution networks highlights one of the most important but frequently disregarded facets of pharmaceutical success in India. The complicated web of connections between producers, distributors, stockists, and retailers determines the effective and economical delivery of life-saving drugs. The writers' thorough field experience and understanding of these relationships give readers insights that are usually only obtained through years of direct experience in the field.

The revolutionary effect of technology on pharmaceutical sales is addressed in a forward-looking manner that takes into account both the present and the potential for the future. From digital detailing to artificial intelligence applications, from sales force automation to predictive analytics, the guide equips readers to adjust to technology advancements and strategically use them to gain a competitive edge.

The writers emphasise ethical and regulatory issues, reflecting their understanding that pharmaceutical sales operate within a context of social responsibility that goes far beyond commercial goals. A thorough examination of ethical marketing practices, compliance standards, and the changing regulatory environment gives readers the information they need to confidently and honourably traverse these crucial domains.

The human element of pharmaceutical sales is perhaps the most significant topic covered in this guidebook. It acknowledges that the primary objective of enhancing human health outcomes is at the heart of every prescription, product introduction, and market penetration plan. The authors' humanistic approach, which has been moulded by years of interacting with patients, healthcare professionals, and industry stakeholders, transforms pharmaceutical sales from a solely commercial endeavour into a career that is driven by a sense of purpose.

The guidebook is a priceless tool for educational institutions that offer pharmaceutical marketing courses because of its pedagogical approach, which includes case studies, suggested questions, and multiple-choice tests. Simultaneously, its practical focus ensures that working professionals can immediately apply the ideas and tactics provided in their respective organisational settings.

The need for qualified professionals who comprehend both the science and the art of pharmaceutical sales is becoming more and more important as India's pharmaceutical industry continues its impressive growth trajectory, which is being driven by factors like rising healthcare awareness, expanding insurance coverage, demographic shifts, and growing international recognition of Indian pharmaceutical capabilities. This handbook provides a thorough manual for building these kinds of skills.

More than just a professional guide or academic exercise, the "Handbook of Pharmaceutical Sales" reflects the writers' dedication to fostering the next generation of pharmaceutical executives who will guide the sector's future while upholding its core purpose of meeting the health needs of people. Dr. Ray and Mr. Bhowmick have made a significant contribution to pharmaceutical education and professional development with their work, one that will surely impact how pharmaceutical sales are seen, taught, and carried out in India and elsewhere.

With the promise of not only information gain but also a greater understanding of the significant influence that qualified pharmaceutical professionals have on global health outcomes, this handbook invites readers to set out on a life-changing adventure through the intriguing world of pharmaceutical sales.

-Author

Contents

Chapter 9: Pharmaceutical Product Launch and Product Lifecycle Management

Chapter 10: Communications and Promotional Strategies of Pharmaceutical Products

Chapter 11: Data Analysis and Market Research

CHAPTER 1

Overview of the Global Pharmaceutical Industry

The pharmaceutical sector largely fuels the modern era's advancements in biotechnology, medicine, and therapeutic interventions. This economic sector encompasses the research, development, production, and marketing of drugs and treatments for a variety of illnesses. With time, it has grown into a multitrillion-dollar global sector that affects economies and health outcomes all around the world.

The pharmaceutical industry has changed remarkably since its modest beginnings. Tiny apothecaries selling herbal remedies made up the bulk of the industry at the beginning of the 1800s. These apothecaries gave rise to modern pharmaceutical companies thanks to industrialization and scientific advancements. Alexander Fleming made important discoveries in 1928, such as the discovery of penicillin, which completely changed medicine, leading to the development of antibiotics.

A small group of powerful businesses known as "Big Pharma" dominate the pharmaceutical industry. Pfizer, Merck, Johnson & Johnson, and Novartis are the industry leaders, with extensive worldwide distribution networks and strong research pipelines. These businesses invest billions of dollars in research and development (R&D) every year to stay ahead of the curve and stay creative.

Regulatory frameworks, patent laws, and market exclusivity are among the factors that influence the market dynamics of the industry. Using patents to briefly create a monopoly on new drugs allows pharmaceutical corporations to recoup their research and development expenses. However, generic medication manufacturers can reproduce less expensive copies once patents expire, creating competition and often driving down prices.

The research and development industry is essential to the pharmaceutical business. The process of bringing a novel drug to market is challenging, costly, and time-consuming. It can cost up to billions of dollars and often takes more than ten years. Drug discovery is the first step in the process, where scientists look for and evaluate possible molecules. The next step for chosen candidates (NCEs) is preclinical testing, which entails safe and effective animal and laboratory tests.

Three stages of clinical trials follow preclinical testing. Phase I trials use a small, healthy volunteer sample to assess participant safety. Phase II trials expand the focus to encompass side effects and effectiveness in a larger patient population. Phase III studies involve thousands of participants in order to confirm medication efficacy, monitor adverse effects, and assess the drug in comparison to standard medical methods. If the drug development project is successful, they apply for approval of a new drug application (NDA) to regulatory agencies including the FDA and the European Medicines Agency (EMA).

The pharmaceutical industry implements strict regulatory criteria to guarantee the quality, safety, and effectiveness of drugs. The FDA, EMA, and the World Health Organization (WHO) are regulatory bodies that set rules and procedures for the development, testing, and marketing of drugs. These institutions are critical to the approval process, post-marketing surveillance, and enforcement of compliance.

Regional differences in requirements complicate the regulatory landscape for pharmaceuticals. The European Medicines Agency (EMA) oversees the European Union, meaning that companies have to abide by multiple national regulations in addition to EU standards. In contrast, the FDA focuses its regulations primarily on the U.S. market. The highest authority for biomedical research in India is the Indian Council of Medical Research (ICMR). It has led the way in addressing a range of health issues, including non-communicable and infectious diseases. The advances made by ICMR have had a significant impact on both public health and medical understanding. The head of the Central Drugs Standard Control Organization, the Drugs Controller General of India, is located next to DCGI. To protect the public's health and safety, they control the production, marketing, importation, and distribution of pharmaceuticals and cosmetics in India.

Because of scientific and technological advancements, the pharmaceutical industry is continually changing. Precision medicine is becoming increasingly popular. It tailors treatments to the particular genetic profile of every patient. Biotechnology has transformed industries such as vaccinations and cancer treatment. Additionally, the integration of AI and machine learning is improving the process of finding and developing new medications, enabling the identification of potential compounds and more accurate prediction of clinical trial outcomes.

The COVID-19 pandemic highlighted the quick rate of discovery and critical importance of the industry. Organizations like Pfizer-BioNTech and Moderna have demonstrated the benefits of international cooperation and the promise of emerging technologies through their swift development and release of vaccines, particularly mRNA vaccines. By creating and producing vaccines that assisted in shielding millions of people from the virus, Serum Institute of India (SII), Bharat Biotech, Zydus Cadila, Biological E, Panacea Biotec, Indian Immunologicals, and Mynvax significantly contributed to India's response to the COVID-19 pandemic.

The pharmaceutical industry has several challenges despite its successes. The necessity for ongoing innovation, stringent regulations, and high R&D costs present significant barriers to entry and sustainability. Additionally, ethical issues such as advertising methods, medicine accessibility, and prescription pricing often attract public and official attention. The expensive cost of some life-saving drugs raises the question of how to reconcile public health responsibility with business.

Given the continued advancements in genetics, biotechnology, and digital health, the pharmaceutical industry appears to have a promising future. Expected growth factors include rising healthcare spending, the expansion of the middle class, and growing markets in Asia, Latin America, and Africa. Governments, corporations, and academic institutions working together will likely be crucial to resolving global health concerns and encouraging innovation.

Global health is reliant on the intricate and ever-changing global pharmaceutical industry. Despite all of the challenges it encounters, its capacity for innovation and adaptation guarantees that it will keep developing and having an impact on our society. By consistently investing in research and development, adhering to ethical values, and adapting to changing trends, the industry will continue to advance medical knowledge and improve health outcomes internationally.

Introduction to Indian Pharmaceutical Industry

The Indian pharmaceutical industry, sometimes known as the "Pharmacy of the World," is vital to the world health care system. Known for manufacturing generic drugs, the industry has expanded to become a significant player in the global pharmaceutical market, offering competitively priced, high-quality drugs to countries worldwide. This article provides a comprehensive review of the Indian pharmaceutical industry, including its history, growth, key players, regulatory environment, challenges, and opportunities.

The pharmaceutical sector in India dates back to the early 1900s, but it wasn't until independence that it truly took off. Up until the 1970s, multinational corporations—mostly from Western countries—controlled the Indian market. In 1970, the introduction of the Indian Patents Act marked a significant turning point. Because of the act's disregard for product patents, Indian companies were able to produce patented medications at a lower cost using reverse engineering. This change in law made it easier for the generics business to flourish and for domestic pharmaceutical companies to expand.

The Indian pharmaceutical industry has expanded rapidly in recent decades. In 2021, India was the third-largest pharmaceutical manufacturer globally in terms of volume and thirteenth in terms of value. The industry is critical to India's economy, accounting for 8% of all merchandise exports and about 1.72% of the nation's GDP.

One of the primary drivers of this expansion has been the industry's reliance on generic drugs. Indian pharmaceutical companies have mastered the art of producing excellent generic medications at a substantial discount to their name-brand counterparts. Because of these capabilities, India has emerged as a major supplier of affordable pharmaceuticals to both industrialized and poor nations. It's noteworthy to note that Indian generics account for a substantial portion of the drugs used in the US, the world's largest pharmaceutical market.

There are a number of well-known Indian pharmaceutical companies that have achieved success both nationally and globally. Among the prominent figures are:

Sun Pharmaceutical Industries: Founded in 1983, Sun Pharma is one of the largest pharmaceutical companies in India. It creates branded generics, generics with a generic name, and active pharmaceutical ingredients (APIs).

Cipla: Founded in 1935, Cipla is well-known for its creative efforts in creating affordable therapies for various diseases, including HIV/AIDS. It is widely available in more than 80 countries.

Dr. Reddy's Laboratories: Established in 1984, this global pharmaceutical company produces and ships a wide variety of drugs both domestically in India and abroad.

Lupin Limited: Founded in 1968, this firm is well-known for focusing on the therapeutic domains of non-steroidal anti-inflammatory drugs (NSAIDs), cardiology, diabetology, asthma, paediatrics, gastroenterology, and the central nervous system.

Aurobindo Pharma: Founded in 1986, Aurobindo Pharma ranks among the top 10 consolidated revenues. It has a large product selection and is well-known worldwide.

The Central Drugs Standard Control Organization (CDSCO), which falls under the Ministry of Health and Family Welfare, Government of India, is in charge of the legal structure that regulates the pharmaceutical industry in India. Clinical trials, drug standards, approvals for new medications, and import laws are under the purview of the CDSCO.

India's regulatory structure has evolved over time to meet international standards. The 1940 Drugs and Cosmetics Act and its subsequent changes have played a pivotal role in ensuring the efficacy, safety, and quality of pharmaceuticals produced in the country. Furthermore, the establishment of the National Pharmaceutical Pricing Authority (NPPA) in 1997 has significantly regulated the cost of essential medications for the general public.

Despite its extraordinary growth, the Indian pharmaceutical industry faces various obstacles that require resolution to sustain its momentum. Some of them are:

Regulatory Obstacles: Although India's regulatory framework has undergone enhancements, compliance with global standards remains challenging. Innovation and market entry may be hampered by stringent regulations and the drawn-out approval process for new drugs.

Quality Control: Ensuring a consistent standard of quality is crucial in the production of pharmaceuticals. The industry's reputation has occasionally been harmed by instances of subpar and counterfeit drugs. Strengthening quality control procedures is necessary to preserve worldwide trust.

Research and Development (R&D): Historically, the Indian pharmaceutical industry has placed more emphasis on the creation of generic medications than on the identification of novel treatments. Increasing R&D expenditures is essential to promoting innovation and competing with global pharmaceutical conglomerates.

Intellectual Property Rights (IPR): Finding a balance between the need to protect intellectual property and the accessibility of reasonably priced drugs is a challenging task. Finding this balance between fostering innovation and preserving access to essential treatments is vital.

Global Competition: Other low-cost manufacturing hubs, like China, compete fiercely with this industry. Enhancing industrial capabilities and supply chain resilience is necessary to maintain a competitive edge.

The Indian pharmaceutical sector appears to have a promising future due to several factors, including:

Increasing Healthcare Access: The Indian government is focusing on improving healthcare access through initiatives like Ayushman Bharat, public health insurance, and Jan-Aushadhi, reasonably priced quality generic medicines, leading to a significant rise in the need for reasonably priced medications.

Expansion into Biologics: Expected to support further growth, Indian companies are increasingly investing in the production of biologics and biosimilars. These complex molecules possess the ability to significantly alter the treatment of numerous diseases.

Digital Transformation: Utilizing digital technology can make the creation, production, and distribution of pharmaceuticals more patient-friendly, cost-effective, and efficient. Accepting change is necessary to succeed in the digital age.

Global Collaboration: Working together with overseas research facilities and pharmaceutical businesses can help with technology transfer, market expansion, and the creation of novel medicines.

Policy Support: The government must keep offering advantageous policies, incentives, and investments in healthcare infrastructure in order to sustain the industry's growth trajectory.

The Indian pharmaceutical sector is uniquely positioned to take advantage of its capacity to produce generic medications while embracing innovation and quality improvements. Its impact on the provision of affordable healthcare options globally cannot be overstated. The industry can continue to be a pillar of the world healthcare system by addressing legal requirements, enhancing R&D capabilities, and promoting international cooperation. There are many opportunities on the future journey, and the Indian pharmaceutical industry has the potential to go even further and enhance health outcomes around the world if the right strategies are implemented.

Pharmaceutical Companies and their Classification

India's pharmaceutical sector has grown significantly over the last few decades, emerging as a significant global participant in pharmaceutical production and distribution. This evolution is characterized by a number of kinds of pharmaceutical companies, which are based on many factors like ownership, product range, operating type, and market reach. Gaining a thorough understanding of these classifications will help you comprehend the dynamics and structure of the Indian industry.

India's pharmaceutical industry began to flourish after independence thanks to substantial government support and intervention. Public sector undertakings (PSUs) such as Indian Drugs and Pharmaceuticals Limited (IDPL) and Hindustan Antibiotics Limited (HAL) formed a strong industry in the 1950s and 1960s. By enabling domestic companies to reverse engineer copyrighted pharmaceuticals, the 1970 Patent Act—which allowed process patents rather than product patents—helped them advance even further, reducing costs and encouraging innovation.

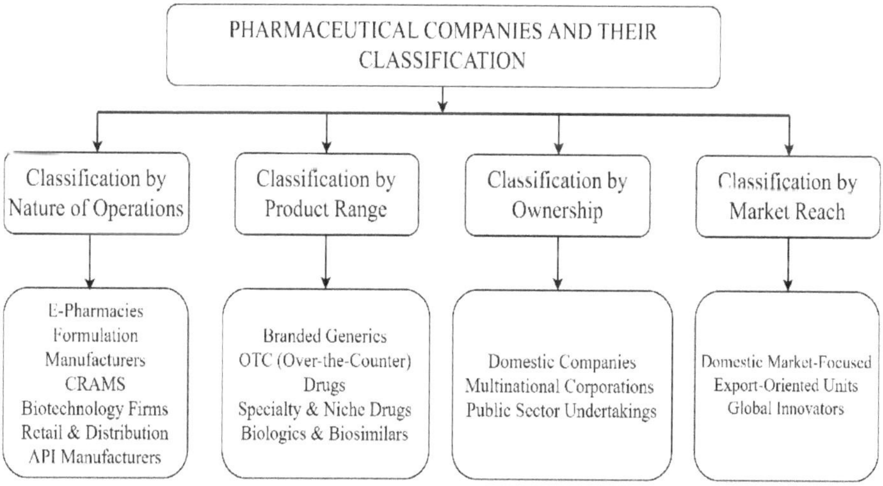

Fig. 1.1 Pharmaceutical Companies and their Classification.

Classification by Nature of Operations

Active Pharmaceutical Ingredient (API) Manufacturers: These companies specialize in making APIs, which are essential components of medications. India manufactures APIs and exports them to a number of countries. Divi's Laboratories and Aurobindo Pharma are two examples of these companies. India's overdependence on China for APIs, however, poses a serious risk. The

PLI programs' purpose is to lessen this reliance by encouraging domestic API production, although it is unclear how successful they will be.

Formulation Manufacturers: These companies are experts in producing finished dosage forms, such as syrups, tablets, capsules, and injectables. Sun Pharmaceutical Industries and Cipla are two of the industry's leading players.

Contract Research and Manufacturing Services (CRAMS): In this industry, businesses provide contract research and manufacturing services. They cater to both domestic and international clients. Jubilant Life Sciences and Piramal Pharma Solutions are well-known CRAMS companies in India.

Biotechnology Firms: These companies develop and produce biopharmaceuticals, which include therapeutic proteins, vaccines, and monoclonal antibodies. The top two biotech businesses in India are Serum Institute and Biocon.

Pharmaceutical Retail and Distribution: This category includes companies that sell and distribute pharmaceutical products. Apollo Pharmacy and MedPlus are two significant players in this industry.

E - Pharmacies: Providing a practical means of making online drug purchases, e-pharmacies have become increasingly popular in India. Popular online pharmacies include 1mg, Pharmeasy, and Netmeds.

Classification by Product Range

Branded Generics: Branded generics make up a significant amount of the Indian pharmaceutical industry. Lupin and Torrent Pharmaceuticals are well-known names in this sector. In this sector, businesses like Torrent Pharmaceuticals and Lupin are well-known.

Over-the-Counter (OTC) Drugs: These are prescription-free medications. Glaxo Smith Kline Consumer Healthcare and Pfizer are two companies with significant over-the-counter product lines.

Specialty and Niche Drugs: These medications aim to treat specific, often chronic medical conditions like diabetes, cancer, and heart disease. Leading providers of specialty pharmaceuticals are Dr. Reddy's Laboratories and Sun Pharma.

Biologics and Biosimilars: Biosimilars are medications that are almost perfect equivalents to biologics, which are sophisticated medications made from living things. In India as well as worldwide, Biocon leads the biosimilars market.

Classification by Ownership

Domestic Companies: These are majority-owned companies founded in India. Among them are Cipla, Sun Pharmaceutical Industries, and Dr Reddy's Laboratories.

Multinational Corporations (MNCs): sometimes known as MNCs, are international pharmaceutical companies with a significant presence in India. They usually bring with them state-of-the-art technologies and standards. Prominent multinational corporations operating in India comprise Novartis, Pfizer, and Glaxo Smith Kline.

Public Sector Undertakings (PSUs): The founding of these state-owned enterprises aimed to supply medicine to meet the urgent needs of the nation. HAL and IDPL are two notable instances.

Classification by Market Reach

Domestic Market-Focused Companies: These enterprises mainly serve the Indian market, satisfying a sizable need there. Companies that put their home market first include Mankind Pharma and Alkem Laboratories.

Export-Oriented Units: India exports a lot of pharmaceuticals, and a lot of its businesses are heavily focused on exports. These businesses supply many countries while adhering to strict international regulatory norms. Well-known companies that put an emphasis on exporting are Glenmark Pharmaceuticals and Aurobindo Pharma.

Global Innovators: These businesses invest a lot of resources in research and development to create innovative medical procedures and technological advancements that appeal to clients both locally and beyond. Biocon and Sun Pharma are two of them that put an emphasis on innovation.

Agencies like the Central Drugs Standard Control Organization (CDSCO) and the Department of Pharmaceuticals regulate the pharmaceutical industry in India. These groups ensure that the industry abides by quality and safety standards on a national and worldwide level. However, the industry faces several challenges, including:

Regulatory Compliance: Adhering to the numerous international regulatory standards can be costly and time-consuming.

Intellectual Property Rights (IPR): Maintaining fair generic prices while adhering to international IPR regulations remains a delicate balance.

Price Control: While government price control programs guarantee that pharmaceuticals are affordable for the masses, they often put pressure on business profits.

Infrastructure and Quality Control: It is a continuous battle to maintain high standards for both infrastructure and quality control in order to meet worldwide requirements.

R&D Investment: Despite growth, India continues to invest less in R&D than other countries.

Rising R&D spending, greater awareness of healthcare issues, and expanding domestic markets all seem to point to a bright future for the Indian pharmaceutical business. Government initiatives like "Make in India" and legislation that support biotechnology and innovation further improve the sector's prospects. Furthermore, we expect new growth and development opportunities as the COVID-19 pandemic intensifies the focus on digital health and telemedicine.

Based on ownership, product range, activities, and market share, the Indian pharmaceutical sector is a vibrant and diverse industry. Its ability to make innovative investments, navigate regulatory obstacles, and expand its global footprint will shape its future trajectory. With a solid foundation and a strategic plan, the industry is well-positioned to sustain development and have a significant impact on global healthcare.

Importance of Marketing in the Pharmaceutical Industry

The pharmaceutical industry, committed to the development, production, and promotion of pharmaceuticals, largely supports modern healthcare. Pharmaceutical product marketing is equally as significant as the scientific research and development (R&D) components of the pharmaceutical industry. Marketing in this industry requires a complex interplay of regulatory compliance, ethical concerns, and strategic planning to guarantee that individuals in need of life-saving and life-improving pharmaceuticals receive them. This chapter explores the many facets of marketing's importance in the pharmaceutical industry, including its effects on education, product awareness, market penetration, and public health in general.

Enhancing Product Awareness

One of the primary marketing goals in the pharmaceutical industry is to raise consumer awareness of new and existing medicines. The pharmaceutical sector is characterized by intense competition among its various players, who vie for the attention of patients and medical professionals. Efficient marketing strategies are essential for making a product stand out in a crowded market, set itself apart from rivals, and highlight its special qualities.

Marketing efforts spread knowledge about new treatments through a range of platforms, such as conferences, print advertisements, medical journals, and online media. These commercials usually highlight the medication's unique features, safety, and effectiveness, providing doctors with the knowledge they need to make informed prescription decisions. By raising awareness, marketing ensures that new drugs will quickly reach their target market, which could expedite illness treatment and improve patient outcomes.

Educating Healthcare Professionals and Patients

In addition to increasing awareness, pharmaceutical marketing is critical for educating. It is imperative for medical professionals to possess comprehensive understanding regarding novel pharmaceuticals, encompassing their modes of operation, potential side effects, compatibility with other drugs, and suggested dose. We generally deliver this knowledge through continuing medical education (CME) programs, webinars, seminars, and thorough product literature.

Giving people clear, concise information about their conditions and the available treatments is a common goal of marketing initiatives. Examples of this include patient handouts, instructional websites, and direct-to-consumer advertising. More adherence to prescribed treatments, early identification of side effects, and proactive engagement with healthcare practitioners are all associated with improved health outcomes for those who are more educated.

Facilitating Market Penetration

Successful market penetration is another critical objective of pharmaceutical marketing. The regulatory body must successfully introduce a new drug onto the market to ensure widespread acceptability. This involves engaging with pharmacies, hospitals, and insurance companies, while also focusing on healthcare providers to secure formulary placements and payment arrangements.

Marketing campaigns regularly send pharmaceutical sales representatives to visit medical professionals and provide them with detailed information about new medications. These delegates play a crucial role in building relationships with medical experts, answering their questions, and providing test specimens. Marketing teams also strive to negotiate with insurance companies to ensure the coverage of new drugs in health plans, thereby expanding patient access.

Navigating Regulatory and Ethical Considerations

Stringent regulatory frameworks govern pharmaceutical marketing, ensuring that promotional actions are truthful, non-misleading, and beneficial to public health. Regulatory authorities such as the U.S. Food and Drug Administration (FDA) and the European Medicines Agency (EMA) have set pharmaceutical marketing standards. Among other things, regulatory authorities prohibit off-label promotion, require risk and benefit information, and monitor advertising tactics.

Ethics is another crucial element in pharmaceutical marketing. Companies need to find a way to balance their duty to market their products with the need to truthfully and fairly represent them. Ethical marketing strategies include openness, avoiding unduly dramatic claims, and prioritizing health care over commercial interests. Adhering to moral principles helps patients, medical experts, and the public gain trust, which eventually boosts the legitimacy and prestige of pharmaceutical companies.

Supporting Public Health Initiatives

Pharmaceutical marketing supports larger public health activities by raising awareness and promoting illness prevention. For example, vaccination campaigns primarily use marketing strategies to dispel myths and educate the public about vaccinations' benefits. These programs could lead to higher vaccination rates, reducing the prevalence of infectious diseases and improving overall health.

Marketing strategies that target specific health problems in marginalized or at-risk populations can also advance public health. Campaigns for targeted marketing can focus on conditions that disproportionately affect specific communities, such as mental health problems, diabetes, or heart disease. By tailoring messages for these communities and ensuring access to necessary medications, pharmaceutical marketing has the ability to greatly improve public health outcomes and reduce health disparities.

Driving Innovation and Economic Growth

The pharmaceutical industry is one of the primary forces driving economic growth and innovation. Pharmaceutical companies can reinvest their income in the development of new medicines and cures since they have earned financial success through their successful marketing strategies. The development of new medications that meet unmet medical needs and the continuous advancement of medical science depend on this reinvestment.

We urge pharmaceutical companies to develop and enhance their products through marketing to gain market share, thereby fostering industry competition. Competition could lead to the development of more accessible, secure, and potent medications, thereby benefiting patients and healthcare systems worldwide.

Marketing is a crucial and intricate component in the pharmaceutical industry that extends beyond mere advertising. It is necessary to increase product awareness among consumers, educate patients and healthcare professionals, open up new markets, resolve ethical and legal issues, support public health initiatives, and encourage innovation and economic growth. Pharmaceutical companies may guarantee that their products reach the intended audience, enhance patient outcomes, and contribute positively to healthcare developments by carrying out marketing campaigns effectively. In an industry where the stakes are so high, marketing plays a critical role in bridging the gap between scientific innovation and real-world health benefits. Its importance cannot be overstated.

Key Stakeholders in Pharmaceutical Marketing in India

There are numerous significant companies engaged in the distribution, consumption, and advertising of pharmaceutical products in India's complex and multifaceted pharmaceutical marketing sector. Comprehending the functions of the pharmaceutical industry and the intricate web of relationships that drives pharmaceutical promotion in the nation requires an understanding of the aforementioned stakeholders.

Medical Retailers

Pharmacies are essential to the pharmaceutical industry because they serve as a crucial link between customers and pharmaceutical companies. These retailers provide pharmaceutical items and facilitate access. They include big-box stores, online vendors, and local pharmacies. Their direct interaction with clients, where they provide essential health advice and assistance in addition to prescription drugs, highlights their importance. In pharmaceutical companies' marketing and sales strategies, retailers are essential since they choose which items to carry, where to put them, and what suggestions to give. These decisions impact consumer choices. Furthermore, they facilitate market knowledge acquisition by providing enterprises with consumer feedback and demand trends, allowing them to adjust their marketing and manufacturing strategies accordingly. India's extensive pharmacy network makes sure that medications go to even the most remote areas, satisfying the wide range of medical requirements of a substantial population. The network's effectiveness influences the cost and accessibility of medicinal products. In addition to managing regulatory requirements, merchants must maintain compliance with government regulations and standards. This solidifies their position as the supply chain's gatekeepers for pharmaceutical quality and safety. Medical merchants are becoming increasingly important as the industry shifts due to advancements in e-commerce and digital health, necessitating their adaptation to new technologies and consumer behavior. In short, drugstores are essential to the healthcare delivery system because they act as a middleman between end users and pharmaceutical companies, ensuring that drugs are accessible, reasonably priced, and utilized appropriately.

Healthcare Professionals

In the pharmaceutical industry, healthcare professionals (HCPs) are essential because they have a significant influence on the success and market penetration of pharmaceutical products. This group includes physicians, pharmacists, nurses, and other health care providers who are crucial in prescribing, recommending, and supplying medications. Pharmaceutical companies employ a range of tactics to connect with healthcare professionals (HCPs), such as sponsoring conferences, arranging direct interactions with medical representatives, and launching continuing medical education (CME) programs. The purpose of these engagements is to inform HCPs about novel drugs, ongoing clinical research, and the most recent developments in treatment options. Medical professionals' suggestions and endorsements directly impact the acceptance and financial success of pharmaceutical products. Patients must feel accepted and trusted in order to produce positive prescribing patterns and high rates of treatment adherence. HCPs also provide incisive analysis on the efficacy and safety of drugs, which can impact marketing strategies and research and development. Given their crucial role in patient care and treatment outcomes, pharmaceutical companies need to have positive relationships with HCPs. Companies can improve patient outcomes and achieve market success by aligning marketing initiatives with healthcare professionals' requirements and preferences.

Patients and Consumers

Patients and consumers now play a more important role as stakeholders in the pharmaceutical industry, which has a significant impact on business practices and market dynamics. Pharmaceutical marketing has traditionally focused on doctors who wrote prescriptions, but this paradigm has shifted as patient empowerment and understanding have increased. Patients today actively seek out information, evaluate offered therapies, and influence pharmaceutical companies' product plans through their input and preferences. Thanks to the advent of patient-centric marketing strategies, pharmaceutical companies increasingly actively engage with patients through patient support programs, educational initiatives, and direct-to-consumer advertising. Thanks to the growing amount of online health information and the growing emphasis on transparency, patients are now better equipped to make informed decisions about their care. As a result, products that meet patients' needs and preferences are in greater demand. Additionally, the experiences and satisfaction of patients with their treatments can significantly impact the success and reputation of pharmaceutical products, underscoring the significance of their feedback. Pharmaceutical companies devote resources to comprehending patient needs, using patient data to enhance product offers, and refining patient interaction strategies. This face-to-face engagement not only builds trust and loyalty but also ensures pharmaceutical companies can handle real-world issues and improve patient outcomes. Patients and consumers have essentially become active participants in the pharmaceutical industry, impacting everything from medication research to marketing techniques and regulations.

Regulatory Authorities

In the pharmaceutical industry, regulatory agencies are essential because they enforce stringent guidelines and provide close supervision, ensuring that drugs are safe, effective, and of high quality. The Central Drugs Standard Control Organization (CDSCO) and the Ministry of Health and Family Welfare are the primary regulatory bodies in India that oversee, regulate, and approve drugs. These bodies set stringent guidelines for clinical trials, manufacturing procedures, and marketing clearances in order to safeguard the integrity of the pharmaceutical market and the public's health. Their work extends beyond basic compliance monitoring; they are essential in putting new rules into place that address issues like pharmacovigilance, ethical marketing, and fake drugs. Regulatory bodies also greatly affect pharmaceutical companies' access to the market by establishing the requirements for drug approval and registration. This regulatory framework safeguards consumers and upholds trust in the pharmaceutical industry by restricting the sale of products to those that can prove their safety and effectiveness. These groups also participate in on-going evaluations and modifications to regulations, modifying them to take into account new developments in science and market trends. As a result, the interaction between pharmaceutical companies and regulatory agencies strikes a dynamic balance between innovation and compliance. Regulations govern corporate practices and cultivate an environment that promotes public health and safety.

Pharmaceutical Industry Associations

The pharmaceutical industry associations, such as the Indian Pharmaceutical Association (IPA), the Indian Drug Manufacturers' Association (IDMA), and the Organisation of Pharmaceutical Producers of India (OPPI), are significant participants in the country's pharmaceutical market. These groups play a crucial role in shaping legislation, setting industry standards, and furthering the interests of pharmaceutical professionals and companies in general. By providing a centralized venue for communication between industry participants and regulatory agencies, these groups help create best practices, address shared concerns, and facilitate regulatory compliance. They actively engage in lobbying to ensure the industry's perspectives are considered during the modification of laws and regulations. These groups also offer helpful resources, such as research papers, networking opportunities, and training courses that promote the general advancement of the industry and the professional development of their members. Pharmaceutical industry associations help to navigate the complicated regulatory landscape, promote innovation, raise industry standards, and strike a balance between the interests of producers and consumers through their advocacy and support. Their participation is critical for stimulating company growth, raising the standard of pharmaceutical goods, and ensuring the industry's continued competitiveness and flexibility in response to demands from both domestic and foreign markets.

Case Studies

Case 1: Recently, a prominent pharmaceutical company in India unveiled GlyCuring, a ground-breaking medication designed to treat diabetes, which is becoming more and more common in both urban and rural areas. The company had to contend with the issue of marketing the medicine in a highly competitive market that was dominated by existing players, even with its strong research and development (R&D) base. In order to increase product recognition, educate healthcare experts, and expand into new markets, the company implemented a complete marketing campaign. Through digital webinars for physicians, direct-to-consumer advertising in regional languages, and targeted efforts at national medical conferences, the company successfully increased awareness about the special advantages of GlyCuring. In order to ensure improved prescription practices, medical representatives were crucial in informing healthcare professionals about the medication's safety profile, possible adverse effects, and effectiveness. In order to increase patient access, the business collaborated with private insurance companies and government health programs to list GlyCuring in formularies. Tight adherence to Indian regulatory rules guaranteed compliance, while moral marketing strategies promoted confidence among physicians. Additionally, the company started diabetes awareness public health campaigns in rural areas, organizing free health camps and distributing instructional materials in collaboration with local healthcare providers. The company was able to reinvest in more inventions since the campaign improved both its financial performance and brand image. This instance illustrates how, in the Indian pharmaceutical landscape, strategic marketing that is in line with ethical and regulatory requirements can result in successful market penetration and advantages for public health.

Case 2: A mid-sized pharmaceutical company found it difficult to establish a foothold in the fiercely competitive Indian pharmaceutical market. To address this, they created a thorough marketing plan that targeted important stakeholders. The business collaborated closely with medical retailers, especially neighborhood pharmacies in remote areas, to ensure that its generic medications were carried at reasonable costs. This collaboration guaranteed that necessary medications reached isolated areas while simultaneously expanding market penetration. Furthermore, the corporation fostered a strong rapport with healthcare professionals (HCPs) by supporting programs for continuing medical education (CME) and maintaining constant communication with doctors through its medical representatives, who provided them with up-to-date clinical data and treatment alternatives. These HCPs' advice became critical for increasing the number of prescriptions written for the company's goods. Recognizing the increasing influence of patients in healthcare decisions, the company introduced patient support initiatives, providing comprehensive educational resources on their medications and utilizing digital health platforms to interact with customers directly. In order to ensure that the company completed all compliance requirements for drug approval, regulatory bodies like the CDSCO played a crucial role. This helped build the company's reputation as a reliable brand. The corporation maintained a lead on legislative changes and implemented industry best practices by actively participating in industry associations, such as the Indian Pharmaceutical Association (IPA). Strategically managing relationships with patients, HCPs, industry associations, regulators, and retailers allowed the company to grow its market share and establish itself as a dependable player in the Indian pharmaceutical landscape. This story highlights the significance of a comprehensive stakeholder-focused strategy in Indian pharmaceutical marketing.

Questions

1. What impact do market exclusivity and patent regulations have on pharmaceutical medicine pricing and competition?
2. In the pharmaceutical sector, what part do the FDA and other regulatory agencies play in guaranteeing the efficacy and safety of drugs?
3. What impact has biotechnology had on the worldwide pharmaceutical industry's efforts to treat cancer and generate vaccines?
4. How did the COVID-19 pandemic emphasize the significance of global collaboration in the creation and dissemination of pharmaceuticals?
5. What role has the Indian Patents Act of 1970 played in the development of the country's generic pharmaceutical market?
6. What role does the Central Drugs Standard Control Organisation (CDSCO) play in Indian pharmaceutical business regulation?
7. What are the biggest obstacles that the Indian pharmaceutical industry must overcome to remain in conformity with international regulations?
8. What effects do national pharmaceutical firms like Cipla and Sun Pharma have on the world pharmaceutical market?
9. In what ways does pharmaceutical marketing enhance patient and healthcare professional education and product knowledge, which in turn improves public health outcomes?

10. How do healthcare professionals and regulatory bodies influence pharmaceutical businesses in India's marketing strategy and product success?

Multiple Choice Questions

1. What is one of the primary objectives of marketing in the pharmaceutical industry?
   (a) Reducing production costs
   (b) Enhancing product awareness
   (c) Increasing the shelf life of drugs
   (d) Regulating drug prices
2. Which of the following stakeholders in the pharmaceutical industry are crucial in prescribing, recommending, and supplying medications?
   (a) Patients (b) Healthcare Professionals
   (c) Regulatory Authorities (d) Medical Retailers
3. Which of the following is a key regulatory authority overseeing the pharmaceutical industry in India?
   (a) IMA (b) WHO (c) CDSCO (d) FDA
4. How do pharmaceutical marketing campaigns contribute to public health initiatives?
   (a) By reducing medication costs
   (b) By raising awareness about disease prevention and promoting health
   (c) By increasing sales quotas for pharmaceutical companies
   (d) By focusing exclusively on direct sales techniques
5. Which of the following pharmaceutical industry associations in India plays a key role in shaping legislation and setting industry standards?
   (a) IPA (b) IMC (c) FIP (d) WHO
6. Which of the following companies specializes in Active Pharmaceutical Ingredient (API) manufacturing in India?
   (a) Sun Pharmaceutical Industries (b) Cipla
   (c) Divi's Laboratories (d) Lupin

7. What was the key feature of the 1970 Patent Act that helped domestic pharmaceutical companies in India?
   (a) Allowed product patents
   (b) Allowed process patents
   (c) Introduced price control mechanisms
   (d) Introduced stringent regulatory standards
8. Which of the following is an example of a biotechnology firm in India?
   (a) Cipla (b) Biocon
   (c) Dr. Reddy's Laboratories (d) Sun Pharma
9. Which category do companies like 1mg, Pharmeasy, and Netmeds fall under?
   (a) Contract Research and Manufacturing Services (CRAMS)
   (b) E-Pharmacies
   (c) Formulation Manufacturers
   (d) API Manufacturers
10. What types of drugs are branded generics?
    (a) Drugs used for treating chronic conditions
    (b) Drugs without a brand name
    (c) Generic drugs sold under a brand name
    (d) OTC medications
11. Which of the following is a public sector undertaking (PSU) in India's pharmaceutical sector?
    (a) Hindustan Unilever
    (b) Indian Drugs and Pharmaceuticals Limited (IDPL)
    (c) Novartis
    (d) Lupin
12. Which company is a well-known player in India's export-oriented pharmaceutical sector?
    (a) Mankind Pharma (b) Glenmark Pharmaceuticals
    (c) Apollo Pharmacy (d) Apollo Hospitals
13. Which Indian pharmaceutical company is recognized as a leader in the biosimilars market?
    (a) Aurobindo Pharma (b) Biocon
    (c) Sun Pharma (d) Glenmark Pharmaceuticals

14. Which of the following is a challenge faced by the Indian pharmaceutical industry?
    (a) Low demand for pharmaceutical products
    (b) Strict international regulatory standards
    (c) Excessive investment in R&D
    (d) Decline in domestic market growth
15. What is the primary regulatory agency for pharmaceuticals in India?
    (a) ICMR
    (b) Ministry of Health and Family Welfare
    (c) CDSCO)
    (d) NPPA
16. What significant law passed in 1970 helped the Indian pharmaceutical industry to grow by enabling the production of low-cost generic drugs?
    (a) Indian Drugs and Cosmetics Act
    (b) Indian Medical Act
    (c) Indian Pharmaceutical Act
    (d) Indian Patents Act
17. Which company is recognized for creating affordable therapies for diseases such as HIV/AIDS?
    (a) Sun Pharma (b) Cipla
    (c) Dr. Reddy's Laboratories (d) Lupin Limited
18. What is the first step in the drug development process?
    (a) Preclinical testing (b) Drug discovery
    (c) Phase I trials (d) Clinical trials
19. Which organization is the primary regulatory body for the pharmaceutical industry in the United States?
    (a) ICMR (b) EMA (c) CDSCO (d) FDA
20. Which of the following is NOT a key player in the global pharmaceutical industry?
    (a) Pfizer (b) Novartis
    (c) Johnson & Johnson (d) Tata Pharma

21. What major discovery by Alexander Fleming revolutionized medicine in 1928?
    (a) Insulin (b) Penicillin
    (c) Aspirin (d) Morphine
22. Which regulatory body oversees the European pharmaceutical market?
    (a) FDA (b) CDSCO (c) EMA (d) WHO
23. What percentage of India's GDP is accounted for by the pharmaceutical industry?
    (a) 8% (b) 1.72% (c) 5.5% (d) 10%
24. What is the purpose of the National Pharmaceutical Pricing Authority (NPPA) in India?
    (a) To regulate the quality of pharmaceuticals
    (b) To set drug prices for essential medicines
    (c) To oversee pharmaceutical exports
    (d) To manage clinical trials
25. Which Indian pharmaceutical company ranks among the top 10 globally by consolidated revenues?
    (a) Sun Pharma (b) Cipla
    (c) Aurobindo Pharma (d) Lupin Limited

CHAPTER

2

The Pharmaceutical Products

Introduction

India's pharmaceutical industry is a major player in the global market and is well-known for making substantial contributions to the availability of reasonably priced, high-quality medications. India is one of the world's top producers of generic medications, making up around 20% of the total volume sold worldwide. This accomplishment is a result of a strong manufacturing infrastructure, a highly qualified labour force, and a regulatory climate that is becoming more and more favourable. Major hubs like Hyderabad, Mumbai, and Bengaluru host a concentration of pharmaceutical businesses, research institutes, and ancillary industries, fostering innovation and large-scale production. With a move towards greater value-added products, the business has changed from making simple generics to creating complicated generics, biosimilars, and even new drug entities.

Indian government policies have heavily influenced this expansion. The Production-Linked Incentive (PLI) Scheme, among other programs, aims to enhance the capabilities of domestic manufacturers and reduce dependence on imported raw materials. Moreover, India's export markets have grown and its credibility strengthened due to its adherence to global standards, including those established by the World Health Organization (WHO) and the US Food and Drug Administration (FDA). The COVID-19 pandemic highlighted India's position as the "pharmacy of the world," since Indian businesses provide essential drugs and vaccinations to more than 150 nations.

Regulating obstacles, concerns about intellectual property, and the requirement for increased investment in research and development (R&D) are some of the difficulties the industry faces. Addressing these issues is necessary to maintain development and improve competitiveness. Enhancing the regulatory environment, fostering innovation with more financing for research and development, and establishing global partnerships are all positive moves. India's pharmaceutical sector continues to be a pillar of the global healthcare system, making a substantial contribution to both public health and economic growth even as the country navigates these challenges.

Prescription Drugs

Prescription medication affordability is a major issue in India. For many people, especially those from lower-income groups, the cost of prescriptions can still be exorbitant, even with the nation's vast production capacity and the availability of generic drugs. In order to keep necessary medications cheap, the National Pharmaceutical Pricing Authority (NPPA) is critical in controlling drug costs. But there's still a persistent conflict between keeping drugs affordable and making sure pharmaceutical companies can continue to innovate and produce.

In India, people are quite concerned about the quality of prescribed medications. The nation has had a number of problems with the distribution of subpar and fake medications, which seriously jeopardize patient safety. Regulatory bodies, such as state drug control organizations and CDSCO, constantly monitor and control drug quality. The regulatory structure intended to guarantee drug safety includes harsh penalties for infractions, frequent inspections, and strict quality control procedures. Despite efforts, this is a constant problem due to the scale and diversity of the Indian pharmaceutical market.

The abuse of prescription medications in India is another urgent problem. Antibiotic resistance, drug addiction, and self-medication are the results of straightforward access to some pharmaceuticals and lax enforcement of prescription guidelines. For example, the over-the-counter sale of antibiotics without the necessary prescriptions exacerbates the issue of antibiotic resistance, which is becoming a greater public health concern. To address this issue, measures to educate the public and healthcare professionals about the dangers of inappropriate drug use are essential, as is the enforcement of prescription restrictions with more severities.

Apart from these obstacles, there are notable developments in the Indian prescription medicine business. Patients now obtain prescription drugs in a completely different way because of the growth of telemedicine and digital health platforms. Obtaining medical prescriptions and pharmaceuticals has become simpler for consumers, particularly those living in rural places, thanks to online pharmacies and tele-consultation services. But this digital revolution also calls for strict regulatory control to stop people from abusing internet resources to obtain prescription medications without the proper medical advice.

Another area of growth in the pharmaceutical industry is research and development (R&D). India has made significant R&D investments, with an emphasis on creating novel medications and enhancing those that already exist. Innovation is essential in order to meet the changing healthcare needs of the populace and maintain the nation's competitive advantage in the international pharmaceutical industry.

The role of pharmacists in India is also changing, with a focus on their obligations to ensure correct prescription drug dispensing and patient education. When it comes to giving advice on how to take medications correctly, possible side effects, and drug interactions, pharmacists are invaluable. Strengthening the role of pharmacists through improved training and regulations can improve patient outcomes and lower the hazards associated with inappropriate drug use.

Prescription drug use in India is a vibrant and complex field with both notable successes and enduring obstacles. Regulators, healthcare professionals, and the pharmaceutical sector must constantly focus on ensuring prescription medication accessibility, cost, and quality, as well as preventing misuse. India is well-positioned to effectively tackle these difficulties and ensure that its populace has access to safe and efficacious prescription pharmaceuticals through continuous efforts and innovations.

Major Categories and Usage of Prescription Drugs

Prescription medications are crucial to modern healthcare, and it is important for consumers and medical professionals to grasp their main uses and types. Cultural norms, economic constraints, and healthcare issues shape the prescription medication usage landscape in India. This chapter delves into the primary categories of prescription medications commonly utilized in India, along with their specific applications in treating medical conditions.

Antibiotics

Antibiotics, which are essential in the fight against bacterial infections, are one of the main classes of prescription medications. India commonly administers antibiotics like cefixime, azithromycin, and amoxicillin to treat a wide range of diseases, including urinary tract infections and respiratory tract infections. The widespread usage of antibiotics in India has brought to light the important public health hazard of antibiotic resistance. Strong public awareness efforts and more stringent regulatory measures are required to prevent the abuse of antibiotics, even in the face of guidelines that support their rational use. Over-the-counter availability and self-medication habits are major contributors to this problem.

Antivirals

Antivirals are essential for treating viral illnesses such as influenza, hepatitis B and C, and HIV in India. People frequently administer medications like Oseltamivir and Acyclovir. Antiretroviral therapy (ART) has become a major public health priority due to the prevalence of HIV/AIDS. Millions of people receive free ART through the government's National AIDS Control Programme, extending and enhancing life expectancy. In order to stop the spread of viral illnesses across the nation, it is crucial that the general public be aware of these drugs and can easily obtain them.

Antifungals

Fungal infections are frequent in India's hot and humid climate, and antifungal drugs are essential for treating them. Medications like Terbinafine and Fluconazole commonly treat illnesses such as systemic fungal infections, dermatophytosis, and candidiasis. Effective treatment is required due to the extensive frequency of fungal infections, especially in rural and tropical areas. Antifungals that are both systemic and topical make it possible to treat patients appropriately, avoiding problems and enhancing skin and general health.

Antiparasitics

In India, where parasitic illnesses such as helminthiasis, leishmaniasis, and malaria are common, antiparasitic medications are indispensable. Commonly used medications include Metronidazole, Albendazole, and Chloroquine. The National Malaria Combat Programme and other attempts to combat parasitic illnesses have dramatically lowered incidence rates. To battle these illnesses, however, on-going efforts in vector management, public health education, and guaranteeing the availability of potent antiparasitic drugs remain essential, especially in rural and underserved areas.

Anti-inflammatory Drugs

In India, doctors frequently prescribe anti-inflammatory medications like corticosteroids and non-steroidal anti-inflammatory drugs (NSAIDs) to treat conditions like inflammatory bowel illnesses, allergies, and arthritis. Prednisone, Diclofenac, and ibuprofen are a few examples of medications that help with pain relief and inflammation reduction. These medications are essential because musculoskeletal diseases and inflammatory illnesses are highly prevalent. Misusing them, however, could have negative effects such as gastrointestinal problems and increased cardiovascular risks, emphasizing the importance of appropriate medical advice and patient education.

Antidepressants

In India, doctors are prescribing antidepressants more frequently to treat mental health issues such as depression, anxiety disorders, and obsessive-compulsive disorder. Commonly used medications include Amitriptyline, Sertraline, and Fluoxetine. As a result of increased awareness of mental health concerns and a decrease in stigma, more people are seeking help. Accessibility to drugs and mental health services is still a problem, especially in rural areas. Primary health care must integrate mental health services to provide comprehensive support to those in need.

Antipsychotics

Antipsychotic drugs are essential for the treatment of serious mental illnesses, including bipolar disorder, schizophrenia, and severe depression exhibiting psychotic symptoms. Prescriptions for medications such as Clozapine, Olanzapine, and Risperidone are common. One of the challenges in India is the scarcity of mental health practitioners and resources. It is imperative to develop the mental health infrastructure, train healthcare professionals, and raise public awareness to ensure patients receive prompt and efficient treatment and lessen the burden of mental disease.

Anxiolytics

In India, doctors frequently prescribe anxiolytics, such as benzodiazepines and non-benzodiazepine substitutes, to treat insomnia, panic attacks, and anxiety disorders. Doctors use medications such as Buspirone, Alprazolam, and Diazepam to temporarily treat anxiety symptoms. These medications can cause dependence and withdrawal symptoms even though they are effective. Thus, healthcare professionals must closely supervise their use. Promoting non-pharmacological therapies and expanding access to psychological therapies are crucial for the comprehensive treatment of anxiety disorders and associated illnesses.

Immunosuppressants

In India, immunosuppressants are essential for treating autoimmune conditions, including lupus and rheumatoid arthritis, as well as for avoiding organ transplant rejection. People frequently utilize medications such as Tacrolimus, Cyclosporine, and Methotrexate. The rise in organ transplant programs and the incidence of autoimmune diseases underscore the significance of these drugs. Assuring their accessibility and cost-effectiveness, as well as consistent monitoring for adverse reactions and infections, is critical for delivering efficient long-term care and improving patient outcomes.

Diuretics

Indians commonly use diuretics to treat edema, heart failure, and hypertension. Drugs that help the body eliminate extra fluid include Spironolactone, Furosemide, and Hydrochlorothiazide. This lowers blood pressure and prevents fluid build-up. Due to the high rate of cardiovascular disease in India, diuretics are essential components of treatment plans. To optimize the advantages and reduce the risk of adverse effects, patient education regarding the significance of adhering to the prescribed regimen and keeping an eye out for electrolyte imbalances is crucial.

Antipyretics and Analgesics

Antipyretics and analgesics are another important class of drugs frequently used to treat pain and fever. In Indian homes, prescription drugs like Ibuprofen and Paracetamol are commonplace. These medications are vital for the treatment of ailments like headaches, musculoskeletal discomfort, and viral fevers. Antipyretics play a particularly important role in a nation where infectious diseases are highly prevalent. However, we should only use these drugs carefully and under medical supervision, as misuse or overuse might lead to negative effects like gastrointestinal problems and liver damage.

Antihypertensives

Due to dietary changes, genetic predispositions, and lifestyle changes in lifestyle, hypertension is becoming a significant concern in India. Antihypertensives are essential for managing this condition. Doctors frequently prescribe antihypertensives like Amlodipine, Losartan, and Atenolol. By assisting in blood pressure regulation, these medications lower the chance of cardiovascular illnesses like heart attacks and strokes. In India, it might be difficult to keep patients taking their medications as prescribed because they frequently stop taking them when their symptoms go away. For successful hypertension management, sustained patient education and monitoring are critical.

Anti-diabetic Drugs

Given the high prevalence of diabetes in India—often referred to as the diabetes capital of the world—antidiabetic drugs are essential. Medication such as Insulin, Glimepiride, and Metformin is essential for controlling blood sugar levels. Because of the high prevalence of Type 1 and Type 2 diabetes, therapy must be comprehensive and include lifestyle changes as well as routine blood sugar testing. Antidiabetic medication price and accessibility are vital, particularly in rural areas with potentially underdeveloped healthcare systems.

Psychotropic Drugs

Psychotropic drugs, such as anxiolytics, antipsychotics, and antidepressants, are critical for treating mental health illnesses, which are becoming more common in India. Medications such as Risperidone, Diazepam, and Fluoxetine treat anxiety disorders, schizophrenia, and depression. In India, the stigma attached to mental health issues frequently results in underreporting and under treatment of these illnesses. In order to guarantee that patients receive prompt and appropriate care, there is an urgent need to raise awareness of mental health issues and integrate mental health services into basic healthcare.

Cardiovascular Drugs

Cardiovascular medications, which include antiplatelets, anticoagulants, and statins, are essential for managing and preventing cardiovascular illnesses, which rank among the top causes of death in India. Drugs that lower cholesterol, stop blood clots, and treat cardiac diseases include Atorvastatin, Aspirin, and Warfarin. Given the cost burden and widespread lack of healthcare coverage, the problem in India is making sure that patients get access to these life-saving medications and follow their prescribed course of treatment.

Respiratory Drugs

Respiratory drugs such as bronchodilators and corticosteroids are essential for treating long-term respiratory conditions like asthma and chronic obstructive pulmonary disease (COPD). Inhalers that are frequently recommended include Budesonide and Salbutamol. These drugs are necessary because of the rising pollution levels in Indian cities, which worsen respiratory ailments. Patients must receive patient education on correct inhaler use and strict adherence to treatment regimens to alleviate symptoms and improve their quality of life.

Gastrointestinal Drugs

Proton pump inhibitors, antacids, and antiemetics are among the many digestive medications used to treat disorders like nausea, peptic ulcers, and acid reflux. Examples of frequently prescribed medications in this category are Ondansetron, Ranitidine, and Omeprazole. In India, eating habits, stress, and the ingestion of tainted food and water are the main causes of digestive diseases. Even if these drugs relieve symptoms, it's just as critical to treat the underlying reasons with better hygiene and lifestyle modifications.

Hormonal Medicines

Thyroid hormones and contraceptives are examples of hormone-based drugs that are important in treating endocrine diseases and reproductive health. Many Indians, especially women, suffer from hypothyroidism, for which Levothyroxine is frequently recommended. People also commonly use hormone replacement treatments and oral contraceptives. Hormonal drugs are essential and should be easily accessible, particularly in remote places where access to healthcare may be restricted. Awareness campaigns and instruction regarding the appropriate use of these drugs can greatly impact the results of public health initiatives.

Anti-Cancer Drugs

In the battle against cancer, which is becoming more common in India, anticancer medications are an essential class of medication. Chemotherapeutic drugs, such as Doxorubicin, Cyclophosphamide, and more recent targeted treatments, treat many cancers effectively. One major obstacle is the high expense of cancer treatment; thus, government programs and health insurance plans are necessary to help patients financially. Improving cancer patients' quality of life and survival rates requires early detection and prompt treatment.

Prescription pharmaceuticals fall into several primary categories in India, including a broad range of drugs necessary for treating chronic illnesses, infectious infections, mental health issues, and other problems. To ensure adequate adherence and reduce misuse, the efficient use of these pharmaceuticals requires not only accessibility and cost, but also education and awareness. To maximize the population's benefits from prescription pharmaceuticals, policy measures, public health campaigns, and enhanced healthcare infrastructure will be critical as the Indian healthcare system develops.

Leading Brands and Manufacturers of Prescription Drugs

India has been a major force in the global pharmaceutical sector, earning the moniker "Pharmacy of the World" thanks to its strong manufacturing base and wide range of generic medications. The nation's pharmaceutical industry is well-known for its capacity to manufacture an extensive range of prescription medications at cost-effective pricing, making it an essential part of the global healthcare system. The existence of numerous top brands and manufacturers who have created names for themselves both domestically and abroad has made this feasible.

Sun Pharmaceutical Industries Ltd., the biggest pharmaceutical firm in India and the fourth-largest specialty generic pharmaceutical company worldwide, is a well-known brand in the Indian pharmaceutical sector. Established in 1983, Sun Pharma boasts a varied range of products covering multiple therapeutic domains, such as neurology, gastrointestinal, psychiatry, cardiology, and diabetology. The company's emphasis on innovation, quality, and cost effectiveness is responsible for its success. Sun Pharma has successfully lowered healthcare costs for patients globally by introducing many generic versions of complicated pharmaceuticals onto the market, placing a heavy emphasis on research and development (R&D).

In 1984, Dr. Reddy's Laboratories emerged as a significant company. Over-the-Counter (OTC) and biosimilar pharmaceuticals, as well as generic treatments, are among Dr. Reddy's specialties. The corporation, which has operations in over 30 countries and manufacturing facilities certified by strict regulatory bodies like the U.S., has made significant gains in growing its global footprint. The European Medicines Agency (EMA) and the Food and Drug Administration (FDA) both accredit the company. Because of its dedication to accessibility and cost, Dr. Reddy has established itself as a reliable brand in the pharmaceutical sector, especially in developing nations.

Established in 1935, Cipla Limited is another well-known brand in the Indian pharmaceutical industry. Cipla has gained global recognition for its humanitarian efforts and for being a leader in the development of cost-effective antiretroviral medications for HIV/AIDS treatment. More than 80 nations market the company's goods, which are well-established in the antiretroviral, cancer, and respiratory markets. Cipla's commitment to patient-centric innovation and high manufacturing standards has cemented its standing as a leader in the global healthcare industry.

Founded in 1968, Lupin Limited is a well-known brand in the biotechnology and generic drug industries. A broad variety of prescription medications covering therapeutic areas like cardiovascular, diabetes, asthma, paediatric, central nervous system (CNS), gastrointestinal, and anti-infective are part of Lupin's product portfolio. One of the main sources of revenue for the corporation's substantial presence in the US market. Lupin's cutting-edge R&D centers and manufacturing capabilities demonstrate its dedication to providing creative and reasonably priced healthcare solutions.

Established in 1986, Aurobindo Pharma is a prominent producer renowned for its wide array of generic formulations and active pharmaceutical ingredients (APIs). This company sells its products in over 150 countries and is well-known in America and Europe. Aurobindo Pharma is able to maintain strict quality control and cost efficiency because of its vertically integrated activities, which span from API manufacture to finished dosage formulations. The company's focus on complicated treatments and strong generic medication pipeline has been major factors in its growth.

Founded in 1959, Torrent Pharmaceuticals holds a prominent position in the Indian pharmaceutical industry. The company specializes in therapeutic areas including pain treatment, gastrointestinal, diabetology, cardiovascular, and central nervous system. With the acquisition of Elder Pharmaceuticals' branded domestic formulations division, Torrent has improved its standing in the Indian market. The company's deliberate R&D and manufacturing investments have allowed it to introduce cutting-edge products and increase its global presence.

Founded in 1952, Zydus Cadila is a prominent pharmaceutical firm offering a wide range of products, including vaccines, innovative biologics, biosimilars, and generic medications. Zydus Cadila is a well-known name in the global healthcare industry because of its commitment to quality and focus on research and innovation. The company has developed India's first vaccine against COVID-19, ZyCoV-D, and has been at the forefront of innovation in the Indian pharmaceutical industry.

Founded in 1977, Glenmark Pharmaceuticals is renowned for both its pioneering research in respiratory therapy, dermatology, and oncology, as well as its strong position in the generic medication market. Glenmark is a major global player, with its products available in more than 80 nations. The secret to the company's success has been its investment in state-of-the-art R&D and its ability to create sophisticated generics and customized goods.

These well-known companies and brands have not only helped the Indian pharmaceutical sector flourish, but they have also been instrumental in enhancing the state of global health. Millions of patients throughout the world now have access to necessary pharmaceuticals thanks to their emphasis on quality, price, and accessibility. The ability of the Indian pharmaceutical industry to mass produce high-quality generic medications has had a significant influence on low- and middle-income nations, where finding inexpensive healthcare is still a major obstacle.

The top brands and producers in the country continue to propel the Indian pharmaceutical sector, which is essential to the global healthcare system. Businesses with a track record of innovation, quality, and cost effectiveness include Sun Pharma, Dr. Reddy's Laboratories, Cipla, Lupin, Aurobindo Pharma, Torrent Pharmaceuticals, Zydus Cadila, and Glenmark Pharmaceuticals. Their efforts have improved India's standing as a major pharmaceutical hub, while also ensuring that individuals in need of important medications receive them, which improves health outcomes globally. As the sector develops, these businesses stand poised to tackle new healthcare issues and meet the growing demand for affordable, high-quality pharmaceuticals.

Over-The-Counter Drugs

In India's healthcare system, over-the-counter (OTC) medications are important since they offer easily available treatment choices for minor illnesses without a prescription. These drugs include painkillers, cough and cold medicines, antihistamines, antacids, and vitamins. Pharmacies and even supermarkets carry them. OTC medications are widely accessible, enabling people to take charge of their health and lessening the strain on the already overburdened healthcare system. OTC medications are an essential source of basic healthcare in isolated and rural locations with limited access to medical institutions. However, the availability of these drugs also raises questions about self-medication and potential abuse. Adverse effects may arise from inappropriate use, incorrect dosage, and possible drug interactions in India, a country with a vast variation in healthcare literacy. To guarantee the security and effectiveness of over-the-counter medications, the government and regulatory organizations, including the Central Drugs Standard Control Organization (CDSCO), have put in place regulations. These laws mandate precise labelling, directions for dosage, and cautions regarding potential adverse effects. Public education regarding the safe use of over-the-counter drugs is still necessary, notwithstanding these safeguards. In addition, pharmacists are essential in providing customers with advice and making sure they make wise decisions. It is critical to strike a balance between accessibility and safety as the over-the-counter (OTC) industry in India grows as a result of rising consumer demand for convenient healthcare solutions and health awareness. India can maximize the benefits of over-the-counter medications while reducing their associated hazards by encouraging appropriate self-medication behaviours and strengthening regulatory control. This strategy will support preserving public health and utilizing over-the-counter drugs as an important part of the nation's healthcare infrastructure.

Popular OTC Drugs in India

Paracetamol

In India, Acetaminophen, sometimes referred to as Paracetamol, is a common over-the-counter medication. People widely use it to lower fever and relieve mild to moderate pain. Brands that carry it include Crocin and Calpol. Because of its affordability and efficacy, it is frequently used in Indian homes to treat common colds, body pains, and headaches. Although Paracetamol is generally safe when taken as prescribed, exceeding the recommended dosage can cause serious liver damage, so it is important to follow the dosage guidelines.

Ibuprofen

India widely uses non-steroidal anti-inflammatory drugs, or NSAIDs, like ibuprofen to treat fever, inflammation, and discomfort. Numerous brands, such as Ibugesic and Brufen, sell it. For the treatment of ailments like arthritis, menstrual cramps, and muscle soreness, ibuprofen works well. Its dual action makes it preferred over other analgesics because of its anti-inflammatory qualities. Users, particularly those with kidney or gastrointestinal disorders, should use it with caution as it can exacerbate these symptoms.

Cetirizine

Cetirizine, a popular antihistamine in India, frequently treats allergy symptoms such as runny nose, sneezing, and itching. This product, which is available under the brands Cetzine and Zirtek, relieves allergic rhinitis and seasonal allergies. Cetirizine is a better option for daytime use because it is less likely to make you sleepy than some other antihistamines. To minimize adverse effects, users should adhere to dosage guidelines and be aware of any potential interactions with other medications.

Ranitidine

Ranitidine, a common over-the-counter drug in India, treats ailments like indigestion and heartburn caused by excess stomach acid. Marketed under names like Zantac and Rantac, it functions by reducing the stomach's acid production. Although it provides short-term comfort, safety concerns have surfaced, prompting the recall of certain items because of possible carcinogenic chemical contamination. Users should speak with healthcare specialists if they are using for an extended period of time or need other treatments.

Domperidone

In India, Domperidone is a commonly used over-the-counter drug for treating nausea and vomiting. Available under names such as Vomistop and Motilium, it functions by obstructing dopamine receptors in the gut and improving motility of the gastrointestinal tract. People frequently use it to treat ailments like medication-induced nausea and motion sickness. While short-term use is usually safe, excessive doses or prolonged use can cause negative effects like dry mouth and light-headedness. When using suggested amounts, users should see a doctor if their symptoms don't go away.

Loperamide

In India, loperamide is a popular antidiarrheal drug that works well. By reducing intestinal motility, this medication—known by brands like Lopamide and Imodium—helps lower the frequency of bowel motions. People frequently use it to treat acute diarrhoea resulting from food errors or infections. Although it works well to relieve symptoms, it should not be used to treat diarrhoea caused by bacterial infections or fever. Following dosing instructions is essential to avoid constipation and abdominal pain.

Topical Analgesics

Indians widely use topical analgesics to treat localized pain in the joints and muscles. Products from companies like Iodex and Volini provide prompt relief from aches and pains, including sprains and strains in the muscles. These products directly apply anti-inflammatory and pain-relieving chemicals to the affected area. External use usually deems them safe with minimal adverse effects on the body. Instead, users should avoid using them on open wounds or damaged skin and stop using them if irritation occurs.

Antacids

Indians frequently use antacids to reduce stomach acid and relieve indigestion and heartburn. Acid reflux sufferers turn to well-known brands like Eno, Digene, and Gelusil for their quick relief from symptoms. People usually use these drugs to treat sporadic discomfort because they neutralize excess stomach acid. While these drugs can provide temporary comfort, their continuous use may mask underlying issues that require medical attention. Users should adhere to the dosage guidelines and seek medical attention if their symptoms worsen or persist.

Regulatory Requirements of OTC Drugs in India

A complex regulatory structure oversees over-the-counter (OTC) medicine regulations in India, striving to ensure the efficacy, safety, and quality of pharmaceuticals. OTC medications, which are available over the counter and do not require a prescription, are essential to the Indian healthcare system because they offer affordable solutions for a variety of common illnesses. This article examines the legal requirements for over-the-counter medications in India, highlighting the main regulatory bodies, legislative frameworks, and associated processes.

1. ***Legislative Framework***

   The Drugs and Cosmetics Rules, 1945, and the Drugs and Cosmetics Act, 1940, have a significant impact on India's regulatory environment for over-the-counter medications. The Rules specify the processes for approving, producing, and distributing pharmaceuticals, while the Act establishes the legal framework for drug regulation, including OTC goods.

2. ***Classification of OTC Drugs***

   OTC drug classification in India is not specifically defined by the Drugs and Cosmetics Act. Instead, the classification process takes into account the drug's qualities and intended purpose. Generally, self-medication using over-the-counter (OTC) medications does not require a doctor's supervision. These medications frequently treat common ailments like colds and coughs, pain management, stomach problems, and mild skin diseases.

   An important factor in categorization and control of over-the-counter medications is the Central Drugs Standard Control Organization, or CDSCO. The Act does not classify OTC medications, but it does classify some drugs based on their consumption patterns and safety profile.

3. ***Regulatory Authorities***

   The central regulatory body in charge of policing over-the-counter (OTC) medicine regulations in India is the CDSCO, which operates under the Ministry of Health and Family Welfare. The CDSCO is in charge of making sure that medications fulfil the necessary requirements for quality, safety, and efficacy. Furthermore, the implementation and enforcement of regulatory requirements at the state level are under the purview of the State Drug Control Authorities (SDCAs).

4. ***Approval and Licensing***

   An extensive approval procedure must be completed before an OTC medication is allowed to be sold in India. The manufacturer is required to apply to the CDSCO and include detailed information about the quality, safety, and efficacy of the medication. This contains information on labelling, manufacturing procedures, and clinical trial specifics.

   To make sure the medication meets the requirements, the CDSCO examines the application. If authorized, the CDSCO grants a license for the medicine's production and sale. The licencing process involves the following steps:

   Pre-Approval Inspection: The manufacturing facility undergoes an inspection (GMP) to ensure adherence to Good Manufacturing Practices.

Clinical Data Evaluation: We evaluate the safety and efficacy data of the medication based on clinical trials and other pertinent studies.

Labelling Review: The label must clearly state the medication's usage, dosage, adverse effects, and precautions.

5. ***Manufacturing and Quality Control***

Producers of over-the-counter medications must adhere to the GMP guidelines set forth by the CDSCO. GMP regulations ensure the regular manufacturing and inspection of medications to meet quality requirements. Implementing quality control procedures and documenting the production process is necessary to ensure the uniformity and purity of the medicine.

Quality control includes regular testing of raw materials, processing materials, and finished products. An additional requirement for the manufacturing plant is a quality assurance system to monitor adherence to legal requirements.

6. ***Post-Marketing Surveillance***

Post-marketing surveillance monitors an over-the-counter medication's effectiveness and safety in the general public after it enters the market. The CDSCO gathers adverse drug reaction (ADR) reports and performs routine inspections in conjunction with state authorities. Manufacturers are required to report all ADRs and take the necessary steps to resolve any safety issues.

7. ***Labelling and Packaging Requirements***

Labelling over-the-counter medications requires adherence to the CDSCO's regulations. The label needs to say:

Drug Name: Both brand and generic names.

Composition: A breakdown of the amounts of the active components.

Indications: The conditions or signs that the medication is intended to treat.

Dosage Instructions: Suggested dosage and guidelines for administration.

Warnings and Precautions: Details on possible adverse reactions and non-suitability for use.

Manufacturing Details: Name and address of the manufacturer, batch number, and expiry date.

The packaging must also ensure that the medication remains protected from deterioration and contamination. In order to prevent unwanted access, tamper-evident packaging is frequently necessary.

8. ***Advertising and Promotion***

   In order to avoid false claims and guarantee that commercials present accurate information, the promotion of over-the-counter pharmaceuticals is subject to regulations. Under the Drug and Magic Remedies (Objectionable Advertisements) Act of 1954, it is illegal to market drugs that purport to heal serious illnesses or make deceptive claims without supporting documentation.

9. ***Challenges and Future Directions***

   India's OTC medicine regulatory framework has a number of difficulties, such as keeping up with GMP requirements, handling the large volume of OTC products, and dealing with problems involving counterfeit medications. The Indian government and regulatory agencies are always striving to improve consumer knowledge, enforce the law more effectively, and fortify the regulatory framework.

   A comprehensive system governs over-the-counter drug regulations in India, with the aim of protecting public health and ensuring people have access to essential pharmaceuticals. The regulatory framework seeks to ensure that over-the-counter medications satisfy the highest safety and effectiveness requirements through strict clearance procedures, strict manufacturing standards, and extensive post-marketing surveillance. On-going efforts to improve and refine regulatory standards will be essential in addressing new issues and guaranteeing the on-going protection of consumer health as the pharmaceutical industry changes.

Biopharmaceuticals

Biopharmaceuticals, a novel class of medications produced from biological sources, including India, have dramatically transformed the world of healthcare. Biopharmaceuticals, as opposed to conventional chemical-based pharmaceuticals, are a broad category of goods that include recombinant proteins, gene treatments, vaccinations, and monoclonal antibodies. Living systems such as yeast, bacteria, and mammalian cells make these molecules, which are extremely complicated and highly specialized in their growth and synthesis. Over the past 20 years, India's biopharmaceutical industry has grown remarkably thanks to developments in biotechnology, encouraging government regulations, and rising investments from both local and foreign businesses.

India's biopharmaceutical sector has grown to be a major player in the worldwide market because of its competent workforce, affordable production, and strong R&D capabilities. Prominent Indian businesses that produce novel biopharmaceutical products and biosimilars for both domestic and foreign markets include Biocon, Dr. Reddy's Laboratories, and Cipla. These companies have become major players in the industry. Particularly in India, biosimilars have become more well-known as more accessible substitutes for costly biologics, allowing a larger population to have access to cutting-edge treatments. India's regulatory environment has also changed to facilitate industry expansion. The Department of Biotechnology (DBT) and the Central Drugs Standard Control Organization (CDSCO) are essential in regulating and approving biopharmaceuticals and making sure they adhere to strict safety, effectiveness, and quality criteria.

The biopharmaceutical industry is expected to flourish thanks to a number of initiatives that the Indian government has launched. The Biotechnology Industry Research Assistance Council (BIRAC) established the National Biopharma Mission with the goal of expediting the growth of biopharmaceuticals in India by offering infrastructure, capital, and assistance to research institutes and start-ups. Additionally, programs like Made in India and Start-up India have strengthened the industry even more by promoting entrepreneurship and innovation.

The Indian biopharmaceutical industry still has to overcome obstacles like high development costs, strict regulations, and the need for ongoing innovation. However, partnerships between government, business, and academics are paving the path to eliminate these obstacles. We anticipate that the incorporation of state-of-the-art technology like artificial intelligence, machine learning, and sophisticated manufacturing processes will enhance the productivity and expandability of biopharmaceutical manufacturing in India.

Biopharmaceuticals are a vibrant and rapidly developing sector of the Indian healthcare market. With continued efforts in research, development, and regulatory assistance, India positions itself to lead the world in the biopharmaceutical industry, greatly enhancing healthcare outcomes and meeting unmet medical needs both at home and abroad.

Types of Biopharmaceuticals

Biologics, another name for biopharmaceuticals, are medications made by biotechnology. They cover a broad spectrum of goods, including tissues, allergenics, vaccines, blood components, somatic cells, gene treatments, and recombinant therapeutic proteins. Biopharmaceuticals derive from living organisms, unlike conventional medications that undergo chemical manufacturing. The biopharmaceutical sector in India is expanding quickly due to advances in biotechnology and a rising need for novel therapies.

Monoclonal Antibodies (mAbs)

Immune cells that are clones of a single parent cell are identical and constitute monoclonal antibodies. They are effective treatments for a variety of illnesses, particularly cancer, autoimmune disorders, and infectious diseases, because of their strong specificity and affinity for certain antigens.

Examples and Usage:

Trastuzumab (Herceptin): Used in the treatment of HER2-positive breast cancer.

Rituximab (Rituxan): Used for non-Hodgkin's lymphoma and chronic lymphocytic leukemia.

Adalimumab (Humira): Effective in treating rheumatoid arthritis, psoriatic arthritis, and Crohn's disease.

Businesses like Biocon and Dr. Reddy's Laboratories have created biosimilar mAbs in India, lowering the cost and increasing the accessibility of these medicines.

Vaccines

Biological preparations known as vaccines offer active, acquired immunity against specific infectious illnesses. They have a significant impact on public health and are among the best tools for preventing illness.

Examples and Usage:

Covaxin: Developed by Bharat Biotech, it is an inactivated virus-based COVID-19 vaccine.

BCG Vaccine: Used for tuberculosis (TB) prevention.

Rotavac: An indigenous rotavirus vaccine by Bharat Biotech, used to prevent rotavirus infections, which are a leading cause of severe diarrhoea among infants and young children.

With organizations like the Serum Institute of India ranking among the world's biggest vaccine makers, India is a significant player in the global vaccine market.

Recombinant Proteins

Recombinant DNA encodes cloned proteins in an expression system. Recombinant proteins serve as therapeutic agents for a range of disorders, including hormone and enzyme replacement.

Examples and Usage:

Insulin (Humulin, Novolin): Used in the treatment of diabetes. Recombinant human insulin is produced using E. coli or yeast.

Erythropoietin (EPO): Used to treat anemia, particularly in chronic kidney disease and cancer patients undergoing chemotherapy.

Growth Hormone (Somatropin): Used to treat growth hormone deficiencies in children and adults.

Indian companies like Wockhardt and Biocon produce recombinant insulin and other proteins for both local and foreign markets.

Gene Therapy

In order to treat disease, gene therapy entails adding, removing, or changing genetic material within a patient's cells. It has potential use in the treatment of viral infections, some cancers, and a range of genetic diseases.

Examples and Usage:

Luxturna: A gene therapy for inherited retinal disease caused by mutations in the RPE65 gene.

Zolgensma: Used for spinal muscular atrophy (SMA), a severe neuromuscular disorder.

While research on gene therapy is still in its infancy in India, organizations such as the Indian Council of Medical Research (ICMR) are funding a number of gene therapy initiatives.

Cell Therapy

Patients receive living cells as part of a cell therapy procedure to treat their illness. Patients can receive their own cells, autologous cells, donor cells, or a combination of both (allogeneic) cells.

Examples and Usage:

CAR-T Cell Therapy: Involves modifying a patient’s T cells to attack cancer cells. It's used in treating certain types of lymphoma and leukemia.

Stem Cell Therapy: Used for regenerative purposes, such as repairing damaged tissues in conditions like osteoarthritis and spinal cord injuries.

Multiple clinical trials in India are investigating stem cell therapy, and it is available for treatment at a number of private clinics, even though the regulatory landscape is still developing.

Biosimilars

Biosimilars are pharmaceuticals that are very similar to reference drugs that have already received approval, with no discernible clinical variations in terms of potency, purity, or safety.

Examples and Usage:

Bevacizumab (BevaciRel): A biosimilar of Avastin, used for treating various cancers.

Etanercept (Enbrel): Used for autoimmune diseases such as rheumatoid arthritis and ankylosing spondylitis.

With companies like Biocon, Dr. Reddy's Laboratories, and Lupin setting the standard for the development and marketing of these goods, the biosimilar market in India is expanding.

Blood Products

Blood products made from human plasma and blood is crucial for treating a number of illnesses, such as immune system deficits, coagulation abnormalities, and bleeding injuries. Surgical procedures also utilize them.

Examples and Usage:

Factor VIII Concentrates: Used for treating hemophilia A.

Immunoglobulins: Used in immune therapy for conditions like primary immunodeficiency diseases and certain autoimmune disorders.

Albumin: Used in treating burns, shock, and other conditions where blood volume expansion is necessary.

In India, the National Blood Transfusion Council is in charge of regulating and inspecting blood products to guarantee their efficacy and safety.

India's biopharmaceutical industry is expected to grow significantly due to advances in biotechnology, favourable government policies, and a strong industrial base. In addition to satisfying the country's healthcare needs, Indian biopharmaceutical companies are becoming well-known worldwide. Clinical practice is increasingly using biopharmaceuticals, transforming the therapeutic environment and instilling new hope in patients with previously incurable diseases.

Sustained research, inventiveness, and cooperation will be essential in overcoming the obstacles and realizing the full potential of biopharmaceuticals in enhancing medical results as the sector develops.

Biopharmaceuticals Companies

India's biopharmaceutical business has seen significant growth because of its cost-effective production capabilities, competent workforce, and strong pharmaceutical infrastructure. In the biopharmaceuticals industry, a number of Indian businesses have achieved notable progress by concentrating on the creation of cutting-edge treatments, vaccines, biosimilars, and novel drug delivery methods. Strategic investments in research and development (R&D), partnerships with global pharmaceutical behemoths and a supportive regulatory framework all contribute to this achievement.

Biocon Ltd.

With its Bengaluru headquarters, the business is a trailblazer in India's biopharmaceutical industry. Kiran Mazumdar-Shaw founded Biocon in the year 1978 with the intention of producing industrial enzymes. However, the company quickly grew to become a major force in the biopharmaceuticals industry. The company is primarily focused on developing complex APIs (active pharmaceutical ingredients), new biologics, and biosimilars. Monoclonal antibodies, immunosuppressants, and insulin analogs are among Biocon's main products. Global pharmaceutical businesses can also receive integrated drug discovery and development services from Biocon through its subsidiary, Syngene International Ltd. The company, known globally for its reasonably priced insulin products, is actively fighting diabetes, a significant global and Indian public health concern.

Dr. Reddy's Laboratories

Dr. Reddy's Laboratory, based in Hyderabad, is another notable participant. Dr. K. Anji Reddy founded the business in 1984, and at first it concentrated on producing generic medications. Over time, it has branched out into biopharmaceuticals, focusing on the creation of complex generics and biosimilars. In the fields of gastroenterology, cardiovascular therapy, and oncology, Dr. Reddy is highly prominent. Its biopharmaceutical branch is especially well-known for its biosimilars, which have lowered the cost and increased accessibility to life-saving therapies like trastuzumab and rituximab. The company's significant R&D investment, along with its several locations devoted to furthering biopharmaceutical research; highlight its dedication to innovation.

Sun Pharmaceutical Industries Ltd.

With its headquarters in Mumbai, it is a significant contributor to India's biopharmaceutical industry. Dilip Shanghvi founded Sun Pharma in 1983, and since then, it has expanded to rank among the biggest specialty generic pharmaceutical firms worldwide as well as the largest in India. The biopharmaceutical portfolio of the company comprises specialty generics, innovative biologics, and biosimilars. Sun Pharma primarily focuses on oncology, dermatology, and ophthalmology, providing solutions that address the medical gaps in these therapeutic areas. 2014 saw Sun Pharma acquire Ranbaxy Laboratories, which greatly strengthened the company's biopharmaceuticals capabilities and expanded its product line and global reach.

Cipla Ltd.

Dr. Khwaja Abdul Hamied founded the business in 1935, and it is currently one of the major participants in the Indian biopharmaceutical market. Cipla is well known for its reasonably priced drugs and for being the first to make HIV/AIDS therapy available in underdeveloped nations. The biopharmaceutical initiatives of the company encompass the creation of innovative drug delivery systems, inhalation treatment products, and biosimilars. Cipla has a solid reputation in India and beyond thanks to its dedication to innovation and quality. The company is able to develop biopharmaceutical products that are up to par with international standards because of its advanced production facilities and strong R&D infrastructure.

Lupin Ltd.

Founded by Dr. Desh Bandhu Gupta in 1968, the company has its headquarters in Mumbai and has made considerable strides in the biopharmaceutical industry. Lupin's portfolio has expanded to cover a variety of therapeutic categories, including cardiovascular, diabetes, and respiratory disorders, from its initial focus on anti-tuberculosis medications. The corporation's biopharmaceutical section actively engages in the development of innovative biologics and biosimilars. Lupin has established itself as a major participant in the market because of its significant emphasis on R&D and strategic alliances with international biopharmaceutical businesses. The company produces safe and effective biopharmaceutical products thanks to its state-of-the-art manufacturing facilities and strict adherence to quality standards.

Zydus Cadila

Ramanbhai Patel established another well-known biopharmaceutical company in India in 1952, with its headquarters in Ahmedabad. Zydus Cadila offers a wide range of products, including vaccinations, innovative treatments, and biosimilars. The corporation's biopharmaceutical section is renowned for its efforts in developing biosimilars in the fields of rheumatology, nephrology, and oncology. Numerous research facilities and partnerships with foreign research universities support Zydus Cadila's strong R&D capabilities. The organization has a significant presence in both domestic and international markets and has received numerous accolades for its dedication to innovation and excellence.

Serum Institute of India

Founded by Dr. Cyrus Poonawalla in 1966, this Pune-based company is the largest vaccine maker globally in terms of volume. The company has received praise from all around the world for its efforts to combat infectious diseases, particularly for playing a crucial part in the development of COVID-19 vaccinations. Among the many vaccines offered by Serum Institute are those for hepatitis B, tetanus, diphtheria, and polio. Millions of people around the world now have access to life-saving vaccines because of the company's cutting-edge manufacturing facilities and dedication to providing affordable healthcare. Serum Institute's continued efforts to create and manufacture cutting-edge vaccines highlight its industry leadership in the biopharmaceutical sector.

Wockhardt Ltd.

Dr. Habil Khorakiwala formed this major player in India's biopharmaceutical industry in 1960, with its headquarters located in Mumbai. The corporation dedicates its biopharmaceutical division to the development of vaccines, new biologics, and biosimilars. Wockhardt's notable accomplishments include the creation of India's first native recombinant insulin and his ongoing efforts to create biosimilars for immunology and oncology. The company's robust R&D infrastructure and state-of-the-art production facilities underpin its global position. Wockhardt is a leader in the biopharmaceutical sector thanks to its dedication to innovation and patient-centered healthcare.

These businesses, among others, have established India as a major player in the world's biopharmaceutical market. Their emphasis on quality, affordability, and innovation has sparked the creation of novel cures and life-saving procedures, increasing access to healthcare for millions of people throughout the globe. As the biopharmaceutical sector develops, Indian businesses are well-positioned to make a significant contribution to the advancement of medical knowledge and the resolution of global health issues.

Case Studies

Case 1: Places with poor healthcare infrastructure, such as rural and underserved areas, face significant challenges. To address these issues, the government has launched programs like the National Programme for Prevention and Control of Cancer, Diabetes, Cardiovascular Diseases, and Stroke (NPCDCS), which aims to increase awareness about diabetes care and improve access to necessary medications. Anticoagulants treat and prevent blood clots, which can lead to major health problems such as stroke, heart attack, and pulmonary embolism. In India, doctors frequently prescribe heparin, warfarin, and more recent medications like Dabigatran and Rivaroxaban as anticoagulants. Anticoagulants are now critical for the treatment and prevention of thrombotic disorders because of the increased prevalence of cardiovascular illnesses. Anticoagulant therapy necessitates close monitoring to prevent problems like excessive bleeding, which is why patient education and follow-up are essential parts of the treatment. India's prescription medicine market is a reflection of both the nation's expanding pharmaceutical industry and its extensive healthcare needs. Despite India's impressive progress in guaranteeing the accessibility and cost-effectiveness of necessary pharmaceuticals, issues with drug quality, availability, and abuse still exist. In order to solve these issues, the pharmaceutical industry, public health programs, and government restrictions are essential. Prescription drug usage and regulation will continue to be crucial to enhancing public health outcomes throughout India as the nation invests in pharmaceutical research and development and builds its healthcare infrastructure.

Case 2: India's biopharmaceutical industry is a prime example of how to successfully combine market potential, regulatory backing, and innovation to change healthcare delivery and access. India has been a global hub for biopharmaceuticals for the past 20 years, thanks to improvements in biotechnology and a highly qualified labour pool. Companies like Biocon, Cipla, and Dr. Reddy's Laboratories have led the way in producing innovative therapies and biosimilars, meeting the urgent need for cost-effective healthcare solutions. For example, the introduction of biosimilars has improved access to innovative therapies for a larger population, leading to better health outcomes. Through programs like Make in India and Start-up India, as well as initiatives like the National Biopharma Mission, of the Indian government has supported this expansion by offering crucial financial, physical, and regulatory support. The industry does, however, confront difficulties, including expensive development expenses and strict regulatory restrictions. Strategic partnerships between government, business, and academia are crucial to overcoming these obstacles. Indian biopharmaceutical businesses can improve production efficiency and scalability by incorporating sophisticated manufacturing techniques and artificial intelligence. India is well-positioned to emerge as a worldwide leader in biopharmaceuticals, making a substantial contribution to the healthcare ecosystem and meeting unmet medical needs in the country and beyond, with continued efforts in research, innovation, and regulatory alignment. This ever-changing environment offers investors and business owners the chance to participate in a booming industry that is both socially and economically significant, improving millions of people's health results.

Suggestive Questions from the Chapter

1. India is known as the "pharmacy of the world." What role does this play in the global pharmaceutical industry?
2. What initiatives are in place to increase the affordability and accessibility of prescription drugs in rural India?
3. What issues with prescription medicine quality and usage does the Indian pharmaceutical industry face?
4. Which medical ailments are treated by the main prescription medicine types that are most frequently used in India?
5. What impact do drug abuse and antibiotic resistance problems have on India's public health?
6. How do government programs and public health initiatives help people in India get access to the necessary drugs for treating infectious and chronic illnesses?
7. What are the typical applications and brand names for paracetamol, an OTC medication that is popular in India?
8. What are the recommended safety measures for using Loperamide as a medicine to prevent diarrhoea?
9. What are the main areas of concentration for significant Indian biopharmaceutical businesses, and what impact have their approaches had on the global biopharmaceutical environment?
10. What role has the Serum Institute of India played in the global fight against infectious diseases, and how did it earn its reputation as a pioneer in vaccine production?

Multiple Choice Questions

1. Which of the following is a key factor contributing to India's success in the global pharmaceutical market?
   (a) A focus on imported raw materials
   (b) High investment in simple generics
   (c) A highly qualified labour force and a robust manufacturing infrastructure
   (d) Limited production of biosimilars

2. What is the role of the National Pharmaceutical Pricing Authority (NPPA) in India?
   (a) Monitoring the quality of prescription drugs
   (b) Regulating the prices of essential medicines
   (c) Promoting the export of Indian pharmaceuticals
   (d) Managing research and development in the pharmaceutical sector
3. What challenge does India face despite its strong pharmaceutical infrastructure?
   (a) Lack of a qualified labour force
   (b) Difficulty in manufacturing generic drugs
   (c) Distribution of substandard and counterfeit medications
   (d) Inability to comply with global standards such as those from the US FDA and WHO
4. What issue arises from the over-the-counter sale of antibiotics in India?
   (a) Increased demand for generic medications
   (b) Growing public trust in pharmaceutical products
   (c) Development of antibiotic resistance
   (d) Decrease in prescription drug misuse
5. How has telemedicine impacted the prescription drug market in India?
   (a) It has led to a decrease in drug prices
   (b) It has made obtaining prescriptions easier, especially in rural areas
   (c) It has reduced the demand for online pharmacies
   (d) It has eliminated the need for prescription regulations
6. Which of the following is a commonly used antibiotic in India?
   (a) Fluconazole (b) Oseltamivir
   (c) Cefixime (d) Risperidone
7. Which class of drugs is essential for the treatment of autoimmune diseases and organ transplant rejection?
   (a) Diuretics (b) Immunosuppressants
   (c) Antipsychotics (d) Antibiotics
8. Which of the following is a key medication used in antiretroviral therapy (ART) in India for HIV treatment?
   (a) Acyclovir (b) Oseltamivir
   (c) Tacrolimus (d) Antiretroviral drugs

9. What is the major public health issue related to the widespread use of antibiotics in India?
   (a) Gastrointestinal issues (b) Hypertension
   (c) Antibiotic resistance (d) Cardiovascular disease
10. Which drug is commonly prescribed in India for managing Type 2 diabetes?
    (a) Metformin (b) Prednisone
    (c) Warfarin (d) Hydrochlorothiazide
11. Which Indian pharmaceutical company is the largest specialty generic pharmaceutical company in the world?
    (a) Cipla Limited
    (b) Dr. Reddy's Laboratories
    (c) Sun Pharmaceutical Industries Ltd.
    (d) Lupin Limited
12. Which company is known for developing India's first COVID-19 vaccine, ZyCoV-D?
    (a) Aurobindo Pharma
    (b) Glenmark Pharmaceuticals
    (c) Sun Pharmaceutical Industries Ltd.
    (d) Zydus Cadila
13. Dr. Reddy's Laboratories specializes in which of the following products?
    (a) Vaccines and biologics
    (b) OTC drugs, biosimilars, and generic treatments
    (c) Anti-retroviral treatments
    (d) Topical analgesics
14. Which company is recognized for providing cost-effective antiretroviral medications for HIV/AIDS treatment?
    (a) Lupin Limited (b) Cipla Limited
    (c) Torrent Pharmaceuticals (d) Aurobindo Pharma
15. Lupin Limited has a significant presence in which market, contributing greatly to its revenue?
    (a) Europe (b) Africa
    (c) United States (d) Latin America

16. Which legislative act primarily governs the regulation of over-the-counter (OTC) drugs in India?
    (a) Drugs and Magic Remedies Act, 1954
    (b) Narcotic Drugs and Psychotropic Substances Act, 1985
    (c) Drugs and Cosmetics Act, 1940
    (d) Indian Penal Code, 1860
17. Which organization is responsible for ensuring the quality, safety, and efficacy of OTC drugs in India?
    (a) IMA (b) CDSCO (c) NPPA (d) BIS
18. What is a critical requirement for the packaging of over-the-counter drugs in India?
    (a) Attractive design (b) Multi-language labelling
    (c) Tamper-evident packaging (d) Eco-friendly packaging
19. The process of monitoring the safety of OTC drugs after they have been released to the market is called:
    (a) Pre-Approval Inspection
    (b) Good Manufacturing Practices (GMP)
    (c) Post-Marketing Surveillance
    (d) Clinical Data Evaluation
20. Which act regulates the advertising of OTC drugs to prevent misleading claims?
    (a) Drugs and Magic Remedies (Objectionable Advertisements) Act, 1954
    (b) Drugs and Cosmetics Act, 1940
    (c) Advertising Standards Act, 1982
    (d) Consumer Protection Act, 1986
21. Which of the following companies is known for its reasonably priced insulin products and active contribution to the fight against diabetes?
    (a) Cipla Ltd. (b) Biocon Ltd.
    (c) Lupin Ltd. (d) Wockhardt Ltd.
22. Dr. Reddy's Laboratories is well-known for its contribution to which of the following therapeutic areas?
    (a) Gastroenterology, cardiovascular therapy, and oncology
    (b) Diabetes and respiratory disorders

(c) Rheumatology, nephrology, and oncology
(d) Dermatology and ophthalmology

23. Which company is the largest vaccine maker globally in terms of volume and has played a crucial role in developing COVID-19 vaccines?
    (a) Serum Institute of India
    (b) Sun Pharmaceutical Industries Ltd.
    (c) Zydus Cadila
    (d) Cipla Ltd.

24. Which biopharmaceutical company expanded its portfolio by acquiring Ranbaxy Laboratories in 2014, significantly strengthening its biopharmaceuticals capabilities?
    (a) Dr. Reddy's Laboratories
    (b) Biocon Ltd.
    (c) Sun Pharmaceutical Industries Ltd.
    (d) Wockhardt Ltd.

25. Wockhardt Ltd. is noted for developing which of the following biopharmaceutical products?
    (a) India's first native recombinant insulin
    (b) Biosimilars for cardiovascular diseases
    (c) Innovative inhalation therapy products
    (d) Vaccines for polio and hepatitis B

CHAPTER

3

Understanding the Medical Representative

Who is a Medical Representative?

It's often observed that a Medical Representative is frequently called a pharmaceutical sales representative, especially in the marketing circuit. More specifically, a Medical Representative (MR) is an official who works for a pharmaceutical company. Their job is to market medicine brands or medical devices to healthcare providers such as doctors, hospitals, pharmacies, etc. and provide prescriptions or recommendations for the promoted brands or devices. These people are an essential conduit between the pharmaceutical industry and the medical community. Assuring that healthcare personnel are knowledgeable about the newest medications, therapies, and medical innovations created by the pharmaceutical companies they represent is the main duty of a Medical Representative (MR).

Medical representatives are essential to the healthcare sector, and they have a wide range of responsibilities based on pharmaceutical product sales. They are consultants and educators in as well as salespeople. MRs must possess comprehensive knowledge about the applications, benefits, limitations, and potential drug interactions of the products they promote. With this information, individuals may have meaningful discussions with medical professionals and make well-informed judgments regarding the drugs and therapies they recommend for their patients.

Making routine trips to hospitals, pharmacies, and doctor's offices is one of an MR's main responsibilities. They give information about both new and current pharmaceutical items during these visits, supporting their talks with samples, pamphlets, and scholarly publications. For the purpose of sharing current knowledge on medication therapy and medical developments, they frequently plan and run educational conferences, workshops, and seminars. By engaging in these activities, MRs cultivates enduring connections with healthcare providers, gradually establishing credibility and trust.

The MRs use a variety of communication methods in addition to in-person sales calls to connect with their target market. The MRs uses these methods, such as phone conversations, emails, and virtual meetings, in the current era of widespread digital communication. It is advisable that the MRs must be able to adjust to many communication modalities in order to be effective and connect with a larger audience.

Medical representatives also need to keep up with the most recent advancements in the pharmaceutical sector, such as the introduction of new products, modifications to regulations, and shifts in consumer preferences. Professional growth and on-going learning are necessary for this. Pharmaceutical companies often provide MRs with on-going training to ensure they possess the latest knowledge and skills. The MRs are able to maintain their competitiveness and provide value to their clients because of their dedication to lifelong learning.

Additionally, the MRs are in charge of getting input on their brands and goods from healthcare providers. Pharmaceutical businesses benefit greatly from this feedback since it helps them understand potential adverse effects, areas for improvement, and the effectiveness of their products. By serving as a channel for this data, the MRs help continuously improve pharmaceutical goods and services.

A medical representative's job is tough and demanding. A Medical Representative (MR) must possess strong interpersonal and communication skills to effectively communicate complex medical information in a clear and persuasive manner, often within a short timeframe. Since gaining and retaining the trust of healthcare practitioners is crucial to their success, they must be skilled at networking and forming connections. MRs, sometimes are expected to oversee a sizable territory and meet predetermined sales goals, also need to possess excellent organizational and time management abilities. Experience and time help further hone these skill sets.

It is crucial for medical representatives to act ethically. Their companies and the industry's governing bodies have strong ethical norms and regulations that they must follow. They must avoid any form of coercion or undue influence, ensure their promotional efforts are based on factual and fair information, and maintain transparency in all their interactions with healthcare professionals.

Moreover, as technology has advanced, so too has the role of the MRs. The MRs work has changed as a result of the integration of digital tools and platforms, making it possible to implement more effective and focused marketing campaigns. CRM (Customer Relationship Management) systems, for example, are letting MRs to keep track of their contacts with healthcare providers, schedule their appointments, and analyse data to spot patterns and opportunities.

Utilizing digital marketing strategies, such as email campaigns and social media interaction, has also grown in significance as a means of expanding the reach and improving the visibility of pharmaceutical items. The Product Management Team (PMT) in the head office (HO) is primarily responsible for executing these digital efforts, but the marketing representatives (MRs) also have a significant impact on engaging their own clientele, such as physicians.

We all know that in the healthcare sector, a Medical Representative plays a crucial role in facilitating communication between pharmaceutical companies and healthcare providers. Their responsibilities include sales, instruction, and advice; they also need to have strong communication skills and a thorough understanding of medical items. To effectively carry out their duties in the ever-evolving healthcare landscape, MRs must continue to be flexible, updating their knowledge on a regular basis and embracing new technologies. Medical representatives make a substantial contribution to the development of medical science and the enhancement of patient care through their work.

Qualities of a Medical Representative

The personal sales, account for majority of the pharmaceutical sales. In the highly competitive market where several pharmaceutical conglomerates advertise their own branded generics, face-to-face selling may be an effective way to market a brand's quality, efficacy, safety, side effects, and other attributes. In the pharmaceutical sales environment, the role of the Medical Representative (MR) is very essential, particularly in a market as vast and dynamic as in India. Their main duty is to market and promote the company's products to the medical professionals, such as physicians, pharmacists, and hospitals, by means of an indirect system that generates prescriptions. Additionally, they receive payment when a patient buys a product directly from a retailer or via hospital purchase departments. A MR has to be quick to pick things up and flexible in order to stay effective in the Indian pharmaceutical market, which is complicated due to its vast range of therapeutic areas and mix of urban and rural healthcare settings. The following characteristics are necessary for a medical representative to be successful:

In-depth Product Knowledge: A medical representative (MR) needs to be well-versed in the pharmaceutical items they are endorsing. This entails being aware of the products advantages over rivals' as well as the active substances, dosage forms, indications, and possible adverse effects. They may confidently and accurately respond to any questions from healthcare professionals thanks to this expertise.

Good Communication Skills: An MR must be able to communicate effectively. They have to be able to communicate intricate medical facts in an understandable and efficient way. Understanding the wants and worries of patients as well as healthcare providers requires excellent listening skills.

Interpersonal Skills: One of the most important aspects of an MR's work is establishing and preserving solid bonds with healthcare professionals. They must be able to establish rapport and trust with their clients and be personable and sympathetic.

Sales Acumen: A successful salesperson must be able to convince and sway medical professionals to prescribe or suggest their products. They ought to be skilled at seeing possible connections, getting past obstacles, and making sales.

Time Management and Organizational Skills: Since the MRs often covers a wide area; they must have excellent time management skills. They need to be able to organize and prioritize their appointments with medical specialists, control their calendars, and maintain tabs on their correspondence and follow-ups.

Persistence and Resilience: Dealing with rejection and disappointments on a regular basis can be difficult in the pharmaceutical sales industry. An MR must be resilient and persistent, keeping a positive outlook and pursuing their sales goals in the face of setbacks.

Technical Proficiency: An MR needs to be at ease with technology given the growing usage of digital tools and platforms in pharmaceutical marketing. This involves being adept at using online meeting platforms, CRM software, and other digital tools for reporting and planning.

Analytical Skills: A market researcher should be able to examine sales data, market trends, and comments from medical professionals. This helps in determining areas in need of development and prospects for growth.

Adaptability and Flexibility: Rules, goods, and market conditions are constantly changing in the pharmaceutical industry, which is a dynamic industry. An MR needs to be fluid and adaptive, able to quickly modify their methods and techniques as circumstances demand.

Ethical Conduct: In the pharmaceutical sales industry, honesty and moral behaviour are crucial. An MR must always abide by ethical standards, making sure that their communications with medical professionals and the data they offer are truthful and correct.

Product Presentation Skills: The ability to give engaging product presentations is a must for an MR. This entails having the skills necessary to provide captivating visual aids, respond tactfully to criticism, and modify presentations to meet the needs of the target audience.

Knowledge of the Healthcare System: It is crucial to comprehend the composition and operation of India's healthcare system. This entails familiarity with the ecosystem of reimbursement, regulatory agencies, and different healthcare providers.

Customer Focus: A MR should constantly put the needs and satisfaction of their clients first, adopting a strong customer-centric approach. This entails giving prompt, pertinent information, solving issues, and efficiently following up.

Networking Skills: Building a strong network within the healthcare sector can greatly increase an MR's efficacy. Relationships with administrators of healthcare facilities, key opinion leaders (KOLs), and other stakeholders are part of this.

Self-Motivation and Discipline: Since MRs frequently works alone; they must possess a high level of discipline and self-motivation. They must be self-aware, retain attention, and put up a constant amount of effort.

Cultural Sensitivity: An MR needs to be able to adjust their approach to various cultural norms and practices, considering the varied cultural environment of India. This facilitates the development of closer bonds and a greater awareness of the particular requirements of various groups.

Continuous Learning: The pharmaceutical sector is always changing, constantly developing new products, technology, and research. An MR must commit to lifelong learning and stay abreast of the latest developments in the industry.

Presentation of Self: Making a favourable first impression requires professional appearance and personal upkeep. An MR should conduct oneself in a way that embodies the integrity and professionalism of their organization.

Problem-Solving Skills: A problem-solving The MR should be able to identify and resolve issues with medical professionals. This covers responding to complaints, settling disputes, and coming up with original solutions to issues.

Collaboration Skills: Although an MR works independently most of the time, they also need to interact well with others in their team, including management, marketing staff, and sales associates. This requires strong communication and teamwork abilities.

Regulatory Knowledge: It is essential to be aware of the regulatory framework that governs pharmaceutical marketing and sales in India. To make sure that their actions are morally and legally acceptable, MRs should be aware of the rules and compliance specifications.

Financial Acumen: An MR may make better judgments and improve the financial health of their company by having a thorough understanding of the financial facets of their work, such as budgeting, pricing strategies, and return on investment.

Emotional Intelligence: An MR with high emotional intelligence may successfully negotiate the complicated emotional terrain that patients and healthcare providers inhabit. This means being aware of, in control of, and sensitive to one's own and others' emotions.

Strategic Thinking: An MR should be able to plan long-term objectives, think strategically, and coordinate everyday tasks with the organization's overarching goals.

Attention to Detail: In the pharmaceutical sales industry, even the smallest mistakes can have far-reaching effects; therefore, accuracy is essential. To ensure accuracy in all of their contacts and paperwork, MRs needs to have excellent attention to detail.

In India's pharmaceutical sales ecosystem, a medical representative needs to have a wide range of skills to effectively market and sell pharmaceuticals in a complicated and competitive industry. These attributes, which range from emotional intelligence and strategic thinking to technical skill and ethical behaviour, guarantee that MRs can forge meaningful connections with healthcare professionals, hit their sales goals, and make a positive impact on the organization as a whole.

The healthcare industry prioritizes the health and well-being of the general public, necessitating individual commitment and integrity to meet the ecosystem's expectations. The company's training department imparts most of these skills, including understanding fundamentals, therapeutic areas, product knowledge, competitive scenarios, and better selling techniques. This training not only equips employees with essential knowledge but also fosters a culture of accountability and excellence. When each team member embodies these values, it creates a ripple effect that enhances collaboration, patient care, and ultimately, the organization's reputation within the community.

Qualifications & Skills Required for Hiring a Medical Representative

Educational Background: A minimum qualification of a bachelor's degree in pharmacy (B.Pharm), life sciences, biology, or a related field is typically required. However, graduates are also considered in many pharmaceutical companies. Degrees in business or marketing can also be advantageous.

Postgraduate degrees such as M.Pharm or MBA can provide an added advantage, enhancing a candidate's prospects and potential career growth.

Knowledge of Medical Terminology: A strong understanding of medical terms, drug formulations, and therapeutic areas is essential. This knowledge enables Medical Representatives (MRs) to communicate effectively with healthcare professionals (HCPs) and understand the products they are promoting.

Certification and Training: While not always mandatory, certifications in pharmaceutical sales or marketing can be beneficial. Various training programs are available that equip candidates with essential skills and knowledge about the pharmaceutical industry.

Continuous professional development and participation in workshops and seminars are highly recommended to stay updated with industry trends.

Communication Skills: Good verbal and written communication skills are crucial for MRs. They must be able to present information clearly and persuasively to doctors, pharmacists, and other HCPs.

Proficiency in multiple languages can be an asset, especially in a diverse country like India.

Sales and Marketing Acumen: A sound understanding of sales strategies, market dynamics, and customer relationship management is vital. MRs should be adept at identifying opportunities, negotiating, and closing deals.

Previous experience in sales or marketing, even in non-pharmaceutical sectors, can be beneficial.

Interpersonal Skills: Building and maintaining strong relationships with HCPs, colleagues, and stakeholders is fundamental. Good interpersonal skills help in establishing trust and rapport, which are critical for successful sales.

Adaptability and Resilience: The pharmaceutical sales environment is dynamic and often challenging. MRs must be adaptable, resilient, and able to handle rejection and setbacks constructively.

Technical Proficiency: Proficiency in using digital tools and platforms for sales tracking, reporting, and presentations is increasingly important. Familiarity with CRM software, Microsoft Office Suite, and other relevant technologies is beneficial.

Understanding digital marketing and social media platforms can also be advantageous as the industry moves towards digital engagement.

Analytical Skills: Ability to analyse sales data, market trends, and customer feedback to make informed decisions and strategies is crucial. Analytical skills help in understanding market needs and adjusting approaches accordingly.

Ethical Standards: High ethical standards and integrity are non-negotiable in the pharmaceutical industry. MRs must adhere to regulatory guidelines and company policies, ensuring that their practices are ethical and compliant.

Time Management and Organizational Skills: Effective time management and organizational skills are essential to balance multiple tasks, meet deadlines, and manage territories efficiently.

Ability to prioritize tasks and manage time efficiently is crucial for meeting sales targets and maintaining a balanced workload.

Networking Abilities: Building a strong network within the medical community, including doctors, pharmacists, and healthcare organizations, can significantly enhance an MR's effectiveness.

Networking abilities facilitate better access to key decision-makers and influencers in the healthcare sector.

Problem-Solving Skills: MRs should be adept at identifying and resolving issues that may arise in the field, from addressing customer concerns to overcoming sales obstacles.

Creative problem-solving can help in finding innovative ways to market products and achieve sales targets.

Product Knowledge: In-depth knowledge of the products being promoted, including their benefits, side effects, and contraindications, is essential. MRs must be able to answer detailed questions from HCPs and provide comprehensive information.

Continuous learning about new products and advancements in the pharmaceutical field is necessary to maintain a competitive edge.

Presentation Skills: Strong presentation skills are required for delivering product information and sales pitches effectively. MRs often conducts seminars, workshops, and meetings, requiring them to present confidently and engagingly.

Customer Orientation: A customer-oriented approach is vital for understanding the needs and preferences of HCPs and providing tailored solutions. Building customer loyalty and satisfaction is key to long-term success.

Developing a deep understanding of customer needs and preferences helps in providing personalized solutions and building strong relationships.

Regulatory Knowledge: Understanding the regulatory environment governing pharmaceuticals in India, including the Drugs and Cosmetics Act and guidelines from bodies like the Central Drugs Standard Control Organization (CDSCO), is crucial.

Compliance with regulations ensures that promotional practices are legal and ethical.

Self-Motivation and Independence: MRs often works independently and need to be self-motivated to achieve their targets. A proactive approach and the ability to work without constant supervision are important traits.

Self-motivation drives performance and helps in achieving and exceeding sales targets.

Team Collaboration: While much of the work is independent, collaborating with colleagues, marketing teams, and management is essential for cohesive strategy implementation and achieving organizational goals.

Teamwork and collaboration enhance overall performance and contribute to the success of the organization.

Experience: Prior experience in pharmaceutical sales or a related field is often preferred. Experienced candidates bring valuable insights, established networks, and a proven track record of success.

Even candidates with experience in other sales sectors can bring transferable skills and fresh perspectives.

By emphasizing these qualifications and skills, companies can ensure they hire competent, capable, and dedicated Medical Representatives who can effectively promote their products and contribute to the company's success.

Personal Attributes Required for a Medical Representative

The personal attributes of a Medical Representative include effective communication, in-depth product knowledge, interpersonal skills, sales acumen, self-motivation, organizational skills, technical proficiency, emotional intelligence, patience, customer focus, analytical skills, stress management, attention to detail, leadership potential, and professional demeanour.

Being a Medical Representative (MR) in the Indian pharmaceutical sales ecosystem demands a unique blend of personal attributes that ensure success in this challenging yet rewarding profession. Here are some of the key attributes:

Communication Attribute

Clarity and Precision: An MR must communicate product information clearly and accurately to healthcare professionals.

Listening Skills: Active listening is crucial to understand the needs and concerns of doctors and pharmacists.

Persuasiveness: The ability to persuade healthcare providers about the benefits and efficacy of a product is essential.

Knowledge Attribute

Scientific Understanding: Comprehensive knowledge of the pharmaceutical products, including their composition, mechanism of action, side effects, and contraindications.

Competitive Awareness: Understanding the competitor products to effectively position their own product in the market.

Continuous Learning: Keeping up-to-date with the latest developments in the pharmaceutical industry.

Self - Motivative Attribute

Goal-oriented: Setting personal and professional goals and working diligently to achieve them.

Proactive Approach: Taking the initiative to solve problems and find new opportunities.

Resilience: Ability to handle rejection and setbacks without losing motivation.

Organizational Attribute

Time Management: Efficiently managing time to cover all assigned territories and meet with healthcare providers regularly.

Documentation: Keeping accurate records of sales calls, meetings, and follow-ups.

Prioritization: Identifying and focusing on high-potential doctors and pharmacists.

Technical Attribute

Use of Technology: Proficiency in using CRM software, email, and other digital tools to manage customer relationships and sales activities.

Data Analysis: Ability to analyse sales data to identify trends and opportunities for growth.

Presentation Skills: Creating and delivering engaging presentations to healthcare professionals.

Adapting Attribute

Handling Change: Ability to adapt to changes in product lines, sales strategies, and market conditions.

Cultural Sensitivity: Understanding and respecting cultural differences in diverse regions.

Flexible Working Hours: Willingness to work beyond regular hours to meet healthcare professionals.

Ethical Conduct

Integrity: Maintaining honesty and transparency in all dealings.

Compliance: Adhering to all regulatory and company guidelines.

Trustworthiness: Building trust with healthcare professionals through consistent and ethical behaviour.

Problem-solving Attribute

Critical Thinking: Analysing situations and making informed decisions.

Creative Solutions: Finding innovative ways to overcome challenges and achieve sales targets.

Resourcefulness: Utilizing available resources effectively to achieve objectives.

Collaborative Attribute

Team Player: Working effectively with other MRs and team members to achieve common goals.

Knowledge Sharing: Sharing insights and information with colleagues to enhance overall team performance.

Supportive Attitude: Offering assistance and support to team members when needed.

Emotional Intelligence

Self-awareness: Understanding one's own emotions and their impact on work performance.

Self-regulation: Managing emotions to remain calm and effective under pressure.

Empathy: Recognizing and understanding the emotions of others, fostering better relationships.

Presenting Attribute

Engaging Presentations: Creating and delivering presentations that effectively communicate product benefits.

Adaptability: Tailoring presentations to the audience, whether it's a group of doctors or a single pharmacist.

Confidence: Presenting with confidence to establish credibility and influence.

Patience and Persistence

Long Sales Cycles: Patience to handle the often long and complex sales cycles in the pharmaceutical industry.

Follow-up: Persistence in following up with healthcare providers without being intrusive.

Consistency: Consistent effort in maintaining relationships and pushing for sales.

Customer - focused Attribute

Customer Needs: Prioritizing the needs and concerns of healthcare professionals.

Service Orientation: Providing exceptional service and support to build lasting relationships.

Feedback Handling: Actively seeking and constructively handling feedback from customers.

Analytical Attribute

Market Analysis: Analysing market trends and identifying potential opportunities for growth.

Performance Metrics: Tracking and analysing sales performance metrics to improve strategies.

Problem Identification: Identifying potential issues and proactively addressing them.

Stress Managing Attribute

Handling Pressure: Ability to remain composed and effective under high-pressure situations.

Coping Strategies: Developing effective coping strategies to manage stress and maintain performance.

Positive Attitude: Maintaining a positive outlook despite challenges and setbacks.

Detailing Attribute

Accuracy: Ensuring all information provided to healthcare professionals is accurate and up-to-date.

Compliance: Meticulous in following all compliance and regulatory requirements.

Quality Focus: Commitment to providing high-quality service and support.

Leadership Attribute

Influence: Ability to influence and inspire others within the team.

Mentorship: Willingness to mentor and guide junior MEDICAL REPRESENTATIVEs.

Vision: Demonstrating a clear vision and direction for achieving sales objectives.

Professional Appearance and Demeanour

Presentation: Maintaining a professional appearance that reflects positively on the company.

Confidence: Projecting confidence and competence in all interactions.

Etiquette: Adhering to professional etiquette and norms in all dealings.

A medical representative can successfully negotiate the intricacies of the Indian pharmaceutical sales ecosystem by exhibiting these qualities, forging close bonds with medical professionals, and attaining success in the sales process.

Importance of a Medical Representative in the Pharmaceutical Industry

One of the main pillars of healthcare is the pharmaceutical sector, which develops, produces, and distributes medications that prolong and save lives. Medical representatives are vital to this large ecology. By acting as a liaison between pharmaceutical corporations and medical professionals, they guarantee that patients receive the newest and most potent therapies available. The function of the medical representative is especially important in the context of the pharmaceutical market in India, which is among the largest and fastest-growing in the world.

The Role of a Medical Representative

In the field, a medical representative serves as a pharmaceutical company's face. Promoting and selling their company's products to medical professionals—such as physicians, pharmacists, and hospitals—is their main duty. This entails giving thorough product demonstrations, giving free samples, and giving medical professionals the clinical and scientific data they want in order to decide whether or not to prescribe or suggest a medication.

Product Promotion and Awareness

There is fierce competition among the many companies in the Indian pharmaceutical market to get the attention of healthcare practitioners. The responsibility of medical representatives is to ensure that the products of their company are distinctive. They accomplish this by setting up meetings with physicians and pharmacists to go over the advantages of their products, talk about the most recent research, and give product samples for assessment. If the firm launches a new antibiotic, the medical representative would be responsible for educating physicians about its effectiveness, dosage, side effects, and comparison to current therapies.

Building and Maintaining Relationships

Personal ties are important in commercial dealings in India, and the pharmaceutical sector is no exception. Developing trusting relationships with medical experts is the responsibility of medical representatives. These connections entail constant information sharing, mutual respect, and trust in addition to sales. A well-liked and trusted medical representative can significantly influence a physician's prescription practices. In the Indian setting, friends and family recommendations hold significant importance.

Providing Feedback to the Company

The pharmaceutical company relies on its medical representatives to monitor the field. They get insightful input on the company's products from medical specialists as well as details on those of rival companies. The company's marketing and product development plans rely heavily on this input. For instance, if physicians frequently report adverse effects linked to a specific medication, the business can utilize this data to look into and resolve the problem, potentially producing a safer or more efficient product.

Supporting Pharmacovigilance Efforts

Pharmacovigilance, the process of monitoring the safety of medications, is a crucial component of the pharmaceutical industry. By disclosing any negative reactions or other safety concerns they learn about from patients or healthcare providers, medical representatives play a crucial part in this. The importance of medical representatives in guaranteeing drug safety is growing in India, where the regulatory landscape is changing. Their front-line position enables them to promptly recognize and report problems, assisting businesses in acting quickly to safeguard people.

Driving Sales and Market Penetration

Pharmaceutical companies want to market their products, and medical representatives are the ones who have to drive these sales. They achieve this by raising the awareness of and perceived worth of their products among medical professionals. Medical Representatives must modify their tactics for various marketplaces in a nation as diverse as India, where availability to pharmaceuticals and healthcare procedures range greatly between areas. For instance, a medical representative in a city would concentrate on marketing high-end, pricey medications, but one in a rural location might prioritize affordable, necessary medications.

The context of the Indian pharmaceutical market

The Indian Pharmaceutical Market Context

India has one of the biggest pharmaceutical industries globally, renowned for its capacity to manufacture affordable, high-quality generic medications. The nation is the world's top supplier of generic medications and meets more than

50% of the demand for various vaccines globally. The domestic market is likewise sizable, with rising demand for OTC and prescription medications due to a large population, rising health consciousness, and government programs to enhance access to healthcare.

In light of this, the medical representative's job assumes even greater significance. The diversity of the Indian market is evident in the types of healthcare providers it offers, the availability of healthcare infrastructure, and the regulatory framework, in addition to its geographic location and demographic makeup. Medical representatives have to negotiate this complexity by adjusting their strategy to meet the unique requirements of various geographic areas and clientele groups.

Some Examples

Rural Healthcare Access

Lack of infrastructure and medical staff frequently restricts access to healthcare in rural India. Medical representatives play a crucial role in these fields by ensuring that physicians and pharmacists receive necessary medications. For instance, medical representatives played a crucial role in raising awareness of the COVID-19 pandemic and distributing vaccinations and antiviral medications to isolated locations. Their work made it possible for even the most marginalized groups to obtain therapies that could save lives

Introducing New Therapies

New therapy introductions necessitate extensive education and relationship-building, especially in specialty areas like diabetes or oncology. Those at the forefront of these initiatives are frequently medical representatives. For example, when a pharmaceutical company introduces a new cancer medication, medical representatives have to collaborate closely with oncologists to make sure they comprehend the drug's advantages, mode of action, and compatibility with current treatment regimens. In India, where there is a significant prevalence of chronic illnesses like diabetes, medical representatives are essential in making sure patients receive the newest and most potent medicines available.

Managing the Competitive Landscape

The pharmaceutical industry in India is extremely fragmented, with several businesses selling comparable goods. It is the duty of medical representatives to set their products apart in this competitive industry. When several companies are selling the same generic medication, for instance, a medical representative's ability to establish rapport and offer value-added services—like comprehensive product details, patient education materials, or frequent follow-ups—may determine whether a doctor selects their product over a rival's.

Supporting Government Health Initiatives

The Indian government has introduced several programs, such as Ayushman Bharat and the National Health Mission (NHM), to enhance public health. By making sure that medical professionals have access to the required pharmaceuticals and are aware of the most recent guidelines, medical representatives can contribute positively to these initiatives. For instance, in the fight against tuberculosis (TB), medical representatives, in collaboration with pharmaceutical companies producing anti-TB treatments, play a crucial role in ensuring doctors receive up-to-date treatment procedures and have easy access to these medications.

Challenges Faced by Medical Representatives

Despite its importance, the position of medical representative is not without difficulties. Working in a highly competitive and price-sensitive market is a challenge that medical representatives in India frequently encounter. They have to strike a balance between the ethical requirements of patient care and the desire to advertise their products. Furthermore, India's regulatory landscape is evolving, placing heightened scrutiny on the marketing and sale of pharmaceuticals. Medical representatives have to follow these rules and still meet their sales goals.

Moreover, medical representatives need to be extremely flexible because of the great diversity of the Indian market. Depending on the area they are operating in, Medical Representatives may need to adapt their sales approach, communication style, and product focus. Unlike a medical representative operating in the North, one operating in the South of India may encounter distinct linguistic barriers, cultural norms, and medical procedures.

A crucial element in the value chain of the pharmaceutical industry is the medical representative. In addition to increasing sales, they make sure medical staff members have access to the resources and assistance they need to give their patients the best treatment possible. Given the complexity, diversity, and explosive growth of the Indian pharmaceutical business, the function of the MR is especially critical. MRs foster strong bonds, offer insightful criticism, and endorse public health campaigns to ensure the nation feels the benefits of contemporary medicine. Their efforts are essential to the pharmaceutical industry's success and, eventually, to the general public's health and well-being.

Responsibilities of a Medical Representative

Medical representatives (MRs) are essential in the pharmaceutical sector because they help close the communication gap between drug manufacturers and healthcare providers (HCPs), such as physicians, pharmacists, and hospitals. They are the main employees in charge of marketing and selling the company's goods, which include both prescription and over-the-counter (OTC) pharmaceuticals. A medical representative's duties are varied and important since they have a direct impact on a product's commercial success. These duties become even more complicated in the context of the Indian pharmaceutical sales ecosystem because of the country's unique healthcare dynamics, diverse medical landscape, and regulatory framework.

Product Promotion and Sales

A medical representative's one of the main roles is to market their company's pharmaceutical products to medical practitioners. This entails visiting physicians, hospitals, and pharmacies on a regular basis to update them on the advantages, applications, and adverse reactions of the company's products. MRs must be knowledgeable about the clinical and scientific elements of the medications they recommend since they frequently discuss intricate medical details with physicians, who need precise and comprehensive information before writing a prescription.

In the highly competitive Indian pharmaceutical market, MRs needs to set their goods apart from rivals' offerings. The MRs achieves this not only through the quality of their product, but also through the effectiveness of their presentation and the rapport they build with medical practitioners. The MR's persuasive skills, product expertise, and awareness of the unique requirements of the physicians they are trying to reach can frequently greatly influence the effectiveness of a medicine in a certain area.

Effective and Impactful Communications

Medical representatives use an effective and powerful communication strategy that directly impacts strong connections with healthcare professionals, product sales, and corporate representation. Clear and succinct communication makes it easier to deliver important product information, respond to doctors' concerns, and convince them of the advantages of particular drugs. Understanding doctors' requirements and offering specialized solutions requires active listening, empathy, and flexibility in interactions. Moreover, proficient communication cultivates reliance, legitimacy, and enduring collaborations, augmenting the function of the medical representative in the pharmaceutical sales procedure.

Building and Maintaining Relationships

With thousands of medical professionals operating in different specialties and regions, the Indian pharmaceutical business is enormous and diverse. One of a medical representative's most important duties is to develop a solid rapport based on trust with these HCPs. This is especially crucial in India, where business dealings heavily rely on trust and interpersonal relationships.

MRs should thoroughly understand the needs and preferences of the physicians practicing in their region. They can then better cater their product offers and communication to these professionals' demands. MRs fosters these relationships through a variety of means, including offering samples for patient trials, timely information, and regular follow-ups. Doctors view a successful MR as a reliable resource, one who offers helpful advice and assistance rather than just marketing goods.

Market Intelligence and Feedback Collection

The pharmaceutical corporations' eyes and ears on the market are medical representatives. They offer vital information about competitive activity, market trends, and the changing demands of patients and healthcare professionals. Pharmaceutical firms need this market data to develop new products, adjust their marketing and sales tactics, and develop new products.

In India, where the pharmaceutical industry is changing quickly, medical professionals are the primary source of information for MRs regarding the safety and effectiveness of medications. They collect data regarding any negative reactions, problems with patient compliance, or worries expressed by medical experts. The company's quality assurance and research and development (R&D) departments receive this input, enabling them to make any necessary modifications to improve the final product.

Achieving Sales Targets

Medical representatives are accountable for reaching predetermined sales goals established by their employers, just like in any other sales-oriented profession. Typically, employers connect these goals to the amount of product sold, the number of prescriptions written, or the market share attained in a specific area. In order to meet these goals, MRs need to carefully develop and carry out their sales tactics.

Reaching sales goals in India can be especially difficult because of the country's varied healthcare system. It is imperative to consider several factors, including but not limited to geographical variations in disease prevalence, doctor prescribing habits, and economic inequities across the nation. MRs must be resourceful and flexible, frequently collaborating closely with their sales managers to customize their strategies for various markets.

Conducting Continuing Medical Education (CME) Programs

Programs for Continuing Medical Education (CME) are a crucial part of a medical representative's duties. The purpose of these programs is to provide healthcare workers with up-to-date information about new medications, treatment guidelines, and developing health issues. MRs frequently plan and lead these programs, which can take the form of online webinars, seminars, or workshops.

CME programs are essential to the standardization of medical practitioners' knowledge and practices in India, where regional variations in medical practices can be substantial. The managers who run these programs have to make sure the material is appropriate for the audience, relevant, and supported by science. By offering worthwhile training programs, MRs establish stronger bonds with healthcare professionals and raise the profile of their business as an industry leader while also improving the understanding of healthcare professionals. Webinars provide an online and onsite option for CMEs.

Regulatory Compliance and Ethical Practices

Organizations like the Medical Council of India (MCI) and the Central Drugs Standard Control Organization (CDSCO) have tight regulatory oversight over the pharmaceutical business in India. When engaging in promotional activities, medical representatives must ensure compliance with all applicable laws and ethical standards. Adhering to the laws governing the promotion of prescription medications, providing accurate information, and refraining from any actions perceived as manipulative or unethical are all necessary.

MRs must be conscious of the regulatory landscape and take care to avoid any actions that can endanger their company's brand or have legal ramifications. This is especially crucial in the Indian market, where ethical marketing techniques are becoming more and more significant and regulatory scrutiny is rising.

Managing Samples and Promotional Materials

Medical representatives are in charge of giving promotional materials and medication samples or trial packs to medical practitioners. Samples are important to the pharmaceutical sales process in India since they let physicians evaluate a medication's effectiveness before recommending it to a broader patient base. MRs must handle these samples effectively to ensure they reach the right doctors and receive them appropriately.

Doctors get a variety of promotional materials from MRs, including pamphlets, visual aids, and product monographs, in addition to samples. These resources aim to bolster the discussions in their sessions and serve as a roadmap for physicians during prescription writing.

Handling Objections and Addressing Concerns

Medical representatives frequently run against objections or reservations regarding the items they are pushing during their interactions with healthcare professionals. These could include questions about the medication's effectiveness as well as worrics about its cost or adverse effects. One of the main responsibilities of the MR is to properly respond to these concerns by offering concise, fact-based answers that can dispel any lingering questions.

In the Indian pharmaceutical market, doctors face a plethora of options and intense competition, making the ability to deal with objections especially crucial. To overcome any unfavourable opinions and eventually convince the physician to prescribe their medication, MRs need to be well-prepared, informed, and assured of the benefits of their product.

Territory Management and Reporting

Usually given a certain geographic zone, medical representatives are in charge of overseeing all sales efforts within that region. This involves planning their weekly and daily schedules, prioritizing high-potential doctor visits, and ensuring coverage of all significant healthcare facilities in their region.

MRs are expected to keep thorough records of their operations, including the quantity of visits, products advertised, and feedback from medical professionals, in addition to overseeing their territory. Their sales managers typically receive a report containing this data, which they use to track performance, identify areas for improvement, and adjust their sales strategies as needed.

Adapting to Technological Advancements

Medical Representatives need to adjust to the digital transition that the pharmaceutical sector, like many others, is going through. The use of digital tools for marketing and sales has increased in India, especially since the COVID-19 pandemic. MRs are increasingly exchanging information online, conducting virtual meetings, and interacting with other healthcare professionals via digital platforms.

It is becoming increasingly important for MRs to stay abreast of technological developments and learn how to use digital tools. This includes knowing how to use CRM (customer relationship management) software, digital marketing tools, and online platforms for conducting CME programs. MARS may improve their effectiveness, reach a wider audience, and maintain their competitiveness in the changing market landscape by embracing these developments.

Conducting Sales Events

Within the Indian pharmaceutical sales ecosystem, one of a medical representative's (MR) most important responsibilities is organizing sales events. Product launches, physician conferences, and health camps are a few examples of these events. They provide a venue to present novel medications, strengthen ties with medical experts, and inform them of the most recent products available. MRs may directly interact with important stakeholders, obtain insightful feedback, and increase the awareness of their goods by planning such events. Sales events are an essential component of an MR's plan to meet sales goals and cultivate enduring relationships with the healthcare industry since they not only increase sales but also bolster the legitimacy of the pharmaceutical brand.

Within the Indian pharmaceutical sales ecosystem, medical representatives are essential. Their duties go well beyond simply promoting products; they are essential for establishing credibility, offering market intelligence, guaranteeing legal compliance, and adjusting to emerging technologies. A pharmaceutical product's ability to succeed in the Indian market frequently depends on how well the MR performs these duties. The need for MRs to continuously improve their abilities, stay up to date on industry developments, and uphold the highest levels of professionalism and ethical behaviour will only increase as India's healthcare system continues to change.

Case Studies

Case 1: A Medical Representative (MR) is an important link between drug companies and healthcare workers in India's fast-paced and competitive drug market. Take the case of Rajesh, an MR who works for a big drug business and is supposed to promote a new drug for heart problems. Rajesh is very successful because he knows a lot about his product's benefits, dosage forms, and possible side effects, and he can explain them to doctors and pharmacies in a clear way. He uses digital tools, such as CRM software, to keep track of his meetings and conversations with medical professionals. Rajesh is excellent at sales, persistent, and emotionally intelligent. He builds strong, trusting relationships with doctors through regular visits and educational seminars, all while working in a very competitive workplace. He also deals with India's huge and culturally diverse healthcare system by changing how he does things, following the rules of ethics, and always learning about the newest medical advances and changes to the rules. Because he works hard and plans ahead, Rajesh not only meets his sales goals, but he also helps patients get better care by making sure they can get and understand lifesaving drugs. His example demonstrates how MRs, who possess extensive product knowledge, effective communication skills, flexibility, and a customer-centric approach, play a crucial role in advancing medical science and healthcare in India.

Case 2: The pharmaceutical market in India is very competitive, and medical representatives like Rahul are very important for connecting drug makers with doctors and nurses. Rahul, a medical sales agent with a lot of experience, was told to promote a new antibiotic in both cities and rural areas. In cities, he talked about how effective, safe, and better than other treatments the drug was. He built strong relationships with doctors by sharing clinical reports on a regular basis. In rural areas, where price is very important, Rahul focused on making the antibiotic affordable by giving primary care doctors free samples and hands-on demos. Rahul gave his company useful information about side effects and how patients responded from both settings. This helped make the product safer and more successful. His comments also helped the company with pharmacovigilance, which made patients safer. Rahul increased sales and marketed the drug as a reliable treatment by using customized strategies, building relationships, and timely reports. This helped the drug reach people in many parts of India. His method shows how important medical representatives are in navigating the complicated Indian pharmaceutical market, meeting the specific needs of different healthcare professionals while also making sure patient safety and product success.

Suggestive Questions from the Chapter

1. In the pharmaceutical industry, how does a medical representative manage their responsibilities as a salesman, trainer, and consultant?
2. What particular attributes and abilities are necessary for a medical representative to gain the confidence of healthcare professionals and create enduring relationships?
3. In the current healthcare environment, how has the function of a medical representative changed as a result of the integration of digital tools and platforms?
4. In what ways might a medical representative's proficiency with medical terminology improve their efficacy when selling pharmaceuticals?
5. How can a medical representative succeed in a fast-paced, demanding pharmaceutical sales market with adaptability and resilience?
6. Why is product knowledge crucial for medical representatives in the marketing of pharmaceutical items to healthcare professionals?
7. In India's pharmaceutical sales ecosystem, what is the role of a medical representative in terms of helping to close the communication gap between healthcare practitioners and pharmaceutical companies?
8. How do medical representatives manage competition in the extremely fragmented Indian pharmaceutical industry and affect the uptake of innovative therapies?
9. In a highly competitive market, how do medical representatives in the Indian pharmaceutical industry establish credibility and set themselves apart with their products?
10. How can medical representatives improve their performance and sales techniques in the changing pharmaceutical industry by utilizing technological advancements?

Multiple Choice Questions

1. What is the primary role of a Medical Representative (MR)?
   (a) Conducting medical research for pharmaceutical companies
   (b) Marketing and promoting medical devices and drugs to healthcare professionals
   (c) Administering medications in hospitals
   (d) Creating and enforcing healthcare policies

2. Which of the following is NOT a quality essential for a Medical Representative (MR)?
   (a) Time management and organizational skills
   (b) Sales acumen
   (c) Technical proficiency
   (d) Conducting clinical trials
3. How does an MR primarily connect with healthcare providers in the modern digital age?
   (a) Conducting face-to-face meetings only
   (b) Through telemedicine services
   (c) Using various communication methods like emails, phone calls, and virtual meetings
   (d) Through pharmaceutical trade fairs exclusively
4. Why is on-going learning important for a Medical Representative?
   (a) To maintain a competitive edge and provide value to healthcare providers
   (b) To switch from pharmaceutical sales to medical practice
   (c) To increase their salary rapidly
   (d) To create new pharmaceutical drugs
5. What is the typical minimum educational qualification required for a Medical Representative?
   (a) High School Diploma
   (b) Bachelor's Degree in Pharmacy or Life Sciences
   (c) Master's Degree in Marketing
   (d) Diploma in Computer Science
6. Which of the following skills is essential for a Medical Representative when interacting with healthcare professionals?
   (a) Strong technical skills
   (b) Public speaking ability
   (c) Knowledge of medical terminology
   (d) Programming skills

7. Which of the following degrees can give candidates an added advantage in the pharmaceutical industry?
   (a) B.Sc or MBA (b) B.Com
   (c) BE in Mechanical Engineering (d) LLB

8. What is the primary role of communication skills in a Medical Representative's job?
   (a) To present information clearly and persuasively
   (b) To create digital marketing campaigns
   (c) To design promotional products
   (d) To code CRM software

9. Which skill is increasingly important for MRs as the pharmaceutical industry moves towards digital engagement?
   (a) Adaptability
   (b) Familiarity with digital tools and platforms
   (c) Leadership qualities
   (d) Mechanical proficiency

10. What trait is essential for handling rejection and setbacks in the pharmaceutical sales environment?
    (a) Confidence (b) Problem-solving skills
    (c) Resilience (d) Team management

11. Which of the following is not an advantage of having good networking abilities in the pharmaceutical industry?
    (a) Building strong relationships with healthcare professionals
    (b) Improving access to key decision-makers
    (c) Learning computer programming languages
    (d) Enhancing effectiveness in sales

12. What is a critical ethical requirement for a Medical Representative?
    (a) Following regulatory guidelines and company policies
    (b) Developing new medical products
    (c) Creating financial reports
    (d) Supervising clinical trials

13. What is the importance of product knowledge for a Medical Representative?
    (a) It helps in administrative work.
    (b) It allows MRs to answer detailed questions from HCPs and provide comprehensive information.
    (c) It aids in preparing financial reports.
    (d) It helps MRs write programming code for marketing.
14. Which skill is essential for creating and delivering effective sales pitches to healthcare professionals?
    (a) Time management
    (b) Technical writing
    (c) Presentation skills
    (d) Administrative skills
15. Which organization in India provides regulatory guidelines that Medical Representatives must be familiar with?
    (a) CDSCO (Central Drugs Standard Control Organization)
    (b) NASSCOM
    (c) RBI (Reserve Bank of India)
    (d) IRDA (Insurance Regulatory and Development Authority)
16. What is one of the primary roles of a medical representative (MR)?
    (a) Conducting surgeries
    (b) Marketing and selling pharmaceutical products
    (c) Developing new drugs
    (d) Managing hospital staff
17. What is essential for medical representatives when discussing products with healthcare professionals?
    (a) Advanced technical skills
    (b) Clinical and scientific knowledge of the medications
    (c) Personal relationships with patients
    (d) Knowledge of insurance policies
18. Why is effective communication crucial for MRs?
    (a) It reduces the need for samples
    (b) It helps in delivering product information and building trust
    (c) It increases the number of products sold
    (d) It eliminates the need for promotional materials

19. What aspect of the Indian pharmaceutical market makes relationship building particularly important for MRs?
    (a) High competition
    (b) Lack of regulations
    (c) Heavy reliance on trust and interpersonal relationships
    (d) Availability of numerous product options
20. What role do MRs play in market intelligence?
    (a) They are responsible for manufacturing drugs
    (b) They collect information on market trends and competitive activities
    (c) They determine pricing strategies
    (d) They oversee regulatory compliance
21. What is one of the goals medical representatives must achieve?
    (a) Reduce the number of hospital visits
    (b) Maintain a customer database
    (c) Reach predetermined sales targets
    (d) Write prescriptions
22. What do Continuing Medical Education (CME) programs aim to achieve?
    (a) Increase sales directly
    (b) Provide updated information on medications and treatment guidelines
    (c) Train MRs in sales techniques
    (d) Evaluate the effectiveness of drugs
23. How must MRs handle samples and promotional materials?
    (a) By limiting their distribution
    (b) By ensuring they reach the right doctors and are used appropriately
    (c) By using them solely for personal gain
    (d) By avoiding any promotional activities
24. What is a critical skill for MRs when addressing objections from healthcare professionals?
    (a) Financial analysis
    (b) Product knowledge and effective communication
    (c) Negotiation skills
    (d) Time management

25. What is the significance of adapting to technological advancements for MRs?
    (a) It helps them avoid compliance issues
    (b) It allows them to conduct virtual meetings and enhance marketing strategies
    (c) It reduces their workload
    (d) It replaces the need for in-person visits

CHAPTER 4

Understanding the Doctor by a Medical Representative

Doctors, as understood by a Typical Indian

Middle-class Indians frequently hold the idea of a doctor in high regard, viewing them as the embodiment of social respect and professional success. Being a doctor is a difficult career path that requires years of intense study and commitment. Prospective physicians typically spend a minimum of five years earning their MBBS degree, with an extra three years typically spent in internships and housekeeping roles. In addition to rigorous academic instruction, this intensive training includes practical hospital experience where they learn how to diagnose and treat patients under the guidance of seasoned specialists. They have spent at least eight years in formal school and training by the time they start their own practice. This is just the beginning for many. After starting their practice, they might invest ten or more years in developing their reputation, perfecting their craft, and improving the community's health. In this regard, the function of a pharmaceutical business salesperson or medical representative assumes a more nuanced meaning. These agents serve as a crucial intermediary between pharmaceutical firms and medical professionals, acting as more than just drug dealers. They need to approach physicians with a thorough awareness of the medical field and the difficulties that practitioners deal with on a daily basis. It becomes imperative for a medical representative to have empathy for doctors, who are frequently the most educated and affluent members of society. Following a lifetime of service and patient care, doctors demand honesty and knowledge from anyone approaching them with a product to promote. Thus, in addition to product expertise, a representative needs to be able to speak in a way that aligns with a physician's moral principles and dedication to patient care.

Furthermore, the complexity of a doctor's occupation frequently influences their perspective. They understand first-hand the difficulties involved in overseeing patient care, keeping up with the most recent findings in medicine, and resolving the moral conundrums that arise in the provision of healthcare. Recognizing this complex terrain, a competent medical representative approaches the physician not just as a client but as a collaborator in health. They must carefully balance salesmanship and empathy to promote their products in a way that supports doctors' objectives of providing patients with the best treatment possible. Comprehending the motives of physicians—be they to enhance patient outcomes or maintain competitiveness in a quickly changing medical field—allows the representative to customize their approach. Having meaningful conversations, attending to concerns, and sharing pertinent information can foster trust and rapport, essential for long-term professional relationships. A typical middle-class family views the doctor as a symbol of health and hope, someone who embodies the goals and dreams they have for their kids. Medical representatives should approach their work with the same seriousness and respect that this profession deserves. Representatives can successfully position themselves as allies in the healthcare ecosystem by acknowledging the commitment and sacrifices made by doctors, so guaranteeing that they positively contribute to the noble goal of healing and caring that doctors uphold. By doing this, they uphold the notion that their goods are useful instruments that enable physicians to carry out their noble profession rather than only being commodities.

Understanding the Doctors as Customers

In the Indian pharmaceutical sector, medical representatives must possess a comprehensive understanding of doctors. A medical representative's relationship with a doctor is the foundation of pharmaceutical sales. Building trust, offering useful information, and assisting doctors in their practices are all part of the responsibilities of the Medical Representative in India, where the healthcare system is a combination of public and private sectors. Physicians, being the primary decision-makers when prescribing medications, require a thorough understanding of pharmaceutical products, including their overall impact on patient care, side effects, and efficacy. To build a successful partnership that benefits the pharmaceutical firm as well as the physician, a medical representative must have a thorough awareness of the unique requirements, preferences, and expectations of physicians.

Recognizing the time restrictions of doctors is a fundamental part of knowing them. Indian physicians frequently manage patient consultations, surgery, research, and administrative responsibilities with hectic schedules. Medical representatives need to consider this when scheduling their visits. Being on time, succinct, and prepared for every meeting is how a good medical representative shows respect for the doctor's time. This entails setting up a well-defined agenda, being aware of the physician's current areas of interest, and adjusting the discussion to include pertinent details that will benefit the physician's practice. For example, if a physician specializes in cardiology, the medical representative should make the talk immediately valuable to the physician by focusing on the most recent developments, clinical data, and product options in cardiovascular medications.

Medical representatives must also possess a thorough understanding of the therapeutic domains that are pertinent to the physicians they see. Physicians anticipate that medical representatives will have a thorough understanding of both their drugs and the larger therapeutic environment. This entails knowing not just the pharmacology of the medications but also the most recent findings, recommended courses of action, and rival goods. Doctors in India, a country that places great importance on medical education and on-going professional growth, highly value medical representatives who can offer fresh perspectives, share study data, and discuss current medical trends. This helps the physician stay current and establishes the medical representative as a trustworthy and knowledgeable associate.

Cultural awareness is another crucial factor. India is a multicultural nation with wide geographical differences in patient demographics, language, and culture. Depending on the local environment, doctors may have various tastes, practices, and ways of interacting with patients in different areas. A medical representative can build stronger relationships with doctors if they are aware of and respectful of these cultural quirks. For instance, doctors in larger cities like Delhi or Mumbai might communicate differently than those in smaller towns or rural areas. While doctors in rural areas may prefer a more personal touch, where medical representatives take the time to establish a relationship before introducing products, doctors in urban environments may prefer rapid, data-driven talks.

In the interaction between a physician and a medical representative, trust is essential. Earning trust requires reliability, integrity, and the capacity to successfully address the doctor's needs. Medical representatives should avoid making overly dramatic statements that could negatively impact patient care and the doctor's practice by being open and honest about the advantages and limitations of their goods. Medical representatives can establish and preserve trust by giving precise, current information, answering questions right away, and keeping their word. In India, where reputation and word-of-mouth hold significant value, a reliable medical representative can influence not only individual doctors but entire networks of healthcare providers.

A crucial component of comprehending physicians is appreciating the significance of continuing medical education (CME). Indian doctors frequently have to participate in continuing medical education (CME) programs to keep their licenses current and stay abreast of medical breakthroughs. Medical representatives can be extremely helpful in this by setting up or leading CME meetings, inviting specialists, and supplying learning resources. Viewed as a supporter of the doctor's professional development, the Medical Representative not only helps the doctor stay up to date on medical knowledge but also enhances the doctor-Medical Representative relationship.

Medical representatives need to be knowledgeable about the practice dynamics of the doctor in addition to CME. This includes knowing patient demographics, prevalent ailments handled, and the doctor's prescription practices. Medical representatives can present their products more successfully if they adjust their approach to take these aspects into account. For instance, the medical representative may highlight medications that are safer for senior citizens and have fewer side effects or drug interactions if the physician specializes in treating elderly patients. Knowing these subtleties enables the medical representative to market their products in a way that aligns with the priorities of patient care and the doctor's everyday practice.

Ultimately, the secret to understanding doctors is excellent communication. Speaking and active listening are both required for this. Medical representatives ought to consider the opinions, desires, and concerns of the physician. This knowledge can help the medical representative tailor their approach, address specific requirements, and offer unique solutions, making it extremely helpful. A medical representative can stand out from the crowd and establish a long-lasting, mutually beneficial relationship by listening and responding effectively in the Indian environment, where relationships and personal connections frequently impact professional encounters.

It takes a combination of product expertise, cultural sensitivity, time management, and effective communication to understand doctors in the Indian pharmaceutical landscape. Proficiency in these domains can develop strong, trustworthy connections between medical representatives and doctors, ultimately improving patient outcomes and fostering fruitful collaborations.

Importance of Understanding Doctors as a Customer

Recognizing physicians as clients is essential to any pharmaceutical company's success in the Indian market. In the healthcare system, physicians play a pivotal role as the main intermediaries between pharmaceutical corporations and patients. Their impact goes beyond simply writing prescriptions; they are influential thought leaders, reliable counsellors, and the final decision-makers in the patient care process. Pharmaceutical businesses must customize their tactics to cater to the unique requirements and preferences of physicians in a market as diverse and complicated as India's, where patient demographics and healthcare practices differ greatly between areas.

The need to view doctors as customers is mostly due to the individualized approach needed for productive dialogue and the development of relationships. In contrast to ordinary customers, physicians are highly skilled professionals who require a high standard of clinical and scientific proof when evaluating novel medications or treatments. Hence, pharmaceutical sales representatives—also referred to as medical representatives—must be knowledgeable about the medical applications of their goods and able to hold fruitful, fact-based conversations with physicians. Gaining a doctor's trust and changing their prescribing behaviour requires the capacity to properly express the therapeutic benefits of a product in illness remission and the positive improvements it delivers in a patient's life.

Ayurveda, homeopathy, allopathy, and other traditional medicinal systems are among the many medical practices that define the Indian healthcare system. There are important opinion leaders associated with each of these professions who frequently impact the treatment decisions made by a sizable number of patients and practitioners. Pharmaceutical businesses need to understand how important these influencers are and interact with them wisely. Companies can create more specialized marketing tactics that appeal to various medical community groups by learning about the unique demands, preferences, and difficulties that physicians encounter in these diverse medical systems.

Studying the socioeconomic issues that affect doctors' decisions is just as important as studying the clinical aspects. Numerous factors, such as patient socioeconomic status, local healthcare facilities, and governmental policy, influence healthcare delivery in India. For example, physicians in rural areas might give priority to low-cost treatments since their patients are on a tight budget, but physicians in urban areas might be more likely to use the newest, most advanced treatments. Pharmaceutical companies need to be aware of these subtleties and provide solutions that fit the demands of the real-world practice environment for doctors. To guarantee that doctors can confidently prescribe their products, this may entail offering various price alternatives, patient education programs, or access to patient support programs.

Realizing the growing significance of digital interaction is another essential component of viewing physicians as clients. The COVID-19 pandemic hastened the healthcare industry's adoption of digital tools, and a growing number of physicians now anticipate that pharmaceutical companies will provide digital solutions that enhance their clinical practices. Whether it's through digital detailing, telemedicine platforms, or online medical education, businesses need to be ready to meet physicians where they are and use the channels and technology that their preferred. A deeper understanding of doctors' digital behaviour and preferences is also necessary in light of this trend towards digital engagement, as they can vary greatly according on age, specialty, and geography, among other aspects.

Furthermore, physicians in India are becoming more and more interested in comprehensive solutions that go beyond just prescribing medications. The complete patient journey, encompassing prevention, diagnosis, treatment, and aftercare, resent their interest. Strong, long-lasting relationships with doctors are more likely to be formed by pharmaceutical companies that can offer comprehensive assistance, including patient education, diagnostic tools, and post-treatment care. This strategy not only fosters trust but also presents the business as a collaborator with the physician in their endeavour to deliver optimal healthcare to their patients.

Finally, it's critical to recognize the regulatory framework that governs the practice of medicine. Physicians in India are subject to legislation and ethical guidelines that control their relationships with pharmaceutical corporations. It is imperative that pharmaceutical organizations comprehend these standards in order to guarantee that their marketing and promotional endeavours are both ethical and lawful. Businesses may establish partnerships based on mutual respect and trust by adhering to ethical guidelines and putting their attention on giving physicians real value.

Recognizing physicians as clients entail more than simply influencing their prescription practices; it also entails forming a collaboration that upholds their function as medical professionals. Pharmaceutical businesses can create strategies that boost sales and enhance healthcare delivery in India by acknowledging the distinct constraints and requirements faced by doctors in the nation. In the context of Indian pharmaceuticals, it is critical to comprehend doctors as clients, whether via individualized communication, digital engagement, or comprehensive solutions.

Characteristics of Doctors as Customers

Doctors are an important customer group in the ever-changing Indian pharmaceutical market. Pharmaceutical corporations and physicians have a complex relationship that is based on mutual understanding, ethics, and trust rather than being purely transactional. Pharmaceutical businesses must acknowledge the distinct attributes of physicians as clients in order to properly customize their approaches. It is important for anyone working in pharmaceutical sales, marketing, or product management to explore the unique traits of Indian doctors as customers.

1. **Highly Informed and Knowledgeable:** Doctors are extremely aware and knowledgeable about medical issues, treatments, and the most recent developments in medicines because of their considerable schooling and on-going professional growth. They are therefore discriminating against consumers who seek information based on facts and scientific accuracy. Doctors are more likely than average customers to have in-depth conversations regarding the pharmacodynamics, pharmacokinetics, and clinical effectiveness of medications.

   This implies that pharmaceutical businesses need to support their marketing initiatives with reliable scientific evidence. To win doctors' trust and confidence, marketing strategies should emphasize the provision of comprehensive information, clinical study findings, and empirical proof.

2. **Ethical Considerations:** Like in other countries, doctors in India are subject to a stringent code of ethics that puts the needs of their patients before business interests. As an indirect customer, this ethical obligation affects how they make decisions. Physicians should recommend drugs based on clinical necessity, not external factors such as the incentives of pharmaceutical corporations.

   Pharmaceutical firms must therefore present the physicians with a value-driven offer that highlights how their goods might enhance patient outcomes. Any marketing tactics that seems to undermine the physician's moral principles, risks losing patients' trust and thereby harming the business's reputation over time.

3. **Time-Constrained and Efficiency-Oriented:** Doctors in India typically face a significant workload, as many of them treat a large number of patients daily. Time becomes a valuable resource as a result of this. Doctors frequently have little time and are not amenable to lengthy sales pitches. They prefer brief, direct conversations that value their time and give them the information they need in a timely manner.

Therefore, pharmaceutical reps need to be well-prepared, concentrating on the most important points and omitting extraneous details. Facilitating prompt access to digital resources, such as web portals or mobile apps, can also improve contact efficiency and meet the demands of time-pressed physicians.

4. **Relationship-Oriented:** In Indian culture, interpersonal interactions are important, despite a focus on ethical issues and scientific data. Doctors often value long-term partnerships with pharmaceutical firms and representatives. Reliability, familiarity, and trust are important variables that affect how they prescribe.

   It takes regular contact, openness, and a sincere concern for doctors' professional needs to establish and preserve solid relationships with them. The on-going knowledge upgrade opportunities, frequent product updates, and routine follow-ups are all efficient methods to foster these connections.

5. **Preference for Continuing Medical Education (CME):** Like their colleagues around the world, Indian doctors are constantly in need of professional growth. They are eager to keep abreast of the most recent developments in medicine and therapeutic techniques. For this reason, physicians place a high emphasis on continuing medical education (CME) programs. These programs offer physicians a systematic, accredited way to learn about new medications, technology, and treatment modalities.

   Pharmaceutical firms might take advantage of this tendency by planning and funding CME events. This not only aids in physician education but also establishes the business as a significant collaborator in the advancement of the physician's career. However, these programs must persist in delivering top-notch educational content, not merely serving as promotional tools.

6. **Diverse and Segmented:** Doctors in India work in a wide range of environments, including government agencies, private offices, rural clinics, and urban hospitals. Their specializations, degrees of expertise, and patient demographics all reflect this diversity. As a result, their clientele may exhibit a wide range of desires and preferences.

   Pharmaceutical businesses must adopt a segmented strategy in their marketing tactics to acknowledge this diversity. Customizing messaging and products to meet the unique requirements of various market segments, such as specialists versus general practitioners or urban versus rural physicians, can greatly increase the efficacy of marketing initiatives.

7. **Influenced by Peer Opinion and Thought Leaders:** Peer opinion and the advice of thought leaders, or Key Opinion Leaders (KOLs), are highly influential in the Indian medical community. For advice on novel therapies and drugs, doctors frequently turn to senior specialists and esteemed colleagues. A KOL's good recommendation can greatly impact the prescription practices of a broader group of physicians.

   KOLs and pharmaceutical corporations frequently interact through lecture programs, advisory boards, and cooperative research. Companies can increase the legitimacy of their products and expand their acceptance in the medical community by collaborating closely with these influencers.

8. **Sensitive to Price and Patient Affordability:** In the Indian pharmaceutical market scenario, the doctors generally are very attentive to the cost of pharmaceuticals and their affordability for patients, even if they place a high priority on clinical efficacy and safety. Since many people pay for their medical treatment out of pocket, doctors are careful to prescribe drugs that will be affordable for their patients.

   Pharmaceutical firms need to think about pricing plans that take this sensitivity into account. Providing a variety of goods at various price points, including generic alternatives, might assist physicians in making choices that strike a balance between patient affordability and clinical requirements. Additionally, doctors can be very appreciative of patient aid programs or schemes that lessen the financial strain on patients.

9. **Expectations of Post-Market Support:** Doctors anticipate that the pharmaceutical companies may offer strong post-market support. This entails making sure the product is available, delivering it on time, and handling any problems relating to side effects or product recalls. One important factor influencing a doctor's decision to continue using a product is post-market assistance.

   Businesses can develop more solid, trustworthy connections with physicians by being prompt and proactive in their after-sales care. Providing patient education resources, instruments for tracking treatment results, and help with regulatory compliance are more examples of this support.

10. **Technology Adoption and Digital Engagement:** As India's healthcare industry rapidly digitizes, more physicians are incorporating technology into their operations. This covers the use of digital technologies for patient management, telemedicine platforms, and electronic medical records (EMRs). Doctors are therefore more receptive to pharmaceutical corporations' digital engagement.

In order to interact with physicians, pharmaceutical businesses must incorporate digital channels into their marketing tactics. These channels include smartphone apps, internet platforms, and virtual details. Particularly useful are digital tools that offer quick access to dosage calculators, medication information, and patient management tools.

As clients, Indian doctors are a distinct and complicated group distinguished by their extensive training, moral issues, and time restraints. In addition to being cognizant of patient cost and technical improvements, they place a high importance on relationships, peer-influence, and on-going education. Pharmaceutical businesses must comprehend these traits in order to interact with physicians in an efficient manner, create enduring partnerships, and guarantee that their products satisfy the wants of physicians and their patients.

Pharmaceutical companies can improve their credibility, build trust, and eventually thrive in the fiercely competitive Indian pharmaceutical market by coordinating their strategy with these traits.

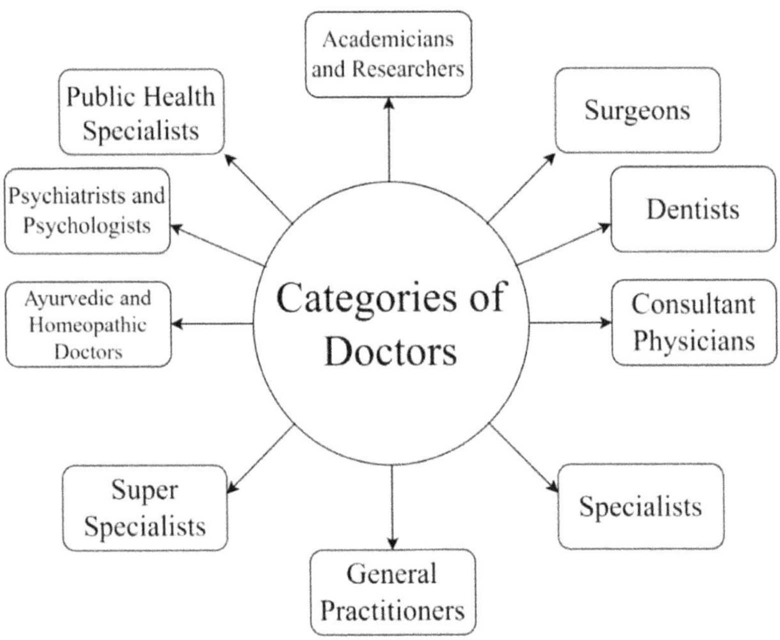

Fig. 4.1 Categories of Doctors.

Categories of Doctors in India: An Overview

India has created a sophisticated and multidimensional healthcare system due to its large population and varied healthcare requirements. Numerous medical professionals with a wide range of specializations support the nation's healthcare system. From primary care to highly specialized medical interventions, these types of physicians are essential in meeting the population's health needs. Anyone wishing to contribute to or navigate the Indian healthcare system must have a solid understanding of these areas.

1. General Practitioners (GPs) and Family Physicians

For the majority of patients in India, general practitioners—also known as family physicians—are their initial point of contact. Regardless of age, gender, or type of illness, these physicians offer families and individuals complete healthcare. They are essential in controlling chronic conditions including diabetes, hypertension, and asthma and are capable of diagnosing and treating a wide range of common illnesses. GPs frequently work in community health centers or private clinics, and they play a crucial role in rural and semi-urban areas where access to specialized treatment may be limited. By providing immunizations, health education, and regular checkups, they also contribute significantly to preventative care.

2. Specialists

Doctors who have completed more training in a particular field of medicine than the requirements for a basic medical degree are known as specialists. For more complicated medical problems, people in India frequently seek the services of highly esteemed professionals. The following are the most common types of specialists in India:

- ***Cardiologists*:** These doctors specialize in diagnosing and treating heart conditions. They manage patients with heart diseases, perform procedures like angioplasty, and provide on-going care for chronic cardiac conditions.

  ***Basic Qualifications* -**

  - **MBBS** (Bachelor of Medicine, Bachelor of Surgery) – 5.5 years (including internship).
  - **MD in General Medicine** – 3 years.
  - **DM in Cardiology** – 3 years (super-specialization).
- ***Neurologists*:** Neurologists focus on disorders of the nervous system. They diagnose and treat conditions such as epilepsy, stroke,

and multiple sclerosis. In India, neurologists are in high demand due to the increasing prevalence of neurological disorders.

Basic Qualifications -

- **MBBS** – 5.5 years (including internship).
- **MD in General Medicine or Paediatrics** – 3 years.
- **DM in Neurology** – 3 years (super-specialization).

- ***Oncologists*:** Oncologists specialize in the diagnosis and treatment of cancer. They work closely with other specialists to provide comprehensive care, including chemotherapy, radiation therapy, and surgical interventions.

  Basic Qualifications -

  - **MBBS** – 5.5 years (including internship).
  - **MD in General Medicine, Radiotherapy, or Paediatrics** – 3 years (depending on the oncological specialization).
  - **DM in Medical Oncology or MCh in Surgical Oncology** – 3 years (super-specialization).

- ***Paediatricians*:** Paediatricians specialize in the care of infants, children, and adolescents. They manage everything from routine childhood illnesses to more severe conditions like congenital disorders and paediatric cancers.

  Basic Qualifications -

  - **MBBS** – 5.5 years (including internship).
  - **MD in Paediatrics** – 3 years.

- ***Gynaecologists and Obstetricians*:** These doctors specialize in women's health, particularly in relation to the reproductive system. They provide care during pregnancy, childbirth, and manage conditions related to the female reproductive organs.

  Basic Qualifications -

  - **MBBS** – 5.5 years (including internship).
  - **MD in Obstetrics and Gynaecology or MS in Obstetrics and Gynaecology** – 3 years.

- ***Orthopedic Surgeons*:** Orthopaedic surgeons focus on the musculoskeletal system. They treat injuries, congenital conditions, and diseases related to bones, joints, and muscles, often performing surgeries such as joint replacements.

Basic Qualifications -

- **MBBS** – 5.5 years (including internship).
- **MS in Orthopaedics** – 3 years.

3. Super Specialists

Super specialists represent the pinnacle of medical expertise. These doctors have completed advanced training in a very narrow field of medicine, often beyond their specialty training. Examples include:

***Cardiothoracic Surgeons*:** These super specialists perform complex surgeries on the heart and chest, such as heart transplants and bypass surgeries.

Qualifications:

MBBS (Bachelor of Medicine, Bachelor of Surgery): A 5.5-year course (including a 1-year internship).

MS (Master of Surgery) in General Surgery: A 3-year postgraduate degree focusing on general surgical procedures.

MCh (Master of Chirurgiae) in Cardiothoracic Surgery: A 3-year super-specialty course that can be pursued after MS in General Surgery. Some institutes also offer direct 6-year MCh courses after MBBS.

***Neurosurgeons*:** Neurosurgeons are highly specialized in performing surgeries on the brain, spine, and other parts of the nervous system. Their work is critical in treating conditions like brain tumours, spinal injuries, and severe neurological disorders.

Qualifications:

MBBS (Bachelor of Medicine, Bachelor of Surgery): A 5.5-year course (including a 1-year internship).

MS (Master of Surgery) in General Surgery or DNB (Diplomate of National Board) in Surgery: A 3-year postgraduate degree.

MCh (Master of Chirurgiae) in Neurosurgery: A 3-year super-specialty course. Some institutes also offer a direct 6-year MCh course in Neurosurgery after MBBS.

Paediatric Cardiologists: These doctors specialize in diagnosing and treating heart conditions in children. Given the complexity of congenital heart diseases, paediatric cardiologists play a crucial role in the healthcare of affected children.

Qualifications:

MBBS (Bachelor of Medicine, Bachelor of Surgery): A 5.5-year course (including a 1-year internship).

MD (Doctor of Medicine) in Paediatrics: A 3-year postgraduate degree focusing on paediatric medicine.

DM (Doctorate of Medicine) in Paediatric Cardiology: A 3-year super-specialty course pursued after completing MD in Paediatrics.

4. Consultant Physicians

Specialists who provide knowledgeable counsel in a specific area of medicine are known as consultant physicians. Consultant physicians concentrate on complicated medical concerns within their specialty, as opposed to general practitioners who may treat a variety of illnesses. They typically work in both public and private hospitals, where other medical professionals refer them because of their particular knowledge. In hospitals, consultant doctors frequently serve as team leaders, directing treatment decisions and plans for patients with severe or complicated medical diseases.

5. Surgeons

Surgeons are medical professionals who operate to address illnesses, wounds, or abnormalities. Surgeons in India may specialize in orthopaedics, neurosurgery, cardiac surgery, or urology, or they may practice general surgery. Surgery is a challenging profession that calls on accuracy, dexterity, and the capacity for rapid decision-making in addition to medical knowledge. When it comes to treating trauma situations, emergencies, and long-term illnesses that call for surgery, surgeons are essential.

6. Ayurvedic and Homeopathic Doctors

Ayurvedic and homeopathic practitioners are essential to India's long history of alternative treatment.

Ayurvedic Doctors: For hundreds of years, people in India have used the traditional Ayurvedic medical method. Trained in this discipline, ayurvedic physicians treat patients using natural cures, lifestyle changes, and detoxifying methods. In rural areas and among those who favour natural remedies over allopathic care, Ayurveda is especially well-liked.

Qualifications

Bachelor of Ayurvedic Medicine and Surgery (BAMS): Duration: 5.5 years (including 1-year internship)

Master's Degree (Optional for specialization): Master of Science (M.Sc.) in Ayurveda or MD (Ayurveda) for further specialization, with an additional 3 years of study.

Homeopathic Doctors: Another alternative form of medicine that is popular in India is homeopathy. Homeopathic doctors use highly diluted drugs to treat various illnesses, adhering to the principle of "like cures like." A lot of people use homeopathy to help long-term conditions like arthritis, allergies, and asthma.

Qualifications

Bachelor of Homeopathic Medicine and Surgery (BHMS): Duration: 5.5 years (including 1-year internship)

Master's Degree (Optional for specialization): Master of Science (M.Sc.) in Homeopathy or MD (Homeopathy) for further specialization, with an additional 3 years of study.

7. Dentists

Dentists are medical professionals who specialize in mouth health. They diagnoses problems with teeth, lips, and other parts of the mouth and treat them. In India, dental care is becoming more important as people learn more about how to keep their teeth clean and how that affects their general health. A dentist can pull out teeth, fix cavities, do orthodontics, and do cosmetic dentistry, among other things. In addition to treating dental issues, dentists play a crucial role in educating individuals about preventive care and maintaining good oral hygiene.

Qualification

Bachelor of Dental Surgery (BDS): The minimum qualification to become a dentist is a BDS degree, which typically takes five years to complete, including four years of academic education and one year of compulsory internship.

Postgraduate Degree (Optional): Dentists can pursue a Master of Dental Surgery (MDS) in various specializations like orthodontics, periodontics, etc., which takes an additional three years.

8. Psychiatrists and Psychologists

Mental health is an area of growing concern in India, and psychiatrists and psychologists are key players in addressing this issue.

Psychiatrists: As the name suggests, psychiatrists are doctors who specialize in diagnosing, treating, and avoiding mental health problems. For a wide range of conditions, such as depression, anxiety, schizophrenia, and bipolar disorder, psychiatrists can give medication and offer psychotherapy.

Qualification

Bachelor of Medicine and Bachelor of Surgery (MBBS): To become a psychiatrist, a person must first complete an MBBS degree, which takes around five and a half years (including one year of internship).

Postgraduate Degree (MD in Psychiatry): After completing MBBS, the individual must pursue a Doctor of Medicine (MD) in Psychiatry, which takes three years.

Psychologists: Psychologists can't give out prescription drugs, but they can help people with mental health problems deal with them through therapy and counselling. Most of the time, they collaborate with psychologists to provide comprehensive mental health care.

Qualification

Bachelor's Degree in Psychology: The minimum qualification to become a psychologist is a Bachelor’s degree in Psychology, which typically takes three years to complete.

Master’s Degree in Psychology: Most psychologists pursue a Master’s degree in Psychology or a related field (e.g., clinical psychology, counselling, etc.), which takes two years.

Doctoral Program (Optional): For clinical psychologists or those seeking higher-level research or academic roles, a PhD or PsyD is required, which may take 3-5 additional years.

9. Public Health Specialists

Public health professionals care more about the health of groups of people than the health of single people. To stop disease outbreaks and improve health on a big scale, they do things like epidemiology, health education, and policymaking. In India, dealing with problems like infectious diseases, malnutrition, and other public health crises is difficult without the help of public health experts. Most of the time, they work for the government, non-governmental organizations (NGOs) or even for the foreign health groups.

10. Academicians and Researchers

In India, many doctors opt to pursue careers in academia or further their studies. In addition to conducting research to enhance medical science, these individuals also pass on their knowledge to the next generation of doctors. Academic doctors typically work in medical schools and universities, where they teach, conduct research, and perform clinical work. Their work is crucial for coming up with new treatments, making medical practices better, and teaching people how to become healthcare professionals in the future.

India has a wide range of medical workers, which shows how complicated the country's health care needs are. Every type of doctor, from general practitioners to super experts, plays a crucial role in ensuring that everyone receives the necessary medical care. You need to know these categories to navigate the healthcare system and ensure patients get enough care. As India continues to change, it's possible that these doctors' jobs will grow and change to fit the new healthcare system.

Doctor's Decision Making Process

The Indian pharmaceutical industry is crucial to the healthcare system of the country, especially when it comes to making decisions about what drugs to prescribe. This process is complicated and depends on many things, such as clinical proof, patient needs, economic concerns, and interactions with pharmaceutical representatives. The way doctors in India make decisions is crucial because it has a direct effect on how well patients do, how much healthcare costs, and how well the healthcare system works generally.

Clinical Evidence and Guidelines

Clinical proof is a crucial factor that guides a doctor's decision-making process. Like doctors around the world, Indian doctors depend on clinical guidelines and medicine that is based on evidence to make decisions about how to care for their patients. Doctors can handle certain conditions more effectively when they follow standardized treatment protocols, like those suggested by the World Health Organization (WHO) or the Indian Council of Medical Research (ICMR). These guidelines are the result of extensive research and clinical trials, ensuring the safety and effectiveness of the suggested treatments.

However, these standards are not as simple to find and understand in all parts of India. In cities, doctors may have easier access to the newest study and clinical guidelines. In rural areas, on the other hand, people may rely more on old-fashioned knowledge and methods. Also, because Indian patients are very different in terms of their genetics, socioeconomic standing, and where they live, doctors often have to change the rules to meet the needs of their individual patients.

Evidence Based Medicine as a Influencing Factor

Evidence-Based Medicine (EBM) is a vital part of how doctors in India make decisions. As healthcare changes, Indian doctors depend on EBM more and more to make clinical decisions that are based on solid research and clinical trials. This method ensures that patients receive care based on the latest scientific evidence, rather than relying solely on tradition or personal experience. India is using EBM because they want to make sure that treatment plans are always the same, patients are becoming more knowledgeable, and medical methods are becoming more consistent around the world. The Indian government and medical schools also support EBM by including it in medical education and programs for doctors to keep learning and improving their skills. Companies that make medicines also help by giving clinical data that shows their goods work and are safe. However, challenges such as resource scarcity, difficulty in accessing quality research, and the diverse health care needs of Indians can hinder the widespread adoption of EBM. Despite these challenges, India's increasing emphasis on EBM is a positive development that is improving patient care and ensuring the success and modernity of medical practices.

Patient-Centric Considerations

The patient's needs, preferences, and socioeconomic status are also important things to think about when making a choice. India has a big problem with the cost of health care, so doctors often have to weigh how well a treatment works against how much it costs. This is particularly true for long-term illnesses that require medical treatment. Doctors must consider the cost of treating their patients and may opt for generic medicines or less expensive alternatives if they are equally effective.

The patient's social and cultural background is also very important. In India, patients often have strong views about certain medicines or treatments, which can make them less likely to follow their doctor's instructions. So, doctors need to use shared decision-making, in which they listen to what the patient wants, talk about the pros and cons of different treatment choices, and come to an agreement that fits the patient's values and expectations.

Influence of Clinical Guidelines

Clinical standards are essential to doctors in India because they help them make decisions and make sure that all of their patients get the same care. Medical groups such as the Indian Council of Medical Study (ICMR) and the Medical Council of India (MCI) typically formulate these rules through extensive research and consensus among experts. These guidelines provide doctors with guidance based on data, enabling them to diagnose and treat a wide range of conditions effectively. These guidelines are very helpful for making sure that everyone follows the same steps and that patients get better care. However, due to the unique characteristics of India's healthcare system, which includes diverse patient groups and varying levels of resource accessibility, doctors frequently need to adapt these guidelines to meet the specific needs of their patients. Also, Indian doctors often have to balance clinical guidelines with their own experience, what the patient wants, and practical issues like the supply of medicines and diagnostic tools. Even with these problems, following clinical standards is becoming more and more important in medical education and practice. This demonstrates the growing commitment to evidence-based medicine. As a result, these guidelines significantly influence treatment choices, ensuring that patient care aligns with the latest scientific discoveries and best practices.

Influence of Medical Representatives

Medical representatives (MRs), who work for pharmaceutical companies, have a big influence on how doctors in India make decisions. These medical representatives are the main link between drug companies and doctors. They inform the doctors about new drugs, updates to old drugs, medical devices, scientific information and treatment plans. The way doctors and MRs talk to each other is crucial in determining how the doctors write prescriptions, especially in India's competitive drug market.

Medical representatives provide the doctors with samples of new drugs, promotional materials, and study data that can help them decide which drugs to prescribe. A lot of the time, these interactions helps doctors stay up to date on the newest medical discoveries and treatment choices. However, drug marketing has influenced the writing of prescriptions, leading to ethical concerns, particularly when business interests may take precedence over patient welfare. For these reasons, it is essential for doctors to think carefully about the information MRs give them and make choices based on fair, strong proof.

Medical Representatives Generates Trust for their Organisations

A Medical Representative's (MR) ability to build trust in a company's brands is a big part of why healthcare professionals choose to suggest those brands' drugs. Regular, dependable contact, where the MR provides accurate, scientifically-based details about the drug's benefits, safety, and effectiveness, builds trust. The MR helps build trust in both the product and the company they work for by giving clear explanations of clinical studies, patient results, and any concerns.

A lot of the time, healthcare workers (HCPs) use MRs to keep up with the latest changes in pharmaceuticals. When an MR constantly gives the HCP useful information, values their time, and keeps their word, they build a strong professional relationship over time. Not only does the MR offer a beneficial product, but it also understands how responsible doctors are to their patients, which is what made this relationship work.

Also, an MR's openness about possible side effects, contraindications, and fair comparisons with competing goods makes trust even stronger. MRs boosts the trustworthiness of their companies' brands in the eyes of HCPs by presenting themselves as trustworthy partners who put patients' health first.

In the end, the level of trust between a medical professional and an MR has a direct effect on the healthcare professional's willingness to give the drugs. Patients trust the MR brand because the doctor does. This builds the company's image and makes sure it stays successful in a very competitive market.

Economic and Regulatory Factors

Economic issues play a crucial role in the decision-making process of physicians in India. The expense of medication, accessibility of insurance, and reimbursement procedures significantly influence treatment selection. In the lack of national health coverage, numerous patients in India incur out-of-pocket expenses for their medications, rendering drug affordability a paramount concern for physicians during prescriptions.

The Indian government has instituted many regulatory steps to guarantee the accessibility of inexpensive medications. The Drug Price Control Order (DPCO) regulates the pricing of key medications, enhancing their accessibility for the overall populace. Physicians must manoeuvre between these rules when making selections, frequently selecting medications that are both efficacious and compliant with the authorized price limits. The advent of Ayushman Bharat, a national health insurance initiative, is transforming the healthcare landscape by offering coverage for an expanded array of therapies, which may influence physicians' decision-making as they evaluate their patients' insurance coverage.

Technological Advancements

Technological developments have progressively integrated into the decision-making process for physicians in India. The emergence of electronic health records (EHRs), telemedicine, and artificial intelligence (AI) in healthcare has equipped physicians with enhanced resources for diagnosis and treatment planning. Electronic Health Records (EHRs) enable physicians to retrieve a patient's comprehensive medical history, thereby guiding their decisions related to drug interactions, allergies, and previous treatments.

Telemedicine has enhanced healthcare accessibility in distant regions of India, enabling physicians to consult with patients who would otherwise have restricted access to medical services. This technology facilitates collaboration among physicians and specialists across the nation and abroad, ultimately improving the quality of care delivered.

Artificial intelligence and machine learning are becoming as formidable instruments in the decision-making process. These tools can analyse extensive data sets to discern trends and propose viable therapies, so aiding physicians in making more precise and fast judgments. The use of these technologies in India remains in its early stages, and their influence on decision-making is anticipated to increase in the forthcoming years.

The decision-making process for physicians in India is complex and dynamic, shaped by clinical data, patient requirements, economic factors, and the changing healthcare environment. As the Indian healthcare system evolves, physicians must adeptly manage these variables while prioritizing optimal patient care. By integrating evidence-based medicine with patient-centered care and rigorously assessing information from pharmaceutical representatives, physicians can make educated decisions that improve patient outcomes while preserving the integrity of the healthcare system.

Understanding Doctors' Needs and Preferences

Comprehending the requirements and preferences of physicians is essential for pharmaceutical companies, particularly within the Indian setting, characterized by a complex and swiftly changing healthcare environment. Diverse elements such as patient demographics, healthcare infrastructure, and geographical disparities shape the complex environment in which Indian physicians operate. These dynamics, along with their professional and personal experiences, shape their demands and tastes.

In India, physicians frequently encounter difficulties with the accessibility of medical resources and the healthcare system's competence. In urban locations, physicians may encounter elevated patient numbers and an abundance of treatment options, but in rural settings, they may contend with constrained resources and fewer alternatives. Comprehending these regional disparities is crucial for pharmaceutical companies aiming to interact effectively with healthcare practitioners.

Medical practitioners in India often emphasize evidence-based medicine, favouring pharmaceutical medicines that are supported by substantial clinical research and demonstrated effectiveness. This choice highlights the necessity of delivering high-quality, scientifically substantiated information. Pharmaceutical companies and medical personnel must be prepared to provide comprehensive clinical data, research studies, and patient outcomes pertaining to their medications. This method not only corresponds with physicians' focus on evidence-based practices but also fosters trust and credibility.

The educational background and on-going learning requirements of Indian physicians significantly influence their preferences. Numerous physicians prioritize opportunities for professional advancement and continuing medical education (CME) as integral to their career progression. Pharmaceutical companies can capitalize on this by providing educational tools, courses, and seminars that enhance their continuous learning. By aligning their products with the training requirements of physicians, pharmaceutical corporations can cultivate beneficial connections and exhibit their dedication to assisting medical professionals.

Alongside clinical efficacy and educational resources, physicians also evaluate the practicality and convenience of pharmacological items. Elements like usability, patient adherence, and adverse effect profiles are essential. In a nation with a heterogeneous population such as India, physicians frequently confront patients possessing differing degrees of health literacy and adherence. Consumers are likely to prefer pharmaceutical goods that are user-friendly and exhibit a low incidence of undesirable effects. Organizations that consider these pragmatic elements in their product development and marketing strategies can more effectively fulfil physicians' requirements.

The impact of legal and policy frameworks on physicians' choices is significant. In India, healthcare rules and regulations are always shifting, influencing the accessibility and utilization of pharmaceutical items. Physicians must adapt to these alterations while guaranteeing optimal treatment for their patients. Pharmaceutical companies that remain abreast of regulatory developments and provide products that adhere to contemporary standards are more effectively positioned to match with physicians' preferences and assist them in their practice.

Moreover, interactions with pharmaceutical reps frequently shape physicians' preferences. The quality of communication and personal interactions significantly influence physicians' perceptions of pharmaceutical products. Representatives who exhibit a comprehensive awareness of medical practices, furnish pertinent information, and participate in substantive discussions are more inclined to establish enduring collaborations with healthcare professionals. The significance of relationship-building is particularly pronounced in India, where personal rapport and trust may greatly influence professional encounters.

Technology significantly influences the preferences of Indian physicians. As digital health solutions and telemedicine proliferate, physicians are increasingly integrating technology into their practice. Pharmaceutical firms providing digital tools, mobile applications, and online materials can address this expanding trend. For example, offering digital platforms for obtaining pharmaceutical information, patient educational resources, and virtual consultations can augment the entire value proposition for physicians.

Cultural sensitivity is an essential element in comprehending the requirements and preferences of physicians in India. The nation's multifaceted cultural environment results in physicians potentially possessing differing perspectives on medical practices and treatments influenced by regional and cultural factors. Pharmaceutical companies must take these cultural variations into account when formulating and marketing their drugs. Customizing marketing techniques and instructional resources to align with local cultural settings can enhance acceptability and participation among physicians.

To fully understand the wants and needs of doctors in India, we need to look at a lot of different factors, such as clinical effectiveness, educational needs, practical concerns, regulatory influences, interpersonal dynamics, technological advances, and cultural aspects. By addressing these factors, pharmaceutical companies can more effectively fulfill the expectations of Indian physicians, cultivate robust professional relationships, and ultimately enhance healthcare results. This comprehensive understanding not only improves the efficacy of pharmaceutical sales techniques but also contributes to the overarching objective of promoting healthcare in India.

Compliance in Maintaining Doctor-Representative Relationship

The relationship between medical representatives (MRs) and physicians in the Indian pharmaceutical sector is essential for successful communication and the promotion of pharmaceutical goods. Several laws and ethical standards regulate this connection, ensuring honest, ethical, and legal interactions between medical representatives and healthcare professionals.

The Indian pharmaceutical industry functions within a framework of rigorous rules aimed at preserving the integrity of medical practices and ensuring that promotional activities do not jeopardize patient care. The Central Drugs Standard Control Organization (CDSCO), the Drug Controller General of India (DCGI), and the Medical Council of India (MCI), which the National Medical Commission (NMC) has since replaced, are the principal regulatory authorities involved. These organizations establish protocols that medical representatives must adhere to in order to guarantee ethical engagements with physicians.

The principal aim of compliance is to avert conflicts of interest and to eliminate any undue influence on healthcare providers. Medical Representatives are responsible for providing accurate and unbiased information about pharmaceutical products, including their benefits, risks, and appropriate use. They must comply with the standards of veracity and transparency, guaranteeing that all promotional materials or assertions are supported by substantial scientific proof. This is vital in the Indian setting, where misinformation can result in severe repercussions due to the diversity of medical practices and the widespread use of traditional and alternative medicine systems.

In India, the Indian Pharmaceutical Alliance (IPA) and the Organization of Pharmaceutical Producers of India (OPPI) offer supplementary rules for ethical engagements between medical representatives and physicians. These rules underscore the necessity of upholding professional decorum and ensuring that any gifts or incentives offered to physicians are modest and non-influential. For instance, offering opulent gifts or funding costly parties may be viewed as efforts to influence medical opinions or choices, contravening the ethical norms established by these organizations. Medical representatives should avoid using forceful or manipulative methods, and refrain from offering personal incentives in exchange for prescribing specific prescriptions.

An essential facet of compliance is the documenting and reporting of contacts between medical representatives and physicians. Medical representatives must maintain precise records of their meetings, encompassing the subjects addressed and any promotional materials distributed. This documentation acts as protection against possible accusations of unethical activity and guarantees that all contacts are executed in a way that is subject to scrutiny and audit if required. Consistent training and updates on compliance rules are crucial for medical representatives to remain apprised of any alterations in the legal and ethical framework.

Moreover, adherence to the Indian government's rules, including the Drugs and Magic Remedies (Objectionable Advertisements) Act, 1954, significantly influences the relationships between medical representatives and physicians. This legislation forbids the advertising of pharmaceuticals or treatments that make inflated or misleading assertions about their effectiveness. Medical representatives are required to back all promotional claims with genuine scientific research and present them in compliance with regulatory guidelines. Failure to adhere to these standards may result in significant fines, including legal repercussions and harm to the reputation of the implicated pharmaceutical company.

Recently, there has been an increasing focus on digital transparency and the ethical utilization of digital platforms within the pharmaceutical sector. With the emergence of digital marketing and online interactions, medical representatives must comply with requirements in both in-person meetings and online contacts. This entails guaranteeing that digital promotions are transparent, accurate, and compliant with regulatory norms. The increasing use of digital tools and platforms necessitates a more stringent compliance strategy, given the scrutiny and wider reach of online interactions compared to traditional methods.

Furthermore, the involvement of pharmaceutical corporations in promoting a culture of compliance is essential. Organizations must create comprehensive compliance programs, offer frequent training for medical representatives, and establish transparent mechanisms for reporting unethical activity. A successful compliance program assures regulatory adherence and fosters a culture of integrity and accountability inside the organization. Regular audits and assessments of compliance activities facilitate the identification of improvement areas and ensure consistent adherence to standards.

Ensuring compliance in the physician-representative relationship in India is a complex process that necessitates adherence to regulatory standards, ethical principles, and thorough documentation. It necessitates a dedication to honesty, precision, and professionalism in all engagements between medical representatives and healthcare professionals. By following these principles, the pharmaceutical sector may establish confidence with healthcare professionals and enhance the overall quality of patient care. Compliance protects the interests of patients and healthcare professionals while simultaneously bolstering the credibility and reputation of pharmaceutical companies in the Indian market.

Case Studies

Case 1: A well-known cardiologist in New Delhi, Dr. Sharma had a busy schedule full of appointments with patients, surgeries, and on-going study. Because of this, he didn't have much time to talk to the medical representatives. He tried to make sure his patients had the best results, and keeping up with the latest developments in cardiology were his top priorities. Ramesh, a medical representative from a major pharmaceutical company, approached Dr. Sharma and suggested they collaborate. Ramesh understood that Dr. Sharma was busy and needed to concentrate on his work, so he gave a brief presentation on cardiology, highlighting the latest clinical data on heart drugs. Instead of giving Dr. Sharma too many general product details, he focused on how effective and safe the medicines were and how they fit with the doctor's goals to improve patient results. Ramesh also knew how important it was to trust. He provided accurate information based on research and refrained from overstating the product's benefits. In addition, he gave Dr. Sharma chances to take part in continuing medical education (CME) programs, which helped the doctor grow as a true healthcare professional. Dr. Sharma eventually trusted Ramesh because he cared about him and was a professional. It wasn't just a sale for the doctor; he saw him as a skilled partner in taking care of patients. Ramesh was able to build a long-lasting relationship with Dr. Sharma that was beneficial for both of them by focusing on the usefulness of the product, respecting the doctor's time, and helping him with his educational needs. This relationship improved both the doctor's practice and the pharmaceutical company's market presence.

Case 2: As a general doctor in a rural village in India, Dr. Srivastava has to deal with the daily challenge of prescribing medications while also taking clinical guidelines, patient needs, and budget limits into account. Mr. Rawat, a 65-year-old patient, comes in with high blood pressure and needs ongoing care. Dr. Srivastava is cognizant of the latest guidelines from the Indian Council of Medical Research (ICMR), which recommend a specific blood pressure medication proven effective through evidence-based medicine (EBM). But this medicine is pricey, and Mr. Rawat, who is a farmer and doesn't make much money, can't afford it. Knowing that Mr. Rawat is on a tight budget, Dr. Srivastava considers recommending a generic alternative. He carefully looks at the clinical evidence to make sure that the alternative drug is safe and effective according to the ICMR standards. He also takes Mr. Rawat's wish for fewer side effects into account. Dr. Srivastava learned about this alternative by talking to a medical representative who gave him clear, evidence-based information, which made him trust the generic name. In this case, Dr. Srivastava makes the right choice by taking into account clinical data, economic realities, and the patient's preferences. He provides high-quality patient care by adjusting to the unique challenges of his rural practice. In this manner, he ensures Mr. Rawat receives cost-effective care, adhering to his duty to employ proven medical practices. This case shows how challenging it is for doctors and patients to make decisions in India's complex healthcare system.

Suggestive Questions from the Chapter

1. Examine the function of medical representatives in fostering trust and collaboration with physicians within the Indian pharmaceutical industry, taking into account cultural and professional subtleties.
2. In what manner do medical representatives tailor their strategies to accommodate the time limitations, therapeutic areas, and regional cultural inclinations of physicians in India?
3. Elucidate the significance of continuous medical education (CME) and the role of medical representatives in facilitating a physician's career advancement in India.
4. How does the fact that pharmaceutical companies in India see doctors as customers change the way they sell their products in the Indian healthcare system?
5. What are the most important things that pharmaceutical businesses need to know about Indian doctors as customers in order to effectively engage them?
6. How can post-sale digital engagement and assistance enhance the relationship between Indian doctors and drug companies?
7. What function do family doctors and general practitioners (GPs) serve in India's healthcare system, especially in rural and semi-urban areas?
8. How do experts like neurologists and cardiologists help treat complicated medical diseases in India?
9. How do homeopathic and ayurvedic physicians in India, especially in rural regions, offer alternative healthcare?
10. How crucial are public health experts to the management of major health problems in India?

Multiple Choice Questions

1. In India, how many years of formal education and training do doctors typically undergo before they start their practice?

   (a) 5 years (b) 8 years

   (c) 10 years (d) 12 years

2. What is a key characteristic that doctors in India expect from pharmaceutical representatives?

   (a) Persuasion (b) Empathy

   (c) Impatience (d) Creativity

3. Which skill is essential for medical representatives to establish long-term professional relationships with doctors?

   (a) Salesmanship (b) Storytelling

   (c) Negotiation (d) Communication

4. What is the primary role of doctors in the pharmaceutical industry?

   (a) Consumers (b) Manufacturers

   (c) Decision-makers (d) Marketers

5. Which therapeutic focus should a medical representative emphasize when speaking to a cardiologist?

   (a) Neurology (b) Cardiovascular

   (c) Oncology (d) Paediatrics

6. In which type of environment do doctors typically expect more personal interaction from medical representatives?

   (a) Urban (b) Rural

   (c) International (d) Corporate

7. Which is a key factor that medical representatives should respect when meeting with doctors?

   (a) Time (b) Style

   (c) Distance (d) Income

8. Trust between doctors and medical representatives are primarily built through which of the following?

   (a) Flattery (b) Honesty

   (c) Negotiation (d) Gifting

9. What can medical representatives organize to help doctors stay updated on the latest medical advancements?
   (a) Conferences (b) Product launches
   (c) CME meetings (d) Sales meetings
10. Which important skill helps a medical representative understand the unique needs of doctors?
    (a) Listening (b) Writing
    (c) Coding (d) Managing
11. Which type of doctor is often the first point of contact for patients in rural areas in India?
    (a) Cardiologist (b) Neurologist
    (c) General Practitioner (d) Surgeon
12. Which specialist is responsible for diagnosing and treating conditions related to the heart?
    (a) Orthopaedist (b) Cardiologist
    (c) Psychiatrist (d) Dentist
13. The minimum qualification to become an Ayurvedic doctor in India is a degree in:
    (a) BAMS (b) BHMS
    (c) MBBS (d) MDS
14. Which medical specialist focuses on the treatment of brain and nervous system disorders?
    (a) Paediatrician (b) Neurosurgeon
    (c) Oncologist (d) Gynaecologist
15. A doctor who specializes in treating cancer is known as a:
    (a) Paediatrician (b) Cardiologist
    (c) Oncologist (d) Psychiatrist

16. The basic qualification required to become a dentist in India is:
    (a) MBBS (b) BHMS
    (c) BAMS (d) BDS

17. Who among the following is considered a super specialist in the medical field?
    (a) General Practitioner (b) Cardiothoracic Surgeon
    (c) Psychologist (d) Family Physician

18. Which medical professional treats mental health disorders and is authorized to prescribe medications?
    (a) Psychologist (b) Paediatrician
    (c) Psychiatrist (d) Orthopaedic Surgeon

19. Which degree is typically pursued after MBBS to specialize in Gynaecology in India?
    (a) MCh (b) MD
    (c) BAMS (d) BDS

20. A doctor who focuses on treating musculoskeletal disorders, including bones and joints, is a:
    (a) Cardiologist (b) Orthopaedic Surgeon
    (c) Dentist (d) Neurologist

21. The primary factor guiding doctors' decision-making in India is:
    (a) Economic concerns (b) Clinical evidence
    (c) Pharmaceutical representatives (d) Patient preferences

22. The Indian Council of Medical Research (ICMR) and the World Health Organization (WHO) provide:
    (a) Clinical guidelines
    (b) Pharmaceutical representatives
    (c) Economic analysis
    (d) Patient preferences

23. A significant challenge in India's adoption of Evidence-Based Medicine is:
    (a) Lack of clinical trials
    (b) Abundance of resources
    (c) Lack of diversity in patient populations
    (d) Difficulty in accessing quality research

24. Medical representatives primarily influence doctors by:
    (a) Prescribing drugs
    (b) Providing clinical evidence
    (c) Conducting clinical trials
    (d) Setting regulations

25. A key factor in building trust between medical representatives and healthcare professionals is:
    (a) Aggressive marketing
    (b) High-pressure sales tactics
    (c) Transparency and honesty
    (d) Limited communication

CHAPTER

5

Importance of the Distribution Network in Pharmaceutical Sales

In the Indian pharmaceutical sales ecosystem, the distribution network is essential to making sure that medications and medical supplies are available everywhere in the nation. Given its size and demographic diversity, India poses special difficulties that call for a strong and effective distribution network to ensure pharmaceutical items are always available. In addition to facilitating the prompt delivery of necessary medications to cities, a well-organized distribution network also enables its reach into rural and isolated areas with potentially inadequate healthcare facilities. In a nation where access to healthcare is still unequal, this broad reach is essential, making distribution networks a crucial public health facilitator.

Additionally, manufacturers, carrying and forwarding agencies (CFAs), distributors, wholesalers, stockists, and retailers are all part of India's multi-tiered pharmaceutical distribution network. Legal requirements dictate the handling, delivery, and storage of goods at every level of the supply chain. The effectiveness of this network directly impacts the availability of medications in pharmacies, hospitals, and clinics, thereby influencing patient outcomes. Stockouts can result from any interruptions or inefficiencies in the distribution system, which can be extremely dangerous, particularly when it comes to life-saving drugs.

Apart from its operational significance, the distribution network also has a strategic function in the pharmaceutical industry's competitive environment. Businesses can guarantee greater market penetration, raise brand awareness, and boost sales performance with a robust distribution network. An effective distribution network can be a major competitive advantage in a market when competition is fierce and product differentiation can be difficult. It enables businesses to efficiently manage inventory, react swiftly to market demands, and cut expenses—all of which can improve pricing tactics and customer happiness.

The increasing demand for over-the-counter (OTC) medications, where the supply chain's speed and efficiency are essential to satisfying customer demands, emphasizes the significance of the distribution network even more. The distribution network's importance will only increase as the Indian pharmaceutical market grows, making it a crucial part of a business's entire sales strategy and a major factor in determining its level of success.

The Distribution Network in Pharmaceuticals

As the backbone that guarantees the prompt and effective supply of medications from producers to consumers, the distribution network is an essential part of the Indian pharmaceutical sales ecosystem. With a wide range of stakeholders, including producers, distributors, wholesalers, retailers, and logistics companies, and the pharmaceutical distribution network in India is intricate and multidimensional. Since each of these stakeholders is essential to preserving the availability and accessibility of medications throughout the nation, the network's success rests on their smooth coordination and integration.

Pharmaceutical manufacturers, who produce a wide range of products from over-the-counter (OTC) goods to life-saving pharmaceuticals, hold a prominent position in the distribution hierarchy. To guarantee that their goods make it to the market, these producers depend on a network of distributors. Distributors often referred to as clearing and forwarding (C&F) agents, act as a bridge between manufacturers and wholesalers. They handle, store, and transport pharmaceutical items to wholesalers in a timely and efficient manner. Distributors in India are usually region-specific, which means they work within a specified geographic area. This helps to minimize logistical issues and streamline the distribution process.

By serving as a link between distributors and retailers, wholesalers are essential to the pharmaceutical distribution network. They buy pharmaceutical supplies in bulk from distributors and resell them to retailers in smaller amounts. Retailers then distribute the medications to final customers. With thousands of businesses operating around the nation, the wholesale industry in India is extremely fragmented. Although this fragmentation poses standards and regulatory issues, it also gives the distribution network flexibility and resilience, enabling it to meet the diverse demands of various geographical areas.

Retailers, including pharmacies and chemist shops, are the final link in the pharmaceutical distribution chain. Customers rely on them as their point of contact in order to obtain necessary medications. The role of retailers is especially crucial in India, where a sizable section of the population resides in rural and semi-urban areas. They support the entire public health system by guaranteeing that medications are accessible even in the most remote areas. Retailers are also crucial in ensuring that subpar or counterfeit goods do not make it to the market, teaching customers how to take pharmaceuticals correctly, and offering advice on dose and possible adverse effects.

The size and diversity of India present a number of significant obstacles for the pharmaceutical delivery network there. With a population of over 1.4 billion dispersed across large geographic areas, it is no small task to guarantee that medications are available everywhere in the nation. The fact that different regions have varying degrees of infrastructure development exacerbates this difficulty, with certain places experiencing restricted access to logistics and transportation services. Pharmaceutical businesses and distributors are increasingly using technology-driven solutions, like automated warehouses, real-time tracking systems, and supply chain management software to address these issues. By cutting down on delays and lowering the possibility of stockouts or overstocking, these improvements have contributed to the distribution network's increased efficiency and transparency.

The problem of fake medications is a major obstacle in the pharmaceutical distribution system. India, one of the world's biggest manufacturers of generic medications, is particularly susceptible to the spread of fake goods. In addition to being a major health risk, counterfeit medications damage the pharmaceutical industry's reputation. The Indian government and industry parties have taken a number of steps to address this problem, including serializing pharmaceutical items and introducing barcoding to track and trace medications across the supply chain. These steps have enhanced the security of the distribution network, ensuring the delivery of only authentic goods to customers.

It is impossible to overestimate the importance of regulatory agencies in monitoring the pharmaceutical distribution system. Organizations such as the Central Drugs Standard Control Organization (CDSCO) and state drug control bodies enforce national laws and regulations on the distribution of pharmaceutical products in India. To make sure that manufacturing plants, storage facilities, and retail establishments follow GDP and preserve the quality and safety of medications, these regulatory agencies regularly check them. They also collaborate closely with industry stakeholders to create standards for the distribution of novel and creative therapies and to solve new issues like the requirement for cold chain management for medications that are sensitive to temperature changes.

In the Indian pharmaceutical sales ecosystem, the distribution network is a dynamic and intricate structure that is essential to guaranteeing the public's access to and availability of medications. Driven by technical developments and regulatory control, the distribution network has continued to evolve and adapt despite the constraints presented by the nation's wide territory, diverse infrastructure, and the threat of counterfeit medications. A strong and effective distribution network will become even more crucial as India's pharmaceutical sector expands, making it an essential part of the nation's healthcare system.

Definition and Purpose of Distribution Network in Pharmaceuticals

The distribution network is essential to the Indian pharmaceutical sales ecosystem because it makes sure that medications and medical supplies are available everywhere in the nation. In the pharmaceutical industry, the word "distribution network" refers to the organized system of middlemen, logistics, and procedures that transport pharmaceutical goods from producers to final customers, including pharmacies, hospitals, and eventually patients. Maintaining the availability, cost, and accessibility of medications throughout India's diverse and expansive geographic area depends on this network.

Definition of Distribution Network

The entire system of channels used to transport pharmaceutical products from the point of manufacture to the point of consumption is known as a distribution network in the pharmaceutical industry. The layers involved in this network include manufacturers, clearing and forwarding agents (CFAs), distributors, wholesalers, stockists, and retailers. Each layer in this network is essential to guarantee the delivery of the appropriate products at the appropriate time to the appropriate location.

The distribution network is a collection of procedures that include order processing, inventory management, transportation, and customer support in addition to being a physical chain of movements. The distribution network aims to maintain the integrity of pharmaceutical products, ensuring their safety, efficacy, and superior quality across the entire supply chain.

Purpose of the Distribution Network

A pharmaceutical distribution network's main goal is to guarantee that medications are always available to patients, healthcare professionals, and retailers. But its importance extends beyond supply; it serves a number of other crucial functions that enhance the ecosystem surrounding pharmaceutical sales as a whole.

1. **Ensuring Product Availability**: The distribution network's primary goal is to ensure that pharmaceutical items are continuously accessible at different points of sale, including pharmacies, clinics, and hospitals. Many pharmaceutical goods have the potential to save lives; thus, any interruption in the supply chain might have serious repercussions for both individuals and healthcare systems.
2. **Maintaining Product Integrity**: Environmental factors like humidity and temperature have a significant impact on pharmaceutical items. The distribution network is responsible for ensuring the proper carriage and storage of these items to maintain their effectiveness and safety. When it comes to vaccinations, biologics, and other medications that are sensitive to temperature, this is especially crucial.
3. **Efficient Inventory Management**: An efficient distribution network simplifies the management of inventory levels at various stages of the supply chain. For distributors, wholesalers, and retailers, it optimizes inventory costs by ensuring that products are neither overstocked nor under stocked. Effective inventory control also reduces the possibility of out-of-date or expired goods entering the supply chain.
4. **Timely Delivery**: The distribution network ensures the timely delivery of pharmaceutical products to meet market demands. This entails organizing a number of logistics processes, such as last-mile delivery, warehousing, and transportation. On-time delivery is essential, particularly during public health emergencies or medical emergencies when demand for some medications may suddenly spike.
5. **Regulatory Compliance**: The Central Drugs Standard Control Organization (CDSCO) and the Drug Controller General of India (DCGI) have established strict regulatory requirements that the pharmaceutical distribution network in India must abide by. The network must ensure that all pharmaceutical items comply with these rules to prevent the sale of fake or inferior medications.

6. **Market Penetration**: India's large and varied geography significantly hinders the distribution of pharmaceuticals. In order to guarantee that pharmaceutical items reach even the most isolated and rural regions of the nation, the distribution network is essential. This is necessary to achieve widespread market penetration and ensure that everyone in the population has access to healthcare.
7. **Cost Efficiency**: Another factor influencing the entire cost of pharmaceutical items is the distribution network. The network lessens the financial burden on the final customer by streamlining logistics and cutting waste. In a price-sensitive market like India, where the affordability of medications is a big problem, cost-effective distribution is especially crucial.
8. **Customer Service and Support**: Manufacturers and merchants or healthcare providers can communicate with each other through the distribution network. Making sure that retailers and healthcare providers have the assistance they need in terms of product availability, information, and after-sales service plays a crucial part in customer service. A healthy distribution network facilitates the development of enduring connections and trust between producers and their clients.

The distribution network is a crucial element of the Indian pharmaceutical sales ecosystem that guarantees the efficient movement of medications from producers to final customers. Its definition includes a sophisticated network of channels and procedures intended to preserve the integrity of the product, guarantee on-time delivery, and accomplish market penetration. Beyond simple logistics, this network is essential to guaranteeing that healthcare supplies are accessible, reasonably priced, and available to everyone. The distribution network will continue to be crucial to the pharmaceutical industry's success as it develops, necessitating constant innovation and modification to satisfy the market's rising expectations.

Key Players in the Distribution Network

The distribution network plays a crucial role in the Indian pharmaceutical sales ecosystem, ensuring the delivery of medications to all regions of the country. The cooperation and effectiveness of a number of important participants, each of whom makes a distinct contribution to the smooth movement of pharmaceutical products from producers to final consumers, are essential to the network's efficacy. To fully comprehend the complexities of the pharmaceutical distribution environment in India, one must be aware of the roles played by these important stakeholders.

1. **Pharmaceutical Manufacturers:** The pharmaceutical companies are at the top of the distribution chain. These businesses are in charge of manufacturing pharmaceuticals, which range from highly specialized therapies to generic medications. One of the world's biggest producers of generic medications is India, whose pharmaceutical companies are renowned for their economical manufacturing techniques. Usually, manufacturers use a vast network to deliver their goods throughout India and work on a massive scale. In addition to their production-related responsibilities, they play a crucial role in setting pricing, selecting supplier networks, and ensuring compliance with legal requirements. To effectively handle the flow of products, leading manufacturers frequently set up their own distribution arms or work with major distributors.
2. **Carrying and Forwarding Agents (CFAs):** Carrying and Forwarding Agents (CFAs) serve as a bridge between manufacturers and distributors. Carrying and Forwarding Agents (CFAs) are responsible for storing numerous pharmaceutical products in their warehouses and ensuring their timely delivery to various distributors or stockists. CFAs typically take care of logistics, inventory management, and distributor orders. Given the vastness and geographic variety of India, CFAs strategically position themselves throughout the country to ensure timely and effective delivery. They are essential for avoiding distribution delays and preserving a stable supply chain.
3. **Distributors/Wholesalers:** An essential component of the pharmaceutical distribution network is distributors or wholesalers. They serve as the main conduit between CFAs and hospitals or retail pharmacies. Distributors offer products to stores, hospitals, and other smaller distributors after buying them in bulk from CFAs or straight from producers. With thousands of distributors working all over the nation, India has a huge and intricate distributor network. Distributors are in charge of making sure the appropriate medications arrive at the appropriate location at the appropriate time. They are crucial in handling transportation logistics, granting retailer's credit, and controlling inventory levels.
4. **Stockists:** Specialized distributors who concentrate on particular regions or drug types are known as stockists. To guarantee that pharmaceutical items are accessible in places that may be difficult to reach, they frequently collaborate closely with distributors. Because accessibility issues may arise in rural and semi urban regions, stockists play a crucial role. They keep tight links with neighbourhood merchants

and frequently offer extra services like credit facilities, which aid in supply chain stabilization in areas that are harder to reach.

5. **Retail Pharmacies:** The most noticeable and approachable participants in the pharmaceutical delivery system are retail pharmacies. They are where customers buy their prescription drugs at the end of the supply chain. Retail pharmacies may operate independently, as a chain, or in clinics and hospitals. With more than 800,000 retail pharmacies in India, they constitute an essential part of the distribution system. Retail pharmacies offer customers crucial healthcare services and advice in addition to dispensing prescription drugs. Their ability to ensure accurate distribution and storage of medications determines the overall effectiveness of the healthcare system.
6. **Online Pharmacies:** Online pharmacies have become important participants in the Indian pharmaceutical distribution network in recent years. Customers may now acquire prescription drugs online and have them delivered right to their door thanks to the growth of e-commerce and digital technologies. Online pharmacies are becoming more and more popular among tech-savvy consumers since they are convenient, particularly in urban regions. To guarantee the availability of a large variety of medications, these platforms work with producers, distributors, and retail pharmacies. But the emergence of internet pharmacies also presents difficulties with regard to legal compliance, guaranteeing the legitimacy of medications, and efficiently handling logistics.
7. **Healthcare Providers:** Healthcare providers like physicians and hospitals play an indirect yet vital part in the distribution network, even though they are not directly involved. They are in charge of writing prescriptions, and the decisions they make affect the demand for particular pharmaceuticals. Since they frequently suggest specific medications based on availability and efficacy, their connections with distributors and pharmaceutical companies may also have an effect on the distribution network.
8. **Regulatory Bodies:** Important participants in the pharmaceutical distribution network are regulatory agencies like the Central Drugs Standard Control Organization (CDSCO) and state-level drug control authorities. These organizations make sure that the distribution of medications complies with all applicable legal and quality requirements. Their supervision is crucial to preserving the integrity of the distribution system since they control the authorization, production, and distribution of pharmaceutical items.

Each participant in India's intricate and varied pharmaceutical distribution network adds to the supply chain's overall dependability and efficiency. Every major participant, from producers to retail pharmacies and, more recently, online platforms, plays a distinct role in ensuring that medications are accessible to patients nationwide. Anyone wishing to navigate or enhance the Indian pharmaceutical sales ecosystem must comprehend these positions.

Types of Distributors in Pharmaceutical Sales

The distribution network is a sophisticated and multidimensional structure that guarantees the effective transfer of medications from producers to customers in the Indian pharmaceutical sales ecosystem. Different distributor types make up the distribution network, and each one is essential to the supply chain. Understanding the various distributor types is crucial for comprehending the operations of the pharmaceutical industry and the nationwide distribution of medications.

1. ***Carrying and Forwarding Agents (CFAs):*** CFAs, or carrying and forwarding agents, are the foundation of the pharmaceutical distribution system. These organizations are in charge of overseeing substantial stock holdings for pharmaceutical producers. Typically, CFAs manage large warehouses, storing medications until they dispatch them directly to wholesalers, smaller distributors, or retailers.

   CFAs work under a contract and receive payment for their services; they do not possess the products. They take care of distribution logistics, such as transportation, inventory control, and warehousing. Given India's vast geographic dispersion, CFAs strategically position themselves across the country to ensure prompt delivery of goods to all areas.

2. ***Stockists:*** Authorized distributors, sometimes referred to as stockists, buy pharmaceutical items in large quantities straight from producers, or CFAs. They deliver medications to hospitals, wholesalers, and retailers from their vast inventory. Stockists frequently concentrate on particular areas or territories, and they might be the only ones having the authority to distribute particular goods there.

   In order to bridge the gap between manufacturers and retailers, stockists play a critical role. They guarantee that there is a steady supply of medications on the market, particularly in places with potentially inadequate healthcare facilities. Additionally, stockists provide shops with credit facilities so they can keep sufficient stock levels without facing immediate financial difficulties.

3. ***Wholesalers:*** In the pharmaceutical distribution network, wholesalers play a crucial role as a bridge connecting retailers and stockists. They buy medications in bulk from wholesalers and resell them to retailers or directly to healthcare facilities like clinics, hospitals, and nursing homes in smaller amounts.

   Generally speaking, there are two sorts of wholesalers: full-line wholesalers and short-line wholesalers. Full-line wholesalers carry pharmaceutical products, including prescription pharmaceuticals, over-the-counter (OTC) treatments, and medical devices. Conversely, short-line distributors concentrate on a small number of therapeutic areas or certain product categories.

   Making sure that medications are easily accessible to merchants, who then provide them to customers, is the main responsibility of wholesalers. They are essential in maintaining the cold chain for products that are susceptible to temperature changes, controlling inventory levels, and guaranteeing on-time delivery.

4. ***Sub-Distributors:*** Smaller companies, known as sub-distributors, work under the direction of wholesalers or stockists. They serve niche local markets, frequently in semi-urban or rural regions where bigger distributors might not be directly present. Sub-distributors buy medications in lesser amounts from stockists or wholesalers and then deliver them to nearby pharmacies or stores.

   Sub-distributors play a critical role in expanding the pharmaceutical distribution network's reach into isolated regions. They improve the nation's general public health by guaranteeing that even the most remote areas have access to necessary medications.

5. ***Retailers:*** The last stop in the pharmaceutical delivery chain is the retailer. They serve as the locations where customers buy their medications, whether they do it online or in real pharmacies. After purchasing medications from wholesalers or sub-distributors, retailers give patients instructions on how to take them.

   India is home to a variety of retail pharmacies, including chain pharmacies, standalone pharmacies, and pharmacies housed in hospitals. The emergence of e-pharmacies has also changed the retail scene by providing customers with the ease of placing online orders for medications and having them delivered right to their door.

   Strict rules apply to retailers to guarantee the ethical and safe distribution of medications. They have to abide by the Pharmacy Act of 1948 and the Drugs and Cosmetics Act of 1940, which regulate the selling of pharmaceuticals in India. Retailers bear the responsibility of monitoring prescription medication records and ensuring the removal of recalled or expired goods from store shelves.

6. ***E-Pharmacies:*** In India, e-pharmacies are a relatively young but quickly expanding sector of the pharmaceutical delivery system. These online platforms provide a high degree of accessibility and convenience, particularly for people living in urban areas, by enabling customers to acquire medications through websites or mobile apps.

   E-pharmacies purchase their goods from stockists or wholesalers and then ship them straight to customers. They frequently provide home delivery choices, prescription management services, and discounts. Despite their growing popularity, e-pharmacies still have to deal with regulatory issues and worries about patient data security and medication authenticity.

The Indian pharmaceutical distribution network benefits from a wide range of distributors, each of whom makes a unique contribution to ensure the effective and safe delivery of medications to customers. Every kind of distributor, from CFAs to e-pharmacies, is essential to the smooth operation of the pharmaceutical supply chain and guarantees that everyone, wherever they may be, can access medications. Gaining knowledge of these distributors' functions and duties will help one better appreciate the size and complexity of India's pharmaceutical sales market.

Types of Stockists in Pharmaceutical Sales

Stockists are essential to the seamless movement of medications from producers to final customers in the Indian pharmaceutical sales ecosystem. Unlike distributors, stockists are mostly in charge of maintaining inventory and making sure that pharmacies are accessible to merchants, medical facilities, and other healthcare professionals as needed. Stockists operate efficiently to maintain the integrity of the supply chain, guarantee on-time delivery, and ultimately assist the healthcare system. Let us find out the various types of stockists in India's pharmaceutical sales market.

1. ***Super Stockists:*** Super stockists are a step up from normal stockists and act as a liaison between local or regional stockists and C&F agents. They typically span a wide geographic area, frequently including several states or regions. Super stockists buy pharmaceutical products in bulk from pharmaceutical companies or C&F agencies, and then distribute them to smaller distributors or stockists in their assigned region.

Super stockists play an especially important role in areas with difficult logistics or strong demand for medicinal supplies. Super stockists serve to shorten delivery lead times and guarantee that stock is available near the point of sale by serving as a mediator between the manufacturer or C&F agent and the smaller stockists. Additionally, they bear the cost of keeping sizable stock levels, which can be essential to guaranteeing a steady supply of medications.

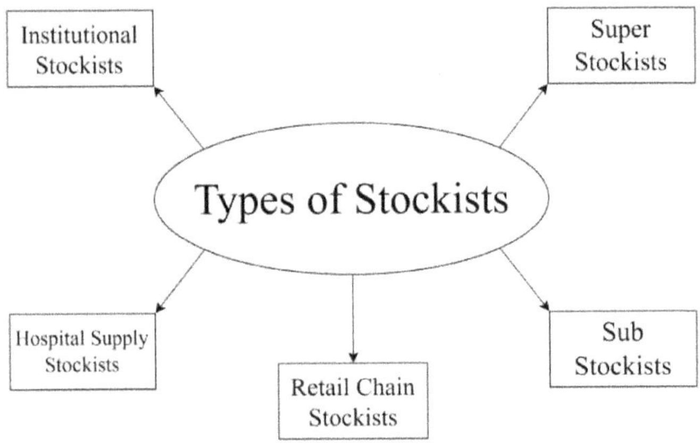

Fig. 5.1 Types of Stockists.

2. ***Sub-Stockists:*** Sub-stockists work on a more regional scale, usually catering to a single city or area within a state. They buy pharmaceutical supplies from supermarkets and then distribute them to local pharmacies, clinics, and smaller hospitals. Sub-stockists are crucial for expanding into new markets, particularly in rural and semi-urban areas where demand may be dispersed but nonetheless substantial.

   Sub-stockists, often family-run companies, possess a deep understanding of the unique characteristics of the local market. They are able to react swiftly to changes in demand because of their strong ties to the local healthcare providers and businesses. They play a vital role in ensuring that medications are accessible even in the most remote regions of the nation.

3. ***Hospital Supply Stockists:*** Providing for the pharmaceutical requirements of hospitals and other large healthcare facilities is the specialty of hospital supply stockists. Unlike general stockists, who supply a wide range of merchants, these stockists exclusively focus on meeting hospital needs, which often involve a wide variety of medications, medical equipment, and surgical supplies.

Hospital supply stockists typically keep a wider variety of goods on hand, including specialty and expensive medications that may not be in demand in retail pharmacies. To guarantee that essential medications are constantly available and that stock levels are sufficient, they collaborate closely with hospital procurement departments. A crucial skill for hospital supply stockists is the capacity to manage unique storage needs, like cold chain management, and provide medications in bulk.

4. ***Retail Chain Stockists:*** A new kind of stockist has appeared as a result of the growth of organized retail chains in the pharmaceutical industry: retail chain stockists. These stockists, who work for big pharmacy chains, are in charge of keeping the supplies for several retail locations in an area stocked. Retail chain stockists typically use a centralized business model, buying pharmaceuticals in large quantities and distributing them to different chain locations.

   Retail chain stockists have the advantage of being able to take advantage of economies of scale, bargain with manufacturers for better terms, and guarantee consistent pricing across all locations. Additionally, they often utilize sophisticated inventory management systems, allowing them to optimize the distribution process and monitor stock levels in real-time. This type of stockist is particularly prevalent in urban areas due to the prominence of organized retail chains.

5. ***Institutional Stockists*:** Institutional stockists provide non-hospital groups that need pharmaceuticals for their workers or beneficiaries, including government departments, non-governmental organizations (NGOs), and big businesses. These stockists frequently deal with large orders, and they might also participate in bidding procedures for the provision of medications to government health programs or major health projects.

   In addition to navigating intricate procurement procedures, institutional stockists frequently have to adhere to strict compliance and quality assurance criteria. They are an essential component of the pharmaceutical supply chain because of their capacity to provide substantial amounts of pharmaceutical products, frequently at discounted prices, especially when it comes to extensive health interventions.

A wide variety of stockists support the Indian pharmaceutical sales ecology, and each one is essential to guaranteeing the accessibility and availability of medications throughout the nation. Every kind of stockist, from C&F agents coordinating logistics to super stockists overseeing vast areas and sub-stockists catering to local markets, adds to the pharmaceutical supply chain's efficacy and efficiency. Stockists will continue to play a crucial role in addressing the public's healthcare demands as the pharmaceutical business develops.

Types of Retailers in Pharmaceutical Sales

Retailers are essential to closing the gap between pharmaceutical corporations and final customers in the Indian pharmaceutical sales ecosystem. Their main responsibility is to guarantee that customers and patients may obtain the prescription drugs and medical supplies they require. The pharmaceutical retail industry is broad and includes a variety of businesses that serve a range of demands and tastes. This section examines the primary categories of pharmaceutical retailers in India, their roles, traits, and ecological importance.

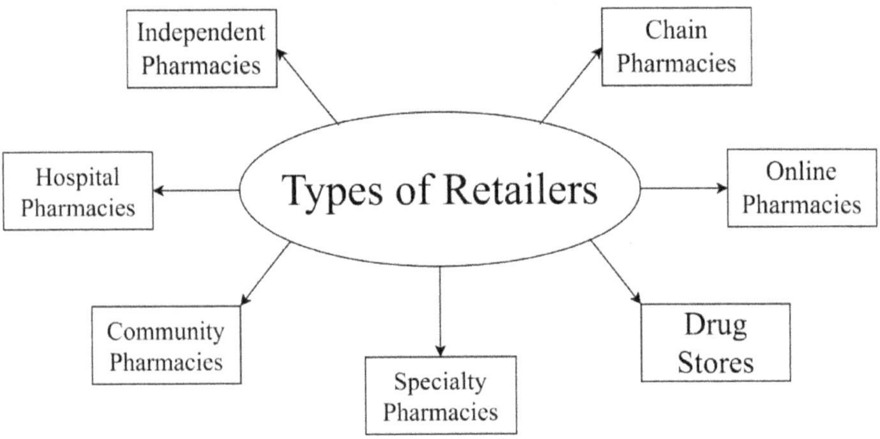

Fig. 5.2 Types of Retailers.

1. ***Chain Pharmacies:*** In India's retail pharmaceutical industry, chain pharmacies are a significant player. These are expansive networks of pharmacies operating under a single management and brand. Chains like Guardian Pharmacy, MedPlus, and Apollo Pharmacy are a few examples. Chain pharmacies offer a multitude of advantages they are:
   - **Standardized Quality and Service**: Chain pharmacies ensure uniform quality and service standards across all their outlets. This consistency is crucial for maintaining customer trust and satisfaction.
   - **Wide Range of Products**: They typically offer a broad range of products, including prescription medications, over-the-counter

(OTC) drugs, personal care items, and sometimes even medical equipment.

- **Convenience**: With multiple locations, chain pharmacies provide convenience to customers who can access their services and products easily.
- **Advanced Technology**: They often use advanced inventory management systems and customer relationship management (CRM) tools to enhance operational efficiency and customer experience.

2. ***Independent Pharmacies:*** Private owners and operators often operate independent pharmacies. They are sometimes known as standalone or single-store pharmacies. These pharmacies are frequently characterised by:
   - **Personalized Service**: Independent pharmacies tend to offer a more personalized service compared to chain pharmacies. The owners and staff often have closer relationships with their regular customers.
   - **Niche Focus**: They may specialize in certain types of medications or therapeutic areas, such as homeopathy, ayurvedic products, or specialized compounds.
   - **Flexibility**: Independent pharmacies can quickly adapt to local market needs and customer preferences, offering tailored solutions and products that might not be available in larger chains.
3. ***Online Pharmacies:*** Online pharmacies have emerged as a result of the substantial impact that the growth of e-commerce has had on the pharmaceutical retail industry. These online pharmacies, such as PharmEasy, 1mg, and Netmeds, provide a number of advantages. They are:
   - **Accessibility**: Online pharmacies provide customers with the convenience of ordering medications from home, which is particularly beneficial for those in remote areas or with mobility issues.
   - **Wide Selection**: They often offer a vast range of products, including medications, health supplements, and personal care items.
   - **Price Comparisons**: Customers can compare prices across different platforms, potentially finding better deals or discounts.
   - **Home Delivery**: Many online pharmacies offer home delivery services, enhancing convenience and accessibility.

4. ***Hospital Pharmacies:*** Hospital pharmacies are essential for today's healthcare facility operations. They primarily cater to inpatients and outpatients of the healthcare facilities and are located within hospitals or nursing homes. The important characteristics of the hospital pharmacies are:
   - **Specialized Medication Management**: Hospital pharmacies manage and dispense medications that are often specific to the hospital's specialty areas, including critical care and oncology.
   - **Collaborative Care**: Pharmacists in hospital settings work closely with medical staff to ensure optimal medication therapy management and patient safety.
   - **Inventory Control**: They handle a wide range of medications, including those that may not be commonly found in community pharmacies, and ensure a steady supply of essential drugs.
5. ***Community Pharmacies:*** Usually smaller than corporate or hospital pharmacies there is a class of pharmaceutical retail outlet known as community pharmacies. In India they are commonly known as chemist & druggist store. They usually cater to their local neighbourhoods. They are characterised by:
   - **Local Focus**: Community pharmacies focus on serving the local population, providing not only medications but also health advice and wellness products.
   - **Health Services**: Many community pharmacies offer additional health services such as blood pressure monitoring, diabetes management, and vaccination.
   - **Community Engagement**: These pharmacies often participate in local health initiatives and provide education on health and wellness topics.
6. ***Specialty Pharmacies:*** Specialty pharmacies concentrate on particular drug classes or patient requirements. They are crucial for the management of chronic or complicated illnesses that need specialized care. Important elements of these speciality pharmacies consist of:
   - **Complex Therapies**: Specialty pharmacies handle medications for conditions such as cancer, HIV/AIDS, and multiple sclerosis, which may require special storage, handling, and administration.
   - **Patient Support**: They often provide additional support services, including patient education, adherence monitoring, and coordination with healthcare providers.

7. ***Drug Stores:*** Drug stores are retail establishments that offer a variety of goods, such as groceries, cosmetics, and household goods, in addition to medications. They provide:
    - **Diverse Product Range:** In addition to medications, drug stores often provide a variety of non-pharmaceutical products, making them a one-stop shop for many customers.
    - **Convenience:** Their broad product offerings and often extended hours make them a convenient option for customers seeking both healthcare and everyday items.

The retail pharmaceutical industry in India is characterized by its diversity, with several kinds of retailers each contributing differently to the population's healthcare requirements. Chain pharmacies, independent pharmacies, internet pharmacies, hospital pharmacies, community pharmacies, specialty pharmacies, and drug stores form a vast network that ensures the availability and accessibility of pharmaceuticals and health-related goods. It is easier to appreciate the intricacy and scope of the Indian pharmaceutical sales ecosystem when one is aware of these many kinds of retailers.

Role of Retailers in the Distribution Network

In India, retailers are crucial to the pharmaceutical distribution network because they connect wholesalers or sellers with end users. Retailers not only oversee sales, but also ensure customer satisfaction, effective material management, and adherence to regulations. Retail pharmacies, also known as chemists, serve as the primary source for prescription drugs, over-the-counter (OTC) medicines, and health vitamins in India.

One of the main jobs of retail pharmacies is to make sure that a lot of different pharmaceutical goods are available. They keep inventory levels that are in line with what they think customers will want, and they keep track of stock movement to avoid shortages and overstocks. This means not only getting goods from authorized sellers, but also keeping track of when they expire and making sure they are stored properly to keep drugs working. Effective inventory management by stores helps keep shelves from running out and makes sure that patients can get their needed medicines on time.

Retailers are also crucial when it comes to educating and counselling patients. In retail settings, pharmacists give advice on how to take medications correctly, as well as possible side effects and how they might mix with other drugs. They are a great place for people to get information about their prescriptions or their over-the-counter medicine, which helps them take their medications as prescribed and improves their health. Often, store pharmacists provide additional services such as blood pressure checks, diabetes management, and immunizations, demonstrating their commitment to providing more than just pharmaceuticals.

Another important part of the retailer's job is to follow the rules set by regulators. Regulatory bodies in India, such as the Drug Controller General of India (DCGI) and the Pharmacy Council of India (PCI), make it very clear what pharmacists must do. This means keeping the right paperwork for controlled substances, labelling them correctly, and making sure that all of their goods come from licensed suppliers. Also, retailers need to know about any changes to the rules and make the necessary changes to their business methods to stay in line.

The standard retail pharmacy scene is also changing because of the rise of digital health platforms and e-pharmacies. Online stores and services that can be used on your phone are becoming more popular because they make picking up medicines easier, especially in rural areas. If retailers can keep up with these changes in technology, they can reach more customers and meet their changing wants in the digital age.

In India, retailers are an important part of the network that moves medicines around the country. They monitor goods, educate patients, ensure adherence to regulations, and adjust to technological advancements. All of these things are necessary to keep the pharmaceutical supply chain running smoothly.

Distributor-Stockist Relationship

A vital part of the Indian pharmaceutical sales ecosystem is the relationship between distributors and stockists. A complicated and ever-changing relationship makes sure that medicines get from the people who make them to the people who buy them without any problems. This partnership is based on trust, speed, and the ability to change with the needs of the market. Coordinating, talking, and making clear decisions are essential for this relationship to work.

Coordination and Communication

The main way that distributors and stores work together is by talking and planning ahead. The supply chain in the Indian pharmaceutical business is very long and involves many people, so good communication is very important. Distributors make sure that the right goods get to the right stores at the right time by acting as go-betweens for manufacturers and stockists.

- **Effective Communication**: Distributors and stores need to be able to talk to each other easily so that there aren't any stock-outs or overstocks, which are both detrimental for business. They discuss product quantities, demand anticipated, delivery dates, and market changes. Regular updates help both sides make changes to their plans as needed. For instance, a wholesaler should promptly inform the stockists of increased demand for a specific drug in a specific area, enabling them to adjust their orders accordingly.
- **Technology in Communication**: Technology makes wholesalers and stockists communicate easier. It is possible for stockists to place orders, track shipments, and handle inventory in real time on many digital platforms and software used by distributors. In addition to communicating better, these tools also make things more clear, so everyone knows the same thing about stock levels, delivery times, and payment statuses.
- **Coordination in Order Management**: Another area where coordination is crucial is order management. To ensure prompt and accurate order fulfilment, stockists and distributors must collaborate. This includes making sure there are enough drugs in stock on a regular basis, ordering faster-moving drugs when they run out, and handling the logistics of delivery. Coordinating well cuts down on delays and makes sure that sellers always have the goods they need to meet customer demand.
- **Problem Resolution**: It's important to be able to quickly solve problems like late arrivals, damaged goods, or differences between orders when they come up. Good lines of contact and coordination facilitate the quick resolution of problems. This keeps the supply chain running smoothly. For instance, if a stockist receives a damaged package, they must promptly inform the distributor. The distributor then needs to replace the damaged goods and look into what went wrong.
- **Feedback Mechanisms**: Another important part of contact between distributors and stockists is feedback. Stockists talk to stores and sometimes even customers directly, which helps them learn a lot about market trends and what customers want. Distributors can make changes to their supply strategies based on regular comments from stockists. This helps them meet market needs more effectively. On the other hand, distributors can let stockists know about new products, sales, and other marketing efforts from makers that might help increase sales.

Contractual Agreements between Distributors and Stockists

The legal foundation for the relationship between a distributor and a stockist is a contract. These contracts or agreements govern each party's responsibilities, expectations, and the relationship rules. This ultimately makes sure that everyone knows what the rules are.

- **Nature of Contracts**: In the Indian pharmaceutical companies, the contracts that exist between distributors and stockists usually cover a number of important topics, such as the terms of supply, payment schedules, credit limits, and ways to settle disagreements. These contracts aim to safeguard the interests of both parties and maintain a smooth business relationship. For instance, a contract might say how many items a stockist has to buy at least once, how long they have to pay (for example, 30 days after delivery), and what happens if they don't pay on time.
- **Credit Terms**: The credit terms are one of the most important parts of these contracts. In the pharmaceutical industry, distributors often sell goods on credit to stockists, who then pay for them over time. The contract usually specifies the credit amount to the stockist, the duration of the credit period, and any interest or penalties for late payments. Stable supply chain finances rely on clear credit terms, which ensure stockists, have the necessary funds to operate their businesses and ensure distributors receive payment for the goods they dispatch.
- **Exclusivity Clauses**: Another common thing in contracts between distributors and stockists is the use of exclusivity clauses. These clauses might make it illegal for stockists to work with competing distributors or sell goods made by other companies. Both distributors and stockists can benefit from exclusivity agreements. Distributors get a dedicated channel for their goods, and stockists may get better pricing, help with promotions, or other benefits in exchange for being exclusive. However, we must carefully manage these types of clauses to ensure they do not hinder the stockist's ability to conduct business or satisfy market demands.
- **Territorial Rights**: Another important part of distributor-stockist arrangements is territorial rights. It is because of these rights, a stockist can only sell products in certain areas of the world. Territorial rights help keep stockists who work in nearby areas from fighting with each other and make sure that wholesalers can reach all of the markets they want to without crossing over into each other's areas. A contract may stipulate that only one stockist is permitted to sell a specific drug in a

specific city or district. This means that no other stockists can go into that area.

- **Pricing Agreements**: Price agreements spell out the amount a stockist can pay the distributers for purchasing the pharmaceutical products. They are often part of contracts. These contracts may also allow prices to change based on market, material, or currency changes. Clear pricing agreements help the stockists' plan their purchases and pricing, which helps them, stay competitive in the market and generate profits at the same time.
- **Legal Obligations and Compliance**: Contracts between distributors and stockists must include more than just commercial terms and terminologies. They must also include legal obligations and compliance with regulatory requirements. Indian pharmaceutical market is governed by strict rules and regulations. Both distributors and stockists must follow these rules and laws, which include those related to drug storage, handling, and sales. There are certain clauses in the contracts that bound the stockists to comply with the rules and laws. If they fail to comply, the contract may terminate or the stockist may face heavy financial penalties.
- **Duration and Termination**: The duration of the contract and its termination procedures are the crucial aspects of distributor-stockist agreements. Most contracts often spell out the ending time of the agreement, which could be anywhere from one year to several years, as well as how either side can prefer to end it. Some examples of termination terms are likely as, breach of contract, not meeting sales goals, or changes in the market. Clear rules for ending the business relationship help both sides prepare for exigency situations and also make sure that the business relationship can end amicably if needed.
- **Dispute Resolution**: Finally, ways to settle disputes are an important part of contracts between distributors and stockists. Despite both parties' best efforts to maintain a friendly relationship, disputes may arise over issues such as late payments, missing goods, or the interpretation of contract terms. Usually, contracts have ways to settle these kinds of disputes, like talking things out, mediating, or arbitrating. Having a clear and agreed-upon way to settle disagreements keeps business relationships strong and keeps disputes from getting worse.

The relationship between a distributor and a stockist in the Indian pharmaceutical marketing environment is very complex and requires careful management. To keep the flow of things and information going smoothly, coordination and communication must be at their best. Well-structured contractual agreements provide the legal framework needed to govern the relationship. Distributors and stockists can work together to meet the needs of the market and make sure that important medicines reach the customers on time by keeping clear lines of communication open and following the terms of their contracts.

Stockist-Retailer Relationship

The stockist-retailer relationship, is a crucial part of the Indian pharmaceutical sales ecosystem, stands out due to its unique dynamics and interdependencies. This partnership guarantees the efficient and successful delivery of medications and healthcare supplies to final consumers. Maintaining the integrity of the supply chain is crucial for the public's access to necessary medications, and this necessitates smooth communication between stockists and merchants. This connection, which is based on mutual benefit, trust, and communication, centres on important topics including order fulfilment and credit management. These elements handle the potential and problems in India's broad and varied pharmaceutical market while ensuring the supply chain runs smoothly.

Order Fulfilment: Ensuring a Steady Supply Chain

The foundation of the stockist-retailer relationship is order fulfilment. By maintaining a sufficient stock of pharmaceutical items, stockists in India's pharmaceutical industry help close the gap between distributors and retailers. They help shops meet client requests by ensuring that they receive the necessary supply on time. The effectiveness of this procedure directly impacts the availability of medications at retail locations, thereby influencing patient satisfaction and the health care system overall.

Stockists frequently serve a wide range of merchants, each with different needs depending on variables including geography, clientele, and seasonal patterns. Stockists must keep up a thorough awareness of the market dynamics and the unique requirements of every shop in order to handle this efficiently. Predicting demand trends, understanding drug use patterns, and ensuring consistent supply of in-demand goods are essential. Prompt order fulfilment for crucial medications can make the difference between life and death, making the stockist's job extremely important.

Communication is essential to the connection between retailers and stockists. Retailers typically place orders in response to their inventory requirements, influenced by local demand. In order to avoid stockouts or overstocking, which can both result in financial losses, stockists must be proactive and responsive while handling these orders. Providing the correct products in the appropriate quantities at the right times is just as important as providing them via an efficient order fulfilment procedure.

In order to streamline the order fulfilment process, technology has started to play an important role. In order to better manage orders, monitor inventory levels, and predict demand, a large number of Indian stockists and retailers are implementing digital platforms. By facilitating real-time communication between retailers and stockists, these solutions lower the possibility of mistakes and delays. To ensure rapid replacement, automated inventory management systems, for example, can notify stockists when a retailer's inventory hits a critical level.

Furthermore, order fulfilment involves more than just product delivery; it also involves guaranteeing the calibre and legitimacy of the medications provided. Stockists are in charge of locating goods from approved manufacturers and distributors and making sure that all medications adhere to the relevant legal requirements. Any failure to uphold this obligation may result in severe repercussions, such as lawsuits and harm to the retailer's reputation. As a result, trust is essential to the connection between the stockist and the retailer, especially when it comes to fulfilling orders.

The speed and effectiveness of order fulfilment can also influence a retailer's competitiveness. Fast and dependable stock delivery puts retailers in a better position to satisfy consumer demand, especially during peak demand periods or when handling essential drugs. This dependability fosters a long-term commercial connection by increasing the retailer's trust in the stockist. However, order fulfilment delays or irregularities might cause tension in the partnership and may lead the retailer to look for other stockists.

Credit Management: Balancing Financial Stability and Business Growth

Another essential component of the stockist-retailer connection is credit management, particularly in the Indian pharmaceutical industry, where credit sales are widespread. Because it has a direct impact on their cash flow and operational efficiency, merchants frequently use the capacity to extend credit as a decisive factor when selecting a stockist. However, there are significant risks linked to credit management, requiring a meticulous equilibrium between credit issuance and maintaining financial stability.

Giving retailer's credit is a long-standing custom in India's pharmaceutical sales industry. Due to their frequently narrow profit margins, retailers might not have the working cash to pay for significant orders up front. As a result, stockists provide credit terms that let shops pay for the merchandise after a predetermined amount of time, typically between 30 and 90 days. With this approach, businesses may better manage their cash flow and maintain a varied inventory without having to worry about imminent financial obligations.

But there are hazards associated with crediting stockists as well. Late or defaulted payments can significantly impact a stockist's liquidity, undermining their ability to pay distributors and maintain stable inventory levels. As a result, maintaining the financial stability of both stockists and retailers depends on efficient credit management. Stockists are required to thoroughly evaluate each retailer's creditworthiness, taking into account elements such as their track record of payments, financial stability, and reputation.

Many stockists create explicit credit policies that specify the terms and conditions for granting credit in order to reduce risks. Credit restrictions, due dates, and late payment penalties are a few examples of these policies. Stockists can shield themselves from undue credit risk exposure while still assisting their retail partners by establishing these limits. In certain situations, stockists may also request personal guarantees or collateral from retailers to safeguard the credit they receive.

When it comes to managing credit, communication is essential. Frequent communication between retailers and stockists ensures that both sides understand their responsibilities and contributes to the preservation of transparency and confidence. Stockists frequently use these exchanges to discuss potential payment concerns or to alert merchants about approaching payment deadlines. Proactive communication can prevent misunderstandings and resolve payment issues before they worsen.

Technology has also begun to impact the credit management procedures in the Indian pharmaceutical industry in recent years. Stockists may now more easily track past-due payments, send automatic reminders, and handle their accounts receivable more effectively thanks to digital payment networks and credit management tools. Stockists may reduce their risks and make well-informed decisions thanks to these technologies, which give them real-time information about their credit exposure.

Order fulfilment and credit management have a substantial relationship. Stockists may prioritize order fulfilment for shops with a clean payment history, while those with past-due payments may experience delays or limitations on additional credit. By establishing a feedback loop that rewards consistent payment behaviour with improved service, this strengthens the bonds between stockists and retailers.

In the Indian pharmaceutical sales ecosystem, the stockist-retailer relationship is a complicated and multidimensional cooperation that is essential to guaranteeing the supply of medications and medical supplies throughout the nation. Two important facets of this connection are order fulfilment and credit management, each with unique opportunities and challenges. Stockists and retailers can create solid, win-win alliances that support the general prosperity and sustainability of the Indian pharmaceutical supply chain by concentrating on effective order fulfilment and responsible credit management The interaction between the stockist and the retailer will continue to be a vital component of the Indian pharmaceutical sales ecosystem as the business changes due to developments in technology and shifting market dynamics.

Medical Representative's Role in the Distribution Network

The responsibilities of a Medical Representative (MR) in the Indian pharmaceutical sales ecosystem go well beyond merely marketing and selling goods to medical practitioners. A vital component of the distribution network, the medical representative makes sure that information, goods, and services move smoothly and efficiently. Promoting and selling products, fostering trust, comprehending and assisting the network, and resolving issues inside the distribution network are all aspects of this multifaceted function.

Product Promotion and Sales

Promoting and selling pharmaceutical items is one of a medical representative's main duties. Medical representatives are the front-line salespeople who deal directly with physicians, pharmacists, and other healthcare providers to promote new goods, outline their advantages, and convince them to carry or prescribe them. The function of the medical representative in product promotion is crucial in the fiercely competitive and diverse Indian pharmaceutical business. They offer comprehensive details on the products, such as their ingredients, medicinal advantages, dose schedules, and any adverse effects. By doing this, they assist medical professionals in making well-informed choices on the items they carry or prescribe.

Additionally, when it comes to introducing new products to the market, medical representatives are crucial. To inform medical professionals about the new goods, they host conferences, seminars, and presentations. This frequently entails giving out samples and marketing collateral as well as having one-on-one conversations to resolve any queries or worries. Through these initiatives, Medical Representatives ensure that medical professionals see and accept new products, thereby increasing sales.

To guarantee that the items are available in the market, medical representatives collaborate closely with distributors and wholesalers in addition to marketing the products to medical professionals. They help distributors place orders, estimate sales, and monitor inventory levels to prevent stockouts or overstocks. The distribution network and medical representatives work closely together to guarantee that products are easily accessible to satisfy the demand created by their marketing campaigns.

Trust Building in the Distribution Network

Within the Indian pharmaceutical ecosystem, medical representatives play a crucial role in establishing and maintaining trust, which is the foundation of any successful distribution network. The interaction between medical representatives and healthcare providers is where trust-building begins. Medical representatives establish themselves as trustworthy information sources by offering current, correct information and being receptive to the requirements and worries of medical professionals. For medical practitioners to feel comfortable prescribing or recommending the items that the medical representatives are promoting, they must have this trust.

But developing trust extends beyond interactions with medical personnel. Additionally, medical representatives are essential in building trust between the pharmaceutical firm and its distributors, stockists, and retailers. Medical Representatives contribute to the development of trust and cooperation within the distribution network by keeping lines of communication open, giving prompt information, and making sure that all of their transactions are transparent.

For example, medical representatives frequently serve as the point of contact between distributors and pharmaceutical companies. They make sure the distributors have access to all the information they need regarding the products, such as prices, special offers, and delivery dates. Medical Representatives contribute to the development of a solid, trusting connection between the business and its distribution partners by informing the distributors and resolving any issues they may have.

Understanding and Supporting the Network

The ability of medical representatives to comprehend and meet the needs of the different network stakeholders determines how effective the pharmaceutical distribution network is. This entails having a thorough awareness of the market dynamics, consumer tastes, and the unique requirements of various locations in addition to being familiar with the items they promote.

Medical representatives must thoroughly understand the complexities of the Indian pharmaceutical business, distinguished by its diversity in geography, demographics, and illness prevalence. They must comprehend the unique requirements of the people and medical professionals in the areas they serve and adjust their marketing strategies accordingly. For instance, medical representatives may need to promote reasonably priced, necessary medications in rural areas while highlighting specialized, expensive goods in urban areas.

Providing distributors, stockists, and retailers with reliable and timely information is another aspect of supporting the distribution network. Medical representatives assist these stakeholders in making well-informed decisions regarding when to place new orders, how much inventory to have on hand, and which items to stock. They also help to resolve any problems pertaining to the quality, pricing, or availability of the goods. Medical representatives contribute to the seamless and effective operation of the distribution network by offering this assistance.

Furthermore, medical representatives are essential in educating and training distributors' and retailers' employees. To acquaint them with the products, their applications, and the correct handling and storage techniques, they plan training courses. By ensuring proper handling and storage, this training plays a crucial role in maintaining the safety and effectiveness of the items throughout the distribution chain.

Addressing Challenges in the Network

Medical representatives are frequently at the forefront of tackling the difficulties facing India's pharmaceutical distribution network. The intricate and dispersed structure of the distribution network, which consists of several tiers of distributors, stockists, and retailers, is one of the main obstacles. Medical representatives are responsible for managing this complexity and ensuring prompt and efficient delivery of products to end users.

Ensuring product availability in underprivileged or rural locations is one of the main issues faced by medical representatives. The distribution network may be inadequate in many regions of India, especially in rural areas, which could cause delays in the availability of products. Medical representatives are essential in identifying these gaps and working with distribution partners to close them. To make sure the products get to their destination, this may entail coordinating with several distributors, setting up special delivery, or figuring out other routes.

Controlling the supply-demand balance presents another difficulty. The demand for pharmaceutical items can shift in a dynamic market like India for a number of reasons, including changes in government regulations, disease outbreaks, and seasonal variations. Medical representatives need to closely monitor these developments and work closely with the distribution network to adjust the supply as needed. To guarantee that they have the appropriate items in the appropriate amounts at the appropriate times, this calls for efficient coordination and communication with distributors and stockists.

Another major issue facing the Indian pharmaceutical industry is the prevalence of counterfeit and inferior medications. Medical representatives help tackle this problem by teaching distributors, merchants, and healthcare professionals the value of obtaining items from reputable and approved sources, medical representatives help to tackle this problem. Additionally, they assist in spotting and reporting any dubious products on the market, protecting the distribution network's integrity in the process.

Additionally, medical representatives play a crucial role in overseeing and settling any conflicts or problems that may emerge within the distribution network. This can entail resolving issues with costs, terms of payment, or delivery dates. Medical Representatives ensure the effective operation of the distribution network by serving as a liaison between the pharmaceutical firm and the distribution partners, assisting in the prompt and friendly resolution of these disputes.

In the distribution network of the Indian pharmaceutical sales ecosystem, a medical representative plays a variety of roles that are essential to the industry's overall prosperity. Medical representatives are the foundation of the distribution network, ensuring that pharmaceutical products reach patients and healthcare professionals who require them through everything from product promotion and trust-building to network comprehension, support, and problem-solving. They are an essential component of the pharmaceutical sales ecosystem in India because of the substantial contributions they make to the distribution network's efficacy, efficiency, and dependability.

Case Studies

Case 1: The distribution network of Shuvankar Pharmaceuticals, a growing Indian pharmaceutical company, ensured that drugs were available and accessible throughout the nation, particularly in rural areas. A multi-tiered network of CFAs, distributors, wholesalers, and more than 5,000 retail pharmacies made up Shuvankar Pharma's distribution platform. However, due to the lack of infrastructure in remote locations, the company faced difficulties with logistics and stock level management prompted them to introduce a new over-the-counter medication aimed at rural and semi-urban areas. Shuvankar Pharma's invested in real-time tracking technology to monitor stock levels at various stages of the supply chain and implement a customized distribution strategy for each location. To improve last mile delivery efficiency, distributors teamed up with regional logistics companies, and the business trained retailers and wholesalers on how to handle products and spot fake drugs. Given India's on-going problems with counterfeit medications, Shuvankar Pharmaceuticals was concerned about the existence of such products. Shuvankar Pharmaceuticals used barcoding and serialization technology to protect their products, guaranteeing product authenticity at every distribution location. Regulatory agencies like the CDSCO played a crucial role in this, conducting regular inspections to enforce standards and ensure that every item in Shuvankar Pharma's network adhered to GDP. Shuvankar was able to effectively enter rural markets because of this strong network, which also greatly decreased stockouts and enhanced the company's reputation in neglected areas. The example of Shuvankar Pharma demonstrates the need for a technologically advanced and well-coordinated distribution network for pharmaceutical businesses looking to expand their market reach and provide long-term public health support in a variety of geographical areas.

Case 2: Aditya, a seasoned medical representative working for a reputed pharmaceutical company, faced a unique challenge in distributing a new diabetes medication to a rural region in Northern India. Recognizing the region's high demand for cost-effective treatments, Aditya adjusted his approach, highlighting the affordability and efficacy of the drug to local healthcare providers and chemists. During his visits, he encountered both logistical and trust-based challenges: distributors hesitated to stock the new product due to limited awareness, and pharmacists were uncertain about patient demand. To address this, Aditya organized a small seminar, inviting local doctors and pharmacists to discuss the benefits, dosage, and potential side effects of the drug. He provided samples, shared promotional materials, and answered questions, building confidence among attendees. Aditya further coordinated with regional distributors to guarantee prompt delivery of the product, offering real-time sales data and advising on optimal inventory levels to prevent stockouts. Despite initial hurdles, Aditya's efforts bore fruit; trust in the product grew, and prescriptions rose steadily. Aditya also tackled counterfeit risks by educating distributors on verifying product authenticity and maintaining robust sourcing channels. By addressing logistical issues, fostering strong relationships, and promoting the drug effectively, Aditya ensured the medication became readily available in the area, meeting patients' needs and reinforcing his company's presence in the region.

Suggestive Questions from the Chapter

1. Describe the functions and significance of the distribution network in ensuring the availability of pharmaceutical items in India's various regions, particularly in the rural areas.
2. Discuss about the important players in India's pharmaceutical distribution system and their exclusive roles for ensuring a smooth supply chain from producers to end users.
3. Describe the geographical diversity, infrastructural constraints, and counterfeit drug problems that Indian pharmaceutical distribution network faces, as well as mention the steps being taken to address them.
4. Describe the roles and responsibilities of the key players in the Indian pharmaceutical distribution network, from the manufacturers to retail pharmacies. How each contributes to the efficient delivery of drugs across the country.
5. Explain the different kinds of distributors that are part of the Indian pharmaceutical sales ecosystem, such as CFAs, stockists, wholesalers, sub-distributors, retailers, and e-pharmacies. How do they make sure that the supply chain operates smoothly?
6. Discuss about the function of healthcare providers and regulatory agencies in the Indian pharmaceutical distribution network? How does their function affect supply chain legal compliance, demand creation, and product quality maintenance?
7. Examine the difficulties medical representatives encounter in guaranteeing efficient product distribution throughout India's many regions, especially in rural areas, and outline the strategies they employ to resolve problems with product availability and supply-demand balance.
8. Examine the importance of trust in the interactions between distributors, healthcare professionals, and medical representatives in the pharmaceutical sector, emphasizing the particular tactics used by medical representatives to establish and preserve this trust.
9. Discuss various roles that the medical representatives play in the Indian pharmaceutical sales ecosystem, including how they help with product promotion and sales, establishing trust, comprehending and assisting the distribution network, and resolving issues within it.
10. Discuss the significance of medical representatives in preserving the integrity and dependability of the pharmaceutical supply chain, as well as their function in thwarting the sale of fake and inferior drugs within the Indian pharmaceutical distribution network.

Multiple Choice Questions

1. Which of the following ensures the availability of medicines in remote areas of India?
   (a) Distribution Network (b) Stockist
   (c) Retailers (d) Logistics
2. What term is used to describe agents who act as intermediaries between manufacturers and wholesalers?
   (a) Retailers (b) Wholesalers
   (c) Distributors (d) Stockists
3. In the Indian pharmaceutical distribution network, which link deals directly with consumers?
   (a) Manufacturer (b) Wholesaler
   (c) Distributor (d) Retailer
4. What organization is responsible for regulating pharmaceuticals in India?
   (a) CDSCO (b) FDA
   (c) WHO (d) CFDA
5. What challenge does the distribution network face related to infrastructure in India?
   (a) Counterfeit Medications (b) Technology Adaptation
   (c) Diverse Infrastructure (d) High Costs
6. Which part of the distribution chain is typically involved in bulk purchasing?
   (a) Wholesaler (b) Retailer
   (c) Distributor (d) Manufacturer
7. Which technology is used to enhance tracking and reduce stockouts in the distribution network?
   (a) Internet (b) Blockchain
   (c) Barcoding (d) Machine Learning
8. The rise of which type of medications emphasizes the need for a speedy supply chain?
   (a) OTC Medications (b) Prescription Medications
   (c) Generic Medications (d) Patent Medications

9. Which level of the pharmaceutical distribution network provides guidance on dosage and possible side effects?
   (a) Manufacturer (b) Distributor
   (c) Retailer (d) Wholesaler
10. What is a significant threat to the Indian pharmaceutical distribution system?
   (a) Inflation (b) Counterfeit Medications
   (c) High Demand (d) Low Demand
11. The primary role of a Carrying and Forwarding Agent (CFA) is to:
   (a) Manufacture drugs (b) Sell drugs to consumers
   (c) Store and distribute drugs (d) Conduct clinical trials
12. Stockists are primarily responsible for:
   (a) Manufacturing drugs
   (b) Distributing drugs to wholesalers
   (c) Selling drugs directly to consumers
   (d) Maintaining drug inventory
13. Wholesalers in the pharmaceutical industry:
   (a) Manufacture drugs
   (b) Directly sell drugs to consumers
   (c) Distribute drugs to retailers
   (d) Conduct clinical trials
14. Sub-distributors are typically involved in:
   (a) Manufacturing drugs
   (b) Distributing drugs to large hospitals
   (c) Distributing drugs to smaller retailers in rural areas
   (d) Conducting clinical trials
15. E-pharmacies primarily operate through:
   (a) Physical stores (b) Online platforms
   (c) Hospital pharmacies (d) Direct sales to doctors
16. Super stockists are responsible for:
   (a) Distributing drugs to individual consumers
   (b) Distributing drugs to smaller stockists in a region
   (c) Manufacturing drugs
   (d) Conducting clinical trials

17. Sub-stockists typically operate in:
    (a) Large metropolitan cities (b) Rural and semi-urban areas
    (c) Industrial zones (d) International markets
18. Hospital supply stockists primarily cater to:
    (a) Individual consumers
    (b) Retail pharmacies
    (c) Hospitals and healthcare institutions
    (d) E-commerce platforms
19. Retail chain stockists supply drugs to:
    (a) Individual consumers (b) Chain pharmacies
    (c) Small, independent pharmacies (d) Hospitals
20. Institutional stockists supply drugs to:
    (a) Individual consumers
    (b) Retail pharmacies
    (c) Government organizations and corporations
    (d) E-commerce platforms
21. Which primary duty involves medical representatives directly engaging with healthcare professionals to promote products?
    (a) Training (b) Marketing
    (c) Manufacturing (d) Research
22. Medical representatives help to build trust within the distribution network primarily through:
    (a) Patents (b) Transparency
    (c) Price cuts (d) Advertising
23. What role do medical representatives play in supporting the distribution network?
    (a) Inspecting (b) Auditing
    (c) Informing (d) Funding
24. Medical representatives face challenges like managing the supply-demand balance due to:
    (a) Advertising (b) Regulatory changes
    (c) Customer loyalty (d) Technology
25. Which type of counterfeit issue do medical representatives actively help to address?
    (a) Warranty (b) Payment
    (c) Product quality (d) Delivery speed

CHAPTER

6

Pharmaceutical Product Sales Strategies and Techniques

Sales Techniques in the Indian Pharmaceutical Sales Ecosystem

In the Indian pharmaceutical sales ecosystem, sales methods are essential, because they act as a link between pharmaceutical companies and healthcare professionals. In order to convince physicians, pharmacists, and other healthcare professionals to prescribe or suggest particular medications, these strategies include in-person meetings, personal marketing, and calculated engagements. One of the key features of selling pharmaceutical products is that it's an indirect sale, means that after a product is marketed to a doctor, the doctor writes a prescription for the product, which results in sales. The distinct features of the Indian market, such as its wide geographic diversity, disparities in healthcare facilities, and intricate regulatory framework, call for customized direct sales strategies that satisfy the requirements and inclinations of various stakeholders.

Personalized Engagement with Healthcare Professionals

Personalized interaction with medical professionals, especially physicians, is one of the most well-known sales strategies in the pharmaceutical sector.

These encounters are conducted by frontline agents known as Medical Representatives (MRs). By giving patients comprehensive knowledge about new medications, clinical trial results, and therapeutic benefits, they are taught to cultivate relationships with physicians. In the Indian environment, where physicians frequently depend on the most recent data to make well-informed decisions regarding patient treatment, this individualized approach is crucial. Medical Representatives can customize their presentations and highlight the advantages of the medications that complement the doctors' treatment philosophies by being aware of the particular requirements of the physicians.

In India, where connections and trust are highly valued, medical representatives frequently do more than just promoting products. They foster relationships between physicians and key opinion leaders (KOLs) in the pharmaceutical sales sector, host seminars, and provide continuing medical education (CME) sessions, in addition to product promotion. All these activities go to the Medical Representatives' credibility. These initiatives establish the pharmaceutical firm as an ally in the on-going professional growth of the physicians and healthcare professionals. In rural areas, where the practicing doctors may have limited access to the most recent medical information, they rely primarily on the knowledge supplied by Medical Representatives. Here also the role of the medical representative for relationship-building is highly crucial.

Strategic Sampling and Free Trials

Strategic sampling and offering free trials are two other important sales strategies in the Indian pharmaceutical industry. Medical representatives frequently provide doctors with trial packs of new or existing medications so they can test the product's safety and effectiveness on a limited scale before writing general prescriptions. This method works especially well in India, where physicians would rather see how a medication works on their patients before giving it their full approval. Because sampling enables medical practitioners to evaluate the drug's effects in the actual world, it fosters confidence and trust.

To entice physicians to prescribe new medications, several pharmaceutical companies provide free trials or temporary discounts for availability of the products in the retail counter, in addition to samples. This strategy is especially helpful when introducing new products for breaking into cutthroat therapeutic competitive markets. These strategies can hasten the product's market adoption by lowering the financial risk involved in trying a new medication. Strategic sampling also aids in obtaining physician input, which can be utilized to improve marketing tactics and resolve any issues that may come up.

Use of Digital Tools and E-Detailing

Pharmaceutical companies are incorporating digital tools and e-detailing techniques into their sales promotion strategies, which is an aftereffect of India's growing digital technology penetration. E-detailing is the process of giving medical practitioners comprehensive product information via digital media. Interactive e-brochures, online seminars, and virtual presentations, etc. fall under this category. Due to the difficulty of in-person connections, the COVID-19 epidemic hastened the adoption of these methods. A hybrid strategy that blends traditional and digital techniques is growing in popularity in the current environment.

In the Indian market, digital tools provide many benefits, including the ability to reach a larger audience, particularly in rural or underdeveloped areas. Additionally, they give medical practitioners a more flexible and easy approach to obtaining information at their own pace. Furthermore, the monitoring and examination of digital interactions provides crucial insights into the preferences and activities of physicians. By using this information, pharmaceutical businesses may improve their sales tactics and make sure they are catering to the unique requirements of various market segments.

Leveraging Key Opinion Leaders (KOLs)

Using Key Opinion Leaders (KOLs) is another successful sales strategy in the Indian pharmaceutical industry. KOLs are well-respected, powerful medical professionals who are known for their proficiency in particular therapeutic fields. Pharmaceutical companies frequently request KOLs to promote their goods or share their experiences with other medical professionals. This endorsement may significantly influence other physicians' prescribing practices, particularly for novel or complex medications.

KOLs can participate in a variety of activities, including conducting clinical trials, publishing research, and giving talks at conferences. People frequently interpret their support as a seal of approval, aiding in overcoming opposition or scepticism regarding new items. KOLs have a particularly significant role in the Indian context, where peer influence and hierarchical respect are powerful cultural elements. Pharmaceutical businesses can successfully increase their reach and reputation in the medical community by partnering with KOLs.

Customized Sales Approaches for Different Segments

It's because of the Indian market's diversity; different pharmaceutical market segments require distinct sales strategies. For example, the sales strategies employed in rural and metropolitan locations may be very different. The emphasis may be on the most recent researches, cutting-edge treatment alternatives, and international guidelines in urban locations where physicians have simple access to a wealth of information and resources. In contrast, in rural locations where information access may be limited, medical representatives might need to provide more fundamental instruction on the drug's use, safety, and advantages.

Additionally, the therapeutic sector may influence the sales strategy. For instance, selling over-the-counter (OTC) medications may require different strategies compared to selling prescription medications. Sales strategies for over-the-counter medications may entail closer interaction with pharmacists, who are essential in suggesting these goods to customers. The emphasis is still on doctors when it comes to prescription medications, but the type and degree of information offered may differ depending on the drug's complexity and the therapeutic setting.

Building Long-Term Relationships through Value Addition

In the Indian pharmaceutical industry, establishing long-term relationship via value addition is a fundamental component of sales strategies. Pharmaceutical companies and medical representatives work to improve the quality of doctors' practices in addition to promoting products. This can involve supplying patient management tools, clinical research support, and teaching materials. Pharmacies might encourage adherence and sustained involvement by presenting themselves as collaborators in the doctors' achievement.

In the Indian context, where personal relationships frequently influence business decisions, this value addition is even more crucial. Physicians are more inclined to regularly recommend a pharmaceutical company's products if they believe it to be a beneficial partner. Furthermore, the additional value can be a differentiator that helps a business stands out in a market with fierce rivalry and several companies offering comparable items.

The requirement to interact personally with healthcare professionals, establish trust, and deliver value makes sales approaches a crucial part of the Indian pharmaceutical sales ecosystem. Pharmaceutical businesses can successfully navigate the intricate and varied Indian market by using digital technologies, KOL leverage, individualized engagement, strategic sampling, tailored strategies, and long-term relationship building. These strategies not only facilitate the adoption of new medications but also ensure that medical personnel make informed and secure prescription choices, thereby enhancing patient outcomes.

Relationship Building with Healthcare Professionals

Developing a relationship with healthcare professionals (HCPs) is essential for success in the fiercely competitive and ever-changing Indian pharmaceutical sales ecosystem. Effective distribution and promotion of pharmaceutical items rely on these connections with doctors, pharmacists, and other medical professionals. In addition to making it easier to promote particular goods, developing solid, moral, and trustworthy relationships with HCPs also helps improve patient outcomes, which is the ultimate goal of all parties involved in the healthcare system.

Understanding the Dynamics of HCP Relationships

Pharmaceutical sales representatives, also known as medical representatives or MRs, have a complex connection with HCPs that encompasses both personal and professional aspects. Fundamentally, the partnership is professional and motivated by both parties' desire to enhance patient care. Nonetheless, building personal rapport is crucial to enhancing these business relationships. In India, where interpersonal relationships and trust hold significant value, the human element of these interactions often determines the commercial success of a pharmaceutical product.

The main conduit between the pharmaceutical manufacturer and HCPs is medical representatives. In addition to promoting medications, their responsibilities also include gathering feedback, disseminating scientific data, and providing updates on novel treatments. Medical representatives must gain a thorough awareness of the requirements, preferences, and difficulties faced by HCPs in order to be effective. This knowledge enables them to modify their product offerings and communications to better suit the practice and patient care priorities of HCPs.

Building Trust and Credibility

The foundation of any fruitful collaboration between MRs and HCPs is trust and credibility. In the Indian pharmaceutical sales environment, where there are many brands and generic alternatives on the market, an HCP's confidence in a given brand frequently depends on the medical representative's reputation. The medical representative must act in a consistent, open, and moral manner in order to earn this trust. This entails giving HCPs accurate and fact-based product information, attending to their requirements promptly, and refraining from any actions that might be interpreted as immoral or deceptive.

Additionally, the medical representative's experience and knowledge contribute to their credibility. Medical representatives should be knowledgeable about both the items they are advertising and the larger therapeutic field, according to HCPs. Because of their knowledge, medical representatives can have fruitful, scientific conversations with HCPs and establish themselves as important collaborators in patient care. To preserve their credibility and successfully assist HCPs in their decision-making, medical representatives must receive regular training and stay current on the most recent developments in medical science.

Ethical Considerations in Relationship Building

Ethics must be the foundation of the interaction between medical representatives and HCPs. India, like many other nations, regulates the pharmaceutical industry to prevent its excessive influence on healthcare professionals' prescribing practices. This includes stringent rules regarding the giving of presents, hospitality, and other inducements. Building relationships is vital, but it should never come at the expense of the HCP's integrity or the profession's ethical norms.

Emphasizing the benefits that the pharmaceutical product offers to patient care is a key component of developing ethical relationships. Instead of using strategies that can be interpreted as inducements, medical representatives should highlight the clinical advantages, safety record, and affordability of their goods. Furthermore, the medical representative must provide solid clinical proof to support any statements they make regarding a product. In addition to building trust, this strategy supports the HCPs' dedication to giving their patients the best treatment possible.

Leveraging Technology in Relationship Building

In today's world, technology is becoming more crucial to developing relationships with HCPs. Medical representatives can interact with HCPs more successfully and efficiently because of digital tools, including e-detailing platforms, virtual meetings, and customer relationship management (CRM) systems. These techniques are especially useful in India, where the geographic dispersion of healthcare institutions can make in-person interactions difficult.

Medical Representatives can monitor their contacts with HCPs, customize their communications, and promptly follow up thanks to CRM systems. Medical representatives can contact HCPs whenever it is most convenient for them and convey information in an engaging and participatory way by using e-detailing platforms and virtual meetings. Furthermore, by using data analytics, medical representatives can spot patterns in the prescription practices of HCPs, adjust their tactics appropriately, and deliver more timely and pertinent information.

But rather than taking the place of interpersonal relationships, technological use should enhance them. Technology tools can increase productivity and effectiveness, but they cannot replace the human aspect. In order to keep their ties with HCPs solid and genuine, medical representatives must strike a balance between their use of technology and the necessity of preserving interpersonal relationships.

Long-Term Relationship Building

Building relationships with HCPs is a continuous activity rather than a one-time event. Mutual respect, trust, and reliable value delivery are the cornerstones of long-term partnerships. This requires medical representatives to maintain regular communication with HCPs, particularly when there are no direct sales opportunities. Maintaining the relationship over time requires constant assistance, information on new developments, and frequent check-ins.

Furthermore, medical representatives ought to see their interactions with HCPs as cooperative ventures. This entails paying attention to the worries of the HCPs, addressing their problems, and being a trustworthy information and support source. Medical representatives can create connections that withstand changes in the market and pressure from competitors by presenting themselves as partners rather than just salespeople.

Having enduring relationships with HCPs gives you a competitive edge in the fiercely competitive and dynamic Indian pharmaceutical sales industry. These connections not only facilitate the successful launch of new items in the future, but also simplify the promotion of existing ones.

In the Indian pharmaceutical sales environment, establishing relationships with medical professionals is essential to success. It calls for a blend of professional knowledge, moral behaviour, clear communication, and technology strategy. Medical representatives may establish solid, long-lasting relationships with HCPs that support the success of their products and the enhancement of patient care in India by emphasizing trust, credibility, and long-term value.

Territory Management

A key component of India's pharmaceutical sales ecosystem, territory management makes sure that sales teams efficiently reach all possible markets, take advantage of opportunities, and meet sales goals. In order to increase sales productivity, this procedure entails carefully structuring and streamlining enormous markets into smaller, easier-to-manage regions, or sales territories. In addition to reaching a large consumer base, effective territory management is crucial for preserving solid ties with medical professionals and guaranteeing the prompt delivery of pharmaceutical products throughout the nation.

Defining Sales Territories

Sales territories in the Indian pharmaceutical industry refer to specific geographical or demographic areas assigned to specific sales agents or teams, enabling them to focus on a specific region or clientele. Common variables used to define these territories include geographic boundaries (such as cities, districts, or states), population density, the concentration of healthcare facilities, the presence of key opinion leaders (KOLs), and the area's sales potential. Furthermore, demographic factors such as the population's age distribution, economic standing, and common health conditions may also influence the definition of territories.

Since it directly affects how successful sales efforts are, the process of creating sales territory is essential. With a well-defined region, salespeople can effectively manage their workload, maintain regular client interactions, and gain a greater understanding of the local market dynamics. Determining territories also requires an understanding of regional healthcare needs, regulatory frameworks, and the competitive landscape in the Indian context, where the healthcare landscape is diverse and rapidly evolving. For example, a territory in a major city like Delhi or Mumbai may have a huge client base and a high concentration of healthcare facilities, necessitating a more aggressive and targeted sales strategy. However, because rural areas have less access to and knowledge of healthcare, they may require a different approach that places more of an emphasis on teaching and relationship-building.

Territory Planning and Optimization

The next crucial stage after defining sales regions is territory planning and optimization. Developing a strategic plan to maximize sales potential in each territory requires efficient allocation of time, money, and personnel. Territory planning aims to guarantee sufficient coverage in each region, enabling sales professionals to reach their goals without feeling overworked or underutilized.

Territory Planning

Analysing each region's market potential in depth is the first step in territory planning. This entails assessing variables such as the quantity and kind of medical facilities, healthcare providers' purchasing trends, the existence of rivals, and the possible demand for particular pharmaceutical items. Sales teams also need to think about practical factors like travel time, how often they need to visit to keep up relationships with healthcare professionals, and whether distribution networks are available. These factors are especially crucial in the Indian pharmaceutical business, where accessibility and infrastructure can differ greatly between regions. For example, the territorial strategy needs to account for the possibility that sales reps will need to travel longer in areas with inadequate infrastructure.

Optimization

Sales territory optimization is a continual process that includes tracking and modifying the territory plan in response to field feedback, market developments, and sales performance. This may include redistributing territories if specific regions are functioning poorly or if the markets are changing. For example, due to the establishment of new medical facilities or changes in consumer behaviour—this can include shifting of the territory. Regular optimization is crucial for staying ahead of the competition and seizing new possibilities in the fiercely competitive and dynamic Indian pharmaceutical market. For example, modifying the sales approach to focus more on a newly opened hospital in a territory may require additional visits or resources.

Technology

In the present pharmaceutical sales environment, technology is very crucial for territory planning and optimization. People are increasingly using Geographic Information Systems (GIS), Customer Relationship Management (CRM) software, and Sales Force Automation (SFA) tools to analyse data, track sales activity, and enhance their territory plans. Sales managers can use these technologies to make data-driven decisions by learning more about territory performance, sales trends, and client contacts. In the Indian pharmaceutical market, where achieving data timeliness and accuracy can be challenging, leveraging technology to focus sales efforts are the most attractive opportunities and allocating resources effectively could provide a competitive advantage.

Challenges

Some of the challenges in the marketing territory management, particularly in India, include the complexity of regulations, the diversity of the healthcare sector, and the need to balance the demands of various client segments. For example, sales personnel must modify their communication and sales tactics while managing territories in areas with a variety of languages and cultures.

Furthermore, the regulatory landscape in India is constantly evolving, introducing new rules and standards for compliance that could influence the administration of territories. To guarantee compliance and preserve client trust, sales teams must remain up to date on these developments and modify their area plans as necessary.

Pharmaceutical companies frequently use a cooperative approach to territory management, incorporating managers, medical representatives, and other stakeholders in the planning process in order to overcome these difficulties. Pharmaceutical companies may develop more effective and realistic territorial plans that take into account the distinctive features of each region by integrating feedback from the field. To guarantee that, medical representatives must have the information and abilities necessary towards successfully negotiating the intricacies of their territory and meet their sales targets, regular training and assistance are also crucial.

A comprehensive approach towards creating and optimizing sales territories is necessary for territory management, which is a crucial part of the Indian pharmaceutical sales ecosystem. Pharmaceutical companies are making sure that their sales teams are in a favourable position to take advantage of opportunities and spur growth by properly defining the marketing territories, preparing efficiently, and continuously optimizing the efforts based on data and market changes. Effective territory management in a competitive and diverse market like India involves more than just covering ground; it also entails doing it in a way that fosters solid customer relationships, fits with the particular requirements of each location, and ultimately helps the firm succeed.

Effective Communication Skills for Medical Representatives

Medical representatives (MRs) are essential in the Indian pharmaceutical sales ecosystem because they help close the gap between pharmaceutical corporations and medical practitioners. Promoting and selling pharmaceutical products to physicians, pharmacists, and other healthcare industry stakeholders is their main duty. Medical representatives need to have outstanding communication skills, especially in presentation and negotiating, to be successful in this cutthroat industry. In addition to successfully communicating the advantages of their products, these abilities help them establish enduring bonds with medical professionals, which eventually boost sales and market share.

Presentation Skills

For a medical representative to succeed, presentation abilities are essential. Medical representatives regularly interact with physicians, pharmacists, and other healthcare professionals in the pharmaceutical industry to show and discuss the characteristics and advantages of their promoted medicine brands. A well-designed presentation can significantly influence a healthcare provider's opinion of a product, potentially influencing their decision to recommend or prescribe it to patients.

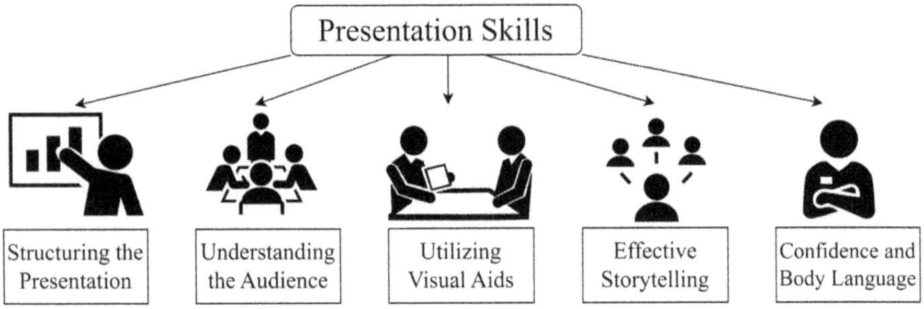

Fig. 6.1 Effective Presentation Skill.

1. ***Structuring the Presentation:*** A presentation's structure has a big impact on how effective it is. Medical representatives need to be able to rationally arrange their information, beginning with an attention-grabbing introduction. Next, they should succinctly and clearly explain the product's characteristics, advantages, and any drawbacks. To persuade the medical professional to consider using the product for their patients, include a summary at the end of the presentation that restates the main ideas and issues a call to action. The ability to give a brief yet powerful presentation is crucial in the Indian environment because patients frequently have limited time during doctor's appointments.
2. ***Understanding the Audience:*** Effective presentations are tailor-made to the needs and preferences of the audience. Medical representatives need to be skilled at comprehending the unique goals and concerns of various healthcare practitioners. For example, a specialist may concentrate on a drug's effectiveness in treating a specific condition, but a general practitioner may be more interested in the drug's broad application. Medical representatives can make their presentation more relevant and compelling by matching it to the interests of the audience. This calls for an extensive planning and study, in addition to the

flexibility to adjust on the fly, in response to audience enquiries as well as reactions.

3. ***Utilizing Visual Aids:*** Charts, graphs, and pictures are examples of visual aids that can improve a presentation's efficacy by simplifying difficult concepts. Visual aids can help make important arguments simpler and more understandable in the Indian pharmaceutical sector, where medical representatives frequently discuss scientific data and clinical trial findings. Medical representatives must, however, use these resources sparingly. Using too many images in a presentation can overload the audience and take attention away from the main point. Finding a balance between supporting the spoken content with visual assistance without overpowering it is crucial.
4. ***Effective Storytelling:*** Medical representatives can utilise storytelling as an effective strategy to enhance the engagement and memorability of their presentations. Medical representatives can showcase the product's practical impact and humanize it by giving case studies or patient stories. This strategy works especially well in the Indian setting, where medical personnel are more receptive to emotional appeal. Connecting the medical representative and the healthcare provider through a well-told story can create a compelling and relatable presentation.
5. ***Confidence and Body Language:*** Medical representatives' presenting style is equally as crucial as the information they cover. Positive body language, clarity, and confidence are essential components of a successful presentation. Medical representatives need to talk in a clear, authoritative tone, make appropriate gestures, and keep eye contact. Nonverbal communication is crucial for establishing confidence and trust in the Indian pharmaceutical sector, where in-person encounters are still the norm. Medical representatives should be aware that their posture, facial expressions, and general mannerisms might influence healthcare professionals' opinions of them and the product.

Negotiation Skills

In the Indian pharmaceutical sales ecosystem, medical representatives also need to have proper negotiation skills for generating sales. Medical representatives must be able to come to mutually advantageous arrangements that meet the requirement for the healthcare professionals and the company's target. Further they also have to negotiate benefits with the pharmacists while placing the products to the Doctors during product presentation. Successful negotiation requires finding common ground, preparation, and active listening.

Fig. 6.2 Effective Negotiation Skillls.

1. ***Preparation and Research:*** The first step in a successful negotiation is preparation. Medical representatives need to be extremely knowledgeable about the product they are endorsing, including its pricing strategy, competitive advantages, and market placement. They should also know the healthcare professional's needs, preferences, and objections. In the highly competitive Indian pharmaceutical market, medical representatives need to be knowledgeable about the advantages and disadvantages of rival goods in order to successfully handle any difficulties that may come up during negotiations. Medical representatives that are well-prepared can confidently begin negotiations, ready to handle any issues and give a strong argument for their product.
2. ***Building Rapport:*** Building a strong relationship with medical professionals is crucial to a fruitful negotiation. Medical representatives need to be able to establish rapport and show that they genuinely care about the objectives and difficulties faced by healthcare professionals. Medical representatives who are able to establish a personal connection have a higher chance of success in India, where commercial relationships are frequently crucial. Active listening, empathy, and the capacity to communicate in ways that appeal to the healthcare provider are all necessary for this. Medical representatives can foster a constructive bargaining environment by being kind and understanding.
3. ***Identifying Common Interests:*** Finding a solution that works for both parties is the goal of effective negotiation. Medical representatives need to be adept at spotting shared interests and using them to establish advantageous contracts. For instance, a medical representative may emphasize the product's cost-effectiveness or provide a discount for large purchases if a doctor is worried about the expense of medication. Medical representatives must be skilled in striking a balance between

the financial limits of healthcare professionals and the company's desire to preserve profitability in the Indian context, where cost considerations are frequently a significant factor. By focusing on common objectives, medical representatives can increase the likelihood of reaching a mutually agreeable agreement.

4. ***Flexibility and Adaptability:*** Flexibility and the capacity to adjust to shifting conditions are frequently necessary for negotiation. Medical representatives ought to be ready to modify their strategy in light of the healthcare provider's comments and answers. In order to close a transaction, this may occasionally include making compromises or providing extra incentives. Medical representatives need to be flexible and sensitive to shifts in the demands of healthcare professionals or the competitive environment in the Indian pharmaceutical sector, where market dynamics can change quickly. Medical representatives can overcome obstacles and come up with innovative solutions that satisfy the goals of both sides by remaining adaptable and receptive.
5. ***Closing the Deal:*** The hallmark of a successful negotiator is the ability to close a deal. Medical representatives need to be aware of when and how to press for a conclusion without coming across as pushy or hostile. Medical Representatives must be cognisant of the healthcare professional's decision-making process in the Indian environment, where interpersonal ties and hierarchy can have an impact on decision-making. This can entail allowing the medical practitioner some time to think about the offer or confer with peers. To guarantee that the negotiation ends successfully, medical representatives should be diligent and patient, following up as necessary.

In the Indian pharmaceutical sales environment, medical representatives must have strong communication skills, especially in the areas of presentation and negotiating. Medical representatives can improve their capacity to market goods, cultivate connections with medical experts, and meet sales goals by developing these abilities. Medical representatives can communicate effectively and convincingly by using presentation skills, and they can negotiate complex situations and come to mutually beneficial solutions by using negotiation skills. These abilities work together as the cornerstone of a prosperous pharmaceutical sales career, enabling medical representatives to prosper in a cutthroat and ever-changing market.

Territory Travel Planning

Territory trip planning is essential to maximizing medical representatives' performances and guaranteeing the efficient coverage of designated territories in the competitive and dynamic Indian pharmaceutical sector. Territory travel planning entails thorough planning and strategic decision-making, with an emphasis on sales territory distribution, cost estimation, itinerary creation, and prudent cost control. Together, these components increase client engagement, boost sales efficiency, and save operating expenses.

Allocating Sales Territory

The distribution of sales territories is the initial stage in the planning of territory travel. This entails breaking up geographical areas into manageable chunks within the Indian pharmaceutical sales ecosystem according to a number of criteria, including the concentration of healthcare professionals (HCPs), the existence of clinics, hospitals, and pharmacies, as well as the possibility of sales growth. Assigning each sales representative a region that is neither too big to be too much to handle nor too little to underuse the representative's ability is the main goal.

A detailed examination of the market dynamics, such as the demand for certain pharmaceutical items, the competitive environment, and the purchasing power of local healthcare institutions, is necessary for territory allocation. The various healthcare requirements in India's urban, semi urban and rural areas call for specialized methods of allocating the sales territory. Rural regions may need fewer visits but longer travel times, whereas urban areas may need more intense coverage because of the larger density of HCPs and healthcare facilities.

Additionally, we consider a territory's past success when assigning sales territories. Representatives seeking to establish a foothold may receive assignments to newer or less explored regions, while territories with a good sales history may receive assignments from more seasoned representatives. This strategic allocation ensures sufficient focus on each territory and the successful achievement of sales targets.

Assessment of Sales Travel Cost

After assigning the sales territories, a critical next step in territory travel planning is the evaluation of sales travel expenses. In the Indian pharmaceutical sector, where medical representatives frequently traverse large geographic areas, travel costs might account for a sizeable amount of the operating budget. Therefore, a thorough evaluation of these costs is necessary to ensure effective use of resources.

Assessing sales travel costs entails looking at a number of variables, such as the distance between medical institutions, the means of transportation, lodging costs, and the number of trips necessary to keep positive connections with HCPs. This evaluation is even more important in India, since accessibility and infrastructure might differ greatly between areas.

For example, delegates may use buses, trains, or ride-sharing services to go to their destinations in large cities with sophisticated public transit networks. However, in rural or isolated places where public transportation is scarce, officials may need to use private automobiles or even employ local transportation, resulting in increased travel expenses. We must also consider the cost of lodging and meals, particularly when delegates need to spend the night in specific areas.

Pharmaceutical businesses can more efficiently distribute budgets by carrying out a thorough evaluation of travel expenses, guaranteeing that each representative has the resources required to cover their territory without going over the allotted budget. Through this process, businesses might also find ways to cut costs, including by streamlining travel itineraries or negotiating lower prices with lodging and transportation suppliers.

Preparation of Travel Plan

After assigning the sales territory and evaluating the trip cost, the next stage of territory travel planning involves creating a comprehensive travel itinerary. For the salespeople, this plan acts as a road map, directing their daily tasks and making the most of their travel time.

Creating a travel itinerary includes planning visits to pharmacies, healthcare facilities, and HCPs in the designated area. It necessitates giving careful thought to elements like visit frequency, HCP availability, and critical account priorities. To establish rapport and trust in the Indian market, where personal connections are crucial to sales, representatives must create a travel itinerary that allows frequent contacts with HCPs.

Additionally, the itinerary should be adaptable enough to take into account unanticipated events like last-minute changes in appointments, traffic jams, or urgent demands from healthcare professionals. In addition to keeping representatives organized, a well-thought-out travel itinerary guarantees that they can adapt to the ever-changing pharmaceutical sales environment.

The use of technology is crucial while making travel arrangements. Representatives of numerous pharmaceutical businesses in India can now plan their routes, monitor their visits, and alter their schedules in real time thanks to specialized software and mobile applications. These instruments not only boost productivity but also provide valuable insights to enhance territory coverage and future trip plans.

Travel Expense Planning

Travel expense planning is the last component of territorial travel planning. Controlling travel costs is essential to preserving profitability and making sure that sales initiatives are lasting in a cost-sensitive sector like pharmaceuticals. Travel expense planning involves creating budgets, monitoring spending, and implementing cost-control measures to prevent overspending.

Setting a reasonable budget based on the evaluation of travel expenses is the first step in the travel expense planning process in the Indian pharmaceutical sales ecosystem. This budget must cover transportation, lodging, meals, and any other unforeseen costs that may arise while the salespeople are on the road. It is crucial to strike a balance between providing representatives with sufficient resources to fulfil their responsibilities and ensuring their wise use.

Another essential element of travel expense planning is real-time monitoring of trip expenditures. Pharmaceutical businesses may now monitor expenses as they happen thanks to the development of digital expense management solutions, which increase control and transparency. In order to make sure that all expenses are reasonable and within budget, representatives can electronically submit their spending for review and approval by managers.

Furthermore, by implementing cost-control measures like limiting daily allowances, encouraging the use of affordable transportation options, and negotiating corporate rates with hotels and restaurants, it is possible to significantly reduce travel expenses without compromising the success of the sales efforts.

Planning for travel expenses also entails routine audits and evaluations to find any inconsistencies or potential areas for cost reduction. Pharmaceutical businesses can guarantee that their sales representatives can efficiently cover their territories while controlling expenses by consistently improving the travel expense plan.

Planning a territory trip is a complex process that is essential to the success of pharmaceutical sales in India. Pharmaceutical businesses may maximize their sales efforts, improve client engagement, and accomplish their company's goals by carefully planning their trips, calculating travel expenditures, distributing sales territory effectively, and managing travel expenses. Effective territory travel planning is crucial for sustaining a strong market presence and promoting long-term growth in a dynamic and competitive sector like pharmaceuticals.

Sales Reporting and Documentation

The pharmaceutical sales process relies heavily on sales reports and documentation, which offer an organized way to monitor performance, guarantee responsibility, and facilitate well-informed decision-making. Effective sales reporting and documentation are even more crucial in the Indian pharmaceutical sales ecosystem, given the size and diversity of the industry. In order to promote smooth communication and operational efficiency throughout the distribution network, this system combines offline and online reporting tools and places a strong emphasis on creating thorough sales statements.

Online Reporting

The sales reporting process in the Indian pharmaceutical industry has changed dramatically since the introduction of modern technology. It's because it enables real-time data entry, analysis, and sharing, online reporting has emerged as a crucial tool for sales teams. Medical representatives, sales managers, and distributors can effectively monitor sales activity and market trends across several regions with the help of this technology. Digital documentation of sales visits, orders, and customer feedback is made possible by online reporting platforms, which are frequently coupled with Customer Relationship Management (CRM) systems. Online reporting's real-time functionality enables instant updates, ensuring that sales managers can keep an eye on their teams' performance every day. Such prompt access to information facilitates quick decision-making, strategy modification, and the identification of problem areas.

Additionally, online reporting makes the sales process more transparent. Having a centralized database system that is accessible to all involved parties, makes it simple to find and fix existing errors. The technology can promptly flag a sharp decline in sales in a specific territory, thus prompting further investigation. Online reporting platforms frequently include automated report production functions to save time and reduce the possibility of human error. By analysing the data gathered by these systems, one can learn more about consumer preferences, market trends, and the effectiveness of sales tactics. Pharmaceutical sector is of no exception. In India's dynamic and cutthroat competitive pharmaceutical industry, staying ahead, demands constant adaptation. In such a scenario this analytical capability is highly necessary.

Offline Reporting

Even though online reporting has many benefits, offline reporting is still essential, especially for medical representatives who prefer more conventional approaches or in places with poor internet connectivity. Manually recording sales activity, such as keeping logbooks, completing daily sales reports, and gathering printed copies of orders and customer reviews, is a common practice in offline reporting. Despite being time-consuming, this approach is still popular throughout India, particularly in rural and semi-urban areas where there may not be as much access to internet infrastructure.

In areas with low levels of digital literacy, offline reporting is essential for ensuring that sales data is still recorded and shared. The sales reps often generate these reports at the conclusion of each workday and provide them to their managers once a week or twice a week. Furthermore, offline reporting provides a physical record that may be consulted when necessary, acting as a backup to online systems. It is because medical representatives physically handle and control their sales documentation, thus it gives them a sense of personal accountability. On the other hand, it can also be found that offline reporting's dependence on human procedures may result in inaccuracies and delays in data compilation. Notwithstanding these difficulties, offline reporting is nevertheless useful, particularly for ensuring thorough coverage of every sales activity, irrespective of technological or geographic limitations.

Sales Statement Preparation

A key component of sales reporting and documentation is the creation of sales statements, which provide an overview of all sales activity during a certain time frame. These statements include a thorough summary of the sales achieved, goals reached, products sold, and the overall performance of the sales force. Sales statements are essential in the Indian pharmaceutical sales ecosystem for evaluating the success of sales strategies, planning future activities, and making sure that sales targets are aligned with the organization's overarching business objectives.

The process of creating sales statements usually entails gathering information from offline and internet sources. Following analysis, this data is packaged into a structured document that offers insights into a number of different facets of the sales process. Total sales volume, sales by product category, geographical sales breakdown, customer acquisition statistics, and a comparison of actual sales against targets are all important parts of a sales statement. Depending on the reporting needs of the business, these statements are typically issued on a monthly, quarterly, or annual basis.

Sales statements are used to communicate with external stakeholders, including distributors, stockists, and management, in addition to being a tool for internal assessment. A well-written sales statement is an essential tool for decision-making since it can point out patterns, pinpoint problems, and recommend areas for development. Sales statements assist in evaluating the success of various product lines and regions in the Indian pharmaceutical market, which is extremely fragmented and diversified. This enables businesses to adjust their plans appropriately.

Expense Statement Preparation

For medical representative, creating expense statements is essential for making sure that all business-related costs are appropriately tracked, justified, and reimbursed by the company. The expense statement needs to be carefully prepared as far as Indian context is concerned. Here the medical representatives frequently travel great distances. Travel, accommodation, meals, entertainment, and promotional activities are usually included in the costs.

A complete expense statement should elaborate expense heads, along with the attached receipts, categorised to the type of expense. For example, transportation expenditures, fuel charges, tolls, and parking fees are further subdivided into travel expenses. Similarly, the price of gifts, samples, or sponsored events for medical professionals may be included in promotional efforts. By classifying these costs, the companies may better analyse spending trends, allocate resources optimally, and make sure that expenditures comply with business standards.

Expense control is essential towards sustaining profitability in the competitive and tightly margined Indian pharmaceutical sales environment. To lessen the administrative load on medical representatives, pharmaceutical companies can use mobile applications and digital technologies to expedite the creation and submission of expense reports. These tools can automatically track expenses, categorize them, and generate reports, thus enabling faster reimbursement cycles and more accurate financial reporting.

Retail Counter Monitoring and Reporting

Retail counter monitoring and reporting is crucial for comprehending the market dynamics at the point of sale and ensuring the effective implementation of sales plans. A wide range of retail counters, from big pharmacy chains to tiny local pharmacist stores, define the pharmaceutical sector in India. Medical representatives must closely monitor these outlets to track product availability, stock levels, and sales performance.

Regular visits to retail locations are necessary for effective retail counter monitoring, during which the medical representatives evaluate the shelf presence of their products, promotional displays, and also monitor the rival activity. Additionally, they get chemist feedback on customer preferences, product demand, and any issues related to supply chain interruptions or product quality. They require this information to make informed decisions about sales targets, marketing strategies, and inventory control.

The medical representative reports to the company's sales and marketing department about the data gathered during these chemist visits by meticulously documenting it. This paperwork usually includes information like the number of products sold, the amount of stock left, and any promotional materials used. Localized retail counter monitoring simultaneously essential for customizing strategies (especially Doctor Visits) for particular regions in the Indian market, where regional variations in prescription generation can have a substantial impact on sales.

For retail counter monitoring, pharmaceutical companies may employ specialized software that enables medical representatives to enter data straight into a centrally controlled system. This method not only increases reporting accuracy, but it also makes it possible to analyse the market trends in real time and react quickly to any new problem arising. It ensures that the concerned company products are always available at the appropriate time and place. This helps the companies to always keep a competitive edge.

Prescription Monitoring and Reporting

Prescription monitoring and reporting are essential for assessing the efficacy of pharmaceutical marketing strategies and ensuring appropriate prescription generated by the healthcare professionals. In India, where medical representative makes a significant influence on doctors' prescribing behaviour, the prescription monitoring is a crucial component of the sales strategies.

Prescription monitoring entails the surveillance of the number and types of prescriptions prescribed by the doctors for particular products. This kind of information helps the sales teams in identifying the products that are gaining popularity, recognizing the patterns in prescription behaviours, and evaluating the effectiveness of their marketing activities. For example, a rapid surge in prescriptions for a specific drug may signify effective marketing strategies or an increasing demand for that therapeutic class.

In the Indian settings that are characterized by a highly fragmented market and diverse physician preferences, the prescription monitoring necessitates a meticulous level of details. The sales team of the pharmaceutical companies frequently conduct in-depth interactions with physicians to comprehend their prescribing behaviours and also the factors affecting their choices. They may additionally get data from pharmacists and other healthcare practitioners to validate their findings.

Prescription scan reporting, often entails aggregating data regarding the quantity of prescriptions, the specialities of the prescribing physicians, and also the geographic dispersion of these prescriptions. The companies subsequently utilise this data to enhance sales strategies, optimise resource allocation, and pinpoint prospective development regions. For instance, the marketing team of the companies may implement focused marketing strategies to enhance awareness and utilisation if a certain area has low prescription rates for a specific medication.

Pharmaceutical businesses in India may use sophisticated analytics technologies to examine the prescription data, allowing them to recognize trends, predict demand, and enhance their marketing strategies. These technologies can also assist in identifying abnormalities in prescribing behaviour, such as probable over prescription or misuse of specific medications, facilitating prompt actions to maintain patient safety and adherence to regulations.

Sales reporting and documentation are essential to the success of pharmaceutical sales in India. The integration of online and offline reporting techniques ensures the comprehensive capture of all sales activity, irrespective of geographical location or technology framework. Sales reporting and documentation within the Indian pharmaceutical sales ecosystem are crucial for ensuring operational efficiency, regulatory compliance, and competitive advantage. Simultaneously, the diligent compilation of sales statements offers a lucid and thorough overview of the sales process, facilitating enhanced decision-making and strategic development. The evolving pharmaceutical sector in India underscores the growing significance of comprehensive sales reporting and documentation, establishing it as a fundamental aspect of effective sales management.

Case Studies

Case 1: Shalini Pharmaceuticals, a promising entrant in India's pharmaceutical sector, sought to market a newly formulated cardiovascular drug brand, CardioHeal, in a highly competitive environment. Acknowledging the essential function of personalised engagement, Shalini Pharma assigned a team of proficient Medical Representatives (MRs) to engage with physicians, offering customised insights into CardioHeal's clinical effectiveness and therapeutic advantages. In areas with restricted access to contemporary medical research, Shalini Pharma's Medical Representatives conducted Continuous Medical Education (CME) sessions and utilised Key Opinion Leaders (KOLs) to provide successful case studies demonstrating the efficacy of CardioHeal. Shalini Pharma employed strategic sampling by supplying trial packs to the targeted physicians, allowing them to evaluate the drug's efficacy on their patients prior to start the formal prescription. Simultaneously, the company implemented a hybrid strategy, integrating conventional sales methods with digital e-detailing technologies to expand their reach in remote regions. This thorough strategy was particularly beneficial, as Shalini Pharma garnered favourable physician comments regarding the drug's results, leading to swift adoption across several market groups. By emphasising long-term relationship cultivation and value-added services, Shalini Pharma established itself as a reliable partner in healthcare, attaining significant growth in the inaugural year of their drug brand CardioHeal's launch and securing a robust presence in India's competitive cardiovascular market.

Case 2: A major pharmaceutical company from India was facing inadequate sales performance and rising travel expenses. To tackle these problems, they executed a thorough territory travel planning strategy for their sales team (Medical Representatives). They systematically assigned sales regions according to market potential, HCP density, and also the presence of the number of healthcare infrastructures. Utilizing sophisticated sales software, the company enhanced travel schedules, minimizing superfluous travel times and fuel costs. Furthermore, the company also instituted stringent expenditure monitoring protocols, secured advantageous prices with hotels and transportation services, and promoted the use of economical travel alternatives. The company made substantial enhancements in sales productivity, decreased travel expenses by 20%, and improved overall operational efficiency. By these measures the company management underlined the crucial importance of effective territory travel planning in boosting sales performance and optimizing resource allocation within the highly competitive Indian pharmaceutical industry.

Suggestive Questions from the Chapter

1. How do pharmaceutical companies work with Indian healthcare providers to meet the different needs of the Indian market?
2. How could digital technologies and e-detailing improve pharmaceutical sales in India, given the COVID-19 epidemic and the country's unique geography?
3. How Indian pharmaceutical companies do use KOLs to influence prescribing and brand reputation?
4. What are the principal characteristics that facilitate the establishment of successful partnerships between medical representatives and healthcare professionals in India?
5. What role does technology play in enhancing these relationships, and what ethical issues must be considered when utilizing it for this purpose?
6. What long-term methods could medical representatives implement to sustain and enhance their connections with healthcare professionals?
7. What is the importance of territory travel planning for the Indian pharmaceutical companies?
8. How can pharmaceutical companies guarantee effective territory coverage and manage costs efficiently?
9. How can integrating online and offline reporting systems improve operational efficiency, transparency, and strategic decision-making in Indian pharmaceutical sales ecosystem?
10. Discuss how prescription monitoring and reporting affect healthcare practitioners' prescribing behaviours and Indian pharmaceutical sales techniques.

Multiple Choice Questions

1. What is the primary role of sales techniques in the Indian pharmaceutical sales ecosystem?

   (a) Finance (b) Link

   (c) Manufacture (d) Logistics

2. Who primarily conducts personalized engagements with healthcare professionals in the Indian pharmaceutical sector?
   (a) Pharmacists (b) Nurses
   (c) Patients (d) Representatives
3. What do Medical Representatives often offer to doctors to build trust in a new product?
   (a) Trials (b) Discounts
   (c) Advertisements (d) Feedback
4. Which tool has become more prominent in pharmaceutical sales due to increased digital adoption?
   (a) E-detailing (b) Packaging
   (c) Printing (d) Telemarketing
5. Who are often sought after to influence other physicians' prescribing habits?
   (a) Distributors (b) Patients
   (c) KOLs (d) Analysts
6. What type of areas benefit from Medical Representatives providing basic drug education?
   (a) Urban (b) Rural
   (c) International (d) Coastal
7. In India, what plays a critical role in doctors' prescribing decisions and business relationships?
   (a) Authority (b) Research
   (c) Trust (d) Sales
8. Which strategy involves Medical Representatives giving doctors sample packs?
   (a) Research (b) Sampling
   (c) Discounting (d) Branding
9. In the Indian context, what is the relationship-based approach often aimed at fostering among healthcare professionals?
   (a) Conflict (b) Awareness
   (c) Compliance (d) Partnership
10. What kind of relationship do pharmaceutical companies aim to build with physicians to support their practice?
    (a) Brief (b) Long-term
    (c) Casual (d) Temporary

11. What is the primary goal of building relationships with HCPs in the Indian pharmaceutical industry?
    (a) Sales (b) Profit
    (c) Patient Care (d) Brand Awareness
12. What is the key role of medical representatives in this context?
    (a) Salesperson (b) Marketer
    (c) Communicator (d) Liaison
13. What is the foundation of any successful relationship between MRs and HCPs?
    (a) Trust (b) Respect
    (c) Empathy (d) Understanding
14. What is the ultimate goal of all parties involved in the healthcare system?
    (a) Profit (b) Market Share
    (c) Patient Outcomes (d) Brand Loyalty
15. What is the human element that often determines the commercial success of a pharmaceutical product in India?
    (a) Marketing (b) Advertising
    (c) Relationships (d) Pricing
16. What is the primary goal of territory travel planning in the Indian pharmaceutical sector?
    (a) Increase market share (b) Enhance brand awareness
    (c) Maximize sales efficiency (d) Reduce marketing costs
17. Which factor is crucial in allocating sales territories in India?
    (a) Population density (b) Geographic size
    (c) Healthcare infrastructure (d) Economic indicators
18. What is the primary challenge in assessing sales travel costs in India?
    (a) Currency fluctuations (b) Varying infrastructure
    (c) High taxation rates (d) Limited transportation options
19. What is the role of technology in territory travel planning?
    (a) Automation of sales calls
    (b) Real-time tracking of representatives
    (c) Predictive analytics for market trends
    (d) AI-powered customer relationship management

20. What is the ultimate goal of travel expense planning?
    (a) Cost minimization (b) Budget optimization
    (c) Profit maximization (d) Expense reduction

21. What is a major benefit of online reporting in the pharmaceutical sales process?
    (a) Transparency (b) Manual
    (c) Delay (d) Print

22. In areas with poor internet connectivity, which type of reporting is essential?
    (a) Online (b) Automated
    (c) Offline (d) Digital

23. What key document offers an overview of all sales activity during a given timeframe?
    (a) Prescription (b) Logbook
    (c) Report (d) Statement

24. Retail counter monitoring helps understand market dynamics at which location?
    (a) Factory (b) Sales
    (c) Distribution (d) Point

25. Prescription monitoring primarily evaluates the effectiveness of:
    (a) Documentation (b) Promotion
    (c) Strategies (d) Costs

CHAPTER

7

Field Sales Force Management

Field sales force management or the Medical Representative management plays a vital role in the Indian pharmaceutical sales environment, considering the intricate and intensely competitive market conditions. Pharmaceutical companies primarily rely on the field sales team, mostly composed of medical representatives, to establish direct communication with healthcare professionals (HCPs), including doctors, pharmacists, and other key players. Ensuring the proper management of this force is crucial to adequately promote the company's products, achieve sales goals, and maintain a robust market presence.

Territory management is another essential aspect of managing a field sales force. The extensive geography of India and its diverse regional markets necessitate a carefully thought-out strategy for allocating territories to sales representatives. Proper territory management allows each representative to optimize their potential by concentrating on a feasible number of HCPs and outlets in their designated area. This entails comprehending the distinct characteristics of each region, such as local competition, doctors' prescribing behaviours, and the regulatory landscape. Frequent performance evaluations and modifications to territory assignments are essential for sustaining optimal coverage and sales efficiency.

Managing motivation and incentives is also essential for enhancing the performance of the field sales team. Considering the challenging aspects of the job, where representatives frequently encounter rejection and need to put in extended hours, maintaining team motivation is crucial. A well-organized incentive program that rewards not just high sales but also other essential performance metrics, like customer satisfaction, compliance with company policies, and market intelligence collection, can accomplish this. Consistent acknowledgement, chances for career growth, and a nurturing workplace play a vital role in sustaining high morale within the sales team.

Effective communication and coordination are crucial for managing a scattered field sales team. The deployment of technology, including CRM systems, mobile apps, and frequent virtual meetings, has become significant for keeping the sales team linked to headquarters and in sync with the organization's goals. These tools enable real-time reporting, improved resource allocation, and faster decision-making, all of which are critical in a dynamic market like India.

Ultimately, compliance and ethical factors are crucial in managing field sales teams. The pharmaceutical sector is subject to strict regulation, and it is crucial for the sales team to comply with all legal and ethical standards in their dealings with HCPs. This not only safeguards the company against legal liabilities but also helps establish a reputation for trust and integrity in the marketplace.

Managing the field sales force or the medical representative team in the Indian pharmaceutical sector presents a complex challenge that necessitates a strategic approach—integrating meticulous recruitment, on-going training, efficient territory management, motivation, and technological utilization—while also ensuring compliance and ethical standards.

Process of Recruitment and Selection

Pharmaceutical companies, particularly in the Indian market characterized by competitive rivalry and varied consumer requirements, rely heavily on the recruitment and selection of appropriate medical representatives for the organisational success. The efficacy of a company's sales strategy frequently depends on the proficiency of its field force, rendering the recruiting and selection process a vital role in the pharmaceutical sector.

A. Qualities Required for an Effective Medical Representative

The position of a medical representative (MR) within the Indian pharmaceutical landscape is challenging and complex. A proficient medical representative must have a blend of technical expertise, interpersonal abilities, and personal qualities that allow them to excel in a competitive setting.

- **Scientific and Product Knowledge:** A medical representative must possess a comprehensive understanding of the pharmaceutical products they endorse. This encompasses understanding of drug formulation, indications, contraindications, adverse effects, and recent advancements in the domain. A comprehensive understanding of medical terminology and the capacity to interpret intricate clinical data are crucial for efficient communication with healthcare professionals (HCPs).
- **Communication Skills:** A key attribute of a medical representative is the capacity for efficient communication. This entails not only articulating product information clearly and convincingly but also attentively considering the concerns and views of physicians, chemists, and other stakeholders. A medical representative must adapt their communication style to various audiences, including experienced physicians and novice chemists.
- **Relationship Building:** Establishing and sustaining relationships with the doctors and healthcare providers is a primary duty of a medical representative. Sustained success in this position requires trust and rapport. A competent medical representative must possess empathy, patience, and networking skills to cultivate robust, mutually advantageous relationships with healthcare professionals.
- **Sales and Negotiation Skills:** The principal role of a medical representative is to stimulate sales. To accomplish this proficiently, they must have robust sales acumen and negotiation abilities. This encompasses the capacity to discern client requirements, articulate convincing solutions, and negotiate mutually advantageous conditions for both the organization and the customer. Persistence and resilience are essential qualities, as medical representatives frequently encounter rejection and must persist in their efforts.
- **Time Management and Organizational Skills:** The position of a Medical Representative necessitates the administration of an extensive area, engagement with numerous clients on a daily basis, and compliance with rigorous reporting standards. Consequently, proficient time management and organizational skills are vital. A medical representative must efficiently arrange their day, prioritize duties, and guarantee target achievement within deadlines.
- **Ethical Integrity:** Medical representatives must adhere to stringent ethical norms due to the rigorous regulation of the pharmaceutical sector. This encompasses maintaining honesty in presentations, upholding patient confidentiality, and adhering to industry laws. A medical representative with robust ethical integrity guarantees the

preservation of their reputation and the credibility of the company they represent.

- **Adaptability and Resilience:** The pharmaceutical market is characterized by its dynamism, marked by rapid alterations in drug legislation, market demands, and competitive landscapes. A medical representative must be versatile, capable of swiftly acquiring and executing new tactics, and robust enough to manage failures and problems without diminishing desire.

B. Hiring Flow of Medical Representatives

The recruiting and selection process for medical representatives in the Indian pharmaceutical sector comprises multiple stages, each aimed at identifying people with the necessary attributes and competencies.

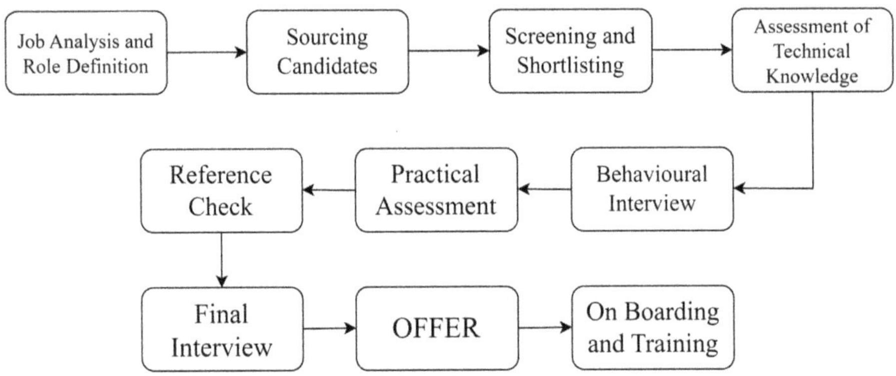

Fig. 7.1 Hiring Flow of Medical Representatives.

- **Job Analysis and Role Definition:** The recruitment process commences with a comprehensive job study to delineate the precise requirements of the Medical Representative position. This entails identifying the requisite qualifications, abilities, experience, and personal traits. After conducting this study, we develop a comprehensive job description that serves as the foundation for the recruitment process.
- **Sourcing Candidates:** Following the finalisation of the job description, the subsequent phase is to identify prospective candidates. Multiple avenues, including employment sites, recruitment firms, university placements, and employee referrals, can accomplish this. In India, numerous pharmaceutical businesses engage in job fairs and industry-specific events to recruit skilled people.

- **Screening and Shortlisting:** The preliminary screening procedure is evaluating resumes and applications to identify applicants who satisfy the fundamental criteria of the position. This phase may also encompass a first telephonic or online interview to evaluate the candidate's communication abilities, comprehension of the pharmaceutical sector, and motivation for pursuing the role.
- **Assessment of Technical Knowledge:** Candidates who successfully pass the preliminary screening are often required to take part in a technical assessment. This may include written assessments or case analyses to assess their comprehension of pharmaceutical products, medical terminology, and the industry at large. Certain firms employ situational judgement exams to evaluate applicants' responses to real-world events they might face as medical representatives.
- **Behavioural Interviews:** Pharmaceutical companies invite candidates who excel in the technical evaluations to participate in behavioural interviews. The purpose of these interviews is to evaluate the candidate's interpersonal abilities, cultural compatibility, and compliance with the organization's ideals. Interviewers frequently employ competency-based inquiries to examine how candidates have handled particular situations previously, emphasizing attributes such as communication, problem solving, and ethical decision-making.
- **Role-Play and Practical Assessments:** To further evaluate the candidate's appropriateness for the medical representative position, organizations may implement role-play exercises or practical evaluations. In a role-play scenario, the candidate may be required to mimic a sales conversation with a physician or chemist, showcasing their proficiency in presenting product information, addressing objections, and finalizing a deal. Practical examinations may include field visits, during which candidates shadow seasoned medical representatives to observe and engage in real sales activities.
- **Reference Checks and Background Verification:** Prior to extending a final offer, organizations generally perform reference checks and background verification to confirm the authenticity of the candidate's qualifications and assess their professional history. This step is essential for preserving the integrity of the recruitment process and reducing the possibility of employing individuals with dubious backgrounds.
- **Final Interview and Offer:** The concluding phase of the recruitment process is an interview with senior management, typically encompassing the regional or national sales manager. This interview

emphasizes the candidate's long-term career objectives, dedication to the organization, and compliance with the company's strategic aims. Once the company deems the candidate suitable, they present a formal job offer that details the remuneration package, job tasks, and additional employment terms.

- **On - Boarding and Training:** Following acceptance of the offer, the new medical representative participates in an extensive on-boarding and training program. This program aims to acquaint them with the company's products, sales procedures, and regulatory obligations. Training may also encompass the development of soft skills, including communication and negotiation tactics, to ensure the new medical representative is adequately prepared to excel in their role.

The recruitment and selection procedure in the Indian pharmaceutical sector is stringent, underscoring the need to employ suitable candidates for the position of medical representatives. By concentrating on the requisite attributes for the role and adhering to a systematic recruitment process, organizations may cultivate a robust and efficient sales team, which propels their success in a competitive landscape.

Online Screening of Candidates

The pharmaceutical sector in India has undergone a significant transformation toward digitalization, encompassing both sales and marketing as well as recruitment processes. Traditional recruitment processes, which mostly included walk-in interviews, campus placements, and manual resume sorting, have transformed with the emergence of internet platforms. Online screening has emerged as a preferred approach for pharmaceutical companies owing to its efficiency, cost-effectiveness, and capacity to access a broader candidate pool.

Multiple forces are driving the transition to online recruitment. The vast magnitude of the Indian pharmaceutical sector demands a more rapid and effective recruitment process. Given the necessity for thousands of MRs nationwide, manual processes have become impractical. Moreover, the growing prevalence of the internet and mobile phones has facilitated connections with prospective candidates in both urban and rural regions. The persistent COVID-19 pandemic has expedited the adoption of online solutions as corporations aim to reduce physical interactions.

Components of Online Screening

The online screening of candidates for the MR role generally has multiple elements, each intended to evaluate distinct facets of a candidate's appropriateness for the position.

1. **Online Application Forms and Resume Submission:** The procedure commences with candidates providing their resumes and completing online application forms on corporate websites or employment platforms. The purpose of these forms is to gather essential details, such as educational qualifications, employment experience, and contact details. Standardizing online forms ensures uniformity in the data collected from all applicants.
2. **Automated Resume Screening:** Automatic screening programs often process resumes upon submission, using algorithms to filter candidates based on predetermined criteria. These criteria may encompass terms pertaining to educational qualifications, pertinent work experience, particular abilities, and geographical location. Automated screening efficiently reduces a vast application pool to a more manageable size, enabling recruiters to concentrate on the most suitable individuals.
3. **Online Assessments:** Candidates who successfully complete the preliminary resume evaluation may be required to participate in online examinations. The purpose of these evaluations is to assess a variety of talents, including technical expertise, problem-solving abilities, and cognitive skills. In the realm of recruiting medical representatives, online examinations may encompass enquiries pertaining to pharmaceutical products, medical terminology, and sales methods. Certain firms employ psychometric assessments to evaluate personality attributes such as resilience, communication abilities, and ethical integrity, which are essential for the position of the Medical Representatives.
4. **Video Interviews:** Video interviews have emerged as a prevalent method for online screening, particularly during the preliminary phases of recruitment. Recruiters can conduct the interviews live or pre-record them. During live video interviews, prospects engage with recruiters instantaneously, facilitating a more dynamic information exchange. Pre-recorded video interviews entail candidates answering a series of pre-set questions, which they record and submit at their convenience. Video interviews have numerous benefits, such as the capacity to evaluate a candidate's communication abilities, nonverbal cues, and confidence without requiring in-person sessions.

5. **Gamified Assessments:** A burgeoning trend in online evaluation is the implementation of gamified exams. These are interactive, gamified situations intended to assess a candidate's decision-making capabilities, problem-solving skills, and adaptability. In the pharmaceutical sector, gamified evaluations may replicate real-world situations that medical representatives are likely to face, such as managing challenging clients or addressing ethical concerns. These evaluations offer a more captivating and immersive method for assessing prospects, enhancing the screening process to be both more efficient and more pleasurable for the candidates.
6. **Social Media Screening:** An additional component of online screening involves the evaluation of a candidate's social media presence. Recruiters may use platforms such as LinkedIn to authenticate professional information and evaluate a candidate's network, endorsements, and industry involvement. Social media screening can yield insights on a candidate's communication style, professionalism, and alignment with the company's ideals. However, careful execution is necessary to avoid biases and ensure that only relevant information is considered.

Process of Online Screening

The selection process for medical representatives in the Indian pharmaceutical sales ecosystem has markedly advanced due to the use of online screening techniques. The need for efficiency, increased outreach and the ability to efficiently evaluate candidates' competencies before in-person interviews motivate this transition.

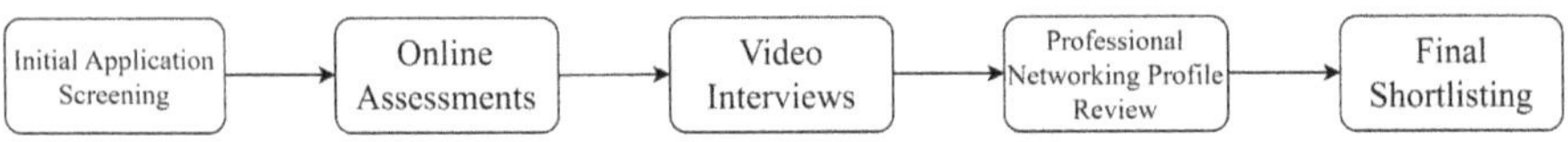

Fig. 7.2 Process Flow of Online Screening.

1. **Initial Application Screening:** The procedure commences with candidates submitting their applications via online job platforms, corporate websites, or professional networks such as LinkedIn. Employers frequently employ Automated Applicant Tracking Systems (ATS) to sift through applications based on established criteria, such as educational credentials, pertinent experience, and competencies. This stage facilitates the rapid identification of individuals who meet the fundamental criteria for the medical representative position.

2. **Online Assessments:** Candidates typically receive an invitation to participate in online examinations after successfully navigating the preliminary screening. These evaluations may encompass aptitude tests, psychometric assessments, and technical knowledge quizzes. Aptitude tests assess a candidate's cognitive capabilities, problem-solving proficiency, and logical reasoning—essential for manoeuvring through the intricate pharmaceutical industry. Psychometric assessments evaluate a candidate's personality characteristics, work ethic, and cultural compatibility. Simultaneously, technical quizzes assess their comprehension of pharmaceutical items, medical terminology, and the regulatory landscape of the sector.
3. **Video Interviews:** Online video interviews are progressively establishing themselves as a common component of the screening procedure. Candidates can respond to a series of predefined questions during live or pre-recorded interviews. Video interviews allow recruiters to assess candidates' communication skills, confidence, and presentation capabilities, which are essential for a medical representative's success. This approach enables firms to evaluate a broader array of candidates from various geographic regions without the logistical difficulties associated with in-person interviews.
4. **Social Media and Professional Networking Profile Review:** During the online screening process, recruiters frequently assess candidates' social media and professional networking profiles. Platforms such as LinkedIn offer insights into a candidate's professional history, endorsements, and connections, assisting in the verification of the information presented in their application. Moreover, social media profiles might provide insight into a candidate's personality, interests, and online conduct, thereby affecting their appropriateness for the position.
5. **Final Shortlisting:** Upon concluding the online screening process, recruiters assemble a shortlist of the most promising individuals. Recruiters subsequently invite these candidates for additional screening, which may include in-person interviews, role-playing scenarios, and practical evaluations. Pharmaceutical firms can optimize their recruiting process by utilizing online screening technologies, thereby efficiently identifying and effectively selecting the most competent applicants for the position of medical representative.

Challenges and Considerations in Online Screening

Although online screening has several advantages, it also presents specific obstacles that organizations must confront in order to guarantee its efficacy.

- **Digital Divide:** The digital gap in India constitutes a substantial obstacle, especially in rural regions where internet access is sometimes restricted. Organizations must take this into account when developing their online screening procedures to ensure they do not unintentionally disqualify skilled individuals who lack access to high-speed internet or cutting-edge technology.
- **Impersonal Nature:** Online screening, particularly when utilizing automated technologies and pre-recorded interviews, may seem impersonal to candidates. This may result in diminished involvement or a feeling of disconnection from the recruitment process. To address this, firms should endeavour to integrate personalized elements, such as prompt contact and feedback, to maintain applicant engagement.
- **Security and Privacy Concerns:** The growing dependence on digital tools has rendered data security and privacy paramount considerations. Organizations must guarantee that the platforms used for online screening are secure and abide by data protection requirements. We must manage candidate information meticulously and establish confidence through clear communication about data utilization.

Online screening has transformed the recruitment process for medical representatives in the Indian pharmaceutical business. By using digital tools and platforms, organizations can effectively find people with the requisite abilities and attributes for the position of a Medical Representative. To fully harness the advantages of online screening, firms must acknowledge the issues it poses and implement measures to ensure a fair, inclusive, and safe recruitment process. As the business progresses, internet screening will certainly assume a more significant role in influencing the future of pharmaceutical sales in India.

Open Application Based Screening Process

The hiring of medical representatives (MRs) in the pharmaceutical sector usually adheres to a well-defined procedure to select individuals with the appropriate skills, attitudes, and understanding to thrive in the position. The combination of open application-based recruitment and a personal interview is a common method for choosing appropriate candidates. This approach strikes a balance between transparency and inclusiveness, permitting a wide array of applicants to submit their applications while allowing recruiters to rigorously evaluate each candidate's qualifications and personal attributes. Here is a summary of this process and its importance.

1. **Open Application Process:** In an Open Application recruitment process, pharmaceutical companies publicly share the job vacancy. They might utilize different channels, including online job portals, corporate websites, social media, newspaper advertisement and industry-specific recruitment agencies, to connect with a wide range of potential candidates. This process draws in candidates from various backgrounds and regions by casting a wide net, which is especially crucial in a field that values local understanding and adaptability.

    - **Job Posting and Advertisement:** The process for open applications recruitment process commences with the creation of an accurate and detailed job listing. The job posting usually contains important details regarding the role, including the duties of a medical representative, desired qualifications, particular skill sets, and other crucial requirements like educational history or applicable work experience.
    - **Eligibility Screening:** Once the job applications are submitted, the HR or recruitment team evaluates them to guarantee that only eligible candidates move on to the next stage. The initial filtering typically takes into account the candidate's educational background, previous work experience, language abilities, and any particular requirements stated in the job description. Pharmaceutical companies usually seek candidates who hold a bachelor's degree in pharmacy, life sciences, or similar areas, though those with robust sales experience might also be taken into account.
    - **Shortlisting Based on Application Quality:** The recruitment team shortlists the candidates from the eligible group whose applications are exceptional. A well-drafted resume and cover letter that showcase pertinent experience and skills, including communication skills, product knowledge, and awareness of the pharmaceutical industry, frequently enhance a candidate's chances of securing an interview.

2. **Personal Interview Stage:** Once the applications are submitted and the initial screening is completed, the chosen candidates are invited for personal interviews. The interview phase is essential for assessing the candidate's hands-on skills, social competence, and suitability for the position. A medical representative's role requires frequent engagement with doctors, medicine retailers and also the whole sellers, making the interview essential for evaluating how well candidates can embody the company and conveys complex information persuasively.

- **Behavioural Interview Questions:** These questions assess a candidate's previous actions in particular circumstances and offer insights into their character and problem-solving methods. Interviewers may inquire about how candidates handled tough sales targets, coped with rejection, or established relationships with clients in past positions. These questions provide insights into the candidate's resilience, adaptability, and sales skills.
- **Role-Specific Competency Assessment:** Medical representatives require a combination of technical and sales expertise, highlighting the importance of role-specific inquiries. Interviewers will evaluate the candidate's understanding of medical terminology, fundamental pharmacology, and principles of pharmaceutical sales. Candidates might be required to showcase their ability to convey intricate medical information in a simplified way because this is an essential skill for MRs engaging with doctors, medicine retailers and also the medicine whole sellers.
- **Communication and Presentation Skills:** Communication and presentation abilities are essential for medical representatives because they act as a bridge between pharmaceutical firms and healthcare professionals. Interviewers frequently notice how the candidates express ideas, sustain eye contact, and convey confidence. A simulated presentation or a situational question can be used to evaluate a candidate's ability to pitch a product effectively.
- **Situational and Problem-Solving Questions:** These questions aim to understand a candidate's decision-making ability, ethical considerations, and problem-solving skills. Candidates may encounter situations in which they must deal with objections from physicians, navigate competition from other pharmaceutical firms, or tackle ethical dilemmas. The answers will assist interviewers in assessing how candidates might deal with actual challenges in the position.

3. **Final Selection and Feedback:** After the interview phase, candidates are assessed on their total performance during both the application screening and interview stages. Typically, the selection panel reviews the strengths, concerns, and potential compatibility of each candidate with the organization's culture and values. Candidates who are selected are given the job offer, whereas those who fail to qualify usually receive feedback on their performance. Constructive feedback can be beneficial because it offers candidate insights into aspects that they can enhance for future opportunities.

Importance of the Open Application-Based with Interview Process

In general, both the organization as well as the candidates benefit from this selection process. The organization guarantees a comprehensive and equitable evaluation, enabling it to identify the candidates who fulfil technical specifications while also possessing the interpersonal skills and attitude necessary for success in the position. The open application procedure offers candidates a clear and reachable way to apply for the role, while the interview allows candidates to highlight their strengths and fit that may not be evident on their resume.

Medical representatives play a crucial role in the pharmaceutical sector by building connections with healthcare professionals and ensuring that medical products are properly conveyed and supported. The open application process combined with personal interviews is an effective method for ensuring that these professionals are adequately prepared to fulfil the requirements of this important role.

Disadvantages of Open Application Screening

Although the open application selection method combined with personal interviews enables a several applicant pool and a detailed candidate assessment process, it has some drawbacks. Initially, the process may require significant time and money, particularly when dealing with large numbers of applications. Initial screenings might miss out on strong candidates who, while not fitting standard criteria, have significant potential. Furthermore, interviews are dependent on subjective assessments, which can lead to biases and impact consistency. Candidates with strong communication skills may excel in interviews but may be deficient in other crucial job-related abilities. Finally, the process may not reveal deeper characteristics, such as resilience and adaptability, which are essential for medical representatives.

Walk-in-Interview Selection Process of Medical Representatives

The need for qualified medical representatives (MRs) in the Indian pharmaceutical sector has prompted a variety of employment practices, with walk-in interviews being a popular way of selection. Managers engaged in hiring often prefer walk-in interviews due to their quickness and effectiveness. During these interviews, candidates can turn up without an appointment and speak with recruitment managers face-to-face to highlight their abilities. Typically, hiring managers plan the walk-in interview process, which encompasses crucial topics such as product knowledge, interpersonal skills, and communication abilities, all essential for the role of a medical representative.

Process of Walk-in Interviews for Selecting Medical Representatives

1. **Advertisement and Notification**: Pharmaceutical Companies usually use a variety of channels, including employment portals, social media, newspapers, and their own website, to promote walk-in interviews. This makes it easier to connect with a large number of applicants, especially recent graduates who are considering a career in sales. The advertisements typically include details like the date, location, eligibility requirements, and required documents.
2. **Document Verification**: Candidates must have certain documents with them when they arrive, such as their resume, identity documents, educational credentials, and any experience letters (if any). Verifying documents is a crucial first step in ensuring that applicants fulfil the fundamental professional and educational requirements for the position of a Medical Representative.
3. **Initial Screening**: To create a shortlist of applicants who have a fundamental understanding of the pharmaceutical sector, as well as strong interpersonal and communication abilities, many organizations perform an initial screening. Junior HR staff members or recruiters frequently carry out this step by determining whether the candidates fulfil the position's minimal requirements.
4. **One-on-One Interview with HR and Sales Managers**: Following their selection, the selected applicants go on to speak with HR and sales managers one-on-one. This phase is essential since it evaluates the candidate's ability to communicate, their familiarity with the product, and their sales prowess. Interviewers look for traits that are essential for a successful medical representative, such as excitement, confidence, and the ability to clearly explain concepts.
5. **Role-Play and Mock Selling**: To assess a candidate's sales and negotiation abilities, some organizations incorporate a role-play or mock selling exercise into the walk-in interview process. This aids the interviewers in determining how well the candidate can manage real-world sales scenarios, such as promoting a product to medical professionals, handling objections, and closing a purchase.
6. **Technical Knowledge Assessment**: Pharmaceutical Companies frequently test candidates' technical knowledge, particularly in relation to drug classifications, medical terminology, and common health issues. Given their expectation to interact with healthcare professionals, medical representatives must possess a basic understanding of the products and the company.

7. **Feedback and Offer**: Candidates who perform well in the aforementioned phases receive feedback, and those who meet all selection requirements may receive an offer of employment immediately or shortly thereafter. Companies may fill critical positions quickly and guarantee minimum delays in territory coverage by using walk-in interviews.

Disadvantages of the Walk-in-Interview Selection Process

Although the walk-in interview procedure has many advantages, it also has drawbacks, particularly when it comes to selecting qualified and dependable applicants for positions as medical representatives Among the principal drawbacks are:

1. **Limited Assessment of Skills**: Walk-in interviews are often constrained by time, making it challenging to assess a candidate's complete range of skills and competencies. Short interview times might not give enough time to discover a candidate's faults or fully grasp their potential, which could affect how well they perform in the job.
2. **High Volume and Lack of Personalization**: Many candidates may participate in walk-in interviews, causing significant stress for both interviewers and candidates. In these situations, it becomes challenging to provide each applicant with individualized attention, and the hiring process may overlook nuanced abilities and qualities that are essential for the position. Hurried or unduly standardised candidate evaluations may result in less-than-ideal recruiting decisions.
3. **Absence of Detailed Background Checks**: Walk-in interviews sometimes lack thorough background checks, because they focus on urgent employment requirements. This may result in differences between the candidates' real ability and qualifications. Without careful screening, businesses risk employing people who don't fully fit the requirements of the position, which could impact both retention and performance.
4. **Focus on Immediate Availability over Long-Term Fit**: Walk-in interviews often aim to fill open positions immediately, potentially favouring applicants who are available immediately over those who may prove to be more qualified for the role over time. This strategy may impact employee retention, as some applicants may quickly leave the organisation if they don't feel the role fulfils them or aligns with their professional objectives.
5. **Higher Risk of Attrition**: The expeditious hiring process of walk-in interviews may attract applicants who lack dedication to the

pharmaceutical sales industry but are actively seeking immediate employment. This could lead to higher turnover rates, as some applicants may seek employment elsewhere. In the pharmaceutical sales industry, where establishing enduring relationships with medical professionals is essential, high attrition rates can be very upsetting.

6. **Limited Understanding of Cultural Fit**: In a brief interview, it might be difficult to determine how well a candidate fits the corporate culture. Due to their speed, walk-in interviews might not give a complete picture of a candidate's ability to fit in with the company's expectations, values, and work culture. This can make it harder for them to follow organizational procedures or collaborate well with others, which could cause problems at work.
7. **Potential for Oversight of Experienced Candidates**: Walk-in interviews are sometimes ineffective in drawing in seasoned professionals because they tend to appeal more to recent graduates and entry-level applicants. Pharmaceutical Companies may lose out on employing more seasoned candidates who would rather have structured scheduled interviews. This restricts the pool of candidates to primarily freshmen, which may have an impact on the sales team's level of experience.

Pharmaceutical Companies must be mindful of the limitations of the walk-in interview procedure, even if it is an effective way to hire medical representatives, particularly when fulfilling urgent staffing demands. Striking a balance between walk-in interviews and more methodical and thorough screening procedures, such as background checks and cultural fit evaluations, can lessen the drawbacks. Companies may create a skilled and dedicated team of medical reps by combining the expediency of walk-in interviews with other hiring techniques.

Experienced Candidate Referral Selection

The Indian pharmaceutical sector frequently employs the reference selection procedure for medical representatives to find and hire qualified applicants. Companies must hire individuals who possess the necessary abilities, industry expertise, and professional networks to effectively function as medical representatives, given their crucial role in marketing pharmaceutical items to healthcare professionals. Experienced candidates, frequently recommended by current employees or through professional connections, possess working knowledge of the pharmaceutical sales environment, making them an effective and reliable means of meeting hiring objectives.

1. **Understanding the Referral Process**

   - A formal or casual referral from an existing employee usually starts the referral selection process in Indian pharmaceutical companies. Indian pharmaceutical companies frequently urge workers to recommend friends, acquaintances, or previous co-workers who possess the necessary medical representative expertise. People with a strong background in pharmaceutical sales who are also knowledgeable about the product, the market, and the expectations of the organization typically make these recommendations.
   - Compared to traditional hiring methods, we typically evaluate referred prospects more quickly. The referred applicant goes through a typical interview procedure following an initial examination of their résumé and pertinent qualifications. Hiring managers may give preference to referred candidates because they have recommendations from reliable staff members, which cuts down on the time required for selection and on-boarding.

2. **Advantages of Referral-Based Selection:** Reduced Recruitment Time: Hiring through referrals is often quicker, as it bypasses the lengthy steps involved in sourcing and shortlisting candidates from scratch. Hiring managers can proceed with the selection process with confidence and efficiency once the recommending employee has attested to the candidate's credibility.

   - **Better Cultural Fit:** Referrals usually have some understanding of the company's work culture through their existing connections. Employees who recommend candidates enhance employee satisfaction and retention, as they tend to select individuals who align with the organization's values and culture.
   - **Higher Job Performance:** Experienced candidates who are hired through referrals often perform better as they bring industry expertise and are aware of the competitive landscape. Additionally, they have a well-established network of healthcare specialists that they can use to boost revenue right away and help the company achieve its growth goals.
   - **Lower Recruitment Costs:** Compared to more conventional approaches like advertising on job boards or using recruiting firms, referral-based hiring is typically less expensive. Businesses looking to control expenses benefit from this strategy since it lowers advertising expenses and eliminates the need for substantial HR staff.

3. **The Referral Process in Practice**
    - In reality, pharmaceutical companies could provide rewards like referral bonuses or recognition initiatives to staff members who recommend qualified applicants. By offering these incentives, companies encourage staff members to take an active role in the hiring process, potentially producing a talented pool of seasoned medical representatives.
    - In order to evaluate a candidate's communication abilities, product knowledge, and attitude toward managing physician interactions, the referral process frequently entails an initial interview with the recruiting manager as well as technical tests or role-playing exercises.

Disadvantages of the Experienced Candidate Referral Selection Process

For experienced candidates, the referral-based selection method has significant disadvantages in addition to its many benefits. To make sure they are not compromising their dedication to diversity or lowering the quality of their talent pools, businesses need to take these drawbacks into account.

1. **Limited Diversity and Innovation**
    - Referral-based hiring can lead to homogeneity within the workforce, as employees tend to refer candidates with similar backgrounds, mind-sets, and experiences. This can lead to a lack of diversity in viewpoints, problem-solving strategies, and ideas, which could hinder the company's capacity for innovation.
    - A bigger workforce with a range of expertise can generate creative sales tactics and strategies in the cutthroat competitive pharmaceutical industry. Some school of thoughts believe that the referral process of recruitment may limit such diversity, making the team less equipped to adjust to emerging challenges and the changing market trends.
2. **Potential Bias and Favouritism**
    - Employees may recommend friends or former co-workers they personally like over those who are best suited for the position, so the referral process of recruitment is somewhat fundamentally subjective. Biasness can also arise when referrals lack impartial evaluations of a candidate’s skills or suitability for the position.

- Favouritism-based hiring could lead to a lack of transparency in the hiring process, potentially aggravating staff members who perceive a subversion of merit-based hiring. This may impact employee morale generally and confidence in the company's hiring procedures.

3. **Overlooking Fresh Talent**

- Relying heavily on referrals may result in missed opportunities to bring in fresh talent, including recent graduates or individuals with non-traditional backgrounds who could contribute positively to the organization. Referral recruitments are frequently made through existing connections, so even if a candidate has the abilities and drive to succeed, they might be looked over if they don't have any references to their credit.

- New talents are more receptive towards learning and training in new techniques, and they frequently bring fresh viewpoints to the forefront. Restricting this selection process to seasoned recommendations can keep away companies from accessing a vibrant pool of upcoming talents.

4. **Over-reliance on Internal Networks**

- Companies that depend too much on referral-based hiring may discover that their internal networks limit their talent pool, which could make it difficult for them towards sufficiently serving the wide range of demands of their sales territories. If the majority of new recruits come through referral system, the organization might unintentionally create a restrictive system that may lack external perspectives.

- The referred candidates may have out-dated knowledge or practices that do not correspond with the most recent developments in technology or pharmaceutical trends. Henceforth, this over-reliance on the referred recruits can also lead to a slower reaction to shifting industry demands.

5. **Reduced Accountability for Performance**

- Recommended candidates are often considered competent due to their relationship with existing employees; this potentially may lead towards lesser scrutiny during the recruitment process. Referred employees may feel a sense of accountability, but when referred individuals fall short of expectations, it can cause conflict within the company and reflect poorly on them.

- In addition to the above, employees may suggest candidates for only the rewards, without properly evaluating their eligibility if at all the referral incentive system in the organisation is unbalanced. Higher turnover rates may result from referred applicants quitting after a brief period of employment because over the time it has been found that their expectations or skill sets mismatches.

To overcome issues with bias, diversity, and dependence on internal networks, Indian pharmaceutical companies most of the time tend to use the referral selection process in conjunction with more conventional recruitment techniques. Pharmaceutical companies may create a strong and diverse workforce that can thrive in a changing market by combining recommendations with open and merit-based hiring procedures.

Training and Development of Medical Representatives

In the Indian pharmaceutical sales ecosystem, medical representatives play a critical role. These sales professionals serve as the primary link between the pharmaceutical companies and healthcare professionals, ensuring that with the proper conveyance and marketing, the pharmaceutical products reaches the appropriate market. A strong framework for medical representatives' training and growth is required due to the dynamic nature of the pharmaceutical sector and the country's complicated as well as competitive market system. In addition to providing them with the necessary knowledge and skills, this framework is crucial for ensuring that they adapt themselves in the marketing environment that is always changing. The Medical Representative Training and development process can generally be divided into two main categories - Introductory Training Programs and Continuous Professional Development (CPD).

Initial Training Programs

The starting of a typical medical representative's profession begins with the introductory training programs provided by the companies who recruit them. However, it's not always mandatory for all companies. These programs aim to provide new recruits with a comprehensive understanding of the pharmaceutical industry, the company's product line, and the necessary skills to engage with doctors, retailers as well as the medicine whole sellers. Given the variety of pharmaceutical products and the different therapeutic areas companies cater, the introductory training programs carefully incorporate both academic knowledge and practical skills.

Understanding the Pharmaceutical Landscape: Educating Medical Representatives about the pharmaceutical environment in the country is the first stage of their basic training program. This entails being aware of the various stakeholder roles, the regulatory environment, and the sales ecosystem as a whole. Medical representatives are generally made aware about the complexities of patent laws, drug approval procedures, and pharmaceutical marketing ethics. This information is essential because it provides the context for the medical representatives' job role and helps them approach complex problems with understanding.

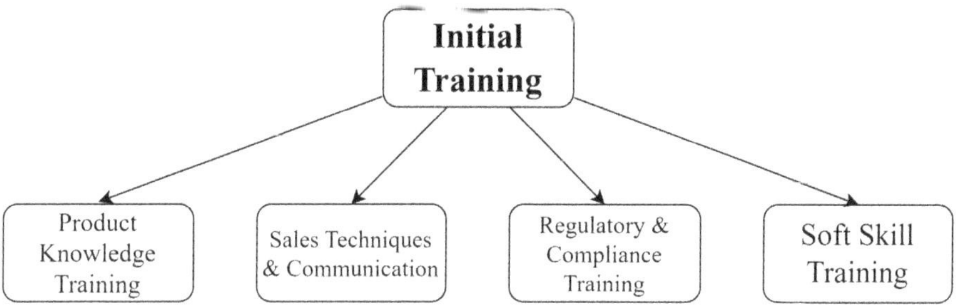

Fig. 7.3 Initial Training Flow for Medical Representatives.

- **Product Knowledge:** A significant portion of the initial training is dedicated towards the product knowledge. A new medical representative is expected to thoroughly understand about the company's products, including their molecular composition, therapeutic advantages, adverse effects, contraindications etc. Through the product knowledge imparting session the Medical Representatives receive in-depth instruction on the science underlying each product during these training sessions. This training session include frequent meetings with the company's product management and R&D teams. The Medical Representatives are also trained to assess their products against their competitors, highlighting the unique selling points that can effectively be communicated to the healthcare professionals.
- **Sales Techniques and Communication Skills:** Persuasive communication and product knowledge are not enough to sell pharmaceutical products; a medical representative also needs outstanding communication abilities. Introductory training programs include modules on effective sales strategies, including how to overcome objections, close deals, and deliver powerful presentations. Role-playing scenarios are frequently used to mimic

real-life interactions with physicians, chemists, and other stakeholders for providing the medical representatives with opportunities to practice and improve their communication techniques.

- **Regulatory and Compliance Training:** Medical Representatives need to be enough knowledgeable about the laws and moral principles that govern their job role in a highly regulated sector i.e. the pharmaceutical industry. Comprehensive lessons on regulatory compliance, including the Drugs and Cosmetics Act, the Medical Council of India's (MCI) recommendations, and industry-specific codes of conduct, are part of the first training programs. Medical representatives receive training to ensure their sales practices are moral and fully compliant with these standards, safeguarding the company's reputation and avoiding legal issues.
- **Soft Skills Development:** Medical Representatives also receive training in soft skills including time management, stress management, and teamwork in addition to technical knowledge and sales abilities. These skills are crucial for maintaining motivation and productivity in a medical representative's job that often involves long hours and frequent travel. Training programs also generally incorporate sessions on cultural sensitivity, particularly in a multicultural market like India where medical representatives interact with doctors, retailers and medical whole sellers from multicultural backgrounds.

Continuous Professional Development (CPD)

Changing market dynamics, regulatory changes, and quick advances in medical knowledge define the pharmaceutical industry. In such a scenario, initial training is insufficient to sustain long-term success for the medical representatives. To guarantee that medical representative's needs to stay updated with the most recent developments in marketing, improve their abilities, and keep adding up value to their interactions with the healthcare providers. For this the continuous professional development, or CPD, is always essential.

- **On-going Product Training:** An essential part of continuing professional development is the on-going product training, because pharmaceutical companies frequently introduce new drugs and upgrade their existing drugs in the market. Medical representatives receive regular updates on new product introductions, formulation modifications, and fresh clinical data associated with the drugs for treatments. This kind of product training generally uses the product briefings, online sessions, and offline seminars. Additionally, the medical representatives have to stay updated on market developments and competing products to effectively position their solutions.

- **Advanced Sales Techniques:** To stay successful in a competitive industry, medical representatives must gradually improve and modify their sales strategies. CPD programs frequently include advanced sales training, covering topics such as customer relationship management (CRM) tools, digital marketing strategies, and strategic customer management etc. Medical representatives receive training on the usage of digital platforms for customer connection and product marketing in light of the pharmaceutical industry's growing reliance on technology.
- **Regulatory Updates and Compliance Refresher:** The pharmaceutical industry experiences a constantly changing regulatory environment due to the frequent introductions of new rules and regulations. CPD programs ensure that medical representatives stay informed about these developments through frequently undergoing refresher training. By obtaining these training sessions, the medical representatives make sure that they remain within the law and understand how the newly introduced rules will affect their sales tactics.
- **Leadership and Career Development:** Continuing Professional Development (CPD) helps the medical representatives get ready for their future roles in the organisation in addition to maintaining their present skill set. In order to prepare high-potential medical representatives for managerial roles, pharmaceutical companies frequently incorporate leadership development topics into the continuing professional development (CPD) programs. These topics might address subjects including strategic planning, decision-making, and team management. Companies may also ensure a consistent supply of talent for future leadership positions by investing in the leadership development for the medical representatives.
- **Soft Skills Enhancement:** The significance of soft skills like emotional intelligence, negotiation, and conflict resolution increases as the medical representatives advances in their careers. CPD programs frequently include advanced soft skills training to help medical representatives manage intricate customer contacts, establish enduring relationships, and overcome the demands of a high-pressure workplace. Recognizing the demanding nature of the medical representative profession, this training also includes courses on mental health and work-life balance.

- **Technology and Digital Tools:** The pharmaceutical sales landscape has changed as a result of the emerging of digital tools and platforms in marketing including pharmaceutical industry. These days, CPD programs include instruction on how to use these tools efficiently. In order to improve their efficiency and client interaction, medical representatives also receives training on how to use CRM software, data analytics tools, and digital communication platforms in some future oriented pharmaceutical companies. Medical Representative training is increasingly including instruction on how to use social media and other internet channels for marketing and sales.

Fig. 7.4 Continuous Professional Development.

For the medical representatives to succeed in the country's pharmaceutical sales ecosystem, training and development are essential. Introductory training programs sets the foundation by giving medical representatives, the fundamental information and abilities they need. The on-going professional development in the companies makes sure that they stay applicable and productive in a field that is always evolving. Generally the pharmaceutical companies have the tendency to improve the skills of their medical representatives and support the expansion and prosperity of the company as a whole by investing in extensive training and development initiatives. Training and development programs must adapt to the changing needs of the pharmaceutical sector to ensure medical representatives are prepared for future opportunities and challenges.

Motivation and Incentive Programs

India is one of the biggest pharmaceutical industries in the world. It contributes significantly to the healthcare sector by offering a wide range of drugs at reasonable costs. Nonetheless, the sales force in India plays a crucial role in this industry's performance, as they are in charge of product promotion, sales growth, and ultimately the expansion and financial success of pharmaceutical companies. In this situation, attaining and maintaining high performance level, depends on inspiring the sales force and creating incentive schemes that work. There are various motivation techniques and the principles of designing incentive plans tailored to the unique dynamics of the Indian pharmaceutical sales ecosystem.

A. Motivation Techniques

A thorough grasp of the individual and group factors that are influencing a pharmaceutical sales team's performance, is very necessary to inspire them. Contrary to other industries, the pharmaceutical companies require salespeople to be well-versed in their products, understand the intricate medical facts, and maintain relationship with healthcare professionals (HCPs). In light of these demands, motivation strategies in this domain need to be diverse, taking into account both internal and external influences.

I. Intrinsic Motivation

Personal fulfilment, development, and the accomplishment of career objectives are the main sources of intrinsic motivation, which originates from within the person. The pharmaceutical industry can foster these things in a number of ways:

- **Skill Development:** Opportunities for professional growth and on-going education are essential for inspiring salespeople. Companies generally tries to help their sales force feel more capable and secure in their positions by providing training programs that improve their understanding of new therapies, products, and also providing knowledge of the changing healthcare environment. Consequently, this promotes a feeling of accomplishment and individual development within the sales team.
- **Autonomy and Empowerment:** Medical representatives often exhibit greater drive when they are given granted autonomy in their jobs. Increased job satisfaction may result by giving them the freedom to decide sales strategies by themselves, develop their own sales plans, and take charge of their territories. Involving sales people in decision-making procedures, such as marketing plans and product launches, can help empower them by making them feel important and essential to the success of the companies.
- **Recognition and Feedback:** Consistently receiving constructive criticism is a strong incentive. Recognizing the medical representative's achievements and efforts, whether formally with rewards or informally by verbal praises, can greatly raise their morale. In addition towards

boosting self-esteem, positive reinforcement also promotes the repetition of successful behaviours.

II. Extrinsic Motivation

Financial incentives, career promotion, and job security are examples of external benefits that generate extrinsic motivation. There are many extrinsic motivators that are essential in the highly competitive Indian pharmaceutical sales ecosystem. They are:

- **Monetary Rewards:** Conventional yet powerful motivators include incentives, bonuses, and competitive pay. However, to maximize their impact, these monetary rewards should closely align with performance indicators. One way to encourage desired behaviours is to tie bonuses to the successful launch of new products or the achievement of particular sales goals.
- **Career Progression:** Opportunities for clear and attainable job growth are always the powerful extrinsic incentives. In a pharmaceutical company generally the top-performing representatives, can advance to more senior positions like area managers or regional sales managers by following the established career paths that pharmaceutical companies can put in place. This helps to retain top talent in addition to offering other forms of motivational incentives.
- **Non-Monetary Incentives:** In addition to monetary rewards, non-monetary incentives such as paid vacations, luxury goods, or even opportunities for international visits through conferences and seminars as well as tour packages can be highly motivating. These rewards often carry a perceived value beyond their actual cost and can be used to recognize exceptional performance.
- **Work-Life Balance:** Due to the rigorous nature of pharmaceutical sales, long hours and frequent travel are the requirement of the job role. Employers may increase job satisfaction and decrease burnout by providing wellness initiatives, and assistance in preserving a healthy work-life balance. This will inspire workers to perform better.

B. Designing Incentive Plans

Designing effective incentive plans is a complex task that requires a deep understanding of the sales process, the market environment, and the unique challenges faced by the sales force. In the Indian pharmaceutical sector, where the market is diverse and regulatory norms are stringent, incentive plans must be carefully crafted to drive performance while ensuring compliance and ethical standards.

1. **Aligning Incentives with Business Goals:** Any incentive plan's main goal is to match the sales force's interests with the business objectives of the organization. This suggests that the developing the incentive programs should motivate actions that contribute to the achievement of these objectives. For instance, the incentive plan should compensate the medical representatives for surpassing sales targets in a specific product category if the company's objective is to expand the market share of that product.
2. **Customization Based on Roles and Regions:** Medical representatives in the Indian pharmaceutical industry work in diverse geographical regions with different market conditions. Consequently, a one-size-fits-all strategy for incentive programs might not work. Companies generally always tries in developing customised incentive programs according to the unique responsibilities of the medical representatives, customer demographics, and regional market situations. The incentive strategies of many companies takes into account the fact that a medical representative operating in a rural area can encounter different obstacles than one operating in an urban one.
3. **Balancing Short-Term and Long-Term Incentives:** Incentive plans ought to balance long-term incentives with short-term benefits. Long-term incentives like stock options or deferred bonuses can promote loyalty and consistent performance, while short-term incentives like monthly or quarterly bonuses can provide benefits right away. Long-term incentives can be especially useful in encouraging regular engagement and trust-building efforts in the pharmaceutical business, where establishing and preserving relationships with HCPs is essential.
4. **Ensuring Fairness and Transparency:** The way the sales team interprets an incentive scheme has a significant impact on its efficacy. To inspire, the plan has to be perceived as fair and transparent. This means that the criteria for earning incentives should be clearly communicated, and the process for evaluating performance should be objective and consistent. Additionally, companies should make sure that the incentive plan is feasible for each representative, with goals based on individual talents and actual market conditions.
5. **Compliance and Ethical Considerations:** Strict regulations apply to the pharmaceutical sector, especially when it comes in dealing with the HCPs. Companies tries to create incentive plans that comply with the rules and promote ethical behaviour among salespeople. For instance, the sales management of the companies shouldn't set up incentives to support pushing or unethical sales tactics, such as encouraging off-label

drug usage or giving HCPs inappropriate inducements. Instead, incentive plans should reward behaviours that align with both regulatory standards and the company's ethical values.

6. **Regular Review and Adaptation:** Regulations, market conditions, and competitive pressures are always changing in the dynamic pharmaceutical industry. Periodically evaluating and modifying incentive strategies is necessary to ensure their relevance and efficacy. This involves monitoring the sales force's performance, gathering feedback, and making necessary modifications to the incentive structure, goals, or prizes.
7. **Integrating Non-Financial Metrics:** Although most incentive schemes include financial performance as a primary metric, the inclusion of non-financial metrics can also offer a more comprehensive method of performance assessment. Metrics like customer satisfaction, adherence to moral principles, and team goal contribution can be useful to gauge a medical representative's overall performance in the pharmaceutical sector. Incorporating these measures into the incentive plan, promotes a more balanced approach towards sales, prioritizing financial goals without compromising the ethical conducts or enduring customer relationships.

Motivation and incentive programs are the essential instruments for promoting high performance and attaining commercial success in the Indian pharmaceutical sales ecosystem. Companies can develop a motivated and engaged sales force by combining extrinsic and intrinsic motivation strategies. Similar to this, well-crafted incentive programs that are in line with corporate objectives, tailored towards local and position-specific requirements, adhered to legal requirements can successfully encourage the desired behaviours and support the company's long-term expansion.

Performance Evaluation

A key component of effectively leading a sales team in the Indian pharmaceutical sector is performance review. This procedure guarantees that medical representatives and other salespeople are accomplishing their goals and supporting the overarching objectives of the company. In addition to inspiring workers, a well-designed performance review system helps them match their work with the organization's strategic objectives. Conducting performance evaluations and establishing performance metrics are two essential steps in this approach.

Setting Performance Metrics

When it comes to managing a successful sales force in the pharmaceutical sector in India, one of the most important components is setting of the performance metrics. In order to evaluate the efficiency of medical representatives and to make certain that their actions are in line with the organization's strategic objectives, these metrics serve as the basis for the evaluation process. It is necessary to establish the appropriate performance indicators in order to drive growth and accomplish corporate objectives in a market as complicated and highly competitive as India, where different areas, different healthcare demands, and regulatory regimes bring their own distinct problems.

1. **Sales Targets and Revenue Generation:** In terms of performance metrics, the achievement of sales targets is the most clear and widely utilized statistic out there. When determining sales targets, we often consider the potential of the market, historical data, and strategic objectives. In the context of the pharmaceutical ecosystem in India, these aims may include metrics like the number of units sold, money earned, or market share captured. Despite this diversity in the Indian market, companies must adapt these targets to the unique characteristics of each region. For instance, urban areas that have a greater concentration of healthcare facilities might have higher sales targets in comparison to rural locations, which might have a lesser need for pharmaceutical products and hence less access to healthcare.
2. **Prescription Generation and Influence on Prescribing Behaviour:** In the pharmaceutical sales ecosystem, the medical representative's capacity to affect healthcare professionals' (HCPs') prescribing practices is another important statistic. The representative's efforts can determine this metric by tracking the number of prescriptions written for a specific product. One of the most important measures of measuring a medical representative's ability to influence doctors to recommend his/her company's brands in India's highly competitive pharmaceutical market, where several brands frequently vie for the same prescription. Prescription generation metrics may include the quantity of new prescriptions, repeat prescriptions, and the medical representative's capacity to move doctors from a competitor's product to their own.
3. **Customer Relationship Management and Doctor Engagement:** In the context of pharmaceutical sales in India, establishing and preserving solid connections with physicians, chemists, and other healthcare professionals is essential. An assessment of a medical representative's

capacity to build rapport and trust with HCPs must include metrics pertaining to customer relationship management (CRM). These metrics may include the frequency and quality of visits to doctors, the effectiveness of communication, and the ability to address customer needs and concerns. In the Indian context, where personal relationships and trust play a significant role in business transactions, CRM metrics are vital for long-term success.

4. **Product Knowledge and Compliance:** It is essential to make sure that medical representatives are knowledgeable about products and compliance standards in a highly regulated market like pharmaceuticals. Performance metrics in this area can assess the representative's understanding of the products they promote, their ability to communicate complex medical information accurately, and their adherence to ethical and regulatory guidelines. In India, where there are strict regulations and serious penalties for non-compliance, metrics pertaining to product knowledge and compliance are crucial for safeguarding the company's reputation and guaranteeing long-term growth.
5. **Territory Management and Market Penetration:** Efficient territory management constitutes a vital performance metric. Medical representatives frequently bear the responsibility of overseeing extensive geographical regions with varied consumer demographics. Metrics in this domain may encompass the representative's proficiency in effectively covering the designated territory; the quantity of new clients secured, the expansion of current accounts, and overall market penetration. In India, where regions exhibit considerable variation in population density, healthcare infrastructure, and market potential, establishing suitable criteria for territory management is crucial for optimizing sales potential.
6. **Cost-Effectiveness and Expense Management:** Alongside sales and customer-related measures, cost-effectiveness is an essential factor in performance assessment. This indicator evaluates the medical representative's proficiency in managing expenses associated with travel, promotional activities, and other sales-related charges. In a price-sensitive market such as India, where margins may be constrained, managing expenses while meeting sales targets is essential for the company's profitability. Metrics in this domain may include travel costs per sales call, return on investment (ROI) for promotional initiatives, and overall expense management.

7. **Feedback from Healthcare Professionals and Market Insights:** Ultimately, the direct input from healthcare professionals and market insights are essential measures for evaluating a medical representative's effectiveness. Feedback might yield qualitative insights regarding the representative's communication abilities, product expertise, and overall efficacy. In India, where market conditions and the healthcare environment are constantly changing, understanding the market insights and feedback is essential for adapting strategies and maintaining competitiveness.

Setting performance metrics in the Indian pharmaceutical sales ecosystem requires a nuanced understanding of the market's complexities and challenges. By establishing clear, relevant, and achievable metrics, companies can ensure that their sales force is aligned with organizational goals and well-positioned to drive growth in a dynamic and competitive environment.

Conducting Performance Reviews

After establishing performance measures, the subsequent stage is to execute regular performance evaluations. Performance evaluations are an essential component of managing the sales force in the Indian pharmaceutical industry. It guarantees that medical representatives (MRs) and other sales professionals remain aligned with their ambitions and effectively contribute to the organization's goals. The performance review process is complex, involving the assessment of established measurements, delivering feedback, and establishing objectives for future performance. In the Indian pharmaceutical sales environment, characterised by regional diversity, regulatory complexities, and market dynamics, effective performance assessments necessitate a structured and sophisticated methodology.

1. **Timing and Frequency of Reviews:** The Indian pharmaceutical industry typically conducts performance evaluations either quarterly or biannually. This cadence facilitates prompt feedback and strategic adjustments, allowing medical representatives to modify their approaches as necessary. The companies frequently synchronize the timing of these evaluations with their sales cycles, product launches, or fiscal quarters. For instance, the company arranges evaluations immediately after a new drug launch to evaluate the effectiveness of initial promotional activities or at the end of a quarter to evaluate overall sales performance. Consistent performance evaluations guarantee that the medical representatives maintain focus and motivation throughout the year.

2. **Evaluation Criteria:** The foundation of any performance review for a pharmaceutical company is the assessment of its medical representative's performance against established metrics. In the Indian pharmaceutical sector, these measures typically encompass sales objectives, prescription generation, customer relationship management, territorial coverage, and compliance with regulatory standards. Each statistic takes into account the unique challenges and opportunities present in the representative's territory. In a competitive metropolitan market, sales targets may be more ambitious, but in rural areas, the focus may be on expanding market reach and developing connections with healthcare professionals (HCPs). Companies must explicitly communicate the evaluation criteria to the medical representatives at the onset of the review period to ensure transparency and fairness.
3. **Self-Assessment:** Self-evaluation is a crucial component of the performance appraisal process in the pharmaceutical companies. It enables the medical representatives to evaluate their work, pinpoint their advantages and disadvantages, and suggest areas for development. This self-reflection is especially significant in the Indian context, where personal accountability and autonomy are crucial for success. Promoting self-assessment among medical representatives cultivates a sense of accountability for their work and can facilitate more substantive discussions during the evaluation process. It also offers management insights into the medical representative's viewpoint, aiding in the customization of feedback and support.
4. **Managerial Feedback:** Managerial feedback is a critical component of the performance review. Area managers, regional managers and zonal managers provide feedback based on their observations, performance data, and input from HCPs and other stakeholders like company appointed stockists or distributors. In India, where hierarchical relationships are often emphasized, the way feedback is delivered can significantly impact the medical representative's motivation and engagement. In general, the feedback needs to be constructive, specific, and focused on helping the medical representative improve. It generally needs to address both the areas where the medical representative excels and those where improvement is needed. Constructive feedback not only helps in correcting deficiencies but also reinforces positive behaviours and achievements, driving continuous improvement.
5. **Goal Setting for the Future:** A key outcome of the performance review process is the setting of goals for the next review period. These goals need to be Specific, Measurable, Achievable, Relevant, and Time-

Bound (SMART). In the Indian pharmaceutical sales ecosystem, goal-setting must consider the dynamic nature of the market, including factors like changing regulations, new product launches, and evolving customer needs. Goals or targets may include increasing market share in a specific or targeted territory, improving customer engagement (Doctors, Chemists and the Stock points), or enhancing product knowledge. By setting clear and challenging goals, the area managers, regional managers or the zonal managers can keep the medical representatives motivated and focused on achieving the desired outcomes.

6. **Addressing Performance Gaps:** Identifying and addressing performance gaps are an essential aspect of the evaluation process. When performance falls short of expectations, it is important to analyse the underlying causes and develop a plan to address them. This may involve providing additional training, re-examining the sales strategy, or making changes in the medical representative's territory or product portfolio. In India, where market conditions can vary widely across regions, being proactive in addressing performance gaps can prevent small issues from escalating into major challenges. Managers need to work closely with medical representatives to develop actionable plans that are realistic and aligned with the company's objectives.
7. **Continuous Improvement and Development:** Performance reviews should be viewed as a chance for continuous progress and development. In the briskly evolving Indian pharmaceutical market, where new products, regulations, and market conditions are constantly emerging, continuous development is essential for long-term success. The review process should not only focus on past performance but also on the representative's potential for growth. This includes identifying avenues for skill development, providing resources for further training, and supporting career progression. By nurturing a culture of continuous improvement, companies can ensure that their sales force remains competitive and capable of meeting the challenges of a dynamic industry.

Conducting performance reviews in the Indian pharmaceutical sales ecosystem requires a structured and thoughtful approach. By focusing on timely evaluations, clear communication, constructive feedback, and continuous improvement, companies can ensure that their medical representatives are equipped to succeed in a complex and competitive market.

Case Studies

Case 1: Harjeet Remedy, an Indian pharmaceutical firm, encountered a significant rivalry in the respiratory drug market with their asthma drug brand, Asthaheal. To secure a position, Harjeet Remedy meticulously recruited seasoned medical representatives with experience in respiratory healthcare domain, emphasizing essential qualities such as scientific acumen and communication abilities. The management assigned these medical representatives specific territories throughout the country, balancing the urban and rural markets for ensuring comprehensive market coverage. A CRM solution enabled the team to keep an uninterrupted connection with Harjeet Remedy's management, allowing for real-time information of competitor brands and Doctor's feedback. Harjeet Remedy implemented a unique incentive program that recognized not only sales achievements but also customer satisfaction and accurate reporting, thereby boosting the team morale. Rajneesh Desai, a medical representative from Sholapur, Maharashtra, utilized his connections with local Doctors to generate many bulk prescriptions for Asthaheal conducting informative presentations on the drug's efficacy. Regular performance evaluations allowed Harjeet Remedy to optimize its approach and reallocate regions as necessary, ensuring the productivity and efficiency of medical representatives. By means of strategic recruitment, effective territory management, and the innovative application of technology, Harjeet Remedy successfully established Asthaheal brand as a preferred option among the doctors, resulting in a growth of significant market share in the launching year. This instance illustrates how a strategic approach to the field sales team can significantly impact pharmaceutical sales in a competitive market.

Case 2: Jyoticare Pharmaceuticals, a leading pharmaceutical firm, recently encountered difficulties in recruiting medical representatives for the introduction of their new cardiovascular drug brand, CardCure. In a competitive market, Jyoticare Pharma pursued an effective recruitment strategy to swiftly identify qualified candidates. The company first launched an open application process, by promoting the information on online platforms and social media, leading towards a rush of applications. This approach fetched applications from varied backgrounds, and the HR staff selected 50 prospective hires based on relevant qualifications and sales experience. Jyoticare Pharma's top managers invited the candidates to a structured personal interview process, where they assessed each candidate's expertise in the cardiovascular sector, their communication and presentation skills, as well as their ability to handle imaginary sales scenarios. Despite this rigorous process, Jyoticare Pharma faced delays in recruiting, thus the shortage of medical representatives grew in the key regions. This led them to enhance their approach by introducing walk-in interviews in urban areas like Mumbai and Delhi. This strategy facilitated rapid access to applicants available for immediate employment. However, Jyoticare Pharma faced challenges with elevated turnover rates among those recruited through walk-in sessions. Jyoticare Pharma concluded that while walk-in interviews addressed immediate staffing requirements, integrating them with more systematic approaches, such as the open application process, provided a more balanced strategy, improving both immediate coverage and long-term retention of medical representatives.

Suggestive Questions from the Chapter

1. What are the fundamental attributes necessary for a skilful medical representative in the Indian pharmaceutical sector?
2. In what ways does territory management enhance the efficiency of the field sales force within the pharmaceutical sector?
3. What are the essential phases in the recruitment process for medical representatives in the Indian pharmaceutical industry?
4. What are the essential steps in the open application-based screening process for recruiting medical representatives in the pharmaceutical companies?
5. What are the drawbacks of the walk-in interview approach for recruiting medical representatives?
6. What advantages does the open application-based screening procedure offer to both the organization and the candidates?
7. In what ways does the initial training of medical representatives at Indian pharmaceutical companies prepare them to effectively interact with doctors and manoeuvre through the industry's regulatory framework?
8. How does continuous professional development (CPD) augment the competencies of medical representatives as they adapt to the dynamic pharmaceutical market and technological innovations?
9. What are the principal strategies for formulating effective incentive schemes in the Indian pharmaceutical sector that align with business objectives, comply with regulations, and encourage sales personnel to attain optimal performance?
10. What strategies can Indian pharmaceutical companies employ to successfully assess the performance of medical representatives through the establishment of suitable performance measures, comprehensive evaluations, and the promotion of on-going enhancement in a diversified and competitive market?

Multiple Choice Questions

1. What is a primary responsibility of the field sales force in the pharmaceutical industry?
   (a) Product distribution
   (b) Direct communication with healthcare professionals
   (c) Manufacturing medicines

(d) Conducting clinical trials

2. Which aspect is essential in managing field sales territories effectively?
   (a) Understanding local prescribing behaviours
   (b) Increasing drug prices
   (c) Decreasing competition
   (d) Reducing the number of territories
3. What is an important factor in motivating the field sales team?
   (a) Free samples
   (b) Incentive programs
   (c) Regular territory changes
   (d) Limited working hours
4. Which technology is commonly used for maintaining coordination with a field sales team?
   (a) CRM systems
   (b) Laboratory tools
   (c) Prescription software
   (d) Inventory management tools
5. In the recruitment of medical representatives, which quality is essential for understanding drug information?
   (a) Scientific and product knowledge
   (b) Physical endurance
   (c) Social media skills
   (d) Artistic creativity
6. What skill is crucial for a medical representative to adapt communication styles for different audiences?
   (a) Marketing knowledge
   (b) Adaptability
   (c) Product expertise
   (d) Communication skills
7. Which process is conducted at the start of the hiring process to outline the job requirements?
   (a) Reference check
   (b) Job analysis and role definition
   (c) On-boarding
   (d) Field visits
8. How do organizations evaluate candidates' responses to real-life scenarios in recruitment?
   (a) Multiple-choice tests
   (b) Role-play exercises
   (c) Group discussions
   (d) Written essays

9. Which of the following is a primary objective of the on-boarding and training program for new medical representatives?
   (a) Assessing technical skills
   (b) Enhancing soft skills and product knowledge
   (c) Conducting background checks
   (d) Developing sales territories

10. In the final step of the recruitment process, candidates usually meet with:
   (a) Department heads
   (b) Regional or national sales managers
   (c) Field agents
   (d) Product development team

11. What is the purpose of an open application-based recruitment process?
   (a) Transparency (b) Cost
   (c) Time-saving (d) Exclusivity

12. What is the main focus of the walk-in interview selection process?
   (a) Efficiency (b) Detail
   (c) Exclusivity (d) Verification

13. What is the main focus of the walk-in interview selection process?
   (a) Efficiency (b) Detail
   (c) Exclusivity (d) Verification

14. What might the job posting for an open application include?
   (a) Company culture (b) Duties
   (c) Salary (d) References

15. What kind of skills does the role-play exercise test in a walk-in interview?
   (a) Interpersonal (b) Communication
   (c) Analytical (d) Sales

16. What disadvantage of walk-in interviews relates to the inability to thoroughly evaluate each candidate?
   (a) Cost (b) Bias
   (c) Limited assessment (d) Availability

17. Which term best describes the feedback candidates receive after final selection in open application screening?
    (a) Constructive (b) General
    (c) Negative (d) Positive
18. What key factor is often missed in walk-in interviews due to limited time with each candidate?
    (a) Sales knowledge (b) Adaptability
    (c) Technical skills (d) Background
19. Which process allows companies to connect with a large candidate pool, including recent graduates?
    (a) Screening (b) Walk-in
    (c) Interview (d) Application
20. Which drawback of walk-in interviews is associated with a higher likelihood of candidates leaving soon after hiring?
    (a) Cultural (b) Training
    (c) Time (d) Attrition
21. What is the primary focus of introductory training programs for medical representatives?
    (a) Cultural Sensitivity (b) Advanced Sales Techniques
    (c) Product Knowledge (d) Leadership Development
22. Which skill is emphasized during Continuous Professional Development (CPD) to enhance digital engagement in the pharmaceutical industry?
    (a) Time Management (b) Regulatory Compliance
    (c) CRM Tools (d) Stress Management
23. What is the primary source of intrinsic motivation?
    (a) Financial Rewards (b) Career Advancement
    (c) Personal Fulfilment (d) Job Security
24. Which of the following is NOT a non-monetary incentive?
    (a) Paid Vacations
    (b) Luxury Goods
    (c) Competitive Pay
    (d) International Travel Opportunities

25. In the context of the Indian pharmaceutical sales ecosystem, which performance metric evaluates a medical representative's ability to manage travel, promotional activities, and other sales-related expenses?

    (a) Sales Targets
    (b) Compliance
    (c) Cost-Effectiveness
    (d) Goal Setting

CHAPTER

8

Pharmaceutical Sales Territory Management

In India, pharmaceutical sales territory management is an essential part of the operational strategy for pharmaceutical companies. It encompasses the strategic planning, distribution, and oversight of sales activities within specified geographic regions to maximize market coverage, ensure effective resource usage, and meet sales objectives. The Indian pharmaceutical market is extensive and varied, making territory management especially difficult but crucial because of the diverse healthcare requirements, economic situations, and regulatory contexts present in different areas.

The process starts with defining sales territories. Sales territories are regions allocated to medical representatives or teams, generally determined by factors like population density, healthcare facilities, and the potential need for pharmaceutical products in the area. Given the significant disparities in healthcare access and needs between rural and urban regions in India, it is crucial to approach the delineation of areas with careful analysis to ensure comprehensive coverage of all potential markets. Urban regions, characterized by their abundance of healthcare facilities and greater purchasing power, may administer healthcare differently than rural areas, which face limited healthcare access and where generic drugs dominate the market over branded drugs.

The next essential phase is territory planning and optimization. This requires coordinating the sales objectives with the unique attributes of each territory. For example, areas with a high concentration of hospitals and specialized medical facilities may need to concentrate on high-end, innovative pharmaceuticals, whereas regions with a notable number of primary healthcare centres might require greater emphasis on essential medicines and generics. Sales managers should enhance territories by taking into account elements such as the quantity of healthcare providers, the competitive environment, and past sales data. In the Indian scenario, where regional languages and cultural aspects significantly influence it, territory planning must consider these factors, ensuring that sales representatives can effectively engage with local healthcare professionals.

Another crucial element of territory management is resource allocation within territories. It encompasses the allocation of sales teams, marketing budgets, and various resources to enhance sales effectiveness. In India, where the pharmaceutical industry is extremely competitive, effective resource allocation can determine success or failure. Companies need to determine how to distribute their most essential asset—their medical representatives—throughout different territories. This requires guaranteeing that each area possesses the appropriate combination of experience, expertise, and local insight to address its specific challenges. For example, a region with a large number of general practitioners might necessitate more representatives skilled in primary care, whereas a region with many specialists may require medical representatives who have extensive knowledge of speciality medications.

Monitoring and adjusting territories is a continuous process in territory management. As market conditions, healthcare policies, and competitive dynamics change, pharmaceutical companies need to consistently track the performance of their regions and modify their strategies as necessary. In India, where shifts in regulations and government policies can greatly affect the pharmaceutical market, it is essential to remain flexible and responsive. Area or Regional managers need to frequently assess sales data, customer feedback, and market trends to pinpoint underperforming territories and implement corrective measures. This could include reallocating territories, redistributing resources, or potentially redefining regions to more effectively correspond with market opportunities.

A challenge in Indian Pharmaceutical Sales Territory Management is managing the workload distribution in the defined sales territories. Due to the geographical vastness and differences in healthcare infrastructure, certain territories may offer more opportunities than others, resulting in imbalances in the workload of medical representatives. A well-structured territory structure ensures that no representative experiences overload or underutilization.

Companies may employ different tools, such as geographic information systems (GIS) and sales analytics software, to visualize regions and evaluate workload distribution. A fair allocation of workload not only boosts productivity but also leads to increased job satisfaction and retention among medical representatives.

A vital component is customer relationship management (CRM) in regions. Establishing and nurturing robust connections with healthcare professionals and organizations is fundamental to successful pharmaceutical sales. Successful territory management necessitates that medical representatives not only achieve their sales goals but also build trust and loyalty with their clients. In the Indian market, where personal connections and trust are essential, CRM strategies should be thoroughly woven into territory management practices. This could include frequent visits, prompt follow-ups, and a tailored approach to meeting the needs and concerns of healthcare practitioners.

Ultimately, sales reporting and feedback mechanisms play a crucial role in successful territory management. Medical representatives must consistently update their managers on their activities, sales numbers, and market insights. This data is essential for evaluating the performance of regions and making informed choices regarding future strategies. In India, where the market is quickly changing, prompt and precise sales reporting is crucial for remaining competitive. Input from the field helps companies grasp market dynamics, recognize emerging trends, and modify their territory management strategies to remain competitive.

Defining Sales Territories

In the competitive scenario of the Indian pharmaceutical industry, the strategic demarcation of sales territories is crucial for achieving effective market penetration and enhancing salesforce competence. The country like India covers a large area, has a diverse population, and has different healthcare requirements in different regions. It is because of this factor, demarcating the sales territories requires careful planning and a deep understanding of both the market potential and the sales force's skills. The central of this initiative is the even-handed distribution of responsibilities, ensuring that each medical representative is neither overburdened nor under-used; thereby creating an environment that facilitates the attainment of organizational goals.

Defining Sales Territories

In the Indian pharmaceutical sales scenario, delineating sales territories is an essential procedure that directly impacts the efficacy and productivity of the sales team. A medical representative or sales pool team is designated with a sales territory as a specific geographic region for the purpose of promoting and selling the pharmaceutical products. The main aim of outlining these regions is to guarantee optimal market coverage, enhance sales potential, and encourage healthy relationships with healthcare professionals.

Defining the sales territory requires a comprehensive review of various criteria, including the geographic distribution of healthcare facilities, the concentration of potential customers such as physicians, clinics, and hospitals, and the historical sales data of the region. In India, where healthcare infrastructure differs strikingly between urban, semi-urban, and rural areas, it is crucial to customize territories to correspond with the distinct attributes of each location.

Urban regions, characterized by a dense aggregation of healthcare providers, frequently necessitate a smaller yet more specialized sales territory. Medical representatives in these regions must sustain regular communication with numerous physicians and chemists, necessitating the management of territory size. Conversely, semi-urban and rural regions may require larger spaces due to the limited allocation of healthcare resources. In these areas, the difficulty resides in traversing extensive distances while guaranteeing regular visits to essential clients.

Another essential element of delineating sales areas comprehends the market potential within each territory. This entails evaluating the demand for diverse pharmaceutical items, the prescribing behaviours of the doctors, and the competitive environment. In a country like India, it is characterized by a fragmented pharmaceutical industry with several local, regional and global competitors, it is essential to strategically allot territories to optimize the sales force's strengths and enhance market penetration.

The cultural and linguistic variety throughout many regions of India requires a nuanced approach to defining territory. Medical representatives must have knowledge of the local language, culture, and preferences to connect effectively with healthcare providers and establish trust. This is especially crucial in rural regions, where comprehension of local dialects and cultural norms can greatly influence the efficacy of sales initiatives.

Pharmaceutical companies frequently utilize advanced tools and technology, such as geographic information systems (GIS) and customer relationship management (CRM) software, to delineate sales regions efficiently. These technologies allow companies to accurately delineate regions, considering elements such as population density, healthcare infrastructure, and transportation networks. Utilizing data and technology, organizations can establish equitable and effective sales regions that enhance coverage while minimizing the potential for overlaps or market gaps.

Balancing Workloads

Equitably distributing workloads within the sales areas is essential towards enabling the medical representatives to execute their responsibilities efficiently without excessive strain. This is especially, when the territory is demarcated as a pool sales territory. An uneven workload may result in fatigue, diminished productivity, and ultimately, adverse effects on sales success. In the Indian pharmaceutical sector, where the sales force is pivotal in generating income, it is imperative to maintain a balanced workload for ensuring long-term success.

A key factor in workload balance is the number of healthcare professionals, retail outlets and stockists in a specific area. A region with a large concentration of physicians and pharmacies may necessitate more frequent visits and follow-ups, thereby increasing the work load for the medical representative. In contrast, a region with a limited number of healthcare professionals may necessitate increased travel time between doctor visits, thus augmenting the overall burden. In both instances, it is crucial to guarantee that the workload remains manageable and that the medical representative has sufficient time to cultivate healthy relationships with essential customers.

The complexity of the products under marketing is another factor to take into account. Some pharmaceutical molecules (drugs) may necessitate extensive knowledge and regular discussion with physicians to generate appropriate prescriptions. In such instances, the workload may increase, necessitating an adjustment in territory size. A medical representative pushing specialized items, such as oncology drugs, may necessitate a smaller territory to concentrate on a specific set of oncologists, facilitating more in-depth discussions and support.

In the Indian scenario, the heterogeneity of healthcare infrastructure contributes to the equilibrium of workload distribution. Urban areas may necessitate more regular consultations with several doctors, while rural regions may entail extended travel durations between healthcare establishments. It is essential to balance these aspects to ensure that medical representatives can adequately cover their areas while maintaining the quality of their contacts with healthcare providers.

Pharmaceutical companies frequently employ diverse criteria to evaluate and equilibrate workloads across sales territories. These variables may encompass the quantity of healthcare experts, the frequency of required visits, the travel distance between clients, and the past sales success of the region. By assessing these criteria, companies may distribute resources more efficiently and guarantee that each medical representative has a job that is demanding but feasible.

An alternative method for workload balance is pool selling, wherein numerous medical representatives cooperate to encompass a broader territory. This strategy is especially efficacious in places with substantial sales potential or in locales where the workload exceeds the capacity of a single medical representative. Delegating responsibilities allows medical representatives to concentrate on their strengths, enhancing their assistance for healthcare professionals and resulting in superior sales success.

Workload balancing necessitates continuous monitoring and modifications. As market situation progresses by including the launch of new products, alterations in healthcare infrastructure, or modifications in customer preferences, it may be imperative to recalibrate areas and redistribute workloads. Consistent performance evaluations and feedback from medical professionals are also crucial for spotting possible problems and implementing appropriate modifications to maintain balanced workloads.

Example from the Indian Context

An example from the Indian scenario, exemplifies the significance of defining sales territories and equilibrating workloads. A prominent pharmaceutical firm in India, faced problems related to diminishing sales in the eastern region. It conducted a comprehensive study of its sales territories and discovered that specific urban areas in Kolkata were overcrowded with excess medical representatives, resulting in redundant visits and inefficient use of resources. At the same time, medical representatives were unable to travel the long distances required to reach all potential clients, leading to inadequate supply in several rural territories in West Bengal.

The company thus executed a territory realignment strategy—reallocating regions for medical representatives to guarantee a balanced workload in accordance with market potential and travel aspects. The company implemented a tiered strategy, assigning seasoned medical representatives with smaller, concentrated territories to high-potential urban regions. On the other hand, teams equipped with enhanced logistical support, such as company-provided vehicles and digital tools for remote communication with healthcare professionals, were asked to manage the rural territories covered by the company.

This restructuring enhanced the effectiveness of the sales team and resulted in a substantial improvement in market coverage and sales performance in the region. The company achieved a more equitable and efficient sales approach by ensuring each medical representative had a feasible task that adequately addressed all prospective customers.

Establishing sales territory and distributing workloads are essential elements of the sales strategy within the Indian pharmaceutical sector. Through a meticulous analysis of regional, demographic, and market variables, pharmaceutical companies may establish efficient and successful sales territories that enhance coverage and maximize sales potential. Equitably distributing workloads throughout different regions enables medical representatives to execute their responsibilities efficiently, cultivate healthy relationships with healthcare professionals, and enhance the company's overall success. As the Indian pharmaceutical industry evolves, the significance of strategic territory management and workload balancing will increase, necessitating that enterprises invest in the tools, technologies, and procedures that facilitate these goals.

Sales Territory Planning

The foundation for efficient market coverage, resource optimisation, sales territory planning etc. is an essential part of the Indian pharmaceutical sales ecosystem. For this, the pharmaceutical companies can increase their sales potential, enhance customer relationship, and accomplish corporate targets by strategically dividing geographic regions into manageable areas. Successful sales territory planning requires careful consideration of factors such as market dynamics, consumer demographics, and the competitive environment. It is important for the companies to focus on the main facets of sales territory planning, emphasizing the importance of goal-setting and resource allocation.

Setting Objectives and Goals

The first and most important step in sales territory planning in the Indian pharmaceutical business is establishing specific objectives and goals. For the sales team, objectives act as a roadmap and source of guidance, ensuring that all activities are in line with the central business strategy. Well-defined objectives aid in negotiating the difficulties of a diverse and rapid changing market such as India, where regional differences in healthcare facilities, medical practices, consumer behaviour are very much prominent and influential for the market.

1. **Market Penetration and Expansion:** Market penetration is one of the main goals of sales territory planning. Reaching new customers and strengthening ties with current ones are two ways pharmaceutical companies want to grow their market share. Setting clear objectives is

essential for market penetration in India's rural and semi urban territories, which are increasingly significant marketplaces. This is because these rural and semi urban territories could lead to significant growth in sales and subsequently in the company's market share. For instance, a company may set a goal to increase its presence in tier-2 and tier-3 cities by 20% over the next year, with a focus on promoting generic drugs that are more affordable to the local population.

2. **Customer Segmentation:** Effective customer segmentation is another crucial objective in the process of sales territory planning for the pharmaceutical companies. The customers of the Indian pharmaceutical market include small retail pharmacies, individual practitioners, and major hospitals and clinics etc. Companies can customize their sales strategies to each customer segment's specific requirements by segmenting their customers into customer segments according to factors like size, purchasing power, and medical specialties etc. For instance, a company may decide to target cardiologists in urban areas with a new line of cardiovascular molecules (drugs), while concentrating on general practitioners in rural areas with a wider selection of critical medications.

3. **Sales Volume and Revenue Targets:** Establishing revenue and sales volume target is essential for coordinating the sales force's activities with the company's financial objectives. These targets must be reasonable, achievable, and in line with the potential of the market. In India's aggressively competitive pharmaceutical industry, establishing a challenging but reachable goal can stimulate the sales force and improve output. For instance, it may not be difficult to say that, by starting launching promotional campaigns and providing discounts to high volume customers, a company may target to boost sales volume in a particular territory by 15%.

4. **Enhancing Brand Awareness:** Increasing brand awareness among the healthcare professionals, patients as well as that of the medicine retailers is an important target for all pharmaceutical companies operating in a country with a diverse market like India. Pharmaceutical companies frequently try to establish objectives to raise awareness of their products among doctors, medicine retailers and even in patients. This can be achieved through targeted marketing campaigns, sponsorship of medical conferences, and partnerships with key opinion leaders (KOLs). For example, a company may decide to use a mix of digital marketing and in-person contacts with the doctors to raise the brand awareness of its new antibiotic in a specific region by 30% over the next six months.

5. **Customer Satisfaction and Retention:** Long-term success in the pharmaceutical sector depends heavily on maintaining and increasing customer happiness. Establishing objectives to raise customer satisfaction might result in more repeat business and loyalty. In India, where trust and personal ties are frequently the foundation of relationships with healthcare professionals, setting goals to improve customer engagement through frequent follow-ups and individualized services can have a big impact on sales results. For instance, by introducing a feedback system and quickly resolving any customer related issues, a company may set a target to raise customer satisfaction ratings in a particular territory by 10%.

Resource Allocation

The next important stage in the sales territory planning is resource allocation. Following the establishment of objectives and goals, effective resource allocation is essential towards achieving them. In the Indian pharmaceutical sales ecosystem, where resources are frequently limited, effective resource allocation could make the difference between success and failure. Allocating resources includes figuring out how to deploy the sales force, setting aside money for marketing and promotional initiatives, and making sure that the necessary tools and technology are available.

1. **Sales Force Deployment:** One important factor in allocating resources is the sales force's deployment. Assigning the right medical representatives to the right territories is essential in India, a country with a wide range of demographic and geographic diversity. To establish trusting relationships with customers, medical representatives should be conversant with the local language, customs, and healthcare environment. With the help of regional sales managers, a pharmaceutical company may, for instance, assign more experienced medical representatives in the high-potential metropolitan territories while putting younger team members in less competitive rural or semi urban territories.
2. **Budgeting for Marketing and Promotional Activities:** Achieving the goals established during the planning phase requires marketing and promotional activities. Companies in general carefully manage their marketing budgets to maximize their impact in the highly competitive Indian pharmaceutical market. This could entail concentrating on traditional marketing strategies, such as medical camps and health awareness campaigns, in rural and semi urban territories, simultaneously focussing on digital marketing expenditures as a priority in urban and metropolitan territories with high internet usage. For

instance, a company may decide to spend more of its budget in promoting a new drug in metropolitan cities because there are possibilities more doctors of those territories who can prescribe it.

3. **Technology and Tools:** The Indian pharmaceutical sales ecosystem is becoming more and more dependent on the use of tools and technology. To increase productivity and streamline their sales processes, companies are investing in mobile applications, data analytics tools, and customer relationship management (CRM) systems. These technologies are also planned to ensure salespeople have the resources they need to succeed. To make data-driven decisions, a company can, for instance, invest in a CRM system that can let its medical representatives monitor their customer interactions and sales performance in real time.
4. **Training and Development:** Allocating funds for the sales force's training and development is vital towards reaching the goals. Continuous training is required to keep sales personnel abreast of the newest products, laws, and market trends in India, where the pharmaceutical sector is extremely active. Companies in general, partially fund regular training sessions, workshops, and seminars. For example, to ensure that the sales team is prepared to interact with the practicing healthcare professionals in an effective manner, the company could, arrange quarterly training sessions focussing on the introduction of new product launches and therapeutic areas.
5. **Monitoring and Evaluation:** The allocation of resources may include provisions for monitoring and evaluation. This entails allocating funds for frequent evaluations of market conditions, customer feedback, and sales performance. Regular monitoring enables companies to make necessary adjustments to their plans and resource allocation in the Indian pharmaceutical sales ecosystem, where the market conditions can change rapidly. For instance, a company may allocate funds for monthly performance evaluations, where the area managers, regional managers or even the zonal managers assess the achievement of goals and adjust the sales territory strategy accordingly.

In the Indian pharmaceutical sales ecosystem, sales territory planning is a complicated and multidimensional process that calls for careful consideration of a number of variables. Companies may give their sales teams direction and make ensure that all efforts are in line with the principal corporate strategy by establishing defined objectives and targets. On the other hand, resource allocation is vital towards guaranteeing that the money, staff, and equipment required to accomplish these goals are available. Effective sales territory planning can result in notable enhancements in market penetration, customer satisfaction, and overall sales success in a market as diverse and competitive as India. Pharmaceutical companies can successfully negotiate the intricacies of the Indian market and attain continued success by means of strategic planning and effective resource allocation.

Performance Management and Evaluation

Performance management and evaluation are essential elements in the Indian pharmaceutical sales ecosystem. These methods guarantee that the sales force's endeavours are consistent with organizational objectives, fostering growth, competitiveness, and customer happiness. The pharmaceutical industry's dynamic nature, marked by swift innovation, stringent regulations, and fierce competition, requires a comprehensive framework for performance management and evaluation. This approach centres on two fundamental components: establishing performance objectives and determining key performance indicators (KPIs).

Setting Performance Targets

Establishing performance objectives is the initial and arguably the most vital phase in performance management. In the context of Indian pharmaceutical sales, these targets must be pragmatic, precise, and consistent with overarching company goals. Targets frequently include multiple facets of sales operations, such as sales volume, market share, product launches, and the establishment of strong relationship with healthcare professionals (HCPs).

1. **Sales Volume Targets:** Sales volume targets are very much essential in the pharmaceutical sector. These targets generally concentrate on the quantity of units sold, revenue generated, or market share obtained within a chosen span of time. In India pharmaceutical scenario is characterized by a complex and segmented market, establishing the sale volume targets necessitates a comprehensive analysis of regional market potential, an evaluation of the competitive environment, and also an assessment of the purchasing power along with the preferences of distinct customer segments. For example, a pharmaceutical company may aim to increase sales volume by 10% in the rural territories. This is because gradually the healthcare convenience is improving in those areas due to various governmental initiatives.
2. **Product-Specific Targets:** In addition to the total sales volume targets, product-specific targets are regularly set, especially when launching new drugs or promoting key therapeutic areas. The Indian pharmaceutical market is identified for its generic drug production, but there is also a noteworthy emphasis on branded generics and specialty drugs. Setting targets for these products includes measuring the

potential acceptance among healthcare providers, medicine retailers and patients, understanding the competitive products in the market, and identifying the most actual promotional approaches. For example, a target could be to achieve a 15% market share within six months of launching a new cardiovascular drug.

3. **Market Penetration and Expansion Targets:** Intensifying into new territories or increasing penetration in present markets is another critical target-setting area. The Indian pharmaceutical market's diversity, ranging from urban metropolises to remote rural territories, needs tailor-made strategies. Setting targets for market penetration includes identifying potential growth areas, knowledge of local healthcare dynamics, and deploying a suitable sales force. For instance, a pharmaceutical company may set a target to enter five new Tier-2 cities within a year or increase its presence in the rural markets by 20% by improving its distribution network and sales force deployment.
4. **Relationship Management Targets:** Considering the significance of relationship with the healthcare professionals in the pharmaceutical sales ecosystem, establishing targets related to relationship management is essential. These targets may include the number of consultations with doctors, the consistency of follow-up appointments, or the engagement level in medical conferences and conferences. In the Indian pharmaceutical marketing context, where personal connections are crucial in business, establishing these targets ensures that the sales team remains focussed on building and nurturing relationships that foster long term business success.
5. **Compliance and Ethical Targets:** In an industry, heavily regulated by the governmental policies and ethical standards, sales targets related to compliance are indispensable. These targets might comprise - following the Medical Council of India's rules on interactions with doctors, ensuring that all promotional activities are transparent, and avoiding any practices that might be considered unethical. Setting such targets is particularly important in India, where the pharmaceutical industry has faced scrutiny regarding the ethical conduct of its sales and promotional practices.

Key Performance Indicators (KPIs)

Key Performance Indicators (KPIs) are measurements employed to assess the success of objectives established during the performance management process. The Indian pharmaceutical sales sector requires meticulous selection of KPIs to accurately reflect the unique challenges and opportunities of the industry.

1. **Sales Growth:** Sales growth is a major KPI, indicating the rise in sales volume or revenue over certain duration. This KPI is especially relevant in a market like India, where substantial development potential exists due to variables such as higher healthcare access, increased income levels, and an escalating population. Monitoring sales growth enables pharmaceutical companies to evaluate the effectiveness of their sales strategies and the performance of their sales personnel. For instance, a 12% year-on-year sales growth may serve as a KPI reflecting effective market penetration and consumer engagement.
2. **Market Share:** Market share is another serious KPI, indicating the percentage of total sales in the market that a company controls. In the competitive Indian pharmaceutical market, maintaining or increasing market share, is often a key objective. This KPI supports companies to identify their position relative to their competitors and evaluate the efficiency of their sales and marketing efforts. For example, attaining a 25% market share in a specific therapeutic category could be a KPI that signifies the supremacy in that segment.
3. **Doctor Coverage and Engagement:** In the pharmaceutical sector, key performance indicators such as doctor coverage, which refers to the number of doctors reached by the sales team, and engagement levels, are vital. These indicators hold particular significance in India, where doctors' recommendations greatly impact prescription trends. Key Performance Indicators (KPIs) may include the number of new doctors included into the network, the frequency of doctor visits, or the extent of engagement through continuous medical education (CME) programs and additional activities. Monitoring these KPIs ensures that the sales team effectively promotes and maintains relationships with key healthcare providers.
4. **Prescription Volume:** The number of prescriptions generated by the doctors due to sales efforts serves as a direct measure of a medical representative's effectiveness. This KPI is particularly significant in the Indian pharmaceutical sales context, where prescriptions predominantly influence pharmaceutical sales. By monitoring prescription volumes, organizations can assess the efficacy of their product marketing strategies and pinpoint areas requiring further support or training for the sales team.
5. **Distribution Reach:** Due to India's extensive and varied terrain, delivering products to the target customer presents a significant difficulty. Key performance indicators relating to distribution reach include the number of newly appointed distribution channels, the extent of geographical coverage reached, and the time required to introduce

products to the market. These KPIs are vital for measuring the effectiveness of a company's supply chain and ensuring the availability of products at required locations.

6. **Compliance Adherence:** Adherence to regulatory and ethical standards is a vital KPI in the pharmaceutical sector. In India, where the regulatory scenario is growing increasingly challenging, compliance with rules is very vital for protecting a company's reputation and avoiding legal hurdles. Key Performance Indicators in this sphere may include the number of compliance training sessions conducted, the percentage of sales activities that are aligned to the ethical standards, and the incidence of compliance breaches.
7. **Customer Satisfaction:** Customer satisfaction, however often ignored, is an important KPI in the pharmaceutical industry. This measure might include responses from the healthcare providers, patients, and also the distribution partners. In India, where trust and relationships are supreme, safeguarding high levels of customer satisfaction is indispensable for long-term success. KPIs in this area might comprise the net promoter score (NPS), the rate of repeat business from the healthcare providers, or the feedback received during regular customer communications.
8. **Cost Efficiency:** Cost management while achieving sales objectives is another important KPI. This measure may include the cost per visit, the return on investment (ROI) from marketing activities, or the total sales spending in relative to the generated revenue. In a price-sensitive market such as India, where profit margins may be minimal, monitoring cost effectiveness is essential for sustaining profitability.
9. **Training and Development:** Continuing training and development of the sales team are crucial for sustaining a competitive advantage in the pharmaceutical sector. Key Performance Indicators (KPIs) in this domain may include the number of training sessions participated in, the improvement of sales performance after the training, and the attainment of new skills or certifications. In India, where the pharmaceutical market is rapidly progressing, it is essential to ensure that the sales team is well prepared to handle evolving difficulties for continual accomplishment.

Performance Appraisal Methods

In the Indian pharmaceutical industry, performance appraisal is an important tool for handling and assessing the efficiency of medical representatives and the total sales force. The appraisal process includes measuring an individual's performance against predefined metrics, recognizing areas of development, and identifying successes. Numerous procedures are engaged to appraise the performance of the sales personnel, each with its own set of advantages and drawbacks.

1. **Management by Objectives (MBO):** A prevalent performance appraisal tool in the pharmaceutical sales sector is Management by Objectives (MBO). This approach involves setting specific, measurable, achievable, relevant, and time-bound (SMART) objectives for each medical representative. The companies subsequently measure the performance based on the degree of success of these objectives. In the Indian context, MBO is notably beneficial, since it simplifies clear communication of expectations and matches the individual ambitions with organizational goals. A medical representative's objectives may include securing a predetermined number of prescriptions from the doctors or fulfilling sales targets for specific products. The MBO technique promotes a results-driven strategy, essential in the aggressively competitive pharmaceutical industry.
2. **360-Degree Feedback:** Another appraisal method gaining popularity in the Indian pharmaceutical industry is the 360-degree feedback method. This method includes gathering feedback from multiple sources, including peers, supervisors, subordinates, and even the customers. The inclusive nature of this feedback delivers a all-inclusive opinion about the medical representative's performance, comprising of their interpersonal skills, teamwork, and customer relationships. In India, where relationship-building is a vital feature of pharmaceutical sales, the 360-degree feedback provides valuable insights into a representative's capability to engage with the healthcare professionals and other stakeholders. However, applying this method requires cautious management to guarantee that the feedback is productive and impartial.
3. **Behaviourally Anchored Rating Scales (BARS):** BARS method is another performance appraisal technique implemented in the pharmaceutical sales ecosystem. It combines the basics of traditional rating scale and the critical incident technique. Detailed behaviours related with diverse performance levels are recognized, and sales personnel are assessed based on these behaviours. For example, in the Indian pharmaceutical context, behaviours such as punctuality in doctor visits, observance towards ethical sales practices, and effective product presentations might be rated. BARS method delivers a clear and

objective assessment of performance, making it easier to detect areas for upgrading and provide targeted feedback.

4. **Sales Performance Metrics:** Along with qualitative procedures, quantitative sales performance measurements are also essential in the appraisal process. The performances of the medical representatives in India are generally measured by certain indicators such as the volume of doctor visits conducted, the conversion rate of doctor visits to real prescriptions, and the achievement of sales targets. These indicators offer a definitive and impartial assessment of a representative's effectiveness in generating revenue and impacting doctors' prescribing practices. In the competitive Indian pharmaceutical sales market, where market dynamics are always changing, sales performance indicators provide a dependable method for evaluating and controlling the sales team.
5. **Self-Appraisal:** Boosting self-appraisal among medical representatives is also an important aspect of performance management in the Indian pharmaceutical industry. Self-appraisal permits the medical representatives to reflect on their own performance, identify their strengths and weaknesses, and set personal development targets. This method encourages a culture of self-improvement and accountability, which is vital in today's dynamic and demanding environment of the pharmaceutical sales. In India, where individual initiative and self-motivation are greatly appreciated, self-appraisal can be an actual tool for promoting professional growth and improving overall performance.

Sales Budget Preparation

The preparation of a sales budget is a crucial element of performance management and assessment within the Indian pharmaceutical sales landscape. The sales budget defines the expected sales revenue and related expenditures for a chosen timeframe. The sales budge also functions as a financial guide for the sales team. An effective sales budget preparation requires thorough planning, forecasting, as well as a detailed resource allocation proposal to ensure the achievement of sales targets without going beyond the budget. There are various areas of the sales budgeting to be focused upon.

1. **Sales Forecasting:** The initial phase of sales budget formulation involves projecting sales for the forthcoming period. This involves measuring the past sales data, market trends, and competitive dynamics to project expected sales revenue. Sales forecasting in the Indian pharmaceutical sector is notably difficult due to the diverse and swiftly evolving market dynamics. Factors like seasonal fluctuations in disease

occurrence, the launch of new drugs in the market, and alterations in regulatory rules can greatly influence the drug sales. Therefore, sales forecasting in India requires a reflective understanding of market dynamics and the capacity to predict variations in the demand. Detailed sales forecasting is essential for developing the attainable sales targets and ensuring that the budget relates with the organization's financial goals.

2. **Cost Estimation:** After establishing the sales forecast, the next step is to estimate the expenditures associated with achieving the sales targets. The expenses include salary and incentives for the sales team, travel and lodging expenses, promotional activities, and product sampling costs. In the Indian pharmaceutical marketing scenario, the cost estimation must account for the varied geographical territory and the fluctuating expenses across different locations. The expense of marketing pharmaceutical products in big cities such as Mumbai or Delhi may be considerably greater than in semi urban or rural regions. Consequently, region-specific cost estimation is also vital for the detailed sales budget preparation in India. Furthermore, organizations must consider any differences in expenses resulting from economic changes, such as inflation or currency exchange rates.
3. **Resource Allocation:** Effective sales budget preparation necessitates the strategic allocation of resources to optimize the sales outcomes. This includes measuring the budget allocation for various promotional activities, including doctor visits, medical conferences, drug sampling, promotional materials and even for online campaigns. In a highly competitive pharmaceutical market like India, companies must strategically invest resources to effectively engage and influence the important healthcare professionals. Investing in digital marketing may be more efficacious for targeting tech-savvy doctors in urban areas, while conventional tactics, such as medical conferences, may be more appropriate for engaging doctors in rural areas. Strategic resource allocation is vital for enhancing sales performance and guaranteeing optimal budget utilization.
4. **Monitoring and Control:** Once the sales budget is prepared, it becomes essential to regularly compare the actual sales and expenses towards the budget. This allows companies to detect any sort of inconsistencies and thereby implement corrective measures if required. In the Indian pharmaceutical sales scenario, where market conditions can fluctuate rapidly, consistent oversight and management of the sales budget are essential for maintaining alignment and attaining sales objectives. Organizations must implement comprehensive systems to

monitor sales performance and expenditures in real time, facilitating prompt budgetary modifications as necessary. If sales in a specific location fall below expectations, the companies may need to reallocate resources or modify its promotional techniques to enhance sales.

5. **Incentive Planning:** The sales budget is crucial in devising incentives for the sales team. Incentives serve as a powerful motivator for the medical representatives and can evidently influence their performances. The Indian pharmaceutical sector is characterized by aggressive rivalry for sales personnel. So it becomes essential for companies to create attractive incentive schemes to retain the top performers and encourage higher productivity levels. The sales budget must incorporate these incentives, ensuring alignment with the company's financial objectives and sales targets. Incentive planning is nothing but a process of establishing a clear and achievable target for the medical representatives, ensuring their motivation to surpass the company sales targets.
6. **Collaborative Budgeting:** The formulation of the sales budget within the Indian pharmaceutical sales framework frequently requires collaboration among different departments, including sales, marketing, finance, and supply chain. This collaborative method guarantees that the sales budget is detailed and reflects all relevant elements, including product availability, marketing initiatives, and financial limitations etc. In India, where the pharmaceutical market is intricate and varied, the pharmaceutical industry requires cross-functional collaboration for efficient sales budget preparation. It enables companies to utilize the expertise of several departments to develop a realistic and attainable sales budget that aligns with the organization's broad business objectives.

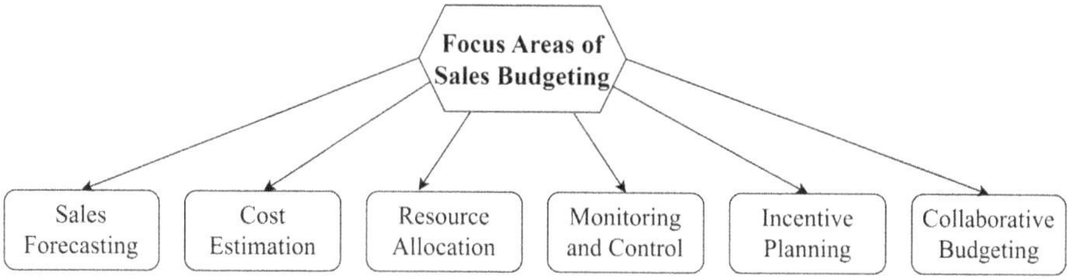

Fig. 8.1 Focus Areas of Sales Budgeting.

Performance management and evaluation within the Indian pharmaceutical sales sector include a blend of rigorous appraisal techniques and careful sales budget preparation. Establishing clear, realistic, and related performance objectives is vital for directing the sales team toward achieving organizational goals. Simultaneously, establishing and monitoring pertinent KPIs produces essential insights for measuring progress, facilitating informed decision-making, and continually enhancing performance. By concentrating on these elements, pharmaceutical companies in India may guarantee their competitiveness, compliance, and responsiveness to market demands.

Territory Optimization

Territory optimization is an essential component of pharmaceutical sales management, especially in a multifaceted and diverse market like India. The widespread geographical spread, wide-ranging healthcare requirements, and multitude of stakeholders in the pharmaceutical sector require that, companies effectively optimize their sales territories. This process entails the strategic alignment of sales resources with market potential to maximize sales effectiveness, minimize expenses, and improve customer satisfaction. In the Indian environment, which is characterized by significant regional inconsistencies in healthcare facilities, illness prevalence, and economic conditions, territorial optimization is not merely a tactical endeavour but a strategic imperative. Two key components of territory optimization are the use of technology and the continuous monitoring and adjusting of plans.

Use of Technology in Territory Optimization

The emergence of technology has transformed the way pharmaceutical companies optimize territories in India. Data-driven methodologies have predominantly replaced orthodox management techniques, which heavily relied on intuition and manual mapping. Today the pharmaceutical companies utilize Geographic Information Systems (GIS) and customer relationship management (CRM) systems to precisely map territories, taking into account the population density, the healthcare infrastructure, and also the disease prevalence.

Pharmaceutical companies can identify places with significant market potential and underserved areas by using the GIS technology to visualise the data geographically. For example, a pharmaceutical company looking forward to promote a new diabetic drug can use the GIS to identify territories with high diabetes prevalence and then it can strategically focus its efforts in those territories. Furthermore, GIS expedites understanding of the competitive environment, allowing the companies to use resources strategically to minimize the overlap with competitors and maximize coverage of the potential customers.

CRM systems offer a central platform for managing customer data, monitoring interactions, and also assessing the sales trends. In the Indian pharmaceutical sales scenario, the relationship between the medical representatives (MRs) and healthcare professionals (HCPs) is vital, where the CRM tools play a role in improving the territory management. Through the exploration of CRM system data, the companies can identify trends in doctor's prescribing behaviour, customize the company's sales strategies towards the concerned healthcare professionals, and thereby optimize the allocation of their medical representatives across various territories.

The integration of artificial intelligence (AI) and machine learning (ML) into these technologies has significantly improved their functionalities. AI-driven analytics can forecast sales trends, improve route optimization for medical representatives, and even suggest the best times to visit specific doctors based on historical data. Machine learning algorithms can perpetually learn from sales data, enhancing the accuracy of territory planning over the time. An AI system can analyse historical sales data to predict which territories will likely to show an increase in demand for specific pharmaceutical products during specific seasons or in response to emerging health trends.

Furthermore, mobile technology also has significantly contributed towards territory optimization. Mobile applications custom-made for pharmaceutical sales teams, allows the medical representatives to obtain real-time data regarding their territories, monitor their daily activities, and document their interactions with healthcare professionals. This enhances the effectiveness of the medical representatives and that the data collected from the field is immediately available for analysis and decision-making. In a country as extensive and diverse as India, where medical representatives frequently travel extensive and diverse territories, mobile technology ensures their continuous connectivity and access to information, regardless of their locations.

Monitoring and Adjusting Plans

Territory optimization is an on-going process that requires constant monitoring and adaptation towards market fluctuations, healthcare dynamics, and internal corporate strategies. In the volatile Indian pharmaceutical industry, where regulatory changes, competitive manoeuvres, and fluctuations in healthcare demand are prevalent, the continuous monitoring and adaptability are very much essential for a long-term success.

A vital element of monitoring is assessing the performance of the sales territory. This involves analysing sales data to determine whether the current territorial alignment aligns with the company's objectives. Companies consistently evaluate key performance indicators (KPIs) such as sales growth, market share, and customer reach to identify underperforming territories or those with an untapped potential. If a territory has a decrease in sales despite considerable market potential, it may suggest that the existing allocation of medical representatives or resources are inadequate, requiring a quick review and reallocation.

The significance of technology in monitoring is very much extensive. Advanced analytics tools offer real-time insights into territory performance, allowing sales managers to make quick and informed decisions. Dashboards that highlight essential indicators, like sales data, customer engagement rates, and medical representative performance, facilitate the quick finding of issues. For example, if a specific territory experiences a rapid decline in sales, the system can notify the management team, enabling them to examine the cause and implement corrective measures, such as increasing medical representative visits or initiating focused marketing campaigns.

Moreover, consistent feedback from medical representatives in the field is essential for evaluating and adjusting territory strategies. The Medical Representatives the first to observe market changes, like the entry of new competitors, changes in doctor's preferences, or the emergence of health concerns within their sales territories. By creating a feedback mechanism for medical representatives to communicate their views, companies can anticipate market fluctuations and adjust their strategies accordingly. In the Indian context, where local knowledge and relationships are essential, the market insights from medical representatives can be very beneficial in readjusting territorial sales strategies.

Redistributing tasks among medical representatives may also be necessary when adjusting territory strategies. In certain instances, specific territories may become very large or complex for a single medical representative to manage efficiently, resulting in burnout and reduced performance.

Conversely, certain regions may be over resourced, leading to under performances. Companies can ensure that each medical representative is assigned a manageable and productive territory by consistently evaluating the workload distribution. This not only enhances sales effectiveness but also increases job satisfaction among the medical representatives, thereby decreasing turnover and developing a more stable and motivated sales force.

The process of modifying plans also involves route optimization. As situations evolve within a territory, the optimal routes for medical representative visits may also change. For example, the establishment of new healthcare facilities or the modification of existing ones,' might shift their priorities, necessitating changes in visit schedules. Route optimization software, frequently coupled with CRM and GIS systems, can dynamically modify medical representatives' routes utilizing real-time data, thereby maximizing their engagement time with HCPs while minimizing travel duration. In a country such as India, where traffic congestion and extensive travel distances create considerable hurdles, effective route planning can significantly improve the efficiency of the sales team.

Furthermore, the regular reassessment of territorial boundaries is essential to accommodate long-term market growths. Population growth, urbanization, variations in disease patterns, and transformations in healthcare infrastructure can all impact the optimal alignment of sales territories. In India, where changes can be rapid and important, a pharmaceutical company frequently reassesses and, if required, redefines their territorial boundaries to retain the market alignment with market opportunities.

Territory optimization within the Indian pharmaceutical sales ecosystem is a dynamic process requiring the combination of advanced technologies and on-going monitoring and adjustment. The use of GIS, CRM, AI, and mobile technology has enabled companies to optimize their territories with greater precision and efficiency, while on-going monitoring and the ability to adjust plans ensure that they remain responsive to the ever-changing market environment. By embracing these practices, pharmaceutical companies can maximize their sales potential, enhance customer satisfaction, and maintain a competitive edge in the diverse and challenging Indian market.

Case Studies

Case 1: A leading pharmaceutical company in India encountered difficulties in managing workloads and attaining adequate sales coverage throughout its territories in West Bengal. The Kolkata market was over allotted with medical representatives resulting in unnecessary doctor visits, while large territories with limited resources in the rest of the rural and semi urban territories remained under staffed. This resulted in inadequate coverage in those markets. This disparity adversely affected sales performance and customer satisfaction. The company performed a widespread scrutiny of its sales territories, taking into account the factors like healthcare infrastructure, population density, and the prescribing trends of local doctors. The company executed a strategic territory realignment strategy, reallocating duties based on market potential and workload. The company allocated experienced medical representatives with smaller targeted territories to high-potential urban regions, enabling them to provide special focus towards the healthcare providers. The company also mailed the teams with logistical assistance, comprising vehicles and digital communication tools, to improve accessibility and efficiency in rural areas. Furthermore, it implemented sophisticated technologies such as Geographic Information Systems (GIS) and Customer Relationship Management (CRM) software to assess territory performance and enable data-driven decision-making. This adjustment enhanced workload distribution, enabling the medical representatives to sustain consistent and significant engagement with the healthcare providers while increasing the market coverage. In one year, the company documented a substantial rise in revenues and enhanced its presence in urban and rural markets.

Case 2: ABC Pharmaceuticals, a midsize pharmaceutical company in India, encountered difficulties in optimizing its sales territories owing to varied healthcare requirements, inconsistent infrastructure distribution, and geographical differences in disease prevalence. To tackle these problems, the company implemented a technology-orientated strategy, employing Geographic Information Systems (GIS) and Customer Relationship Management (CRM) solutions. ABC Pharmaceuticals used GIS to define territories according to population density, healthcare facility allocation, and disease incidence. For example, during the introduction of a new diabetes medication, GIS pinpointed territories with high diabetes prevalence, facilitating targeted resource distribution in states such as Maharashtra and Tamil Nadu. CRM solutions improved the process by integrating physician interaction data, analysing prescribing patterns, and optimizing medical representative allocations. Advanced analytics combined with artificial intelligence (AI) forecasted seasonal surges in demand for respiratory medications during the monsoon season in West Bengal, ensuring sufficient inventory and medical representative availability. Mobile applications provided MRs with real-time data, enhancing field connectivity and facilitating swift decision-making in remote areas such as the North-East. On-going investigation identified inefficiencies in suboptimal territories, including insufficient MR allocation in rural Rajasthan. ABC Pharmaceuticals reduced travel times and enhanced contact with healthcare professionals (HCPs) by reallocating workloads and utilizing route optimization tools. Feedback mechanisms from MRs yielded relevant knowledge, including rival actions in urban Gujarat, facilitating prompt strategic adjustments. Using this dynamic optimization strategy, ABC Pharmaceuticals achieved a 20% increase in sales growth in targeted regions, improved customer satisfaction, and strengthened its market position, illustrating the essential role of technology and adaptability in navigating India's intricate pharmaceutical sales environment.

Suggestive Questions from the Chapter

1. What strategies may the pharmaceutical companies employ to efficiently manage sales territories in India, considering the diverse healthcare scenario and economic inequalities?
2. What are the main challenges in managing sales territories in the Indian pharmaceutical sector, and what are the possible solutions to these challenges?
3. What is the significance of customer relationship management (CRM) for the pharmaceutical sales territory management?
4. What are the essential things to consider while defining sales territory in the Indian pharmaceutical sector?
5. What strategies can the pharmaceutical companies implement to maintain equitable workloads for their medical representatives in India?
6. What are the problems and opportunities in sales territory management within the Indian pharmaceutical industry?
7. What are the essential criteria that pharmaceutical companies must consider while making strategizing for their sales territories?
8. In what ways does efficient resource allocation enhance the effectiveness of sales territory planning for the pharmaceutical companies?
9. In what ways does technology, specifically GIS, CRM, AI, and mobile applications, enhance territorial optimisation within the Indian pharmaceutical sector?

10. What are the essential elements of monitoring and modifying territory plans, and how does technology enhance this process within the Indian context?

Multiple Choice Questions

1. What is the primary purpose of pharmaceutical sales territory management in India?
   (a) Marketing (b) Optimization
   (c) Distribution (d) Monitoring
2. What factor is primarily considered while defining sales territories in India?
   (a) Regional languages (b) Population density
   (c) Regulatory policies (d) Past sales
3. Which tool is often used for workload distribution in sales territories?
   (a) CRM (b) GIS
   (c) ERP (d) KPI
4. What is a key challenge in managing pharmaceutical sales territories in India?
   (a) Limited resources (b) Workload imbalance
   (c) Poor communication (d) Regulatory complexity
5. What is critical for sales representatives to build in their assigned territories?
   (a) Trust (b) Resources
   (c) Data (d) Policies
6. What is the primary purpose of defining sales territories in the Indian pharmaceutical industry?
   (a) Marketing (b) Coverage
   (c) Training (d) Recruitment
7. Which tool is commonly used by pharmaceutical companies to define sales territories?
   (a) CRM (b) ERP
   (c) AI (d) CMS

8. What is a critical factor for balancing workloads in rural territories?
   (a) Competition (b) Travel
   (c) Pricing (d) Branding
9. What approach is recommended for covering larger territories with substantial sales potential?
   (a) Individual selling (b) Pool selling
   (c) Outsourcing (d) Bulk selling
10. Which type of region typically requires smaller yet specialized sales territories?
    (a) Urban (b) Semi-urban
    (c) Rural (d) Coastal
11. What is the primary purpose of sales territory planning in the Indian pharmaceutical industry?
    (a) Marketing (b) Branding
    (c) Resource optimization (d) Advertising
12. Which objective focuses on reaching new customers and strengthening ties with existing ones?
    (a) Brand Awareness (b) Customer Retention
    (c) Market Penetration (d) Sales Target
13. What is an essential tool for medical representatives to monitor customer interactions and sales performance?
    (a) CRM (b) ERP
    (c) POS (d) CMS
14. In resource allocation, what is vital for maintaining relationships with healthcare professionals in diverse territories?
    (a) Sales Force Deployment (b) Budget Management
    (c) Brand Promotion (d) Feedback System
15. What ensures sales personnel remain updated on new products, laws, and market trends?
    (a) CRM Tools (b) Customer Feedback
    (c) Training (d) Technology

16. What is the primary focus of setting sales volume targets in the Indian pharmaceutical sector?
    (a) Compliance (b) Revenue
    (c) Distribution (d) Training

17. Which KPI is used to measure the effectiveness of relationships with healthcare professionals?
    (a) Sales Growth (b) Doctor Coverage
    (c) Distribution Reach (d) Compliance

18. What target-setting area is crucial for launching new drugs or promoting key therapeutic areas?
    (a) Sales Volume Targets (b) Market Penetration
    (c) Product-Specific Targets (d) Cost Efficiency

19. Which KPI directly measures the influence of sales efforts on doctors?
    (a) Prescription Volume (b) Market Share
    (c) Customer Satisfaction (d) Training

20. What KPI ensures ethical sales activities in compliance with governmental policies?
    (a) Sales Growth (b) Compliance Adherence
    (c) Cost Efficiency (d) Customer Satisfaction

21. What technology is used to visualize data geographically for territory optimization in pharmaceutical sales?
    (a) CRM (b) GIS
    (c) AI (d) ML

22. Which system helps monitor interactions and assess sales trends in territory optimization?
    (a) GIS (b) CRM
    (c) AI (d) GPS

23. What technology is used to predict sales trends and optimize routes for medical representatives?
    (a) Machine Learning (b) CRM
    (c) GIS (d) Blockchain

24. What is a key element of continuous monitoring in territory optimization?
    (a) Market Expansion
    (b) Feedback Mechanisms
    (c) Social Media Integration
    (d) Offline Mapping
25. What type of software dynamically modifies medical representative routes based on real-time data?
    (a) CRM
    (b) GIS
    (c) Route Optimization
    (d) AI

CHAPTER

9

Pharmaceutical Product Launch and Product Lifecycle Management

Introduction

The Indian pharmaceutical market ranks among the largest and most dynamic globally, distinguished by a competitive atmosphere, an evolving regulatory framework, and a varied consumer demographic. The pre-launch phase of a pharmaceutical product is essential for ensuring its successful introduction and on-going presence in this market. This phase encompasses a series of carefully orchestrated activities that establish the foundation for the product's acceptance by healthcare professionals, regulatory bodies, and consumers. It integrates strategic marketing, regulatory adherence, market analysis, and stakeholder involvement, rendering it a complex yet vital component of pharmaceutical company operations.

A comprehensive market research process serves as the foundation of pre-launch activities. It entails identifying unmet medical requirements, analysing disease prevalence, and assessing existing treatments to establish a distinct positioning for the product. This phase not only assists in refining the product's value proposition but also facilitates an understanding of the competitive landscape, including pricing strategies and potential challenges from established brands. In India, where regional and demographic differences significantly influence drug utilization, thorough market segmentation and analysis are essential.

Regulatory preparation constitutes another critical element of the pre-launch phase. The Indian regulatory landscape, overseen by entities such as the Central Drugs Standard Control Organization (CDSCO), necessitates that pharmaceutical companies navigate a comprehensive drug approval process. This process includes conducting clinical trials, ensuring adherence to Good Manufacturing Practices (GMP), and securing necessary approvals and certifications. A well-prepared regulatory dossier accelerates the approval process and reduces delays, facilitating a more seamless product launch.

At the same time, organizations concentrate on raising awareness among essential stakeholders, especially healthcare professionals. This process entails focused scientific communication, frequently conducted through advisory board meetings, continuous medical education (CME) initiatives, and the sharing of clinical trial results. Interacting with physicians, pharmacists, and key opinion leaders (KOLs) during this stage is crucial for building credibility and trust in the product, thereby ensuring a positive reception upon its launch.

Pre-launch efforts also encompass the development of a thorough marketing and branding strategy. Crafting a striking brand identity, which includes a distinctive name, packaging design, and promotional materials, is vital for standing out in India's competitive pharmaceutical landscape. Careful planning regarding product pricing, distribution, and logistics is equally critical to guarantee accessibility and availability across various regions, from urban hospitals to rural clinics. Companies frequently utilize digital platforms for pre-launch initiatives, generating excitement and informing potential prescribers and patients about the product's advantages.

Moreover, pharmaceutical companies implement internal training programs to prepare their sales teams for effective product promotion. These programs aim to provide medical representatives with comprehensive knowledge of the product's characteristics, benefits, and usage instructions, empowering them to confidently respond to company inquiries from healthcare professionals.

Lastly, risk management strategies are essential components of pre-launch planning. Tackling potential obstacles, such as pricing pressures, regulatory challenges, or competitor actions, ensures preparedness for unexpected circumstances. Scenario planning and proactive strategies allow companies to swiftly adapt and sustain momentum during the launch period.

Pre-launch activities within the Indian pharmaceutical sector encompass a combination of scientific, regulatory, and commercial strategies. These efforts guarantee that the product complies with regulatory requirements while also appealing to healthcare professionals and patients, thereby facilitating a successful market introduction. By means of careful planning and implementation, these activities establish the groundwork for sustainable growth in a competitive and varied market.

Pre-Launch Activities of Pharmaceutical Products

The launch of pharmaceutical products in the Indian market is a carefully orchestrated and strategically implemented endeavour. Pre-launch activities serve as the foundation for a successful product launch, guaranteeing that the medication aligns with market requirements, adheres to regulations, and effectively meets patient needs. These activities encompass market research, product development, patient-journey mapping, and obtaining regulatory approvals. It is essential to examine these essential steps through real-life examples and scenarios inspired by India.

Market Research

Market research is fundamental to the successful launch of any pharmaceutical product, representing the initial and most vital phase in pre-launch planning. It involves a thorough assessment of unmet medical needs, a detailed examination of the competitive environment, and a sophisticated comprehension of consumer behaviour. This phase is crucial for evaluating potential market demand, developing a strong positioning strategy, and ensuring that the product meets the expectations of both patients and healthcare providers.

Take, for instance, the Indian pharmaceutical company, KashyapMed, which aims to launch an innovative anti-diabetic medication in a aggressively competitive market. Acknowledging the rising incidence of diabetes in India, the company initiated an extensive market research initiative covering Tier 1 cities like Mumbai and Delhi, Tier 2 cities such as Lucknow and Coimbatore, and even Tier 3 cities like Jhansi and Madurai. The research employed both primary and secondary methodologies, including surveys targeting patients and healthcare professionals, analysis of epidemiological statistics, and insights from retail pharmacists.

The results revealed a compelling narrative: diabetes is rapidly increasing, particularly in semi-urban and rural areas, fuelled by more sedentary lifestyles, urban migration, and poor dietary choices. Despite the escalating demand, the research identified considerable gaps in the market. Numerous patients in these regions either could not afford existing treatments or faced challenges with adherence due to the complexities of managing multiple prescriptions. This situation underscored the potential for a cost-effective, fixed-dose combination therapy that provides convenience without sacrificing effectiveness.

In addition to recognizing the needs of patients, KashyapMed performed a competitive analysis to delineate the current market landscape. Key competitors such as DibotCare Ltd. and Gl Care Pvt. Ltd. were thoroughly examined to gain insights into their product offerings, pricing models, marketing strategies, and distribution channels. For example, while DibotCare Ltd. maintained a strong presence in urban locales, their pricing often exceeded the financial capabilities of middle-income populations in rural India. In a similar vein, Gl Care Pvt. Ltd., despite being recognized for their innovative products, demonstrated limited reach in semi-urban areas. These findings emphasized the necessity for a pricing strategy that harmonized affordability with profitability, allowing KashyapMed to position its product as a more accessible option.

The research further illuminated another vital insight: a considerable knowledge deficit among general practitioners (GPs) and primary healthcare providers, especially in rural settings. Numerous doctors and physicians depended on out-dated treatment protocols, remaining oblivious to the latest advancements in diabetes management, including combination therapies. This highlighted a crucial pre-launch initiative—educating physicians and other healthcare professionals about the advantages of the drug through targeted campaigns, workshops, and scientific conferences.

Moreover, the market research encompassed an exploration of the distribution and retail dynamics within India. KashyapMed identified logistical challenges in rural areas, where erratic drug supply frequently resulted in stock shortages. To mitigate this issue, the company opted to partner with local stockists and utilize digital supply chain solutions to guarantee a consistent availability of their product.

By employing a comprehensive strategy for market research, KashyapMed not only obtained actionable insights but also developed a thoroughly informed strategy. These insights served as the basis for creating a product that was both innovative and responsive to the varied requirements of India's healthcare landscape. Through such careful planning, the pharmaceutical company positioned itself to address a significant gap in diabetes care, thereby preparing for a successful product launch.

Product Development

The product development process begins with market research as its foundation, concentrating on formulating a medicine that efficiently fills identified gaps while adhering to stringent standards of quality, safety, and efficacy. This phase is a collaborative effort including teams from research and development (R&D), clinical research, and marketing, ensuring the product is scientifically sound and prepared for the market.

In this context, KashyapMed initiated the development of G-Smart Duo, a fixed-dose combination medication that integrates metformin, a reliable mainstay in diabetes therapy, with an innovative DPP-4 inhibitor aimed at improving glycaemic control. KashyapMed specifically designed this formulation to align with Indian dietary practices, known for their high carbohydrate content and unique challenges in diabetes treatment.

The pharmaceutical company partnered with a prominent chemical technology institute in Hyderabad, known for its proficiency in pharmaceutical advances, to enhance the formulation. This collaboration was important in improving the drug's bioavailability, guaranteeing continuous therapeutic advantages despite the dietary changes prevalent among Indian patients. The formulation underwent rigorous stability testing to verify its effectiveness in India's varied climatic circumstances, especially in hot and humid areas.

To guarantee the drug's effectiveness across India's heterogeneous population, clinical trials were systematically designed and conducted at many centres, including leading hospitals in Delhi, Mumbai, and Chennai. The studies encompassed a broad group of volunteers differing in age, gender, and socio-economic status, mirroring India's diversified patient demographic. The trials validated the drug's efficacy in regulating blood glucose levels and established its tolerance, with minimal adverse effects observed, thereby increasing its attractiveness to both physicians and patients.

An essential element of product development in the Indian pharmaceutical sector is the creation of packaging and dosage forms that address particular market preferences and practical obstacles. Acknowledging the need for preserving drug stability in India's frequently humid atmosphere, KashyapMed selected robust blister packs that prolonged shelf life and safeguarded the medication from moisture. In areas where purchasing behaviour favours smaller quantities due to economic limitations, G-Smart Duo was offered in sachet form, facilitating single-dose acquisitions.

This strategic packaging choice was especially important for rural and semi-urban markets, where patients frequently purchase medications on a daily or weekly basis due to constrained disposable income. The sachet format ensured cost-effectiveness and promoted medicine adherence by streamlining the dosage procedure. Additionally, patient feedback throughout the development process underscored the necessity for explicit labelling in several regional languages, a feature that was incorporated to improve accessibility and comprehension among non-English-speaking patients.

By amalgamating scientific accuracy, patient-focused insights, and market-driven tactics, KashyapMed guaranteed that G-Smart Duo transcended a mere pharmaceutical product, evolving into a holistic solution specifically designed to address the distinct issues and requirements of the Indian diabetes demographic.

Patient Journey Mapping and Its Importance

Comprehending the patient journey is fundamental to pre-launch planning, guaranteeing that the pharmaceutical product is tailored to address the distinct demands, preferences, and obstacles encountered by end users. Patient journey mapping is a thorough examination of a patient's experience, commencing with first symptoms, diagnosis, and therapy, and extending to on-going post-treatment care and follow-ups. This strategy enables pharmaceutical companies to synchronise their medicines and support services with actual patient needs, promoting improved outcomes and increased market acceptance.

In the pre-launch phase, KashyapMed conducted a thorough mapping of the patient journey to identify the issues encountered by diabetic patients in India, namely in Uttar Pradesh and Maharashtra. These states were selected because of their significant diabetes incidence and diverse healthcare access in urban and rural regions. The pharmaceutical company interacted with many stakeholders, such as patients, healthcare providers, and carers, via surveys, focus groups, and individual interviews. This method offered a comprehensive perspective on the challenges patients faced at every phase of their healthcare experience.

A notable discovery was the delayed identification of diabetes in numerous individuals, chiefly attributable to restricted access to diagnostic facilities in rural and semi-urban regions. Numerous individuals were oblivious to their disease until complications emerged, aggravating their health problems and complicating therapy. Moreover, compliance with prescription drugs was disturbingly inadequate. Patients often reported factors such as the exorbitant expense of prescriptions, adverse effects such as gastrointestinal discomfort linked to routinely prescribed pharmaceuticals like metformin, and the hassle of daily polypharmacy. These insights underscored the essential requirement for a cost-effective, well-accepted, and streamlined treatment alternative that overcame both physiological and practical obstacles to adherence.

In response to these issues, KashyapMed created G-Smart Duo, a fixed-dose combo medication intended for once-daily use. This formulation mitigated prevalent adverse effects and diminished the tablet burden, enhancing convenience for patients. The once-daily regimen was especially advantageous for employed individuals and elderly patients who frequently had challenges with intricate dosing schedules. The positioning of G-Smart Duo highlighted its patient-centric approach, demonstrating the pharmaceutical company's dedication to tackling both medical and lifestyle issues.

Understanding that pharmacological treatment alone could not address the challenges encountered by diabetic patients; KashyapMed collaborated with local NGOs and healthcare providers to implement community-orientated initiatives. Health camps were conducted in smaller towns and villages, including blood sugar testing and teaching workshops on diabetes prevention and control. These camps not only offered diagnostic assistance to individuals with limited access but also heightened awareness of the significance of early detection and treatment compliance. Significantly, these outreach initiatives fostered trust within local communities, establishing KashyapMed as a compassionate and dependable healthcare partner.

KashyapMed acknowledged the capacity of digital tools to improve patient involvement and assistance, alongside physical measures. The pharmaceutical company created a mobile application named GlucoGuide, specifically intended to tackle prevalent challenges in diabetes treatment. The application offered customised reminders for prescription regimens, assisting patients in preventing missed doses. It also featured dietary guidance customised to Indian culinary practices, enabling users to make informed eating decisions that corresponded with their treatment regimens. Additionally, the application provided teleconsultation services, linking patients with endocrinologists and diabetes educators. This function was particularly beneficial for persons in distant regions with restricted access to specialised healthcare.

The significance of patient journey mapping is its capacity to develop authentic, patient-centred solutions. By exploring the lived experiences of patients, pharmaceutical companies can discern essential pain sites and gaps that may otherwise be neglected. For KashyapMed, this process guaranteed that G-Smart Duo was not merely another product in the saturated diabetic market but a holistic solution tailored to address the unique issues faced by

Indian patients. The insights derived from patient journey mapping influenced product development and marketing tactics as well as post-launch support services, establishing a whole ecosystem that prioritised patient welfare.

KashyapMed demonstrated that including patient journey mapping into their pre-launch strategy may enhance innovation, foster trust, and ultimately elevate treatment outcomes by comprehending the human dimension of healthcare. This holistic strategy positioned G-Smart Duo to significantly influence the lives of diabetic patients throughout India.

Regulatory Approvals

The Indian pharmaceutical market is regulated by a detailed framework of norms set forth by the Central Drugs Standard Control Organisation (CDSCO) under the Directorate General of Health Services, Ministry of Health and Family Welfare. Moreover, state-level Food and Drug Administrations (FDA) are essential in monitoring local compliance and granting approvals. Obtaining regulatory clearances is fundamental to pre-launch efforts, guaranteeing that the product complies with rigorous quality, safety, and efficacy criteria prior to market introduction.

KashyapMed initiated a thorough regulatory approval process to market G-Smart Duo. The pharmaceutical company commenced the compilation of a comprehensive dossier for submission to the CDSCO. This dossier contained an extensive array of data, including preclinical studies to establish the drug's safety profile, outcomes from multi-phase clinical trials to confirm its efficacy, and thorough manufacturing processes to guarantee consistency and compliance with Good Manufacturing Practices (GMP). Acknowledging the intricacies of Indian regulatory frameworks, KashyapMed enlisted seasoned regulatory advisers. The experts possessed extensive knowledge of CDSCO regulations, guaranteeing that the dossier fulfilled the criteria for an efficient examination.

A major problem faced during this period was achieving the bioequivalence standards for G-Smart Duo, a fixed-dose combination medicine. Such pharmaceuticals frequently necessitate stringent testing to confirm that the combined formulation functions comparably to its individual constituents. Preliminary experiments indicated slight variations in absorption rates across different circumstances. In response, KashyapMed collaborated with a prestigious clinical research institution in Bengaluru to do supplementary bioavailability and bioequivalence tests. This initiative guaranteed that the medicine met all requisite standards and showed reliable therapeutic efficacy among various patient populations.

The regulatory approval process necessitated interaction with state-level FDAs to secure marketing permits. KashyapMed encountered difficulties with region-specific mandates for labelling, storage, and distribution methods in areas such as Tamil Nadu and Gujarat, where local regulatory standards are notably rigorous. The pharmaceutical manufacturer pre-emptively addressed anticipated obstacles by convening consultation meetings with state FDA officials and local health authorities. These sessions offered a venue to discuss compliance issues and promoted the exchange of information regarding the drug's distinctive formulation and advantages.

Obtaining regulatory licenses in India beyond basic compliance basically involves fostering confidence and transparency with the authorities. KashyapMed's strategic involvement facilitated consistent communication and prompt resolution of enquiries during the evaluation process. This cooperative strategy was crucial in fostering confidence among regulators and accelerating the approval process. By cultivating robust partnerships with both CDSCO and state FDAs, the pharmaceutical company successfully mitigated delays, thus ensuring the timely launch of G-Smart Duo.

The meticulous and coordinated efforts illustrate the importance of regulatory compliance as a fundamental component of the pharmaceutical product lifecycle. The efficacy of KashyapMed's strategy underscores the need for rigorous planning and proactive collaboration with regulatory bodies, facilitating the approval process, enabling prompt market entry, and ensuring patient access to novel medications.

Integrated Example of Pre-Launch Activities

The integration of market research, product development, patient path mapping, and regulatory approvals guarantees a comprehensive plan for a successful product launch. For example, as G-Smart Duo readied for its introduction in the Indian market, KashyapMed executed a phased launch strategy. The initial phase focused on metropolitan areas and Tier 1 cities such as Mumbai, Bangalore, and Hyderabad, where awareness and diagnostic rates were elevated. The second phase expanded to semi-urban and rural regions, utilising insights from patient journey mapping to tackle issues of affordability and accessibility.

The pharmaceutical company orchestrated a pre-launch conference in partnership with a premier national medical research institute in New Delhi, where prominent endocrinologists deliberated on the advantages of combination medication for diabetes. The event featured training for medical personnel to acquaint them with the attributes and competitive benefits of G-Smart Duo.

Moreover, digital advertisements on India's premier online health-tech platforms showcased patient testimonials and physician endorsements, enhancing legitimacy and facilitating early uptake. The pharmaceutical industry collaborated with prominent branded retail chains to guarantee extensive availability from the outset.

Pre-launch operations in the Indian pharmaceutical market necessitate a combination of thorough planning, patient-focused tactics, and regulatory expertise. Through comprehensive market analysis, the creation of novel goods, the delineation of patient pathways, and the acquisition of prompt approvals, enterprises can provide a robust foundation for a successful product launch. The hypothetical case of KashyapMed and its anti-diabetic medication G-Smart Duo exemplifies the integration of these efforts to tackle the distinct issues and prospects of the Indian market. This strategic planning guarantees commercial success, while enhancing patient outcomes and overall healthcare accessibility in India.

Launch Strategies of Pharmaceutical Products

The launching of a pharmaceutical product is a strategic endeavour that necessitates thorough planning and precise execution. It entails comprehending market dynamics, defining target demographics, and integrating operational actions with corporate objectives. In India, characterised by a diversified and competitive pharmaceutical market, a good launch plan can dictate a product's success. This document examines two essential components of pharmaceutical product launches: launch planning and the execution of launch strategies, illustrated using Indian examples and fictional names for context.

Launch Planning

Launch planning constitutes the essential phase in the introduction of a pharmaceutical product. It includes many strategic measures such as market analysis, regulatory adherence, price strategies, distribution planning, and stakeholder engagement. Every stage is essential to guarantee the product's successful introduction into the fiercely competitive Indian pharmaceutical industry. Herein, we elaborate on the phases of launch planning, using further hypothetical instances from the Indian setting.

1. ***Market Analysis and Opportunity Identification:*** Market analysis commences with the identification of unmet medical requirements and the examination of the competitive environment. The process entails assessing illness prevalence, evolving healthcare trends, patient demographics, and available treatment modalities. A comprehensive

market analysis enables organisations to strategically position their products and ensures alignment with the target audience's requirements.

Heelax Biotech, a pharmaceutical company located in Chennai, intended to introduce "Astharelief", a novel inhaler for those with asthma. Through the analysis of data from metropolitan hospitals in Tamil Nadu and Andhra Pradesh, the company identified a rise in asthma cases attributable to deteriorating air quality. Furthermore, some patients encountered challenges in financing prolonged inhaler treatment. Heelax strategically positioned Astharelief as an economical, durable inhaler aimed at middle-income households.

Herb Wellness Pharmaceuticals, a Kolkata-based company specialising in ayurvedic formulations, has chosen to introduce "Glooguard," an herbal supplement aimed at diabetic management. Market research in West Bengal and Odisha revealed that a substantial proportion of diabetic patients choose alternative cures over allopathic treatments. This understanding allowed Herb Wellness to emphasise Glooguard's Ayurvedic origins and absence of adverse effects in its marketing strategies.

2. ***Regulatory Compliance:*** Successfully manoeuvring through India's rigorous regulatory system is essential for seamless product launches. Obtaining approvals from the Central Drugs Standard Control Organisation (CDSCO) and adhering to the Drugs and Cosmetics Act is compulsory. Companies must do comprehensive clinical trials to demonstrate the safety and efficacy of their products.

   BagaNivarana Pharmaceuticals, located in Hyderabad, encountered regulatory obstacles with the marketing of its inaugural biologic medicine, "Immune Gard", intended for rheumatoid arthritis. To surmount these obstacles, BagaNivarana established a proficient regulatory team that maintained continuous dialogue with CDSCO officials. They guaranteed that all clinical trial data were thoroughly recorded and submitted in advance of the deadline. BagaNivarana convened an advisory meeting with key authorities to discuss potential obstacles and accelerate approvals.

   The debut of "Brain Briddhi", a nootropic medication by Nara Jivantavagiri Labs, a neuropharmaceutical company based in Bengaluru, necessitated rigorous compliance with safety regulations. The company collaborated with local clinical research organisations (CROs) to execute trials in many locations, including Delhi, Mumbai, and Bengaluru, while adhering to CDSCO's multi-center trial regulations.

3. ***Pricing Strategy:*** Pricing strategies in India must achieve equilibrium between affordability and profitability. The Indian market is sensitive to cost, as many individuals rely on personal healthcare expenses. Furthermore, governmental regulations such as the Drug Price Control Order (DPCO) restrict the pricing of important pharmaceuticals.

   Jeevan Rakshak Pharmaceuticals Pvt. Ltd., a pharmaceutical firm located in New Delhi, launched "CardioChime", a statin for cholesterol reduction, in 2023. In response to the competitive statin market, Jeevan Rakshak Pharmaceuticals implemented a tiered pricing strategy. In urban areas, they focused on affluent clients with premium packaging and branding, whilst in rural areas, they introduced a cost-effective version delivered via government-operated health facilities. This dual pricing technique enabled Jeevan Rakshak Pharmaceuticals to serve various income segments while maintaining profit margins.

   Simultaneously, Ayurjeevanth Wellness, a pharmaceutical company based in Pune, launched "Digyme", an ayurvedic digestive enzyme supplement. To appeal to price-sensitive rural demographics, Ayurjeevanth partnered with microfinance institutions to provide accessible payment plans for bulk acquisitions. This pricing model incentivises local stores to extensively stock Digyme, guaranteeing its availability in tier-2 and tier-3 cities.

4. ***Distribution and Logistics Planning:*** The extensive and diverse geography of India needs a highly efficient distribution network to guarantee prompt product availability across regions. This necessitates meticulous coordination with stockists, distributors, and logistical partners.

   SwasthKhoj Pharma, a pharmaceutical company located in Delhi, introduced "R-Throw," an over-the-counter pain treatment gel. SwasthKhoj Pharma established arrangements with various distribution centres across states, such as Rajasthan, Uttar Pradesh, and Karnataka, to guarantee nationwide availability. In temperature-sensitive areas such as Rajasthan, insulated packing methods were employed to preserve product quality during transportation.

   DawaiAsaan Labs, a pharmaceutical start-up operated from Lucknow, launched "Nutrient+," a dietary supplement designed for youngsters. The company developed a distinctive distribution mechanism using partnerships with schools. DawaiAsaan Labs collaborated with educational institutions in Uttar Pradesh, Bihar, and Jharkhand to disseminate Nutrient+ samples during health camps, thereby providing direct access to target consumers.

5. ***Marketing and Awareness Campaigns:*** Marketing efforts are essential for raising awareness among healthcare professionals (HCPs) and patients. These efforts frequently encompass continuing medical education (CME) sessions, digital outreach, and promotional events.

   Chikitsa Ayuttama Labs, a pharmaceutical company located in Bengaluru, has introduced "NeuroPulsar," a medication for nerve regeneration. Chikitsa Atyuttama Labs conducted a CME series entitled "Nerve Health Revolution" in partnership with prominent neurologists from South India to raise awareness. The gatherings drew physicians from Karnataka, Kerala, and Tamil Nadu, enhancing confidence in NeuroPulsar's therapeutic effectiveness.

   Mahat Sambarn Labs, a pharmaceutical company based in Ahmedabad, has introduced "LivoProtect", a natural liver detoxification product. Mahat Sambarn Labs launched a digital marketing campaign called "Healthy Liver, Happy Life", which includes patient testimonials, animated explanation videos, and interactive quizzes. Their multilingual programming in Hindi, Gujarati, and English facilitated extensive outreach, especially in rural regions.

   Mahat Sambarn Labs collaborated with prominent Indian health influencers on social media platforms to enhance patient awareness. These influencers disseminated informative content on liver health and emphasised LivoProtect as a secure and efficacious remedy, stimulating customers' interest.

   Thorough preparation encompassing market analysis, regulatory compliance, pricing, distribution, and marketing is crucial for a successful pharmaceutical product introduction. By leveraging insights, cultivating partnerships, and incorporating digital solutions, enterprises may strategically position their products in the diverse Indian market.

Execution of Launch Plans

The execution phase of launching a pharmaceutical product is crucial for converting strategic ideas into tangible results. In the Indian setting, where healthcare dynamics are varied and complex, effective coordination among departments such as sales, marketing, supply chain, and medical affairs is essential. The following is a comprehensive examination of the implementation of launch strategies, accompanied by further hypothetical Indian instances.

1. ***Field Force Training***: An informed and self-assured field sales team constitutes the foundation of a successful pharmaceutical launch. Medical representatives (MRs) must be proficient in articulating the

product's unique selling propositions (USPs) to healthcare professionals (HCPs), countering objections, and distinguishing the product from its competitors.

Vaidyakiya Suraksita Labs, located in Bengaluru, conducted a four-week rigorous training for its medical representatives before to the launch of "Dybicure," a novel anti-diabetic medication. The program encompassed workshops on diabetes care, simulated medical consultations, and mock detailing sessions. To enhance interactivity in training, Vaidyakiya Suraksita Labs integrated gamification, incentivising MRs for effectively addressing potential complaints over Dybicure's elevated price relative to generics.

Moreover, Vaidyakiya Suraksita Labs utilised regional training centres in Kolkata, Delhi, and Chennai to guarantee that their sales personnel throughout India received consistent training. Each hub included regional linguistic subtleties and cultural inclinations to render the instruction pertinent and effective.

2. ***Pre-Launch Activities:*** Pre-launch efforts cultivate enthusiasm and guarantee that all stakeholders are ready and synchronised for the product's official introduction. This phase entails strategic collaboration with key opinion leaders (KOLs), pilot testing, and the distribution of samples or starter kits to cultivate initial trust and familiarity.

   Navtara Dawai Company, a pharmaceutical firm located in Delhi, collaborated with a distinguished cardiologist in Ahmedabad for the pre-launch of its heart failure drug, "Cardiorel." The cardiologist organised webinars and seminars on heart failure management in partnership with Navtara Dawai Company. These sessions established Cardiorel as a novel and efficacious therapy.

   Navtara Dawai Company executed a pilot testing initiative in 20 clinics located in Gujarat and Rajasthan. Patients were provided with a complimentary one-month supply of Cardiorel, and input was gathered to refine the product's positioning. The company utilised testimonies from these patients at the launch event to illustrate the drug's effect on actual situations.

3. ***Product Launch Event:*** An effectively coordinated launch event can generate considerable excitement and establish the atmosphere for the product's market introduction. Such events generally encompass healthcare professionals, distributors, journalists, and industry players.

   Suryodayamu Labs, located in Hyderabad, introduced its osteoporosis medication "BoneProtect" during a significant event in Delhi. The event showcased distinguished orthopaedists, live demonstrations of

BoneProtect's distinctive mechanism of action, and a panel discussion regarding osteoporosis in postmenopausal women.

Suryodayamu Labs convened distributors from throughout North India, ensuring they were thoroughly informed of BoneProtect's logistical prerequisites. The event featured an awards ceremony honouring high-achieving distributors in pertinent therapeutic categories, enhancing relationships and fostering dedication to the new product.

Suryodayamu Labs live-streamed the event on social media channels such as YouTube and LinkedIn, achieving over 10,000 views within a week.

4. ***Monitoring and Feedback Mechanisms:*** Ongoing monitoring and feedback are crucial for assessing the product's market performance and implementing prompt improvements. This entails gathering insights from several stakeholders, including physicians, patients, distributors, and sales personnel.

   Following the debut of 'VednaEase', a novel pain-relief gel, Mahatwacha Aushadhi Aikya, a pharmaceutical firm located in Pune, established a specialised feedback helpline for medical professionals and chemists. They cooperated with a healthcare analytics firm to monitor prescription trends and sales in significant markets, including Tamil Nadu and Uttar Pradesh.

   Field research suggested that chemists in rural regions deemed VednaEase's packaging less resilient in humid environments. Mahatwacha Aushadhi Aikya promptly reengineered the packaging to enhance its durability, so averting additional grievances. Furthermore, input from orthopaedic physicians indicated a requirement for more comprehensive pamphlets regarding VednaEase's formulation, leading Mahatwacha Aushadhi Aikya to amend its promotional materials.

5. ***Digital Integration:*** The incorporation of digital tools and platforms has emerged as a fundamental element of successful product launches in India's transforming healthcare sector. These instruments can markedly augment the reach, efficiency, and efficacy of a product launch.

   Marundu Cirappu Solutions, a pharmaceutical firm located in Chennai, introduced "RespyroCare," an inhaler designed for asthma patients, in conjunction with a companion application, "Bryther." The application enabled patients to monitor their inhaler utilisation, arrange refills, and obtain reminders for subsequent sessions.

   Marundu Cirappu Solutions has collaborated with a telemedicine platform, allowing physicians to remotely prescribe RespyroCare to patients in regions with restricted healthcare access. The pharmaceutical company enhanced this with an e-detailing tool for medical representatives, enabling them to provide animated movies and infographics regarding RespyroCare during virtual consultations with physicians.

Marundu Cirappu Solutions conducted a social media campaign titled "Breathe Freely," showcasing authentic narratives of asthma sufferers whose conditions improved with RespyroCare. This campaign profoundly resonated with the audience, yielding over 50,000 engagements on Instagram within a month.

6. ***Post-Launch Promotions*:** Continuous promotional initiatives are essential to preserve momentum and guarantee enduring success. This encompasses routine medical consultations, patient education programs, and marketing incentives for distributors and retailers.

   Chetapeshi Labs, located in Pune, executed a dual-faceted promotional approach following the debut of "ChetaPlus," a cognitive enhancer. The initial phase included bi-weekly consultations with neurologists, psychologists, and general practitioners conducted by MRs, who supplied case studies and sample packets. The second emphasised patient education via health camps in tier-2 towns such as Nagpur and Lucknow.

   Chetapeshi Labs provided complimentary starting kits for each purchase of 10 units of ChetaPlus to motivate retailers. The pharmaceutical company instituted a "Retailer of the Quarter" program, rewarding top-performing locations with prizes including cellphones and coupons. Chetapeshi Labs employed WhatsApp groups for instantaneous contact with distributors and retailers, disseminating updates regarding promotions and stock availability.

7. ***Community Engagement*:** Interacting with the community fosters trust and guarantees that the product aligns with its intended audience. This is especially significant in India, where healthcare knowledge continues to develop in numerous areas.

   Shubh Sewa Labs, a pharmaceutical company located in Jaipur, introduced "Glucostive," a device for monitoring blood glucose levels, employing a community-oriented strategy. They established complimentary diabetes screening camps in communities throughout Rajasthan and provided Glucosure devices to local health practitioners.

   Shubh Sewa partnered with local radio stations to air programs on diabetes treatment, featuring physicians who elucidated how Glucostive may facilitate monitoring for patients. These activities not only enhanced product awareness but also showcased Shubh Sewa's dedication to community welfare.

The successful implementation of launch plans requires strategic vision, operational efficiency, and agility. Pharmaceutical companies can optimise their product's success in the competitive Indian market by training the sales staff, engaging stakeholders through pre-launch activities, organising effective launch events, integrating digital tools, and sustaining vigorous post-launch promotions.

The aforementioned examples demonstrate how companies may customise their tactics to address varied consumers and surmount problems specific to India, so ensuring both commercial success and improved healthcare outcomes. By integrating traditional techniques with modern digital strategies, these enterprises can establish precedents for successful pharmaceutical product launches in India.

Post-Launch Activities of Pharmaceutical Products

The Indian pharmaceutical market is among the fastest-growing globally, propelled by heightened healthcare awareness, increasing disposable income, and governmental efforts like the Ayushman Bharat scheme. Nonetheless, introducing a novel pharmaceutical product in this competitive environment is merely the commencement. Post-launch actions are essential for guaranteeing the product's success and sustainability. These activities encompass market penetration, go-to-market strategies, and distribution channel management, all necessitating a meticulously devised methodology substantiated by practical examples from the Indian pharmaceutical sector.

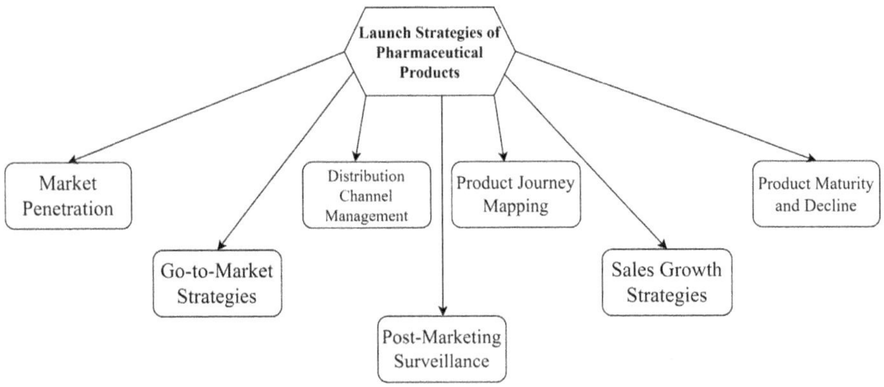

Fig. 9.1 Launch Strategies of Pharmaceutical Products.

Market Penetration

Market penetration in the Indian pharmaceutical company entails enhancing the uptake and use of a newly introduced product among targeted healthcare professionals, chemists, and patients. This procedure necessitates assertive marketing, pricing tactics, and relationship cultivation. A significant issue confronting pharmaceutical companies in India is penetrating the saturated market, where established names prevail.

Mahatwacha Aushadhi Aikya Ltd., a pharmaceutical firm, introduced MadhuRaksha, a novel anti-diabetic medication, in 2023. Given the presence of established brands such as Glycomet and Amaryl in the Indian market, Mahatwacha Aushadhi Aikya implemented a differential pricing approach to enter tier-2 and tier-3 cities, where the prevalence of diabetes is significant; however, affordability poses a challenge. The pharmaceutical industry implemented adaptable pricing strategies, emphasising physician participation initiatives. Utilising digital marketing and direct sales teams, they focused on diabetologists and general practitioners in smaller cities and informed them about the product's enhanced efficacy and cost-effectiveness.

A further element of market penetration is patient awareness. Pharmaceutical companies must proactively establish patient care services in India, where there are restrictions on the connection between doctors and patients. Mahatwacha Aushadhi Aikya collaborated with hospitals to organise complimentary blood sugar screening camps and patient education programmes, hence enhancing brand recognition. Consequently, within six months of its inception, MadhuRaksha secured a 5% market share in designated regions, demonstrating the value of an assertive market penetration strategy.

Go-to-Market Strategies

A go-to-market (GTM) strategy outlines the approach by which a pharmaceutical product engages its target demographic, emphasising sales force allocation, pricing structures, promotional initiatives, and adherence to regulatory standards. Due to the varied characteristics of the Indian pharmaceutical company, companies must customise their go-to-market strategies according to regional demand, physician preferences, and competitor presence.

Chikitsa Upchar Pvt. Ltd., a pharmaceutical company, launched PainRel-X, a novel pain management medication, in India in 2022. Given that the Indian pain management sector is predominantly controlled by established brands such as Combiflam and Voveran, Chikitsa Upchar was compelled to implement an innovative go-to-market strategy. Rather than exclusively targeting allopathic physicians, they broadened their strategy by collaborating with Ayurvedic practitioners and physiotherapists, who often recommend analgesics. This distinctive multi-channel engagement strategy enabled them to access an untapped target nice.

Furthermore, digital marketing has emerged as a crucial element of go-to-market strategy in India, especially during the epidemic. Chikitsa Upchar has introduced an interactive mobile application for healthcare practitioners, with webinars conducted by pain specialists and discussions of case studies. This digital strategy improved physician interaction and guaranteed persistent product recognition. Furthermore, they partnered with online pharmacy platforms such as PharmEasy and 1mg, providing exclusive discounts to stimulate initial sales volume. Employing an omnichannel strategy, PainRel-X swiftly garnered support from both physicians and patients.

Another exemplary case is ChetaPidhi Solutions, which introduced SmritiMax, a cognitive-enhancing pharmaceutical aimed at senior patients. Recognising India's expanding senior population, ChetaPidhi Solutions implemented a targeted go-to-market strategy centred on geriatric clinics and retirement homes. Rather than depending exclusively on physician prescriptions, they implemented direct-to-consumer advertising via television and social media, resulting in a 10% rise in prescription rates within three months. These tactics underscore the importance of a customised go-to-market strategy for achieving product success in India.

Distribution Channel Management

Management of distribution channels is a vital post-launch activity that influences product availability, pricing, and accessibility in diverse locations. India possesses a multifaceted pharmaceutical supply chain, comprising many intermediaries such as stockists, distributors, and retailers. Ensuring uninterrupted distribution is crucial to avert stockouts, regulate pricing variations, and uphold the trust of both doctors and patients.

An exemplary case is JaiwaMed India Ltd., which introduced HridayFit, a cardiovascular medication, in 2021. To guarantee extensive accessibility, they collaborated with major distributors such as HealthMeds Distributors, facilitating efficient last-mile distribution in rural and semi-urban regions. Recognising that stockists and retailers frequently promote high-margin items, JaiwaMed implemented an incentive-based programme for retailers, rewarding those who achieved larger sales volumes of HridayFit. The program led to enhanced visibility and availability in pharmacies, ultimately boosting sales figures.

Moreover, overseeing cold chain logistics is essential for temperature-sensitive pharmaceuticals. SharkaSafe Ltd. introduced InsuCool, a novel insulin version, but had initial distribution challenges owing to cold storage limitations. Through collaboration with cold-chain logistics firms, they guaranteed that the product stayed within the necessary temperature parameters, preventing spoiling and preserving efficacy. Additionally, they implemented a stockist training programme to instruct partners on the significance of appropriate handling and storage.

E-commerce and digital platforms are increasingly significant in distribution. Companies are using online platforms to improve accessibility, especially in metropolitan regions. Chikitsa Upchar, for instance, guaranteed that PainRel-X would be accessible on prominent online pharmacy platforms within two weeks of its introduction, targeting technologically adept clients who favour online medication delivery.

Post-Marketing Surveillance (PMS)

Post-marketing surveillance (PMS) is essential for assessing the safety and efficacy of pharmaceutical products following their introduction to the market. In India, regulatory bodies like the Central Drug Standard Control Organisation (CDSCO) need pharmacovigilance systems to monitor adverse drug reactions (ADRs) and product efficacy.

Mahatwacha Aushadhi Aikya Ltd. noted that a minor percentage of patients reported moderate dizziness following the launch of MadhuRaksha. The pharmaceutical company partnered with CDSCO to conduct a thorough investigation into these occurrences rather than disregarding them. A real-time data-gathering system was established, enabling physicians and patients to report adverse effects through a user-friendly smartphone application. Through this active surveillance, Mahatwacha Aushadhi Aikya modified the product's dosage recommendations to ensure improved patient safety.

Likewise, ChetaPidhi Solutions, a Nashik-based pharmaceutical firm, introduced SmritiMax, a cognitive-enhancing medication aimed at senior patients. One year post-launch, concerns surfaced regarding moderate gastrointestinal complications in a few users. The pharmaceutical company promptly commenced PMS research, evaluating real-world patient input. By making minor adjustments to the formulation and engaging in honest communication with healthcare professionals, ChetaPidhi Solutions averted potential regulatory obstacles and enhanced its market reputation.

Product Journey Mapping

Product journey mapping entails monitoring a pharmaceutical product's success from its launch through multiple growth phases. It assists organisations in evaluating sales trends, patient adoption, physician acceptance, and market competition.

Chikitsa Upchar Pvt. Ltd., a New Delhi based company documented the progression of PainRel-X, a pain management medication, over a two-year period. The initial phase included vigorous physician involvement and internet marketing initiatives, resulting in swift adoption. By the third quarter, however, revenues stabilised as competitors introduced analogous medications. Chikitsa Upchar, using route mapping, recognised the necessity to introduce supplementary strengths (both higher and lower dosages) and penetrate rural markets. Through collaboration with local healthcare practitioners and the initiation of patient education initiatives, the pharmaceutical industry maintained demand.

An alternative method for mapping product journeys involves evaluating prescription behaviour. JaiwaMed India Ltd. employed AI-driven analytics to analyse prescription trends for HridayFit, a cardiovascular medication. Cardiologists preferred known brands; however, general practitioners were receptive to prescribing HridayFit because of its cost-effectiveness. By shifting their sales team's emphasis from cardiologists to general practitioners, JaiwaMed increased sales and optimised marketing strategies.

Sales Growth Strategies

Maintaining and enhancing sales growth after launch necessitates strategic planning. Companies must adopt pricing strategies, broaden their target demographics, launch product extensions, and utilise digital resources.

SharkaSafe Ltd, following the introduction of InsuCool, a novel insulin variation, encountered challenges in acceptance within metropolitan areas owing to competition from international brands. Nevertheless, the pharmaceutical industry concentrated on tier-2 and tier-3 locations, providing promotional discounts to physicians and stores. Furthermore, they organised complimentary diabetes awareness programmes in partnership with NGOs, resulting in a 30% rise in prescription rates.

A further efficacious approach for sales expansion is co-marketing. Chikitsa Upchar Pvt. Ltd. collaborated with a nutrition firm to endorse PainRel-X in conjunction with a joint-health supplement. This integrated strategy enhanced patient adherence and boosted sales. The company launched a patient loyalty program, providing discounts for recurring purchases via online pharmacies.

Omnichannel marketing is essential for revenue growth. ChetaPidhi Solutions launched a AI-driven chatbot on WhatsApp to address enquiries from physicians regarding SmritiMax. This digital project improved physician interaction, resulting in a rise in prescriptions. Furthermore, the chatbot issued reminders to patients about prescription adherence, thereby enhancing compliance and increasing sales.

Product Maturity and Decline

Each pharmaceutical product undergoes a life cycle that commences with introduction, progresses through growth and maturity, and ultimately culminates in decline. Effective management during the maturity and decline stages can optimise revenue and prolong the product's lifespan.

Maturity Stage: During the maturity phase, enterprises concentrate on differentiating and sustaining market share. JaiwaMed India Ltd noted that HridayFit had maximum sales in metropolitan hospitals. To maintain its market presence, the pharmaceutical company launched a sugar-free variation designed for diabetic patients who were reluctant to use conventional formulations. Furthermore, they introduced combination packs with multivitamins, augmenting the value proposition and increasing sales.

Decline Stage: As competition escalates and novel pharmaceuticals emerge, established products experience a downturn. Companies should adopt phase-out techniques rather than abruptly abandoning the product. Mahatwacha Aushadhi Aikya Ltd. possessed a product named PainShield, which began to experience a decline in sales due to emerging pain management alternatives. Instead of allowing it to become out-dated, the company rebranded it as a cost-effective generic replacement aimed at government healthcare programs. Through its collaboration with Ayushman Bharat, PainShield maintained its relevance, albeit within a distinct market sector.

Likewise, ChetaPidhi Solutions experienced a decrease in SmritiMax sales due to the introduction of newer cognitive pharmaceuticals. Rather than ceasing production, they launched an over-the-counter alternative accessible without a prescription, aimed at younger workers facing stress-induced memory impairments. This intentional alteration rejuvenated sales and prolonged the product's life cycle.

Post-launch efforts are pivotal for the enduring success of a pharmaceutical product in India. In the face of fierce competition and varied consumer demands, companies must prioritise market penetration tactics that encompass differential pricing, patient awareness, and physician engagement. An effectively devised go-to-market (GTM) strategy, integrating digital activities and multi-channel engagement, facilitates the establishment of a robust market presence. Efficient management of distribution channels guarantees reliable product availability, especially in rural and semi-urban areas.

Post-marketing surveillance is essential for detecting safety issues and ensuring regulatory adherence. Product path mapping enables companies to evaluate performance and adjust strategy as needed. Strategies for sales growth, including geographic expansion, co-marketing, and digital engagement, are vital to maintaining momentum. Ultimately, overseeing the maturity and decline stages guarantees that products retain their relevance despite escalating competition.

The Indian pharmaceutical companies have distinct hurdles; yet, with effective post-launch initiatives, companies can optimise their product's reach and influence. Hypothetical instances from fictional Indian pharmaceutical companies such as Mahatwacha Aushadhi Aikya, Chikitsa Upchar Pvt. Ltd., ChetaPidhi Solutions, and JaiwaMed illustrate how a methodical strategy can facilitate enduring growth and market supremacy.

Disclaimer: To ensure strict confidentiality, company names and head office locations in the examples cited in this chapter have been intentionally altered to protect confidentiality. Any resemblance to actual entities is purely coincidental.

Case Studies

Case 1: KashyapMed, an innovative Indian pharmaceutical company, has commenced the pre-launch phase of its anti-diabetic medication GLY-Chabrak Duo by emphasizing thorough market analysis and creative product development. With the objective of addressing the growing diabetic demographic in India, especially in semi-urban and rural regions, the company launched an extensive research initiative in cities such as Mumbai, Coimbatore, and Jhansi. The findings highlighted an increase in diabetes cases, challenges related to affordability, issues with medication adherence, and a lack of knowledge among general practitioners. Utilizing these findings, KashyapMed created GLY-Chabrak Duo, a fixed-dose combination of metformin and a new DPP-4 inhibitor, specifically designed to align with Indian diotary habits and climatic conditions. In collaboration with a leading chemical institute in Hyderabad, the company improved the drug's bioavailability and ensured reliable performance. Clinical trials conducted in hospitals across Delhi, Chennai, and Mumbai confirmed the drug's safety and effectiveness. To tackle economic and logistical hurdles, KashyapMed introduced cost-effective sachet packaging, complemented by robust blister packs to ensure stability in humid conditions. Regional labelling improved accessibility; CME programs addressed rural doctors' educational needs. Furthermore, KashyapMed bolstered its distribution strategy by partnering with local stockists and integrating digital supply chain solutions to avoid stock shortages. By merging scientific advancement, market insights, and a profound understanding of patient behaviour, KashyapMed positioned GLY-Chabrak Duo not merely as a medication, but as a comprehensive diabetes care solution tailored to India's varied healthcare environment—establishing a foundation for successful market entry and lasting impact.

Case 2: Several years ago, Sudha Saarvaar Pvt. Ltd., a pharmaceutical company introduced DardLupt-X, an innovative pain management medication, into the fiercely competitive Indian market, which is primarily led by well-established brands such as Combiflam and Voveran. Acknowledging the saturation among allopathic prescribers, the company implemented a distinctive go-to-market strategy by engaging Ayurvedic practitioners and physiotherapists, thereby accessing a relatively neglected segment. To support this strategy, Sudha Saarvaar created a digital platform that included webinars and case study discussions led by pain specialists, enhancing doctor engagement and brand recognition. Additionally, they partnered with online pharmacies to provide initial discounts, attracting early adopters among tech-savvy consumers. Within a fortnight, DardLupt-X was listed on major e-commerce platforms. The distribution was meticulously organized through large stockists and incentivized retail sales programs, ensuring the product's visibility and availability. Concurrently, Sudha Saarvaar established post-marketing surveillance through a mobile application for reporting adverse effects, facilitating real-time safety monitoring. By analysing the product's journey, they recognized stagnating sales in urban areas and shifted their focus towards rural markets and new dosage forms. These integrated strategies enabled DardLupt-X to achieve swift market penetration, positioning Sudha Saarvaar as a significant contender in the pain management sector, while illustrating how a multi-channel, technology-driven, and regionally tailored approach can secure post-launch success in the Indian pharmaceutical landscape.

Suggestive Questions from the Chapter

1. What role does market research play in uncovering gaps and opportunities prior to the introduction of a new pharmaceutical product in India?
2. How can mapping the patient journey assist pharmaceutical companies in developing superior products and support systems for patients?
3. In what ways does proactive communication with regulatory bodies facilitate the acceleration of the pharmaceutical product approval process in India?
4. How does meticulous launch planning affect the success of a pharmaceutical product within the Indian market?
5. What elements render marketing and field training crucial for a successful pharmaceutical product launch in India?
6. What approaches can companies adopt to guarantee on-going product success following its initial launch?
7. How can pharmaceutical companies refine their post-launch strategies to improve market penetration and distribution efficiency?
8. What are the principal factors that impact post-marketing surveillance and sales growth strategies within the pharmaceutical sector?
9. How can pharmaceutical companies effectively manage the maturity and decline phases to prolong a product's market lifespan?
10. What sales strategies can companies implement to stimulate growth in competitive markets and enhance customer engagement?

Multiple Choice Questions

1. What is the primary purpose of market research in the pre-launch phase of a pharmaceutical product?
   (a) Distribution (b) Positioning
   (c) Branding (d) Pricing
2. Which Indian regulatory body is responsible for overseeing pharmaceutical approvals?
   (a) WHO (b) CDSCO
   (c) FDA (d) MHRA

3. Which element is crucial for ensuring timely drug approval during the pre-launch phase?
   - (a) Branding
   - (b) Dossier
   - (c) Packaging
   - (d) Advertising
4. What is a key challenge faced in rural regions related to pharmaceutical supply?
   - (a) Affordability
   - (b) Logistics
   - (c) Education
   - (d) Awareness
5. Which factor was identified as a significant driver for diabetes prevalence in India?
   - (a) Diet
   - (b) Climate
   - (c) Genetics
   - (d) Aging
6. What type of program is typically conducted to prepare the sales force before product launch?
   - (a) Awareness
   - (b) Training
   - (c) Promotion
   - (d) Feedback
7. What kind of compliance is mandatory under Indian pharmaceutical regulations?
   - (a) CSR
   - (b) GMP
   - (c) SEO
   - (d) GDP
8. What region of India showed a significant increase in diabetes cases according to the research?
   - (a) Urban
   - (b) Rural
   - (c) Coastal
   - (d) Semi-urban
9. Which aspect of pre-launch activities is crucial for building trust with healthcare professionals?
   - (a) Product pricing
   - (b) Scientific communication
   - (c) Advertisement
   - (d) Brand design
10. Which digital tool is increasingly used to generate pre-launch excitement and awareness?
    - (a) Logistics
    - (b) Automation
    - (c) Campaigns
    - (d) Audits

11. What is the primary goal of patient journey mapping in pharmaceutical marketing?
    (a) Revenue (b) Compliance
    (c) Understanding (d) Litigation
12. Which phase typically follows the identification of symptoms in the patient journey?
    (a) Awareness (b) Diagnosis
    (c) Treatment (d) Prescription
13. Which regulatory body governs pharmaceutical product approvals at the national level in India?
    (a) WHO (b) CDSCO
    (c) FDA (d) ICMR
14. What is a common challenge associated with fixed-dose combination drugs during regulatory approval?
    (a) Branding (b) Distribution
    (c) Bioequivalence (d) Promotion
15. What element is not typically included in a regulatory dossier?
    (a) Trials (b) Campaigns
    (c) Manufacturing (d) Safety
16. Which phase includes defining pricing and stakeholder communication in a product launch?
    (a) Execution (b) Regulation
    (c) Planning (d) Forecasting
17. Which one of these is a digital strategy to support patient engagement?
    (a) Pamphlets (b) Seminars
    (c) Applications (d) Posters
18. The term 'Good Manufacturing Practices' is commonly abbreviated as:
    (a) GMP (b) GDP
    (c) GPP (d) GSP
19. What is the major benefit of aligning a product with real-world patient needs?
    (a) Profit (b) Efficiency
    (c) Acceptance (d) Expansion

20. Which stakeholder is not typically involved in patient journey mapping?
    (a) Patients (b) Retailers
    (c) Caregivers (d) Providers
21. What is the primary objective of field force training during a product launch?
    (a) Recruitment (b) Communication
    (c) Development (d) Certification
22. Which activity is typically included in pre-launch strategies to build trust among stakeholders?
    (a) Advertising (b) Sampling
    (c) Packaging (d) Branding
23. Which department is primarily responsible for ensuring product availability during launch?
    (a) Legal (b) Finance
    (c) Logistics (d) Compliance
24. Which digital tool can be most usefulk for remote product presentations to doctors?
    (a) App (b) Email
    (c) Webinar (d) Portal
25. What is a key purpose of post-launch promotions?
    (a) Reimbursement (b) Forecasting
    (c) Retention (d) Acquisition

CHAPTER

10

Communications and Promotional Strategies of Pharmaceutical Products

Introduction

Marketing communications and promotional techniques are essential for the success of pharmaceutical products in India, a highly competitive and regulated market. Pharmaceutical marketing, in contrast to traditional consumer goods, is regulated by rigorous legislation, such as the Uniform Code of Pharmaceutical Marketing Practices (UCPMP), which limits direct-to-consumer advertising for prescription medications. Consequently, corporations must implement innovative and ethical techniques to engage essential stakeholders, including healthcare professionals (HCPs), lab scientists, and patients. An effective marketing communication plan combines empirical information with compelling messaging to enhance product credibility, distinguish from competitors, and stimulate prescription growth. The promotional mix for pharmaceutical items generally includes direct sales via medical reps, involvement with key opinion leaders (KOLs), internet marketing, and patient education initiatives. Medical reps function as the principal conduit for brand communication, utilising scientific details, product samples, and on-going relationship cultivation with physicians to impact prescribing practices. Moreover, Key Opinion Leaders—esteemed physicians and researchers—facilitate product acceptance by endorsements and involvement in conferences. In recent years, digital transformation has fundamentally altered pharmaceutical marketing, as corporations utilise webinars, social media, telemedicine platforms, and AI-driven chatbots to convey information and interact with healthcare stakeholders. The emergence of patient-centric marketing has resulted in a proliferation of disease awareness campaigns and patient aid programs that enhance trust and adherence. In contrast, over-the-counter (OTC) products employ more direct promotional techniques, such as mass media advertising, influencer partnerships, and in-store promotions. Navigating the dynamic realm of pharmaceutical marketing necessitates a balance between promotional inventiveness and regulatory adherence. Indian pharmaceutical companies must substantiate marketing claims with clinical data, refrain from deceptive promotions, and uphold ethical contacts with prescribers. Moreover, India's regional variety requires tailored marketing tactics that address the linguistic, cultural, and economic disparities among various markets. Rural marketing approaches frequently encompass health camps, mobile medical units, and collaborations with government healthcare programs to enhance outreach. Conversely, urban marketing emphasises internet engagement, professional seminars, and specialised clinics. Pricing methods impact promotional initiatives, as premium brands highlight product differentiation via enhanced efficacy and safety profiles, whilst generic producers depend on cost-effectiveness and extensive distribution networks. The COVID-19 epidemic expedited the implementation of digital and hybrid marketing methods, transforming conventional pharmaceutical communication strategies. Organisations that adeptly implement omnichannel strategies, merging in-person encounters with digital interfaces, get a competitive advantage in effectively engaging prescribers and patients. As the Indian pharmaceutical company evolves, organisations must remain adaptable, utilising data analytics and customer insights to enhance promotional campaigns while complying with ethical marketing standards. Pharmaceutical companies can enhance brand visibility, stimulate prescription growth, and secure long-term market sustainability by merging scientific communication with strategic promotional initiatives. This chapter examines the fundamental elements of marketing communications and promotional tactics within the pharmaceutical sector, highlighting best practices, practical examples, and developing trends that influence the industry's future.

Marketing Communications for Pharmaceutical Products

Effective marketing communications are essential for the success of pharmaceutical products in India's competitive and regulated market. In a varied healthcare environment, pharmaceutical companies must develop strategic communication plans that effectively involve healthcare providers, lab scientists, and patients while complying with ethical and legal standards. Communicating the appropriate message via the correct channels to the intended audience influences a product's market penetration, brand recognition, and overall sales expansion. The elements of marketing communications and their systematic preparation are essential for ensuring that pharmaceutical products effectively reach their intended users.

Components of Marketing Communications for Pharmaceutical Products

Pharmaceutical marketing communications comprise various components, including direct sales initiatives, scientific details, digital engagement, key opinion leaders' (KOL) advocacy, and patient education programs. Each element contributes independently to the establishment of brand credibility and the influence of prescription behaviour.

1. ***Medical Representatives and Scientific Detailing:*** Medical representatives (MRs) constitute the foundation of pharmaceutical marketing communications in India. Their responsibilities include direct interactions with physicians, delivering clinical data, elucidating the product's mechanism of action, and emphasising its advantages relative to competitors. Niramay Labs, a midsize Indian company, introduced a novel anti-diabetic medication and instructed its medical representatives to deliver scientific information using meticulously crafted visual aids and clinical trial data. Such efforts fostered trust between diabetologists and general practitioners, resulting in heightened prescriptions.
2. ***Key Opinion Leader (KOL) Advocacy:*** Key Opinion Leaders (KOLs), comprising top physicians and researchers, serve as influencers within the medical domain. Their support of a product substantially influences its credibility. Ilaaz Solutions, a pharmaceutical start-up, partnered with respected cardiologists throughout India to host webinars on the efficacy of their recently introduced hypertension medication. The involvement of esteemed clinicians resulted in extensive acceptance by other physicians who participated in these sessions.
3. ***Digital and Social Media Marketing:*** As digitalisation advances, pharmaceutical corporations have adopted social media, email campaigns, and webinars to engage with healthcare professionals and patients. Neomedico India used LinkedIn to interact with oncologists by disseminating case reports and research advancements pertaining to its cancer product portfolio. The organisation employed WhatsApp groups to inform medical practitioners about new guidelines and therapeutic improvements.

4. ***Patient Education and Awareness Campaigns:*** Equipping patients with information regarding diseases and treatments constitutes an essential communication approach. Bhadrate Pharmaceuticals launched a 'Know Your Heart' initiative for its cholesterol-lowering medication. They effectively enhanced patient knowledge and medication compliance using informative videos, social media material, and complimentary cholesterol screening camps.
5. ***Scientific Conferences and CME Programs:*** Continuing Medical Education (CME) programs and industry conferences function as venues for knowledge dissemination and brand enhancement. JiwaVignana Biotech consistently offers continuing medical education events featuring distinguished physicians who provide clinical research on its respiratory care pharmaceuticals. This improves product visibility and fortifies trust among prescribers.
6. ***Print and Online Advertisements:*** Although direct-to-consumer advertising for prescription medications is prohibited in India, pharmaceutical corporations use print and digital media to market over-the-counter (OTC) goods. Atreya Jeevan Herbals effectively introduced an Ayurvedic pain relief balm via strategic newspaper advertisements, influencer marketing, and television advertising, leading to a notable increase in sales.

Developing a Marketing Communications Plan for Pharmaceutical Products

A well-organised marketing communications plan guarantees that messaging is coherent, focused, and efficient when achieving corporate goals. The planning process encompasses goal definition, selection of appropriate communication channels, formulation of content strategies, and assessment of outcomes.

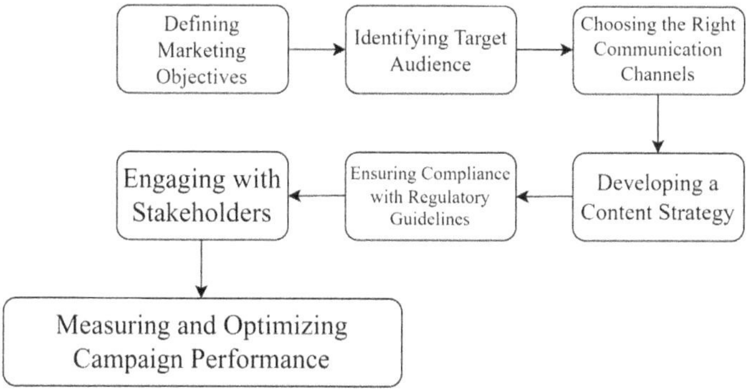

Fig. 10.1 Marketing Communication flow for Pharmaceutical Products.

1. ***Defining Marketing Objectives:*** Prior to initiating a marketing effort, corporations must delineate explicit objectives—such as enhancing brand awareness, boosting prescriptions, or informing patients. Medora Pharmaceuticals sought to enter Tier 2 and Tier 3 cities with its cost-effective antibiotic portfolio. They aimed to inform general practitioners about the drug's effectiveness and establish it as a cost-efficient alternative to premium brands.
2. ***Identifying Target Audience:*** Pharmaceutical communication techniques must be customised for distinct target audiences, including specialists, general practitioners, laboratory scientists, or patients. Vedic Cure Pvt. Ltd., advocating a supplement for diabetes control based on Ayurveda, categorised its target into urban professionals, senior patients, and rural health centres, formulating tailored communication tactics for each sector.
3. ***Choosing the Right Communication Channels:*** The choice of channels is contingent upon the product type, target demographic, and financial constraints. Prescription pharmaceuticals are more effectively promoted through direct medical representatives, key opinion leader interactions, and scientific journals, but over-the-counter products benefit more from social media, television advertisements, and retail promotions. Zithero Labs effectively launched an anti-allergy syrup by combining medical representatives' detailing with internet physician forums, where doctors shared real-world patient experiences.
4. ***Developing a Content Strategy:*** Compelling and scientifically substantiated information is crucial to pharmaceutical marketing communications. CrestGen Biotech guaranteed that its advertising materials for a newly introduced immunosuppressant incorporated peer-reviewed study citations, comprehensible infographics for medical representatives, and patient pamphlets detailing dosing regimens in regional languages.
5. ***Ensuring Compliance with Regulatory Guidelines:*** Pharmaceutical marketing in India is regulated by the Uniform Code of Pharmaceutical Marketing Practices (UCPMP), which requires ethical promotion and prohibits deceptive claims. Nirvana Pharmaceuticals revised its promotional campaign following a regulatory evaluation that indicated its tagline overstated the drug's effectiveness. By optimising communications grounded in empirical clinical data, they maintained compliance while preserving brand allure.
6. ***Engaging with Stakeholders:*** Effective marketing communication necessitates on-going interaction with physicians, laboratory scientists, and patients. Benevolence Healthcare introduced an omnichannel

engagement paradigm for its mental health portfolio, integrating telemedicine consultations, Real time training, and interactive digital Q&A sessions for psychiatrists.

7. ***Measuring and Optimizing Campaign Performance:*** Monitoring the efficacy of marketing communication is crucial for optimisation. Metrics, including prescription growth, physician feedback, patient engagement rates, and digital campaign efficacy, are crucial in evaluating success. Trident JiwaVignanas analysed sales data and physician survey responses to assess its marketing strategies for a gastrointestinal medication, utilising insights to enhance MRs' detailed methods.

Marketing communications in the pharmaceutical sector necessitate a purposeful amalgamation of scientific detailing, stakeholder engagement, internet outreach, and patient education. By using various communication elements and implementing a systematic strategy, pharmaceutical companies in India can improve product visibility, increase prescriptions, promote patient adherence, and comply with regulatory standards. Due to improvements in digital health technologies and changing consumer behaviours, organisations must consistently modify their communication tactics to maintain competitiveness in the dynamic Indian pharmaceutical market. The amalgamation of ethical marketing practices with creative promotional strategies will be pivotal in determining the future of pharmaceutical marketing communications in India.

Digital Marketing in Pharmaceutical Sector in India

The pharmaceutical sector in India has experienced a significant evolution in marketing techniques over the last decade, with digital marketing being a crucial catalyst for growth and engagement. Comprehensive online engagement plans, social media campaigns, and targeted e-marketing activities have now enhanced conventional marketing methods, such as medical representatives consulting with physicians. The digital revolution has empowered pharmaceutical corporations to expand their outreach, ensure compliance, and cultivate more profound relationships with healthcare professionals (HCPs) and patients. This document examines contemporary developments in online engagement methods, e-marketing, and social media marketing within the pharmaceutical sector, illustrated with Indian case studies featuring fake names.

Online Engagement Strategies for Pharmaceutical Products

As more physicians utilise digital platforms for professional advancement and patient management, pharmaceutical corporations are increasingly implementing online engagement techniques to reach healthcare providers. Webinars and virtual Continuing Medical Education (CME) sessions have proven to be among the most successful techniques. Ilaaz Solutions, a prominent pharmaceutical company in India, initiated the "MedicoConnect Webinar Series", offering specialists insights into recent pharmacological advancements, treatment protocols, and research findings. These webinars, frequently sanctioned by medical societies, allow pharmaceutical companies to sustain direct communication with physicians without geographical constraints.

A burgeoning trend is AI-driven, personalised content dissemination. Navarogya Remedies has established an AI-driven engagement platform that evaluates a physician's specialities, prescribing behaviours, and historical interactions to compile pertinent medical papers, clinical trial updates, and pharmaceutical information. This tailored strategy bolsters trust and cultivates enduring partnerships between pharmaceutical brands and physicians.

Moreover, physician-orientated mobile applications are increasingly gaining popularity. Mairunnu Sevanam India introduced "DocAssist", an application enabling physicians to view electronic samples, request patient case studies, and participate in real-time discussions with corporate officials. These internet tools have optimised the dissemination of information by facilitating healthcare professionals' access to updates on novel pharmaceutical items and treatment approaches.

E-Marketing of Pharmaceutical Products in India

E-marketing has become a crucial element of pharmaceutical sales techniques in India, particularly because of the proliferation of telemedicine and e-lab services. Email marketing initiatives aimed at healthcare professionals have demonstrated efficacy in disseminating pharmacological information, regulatory updates, and promotional offers. Navaushad Solutions dispatches tailored email newsletters to cardiologists, offering comprehensive information about its newest cholesterol-lowering medication. The email campaigns incorporate interactive components, including embedded movies, connections to case studies, and AI-generated responses to enquiries.

Additionally, search engine optimisation (SEO) and paid digital advertising are used to improve brand visibility. Shubhayatan Pharmaceuticals carefully allocates resources to Google Ads and SEO initiatives, guaranteeing that its meds rank prominently in search results when physicians and patients seek relevant therapies. The company has markedly enhanced its internet visibility and trustworthiness by using keyword optimisation strategies and referencing credible medical studies.

A vital component of e-marketing is partnership with e-Real time platforms. The emergence of platforms like 1mg, Netmeds, and PharmEasy has afforded pharmaceutical corporations an extra sales avenue. Uyirvalarchi Remedies collaborated with Netmeds to advertise its pain relief medication via targeted digital marketing and discount initiatives. These alliances enhance sales and facilitate patient access to authentic medications.

Moreover, chatbots and AI-driven customer care are transforming pharmaceutical e-marketing. ChikitsaSeba Labs launched an AI-driven chatbot, "SewaNirdeshak", on its website and WhatsApp, enabling physicians and patients to enquire about medication availability, adverse effects, and suggested dosages. The chatbot delivers immediate, dependable information, improving client interaction and contentment.

Social Media Marketing of Pharmaceutical Products in India

Social media has emerged as an essential instrument for pharmaceutical marketing in India, facilitating companies' engagement with healthcare professionals and customers in a more dynamic way. Campaigns on LinkedIn and Twitter aimed at physicians have surged in popularity. Navjivika Biotech initiated a LinkedIn campaign showcasing endorsements from prominent endocrinologists regarding the effectiveness of their newest diabetes treatment. The campaign achieved considerable engagement among healthcare professionals by integrating video content and expert talks.

Likewise, Facebook and Instagram Live sessions have demonstrated efficacy in engaging both physicians and patients. Jivaushadham Remedies, a prominent maker of Ayurvedic medication, hosted an Instagram Live session featuring recognised Ayurveda practitioners who discussed the advantages of herbal remedies for enhancing immunity. This approach not only informed consumers but also bolstered brand trust and credibility.

A highly effective social media strategy encompasses disease awareness campaigns. Ayurpidhi Pharmaceuticals initiated the "Know Your Heart" campaign on Facebook to inform consumers about cardiovascular disorders and to advocate for their heart health products. The campaign featured patient success narratives, expert question-and-answer sessions, and interactive quizzes, leading to heightened brand engagement and product awareness.

Furthermore, cooperation with influencers has gained traction in pharmaceutical marketing. VitaHealth India collaborated with health influencers and fitness coaches to endorse its range of nutritional supplements.

By using Instagram and YouTube influencers that provide testimonies and empirical data, the company successfully enhanced consumer trust and increased sales.

Moreover, WhatsApp marketing has become a potent communication instrument. NavoAushadh Solutions has established specialised WhatsApp groups for physicians and laboratory scientists to disseminate product updates, clinical trial outcomes, and promotional offers. The instant messaging function facilitates prompt replies and immediate interaction, rendering it a preferred medium for healthcare professionals' discussions.

The pharmaceutical industry in India is swiftly adopting digital marketing to improve outreach, engagement, and sales. Online engagement tactics, including AI-driven material, webinars, and mobile applications, have enhanced the interactions between doctors and pharmaceutical companies. E-marketing strategies, like SEO, email marketing, e-Labs, and AI chatbots, have markedly enhanced the accessibility of pharmaceutical medicines. Meanwhile, social media marketing has transformed brand engagement via LinkedIn campaigns, influencer partnerships, and health awareness programs. Through the integration of these digital initiatives, pharmaceutical companies in India are enhancing communication, compliance, and customer happiness within a dynamic healthcare environment.

Traditional Marketing Techniques in the Pharmaceutical Industry

Notwithstanding the swift advancement of digital marketing within the Pharmaceutical sector, conventional marketing methods remain essential for product promotion and relationship cultivation. These methods, fundamentally based on personal involvement and trust, are crucial for the success of pharmaceutical companies in India. Key traditional marketing strategies encompass physician visits, retailer engagements, company-hosted physician conferences, retailer gatherings, and wholesaler meetings, especially for over-the-counter pharmaceutical items. This section examines these strategies through practical examples to demonstrate their influence on the Indian Pharmaceutical market.

Doctor Calls and Retailer Calls

Physician outreach, sometimes referred to as medical detailing, constitutes a critical component of pharmaceutical sales. Medical representatives (MRs) consult physicians to disseminate information regarding novel pharmaceuticals, clinical studies, and therapeutic protocols. This direct engagement fosters trust and guarantees that physicians possess the requisite knowledge to prescribe the company's products.

A current trend in medical consultations is the hybrid detailed approach, which combines in-person appointments with digital follow-ups. Chikwesi Pharmaceuticals has provided its Medical Representatives with AI-enabled tablets to deliver interactive product presentations and immediate access to drug efficacy reports. Subsequent to an in-person consultation, follow-up communications transpire via WhatsApp or email, enhancing the physician's comprehension of the merchandise.

Likewise, retailer communications are essential for ensuring that Real time stocks and endorses particular products. The most recent trend in retail communications encompasses real-time inventory updates and incentive-based sales monitoring. Jibswasthya Labs has just launched a smartphone application for its field sales staff, allowing medical representatives to verify stock availability at laboratories in real time. This approach enables merchants to manage inventory efficiently while permitting MRs to selectively promote fast-moving products.

A novel strategy in retail communications is the geo-tagging system, wherein market representatives document their visits via GPS tracking to guarantee responsibility. Jaruraushadi India has adopted this technology to enhance the efficiency and reach of the sales team. The system produces automatic reporting on physician and store interactions, helping managers analyse sales trends and enhance area planning.

Company-Organized Doctors' Meets

Medical conferences are organised to promote knowledge sharing and networking among healthcare professionals. These assemblies offer a venue for pharmaceutical corporations to unveil new medications, deliberate on research outcomes, and cultivate reputation among the medical community.

The recent trend in medical conferences is the adoption of virtual and hybrid models, wherein in-person meetings are enhanced with live-streamed sessions to increase accessibility. InnovaMed Labs orchestrated a state-wide gathering titled "CardioConnect 2024," convening leading cardiologists to deliberate on breakthroughs in hypertension therapy. A small number attended the event in person, while thousands of doctors throughout India participated electronically, engaging in live Q&A sessions and case discussions.

A notable trend is the emphasis on patient-centric dialogues during medical conferences. NavoAushadh Ltd. conducted an event centred on diabetes care, during which anonymous case studies of actual patients were presented. This method enhanced physicians' comprehension of the practical uses of newly launched pharmaceuticals.

Moreover, immersive learning via simulation workshops has become increasingly popular. Agampidhi Biotech organised a practical session for orthopaedic surgeons, showcasing the use of an innovative pain management medication through a virtual reality (VR) system. This participatory method enhanced physicians' involvement and their readiness to prescribe the product.

Company-Organized Retailers' Meets

Retailers' meetings function as a crucial platform for pharmaceutical companies to educate and motivate laboratory owners and personnel. The main goal is to inform customers about product advantages, pricing tactics, and sales incentives.

A current trend in retail meetings is the implementation of loyalty programs and incentive-driven participation. ChikitsaSeba Labs initiated a "Star Retailer" program, granting member labs significant advantages, including enhanced prices, promotional resources, and incentives for meeting sales objectives. At the annual meeting, high-achieving shops received awards, underscoring their dedication to the brand.

A notable advancement is the implementation of digital engagement tools in retail meetings. Changiaukhad India implemented AI-driven analytics to provide retailers with real-time sales performance dashboards, enabling them to comprehend product demand across various areas. The organisation additionally offered practical training on handling online sales via e-realtime platforms such as PharmEasy and Netmeds.

Themed product launch parties are gaining popularity. HerbiaLife Naturals, an Ayurvedic pharmaceutical company, conducted a "Natural Wellness Meet" for merchants, during which they unveiled a new line of herbal immunity enhancers. The event included live demonstrations, customer testimonials, and product sampling, greatly enhancing retailer confidence in product promotion.

Company-Organized Wholesalers' Meets

Wholesalers are essential in the pharmaceutical supply chain, particularly for over-the-counter drugs that depend on widespread distribution. Effectively engaging distributors guarantees broader market penetration and reliable product supply.

A recent trend in wholesale gatherings is the implementation of bulk purchasing incentives and dynamic pricing techniques. FastMedy Distributors unveiled a volume-based discount plan at its annual wholesalers' conference. Major purchasers obtained tiered pricing advantages, promoting increased order quantities and guaranteeing uninterrupted supply chain flow.

Another innovative strategy involves granting exclusive pre-launch access to new over-the-counter (OTC) products. Jeevrakshit Remedies conducted a wholesalers' meeting to grant early access to a novel pain-relief spray. Participants obtained direct product demos and promotional materials, providing them with a competitive advantage in their markets.

Integration with e-commerce supply chains represents a significant development. OTCWell India convened a wholesalers' seminar centred on digital sales integration, instructing distributors to collaborate with online laboratories. By allowing wholesalers to showcase their inventory on platforms such as 1mg and Amazon Business, the company broadened product accessibility while maintaining distributors as essential participants in the sales process.

Moreover, joint marketing methods between wholesalers and pharmaceutical corporations have become increasingly significant. Vaidyanyas Labs collaborated with distributors to finance co-branded marketing initiatives. At their annual wholesalers' meeting, they introduced collaborative advertising activities featuring wholesalers' contact information on promotional materials sent throughout retail locations. This method enhanced commercial ties and elevated brand visibility.

Company-Organized Rural Pharmaceutical Retailer Meet

Conventional marketing is essential for attracting rural pharmaceutical dealers in India, as many favour in-person encounters and practical demonstrations over internet approaches. Companies conduct rural store meetings through in-person product demonstrations, printed brochures in regional languages, and direct interaction with Medical Representatives (MRs) to establish confidence. Sample distribution, monetary incentives, and volume purchase discounts motivate stores to acquire new products. Numerous companies include local traditions and celebrations into these events, so augmenting engagement. Furthermore, collaborations with Registered Medical Practitioners (RMPs) and Ayurvedic physicians facilitate product promotion in rural areas. DraviMed Pharmaceuticals organised a meeting in Rajasthan, providing complimentary samples and printed guidelines in Hindi, while partnering with local RMPs for health workshops, resulting in a 30% increase in retailer acceptance within three months. Despite technological progress, conventional marketing is essential for informing, engaging, and extending rural pharmaceutical networks in India, hence guaranteeing extensive product availability.

Although digital marketing has revolutionised the pharmaceutical landscape, conventional marketing strategies remain essential in India's pharmaceutical sector. Medical and retail communications have transformed through AI-driven tools and geo-tagging, enhancing efficiency and accountability. Company-organized medical conferences now feature virtual accessibility, patient-focused discussions, and immersive learning via virtual reality. Retailers' meetings concentrate on loyalty initiatives, real-time performance metrics, and thematic product introductions to augment engagement. Wholesalers' meetings have evolved to incorporate bulk purchase incentives, e-commerce integration, and coordinated marketing techniques.

Pharmaceutical companies in India are forging robust ties with healthcare experts, retailers, and wholesalers by integrating classic marketing strategies with contemporary technologies. These tactics guarantee efficient market penetration and on-going corporate expansion in a more competitive environment.

Disclaimer: To ensure strict confidentiality, company names and head office locations in the examples cited in this chapter have been intentionally altered to protect confidentiality. Any resemblance to actual entities is purely coincidental.

Case Studies

Case 1: ManasVeda Labs, a mid-sized Indian pharmaceutical company, adopted digital marketing to improve engagement with healthcare professionals (HCPs) and augment product visibility in a competitive landscape. The corporation implemented a multifaceted strategy integrating online interaction, e-marketing and social media initiatives. The "NeuroConnect Webinar Series" was launched, a virtual CME platform supported by esteemed medical societies, allowing physicians throughout India to access the latest advancements in neurology and psychiatric therapies. The company concurrently implemented an AI-driven platform to provide tailored medical content according to the specific specialities and prescription habits of individual physicians, thereby cultivating enduring partnerships. ManasVeda Labs developed the "DocSphere" smartphone application, granting healthcare professionals access to electronic samples, real-time discussions, and patient case studies. Personalised email campaigns using embedded videos and clickable case study links were initiated in e-marketing, bolstered by SEO and Google Ads to enhance the online visibility of its main medication. The company collaborated with PharmEasy to execute targeted promotions and product awareness initiatives. To augment engagement, ManasVeda implemented an AI chatbot on its website and WhatsApp for instantaneous pharmacological information. The organisation executed a LinkedIn advertisement featuring testimonials from psychiatrists and initiated the "Mind Matters" Facebook campaign to promote mental health awareness. ManasVeda Labs saw heightened healthcare professional involvement, enhanced digital presence, and augmented patient trust and accessibility to its medications through these approaches.

Case 2: ArogyaWell Aushadhi Pvt. Ltd. illustrated how the amalgamation of classic marketing strategies with contemporary technologies could propel success in India's competitive pharmaceutical sector. ArogyaWell Aushadhi had provided its medical representatives with AI-powered tablets for in-person contacts with doctors, leveraging calls from physicians and retailers to facilitate dynamic presentations and immediate access to clinical data. Subsequent to these trips, digital interactions occurred through WhatsApp and email, enhancing product retention. ArogyaWell Aushadhi employed real-time stock monitoring via a mobile application for stores, which facilitated optimised inventory management and smart product positioning. Geo-tagging guaranteed responsibility and effective territorial administration. The company enhanced these initiatives by organising doctors' meetings, including hybrid events where certain specialists participated in person while others joined remotely, which promoted information sharing and product credibility. Retailer meetings were equally comprehensive, featuring loyalty programmes, performance dashboards, and practical training using systems such as PharmEasy. At themed events, such as wellness-orientated product releases, live demonstrations and sampling enhanced product confidence. ArogyaWell Aushadhi incorporated wholesalers by offering bulk purchase incentives, early access to new products, and co-branded marketing campaigns, which augmented market penetration. In rural regions, conventional approaches remained essential—ArogyaWell Aushadhi organised sessions in regional languages, incorporated local customs, engaged rural medical practitioners (RMPs), and distributed samples to enhance outreach and credibility. This comprehensive, hybrid methodology illustrated how the integration of traditional procedures with digital resources fostered robust professional connections and guaranteed extensive accessibility within the Indian pharmaceutical sector.

Suggestive Questions from the Chapter

1. What is the impact of scientific detailing by medical representatives on physicians' prescribing practices in India?
2. What function do key opinion leaders serve in augmenting product credibility and adoption rates?
3. In what ways may digital platforms enhance engagement with healthcare professionals and patients efficiently?
4. What is the significance of regulatory compliance in developing marketing strategies for pharmaceuticals?
5. What techniques may organisations employ to accurately assess and enhance campaign efficacy?
6. In what ways are AI-driven platforms improving pharmaceutical interactions with physicians through digital channels?
7. What is the significance of webinars in enhancing pharmaceutical partnerships with Indian healthcare professionals?
8. What is the efficacy of influencer marketing in promoting pharmaceutical items to health-conscious consumers?
9. How has WhatsApp revolutionised communication between pharmaceutical companies and Indian physicians?
10. What is the effect of SEO methods on the online exposure of items from Indian pharmaceutical companies?

Multiple Choice Questions

1. Which component involves face-to-face interaction with doctors?
   (a) Conferences (b) Medical Representatives
   (c) Advertisements (d) Webinars
2. Who are influential senior doctors supporting product credibility?
   (a) Patients (b) Journalists
   (c) KOLs (d) Chemists
3. What channel is effective for OTC product promotion in India?
   (a) Journals (b) WhatsApp
   (c) Television (d) CMEs

4. Which regulatory code guides ethical drug promotion in India?
   (a) UCPMP (b) FDA
   (c) WHO (d) ICMR
5. What strategy empowers patients with knowledge about diseases?
   (a) Advocacy (b) Education
   (c) Detailing (d) Advertising
6. What platform is used for AI-based personalized content delivery to doctors?
   (a) DocAssist (b) Netmeds
   (c) NeuroHealth (d) SewaNirdeshak
7. Which company launched "MedicoConnect Webinar Series" for HCP engagement?
   (a) Ilaaz (b) Navjivika
   (c) Jivaushadham Remedies (d) ChikitsaSeba
8. What app allows doctors to access e-samples and real-time discussions?
   (a) MediApp (b) DocAssist
   (c) HealLink (d) PharmaTalk
9. Which company uses email marketing for cholesterol-lowering drug promotion?
   (a) Navaushad Solutions (b) NavoAushadh
   (c) Uyirvalarchi (d) Shubhayatan
10. Who uses Google Ads and SEO for brand visibility?
    (a) VitaHealth (b) Shubhayatan
    (c) Netmeds (d) ChikitsaSeba
11. Which Pharmaceutical company partnered with Netmeds for digital promotion?
    (a) Uyirvalarchi (b) Jivaushadham
    (c) Ilaaz (d) Navjivika
12. What chatbot provides drug info via website and WhatsApp?
    (a) MediLink (b) DocBot
    (c) SewaNirdeshak (d) PharmaBot

13. Which company launched LinkedIn campaign with endocrinologist testimonials?
    (a) NeuroHealth (b) Navjivika
    (c) Shubhayatan (d) Navaushad Solutions
14. Which brand conducted Instagram Live with Ayurveda practitioners?
    (a) Ayurpidhi (b) Uyirvalarchi
    (c) Jivaushadham Remedies (d) NavoAushadh
15. What campaign by Ayurpidhi educates users about cardiovascular diseases?
    (a) HeartWise (b) KnowHeart
    (c) HeartHealth (d) Know Your Heart
16. Which strategy involves virtual educational sessions for healthcare professionals?
    (a) SEO (b) Webinars
    (c) Chatbots (d) Instagram
17. What technology enables personalized content for doctors in engagement platforms?
    (a) AI (b) SEO
    (c) Email (d) WhatsApp
18. What mobile app offers doctors real-time interaction with representatives?
    (a) SewaNirdeshak (b) DocAssist
    (c) Netmeds (d) 1MG
19. Which platform provides additional sales channels through online pharmacies?
    (a) DocAssist (b) Webinars
    (c) PharmEasy (d) SEO
20. Which tool offers instant support to patients and doctors on websites?
    (a) Email (b) Webinar
    (c) Chatbot (d) SEO
21. What marketing technique increases website visibility on search engines?
    (a) AI (b) SEO
    (c) Webinar (d) WhatsApp

22. Which platform is used for professional testimonials in LinkedIn campaigns?
    (a) Cardiologists (b) Endocrinologists
    (c) Real times (d) Dermatologists

23. What kind of campaign promotes awareness about diseases like heart conditions?
    (a) Quiz (b) SEO
    (c) Awareness (d) Influencer

24. Which form of marketing uses health experts to promote supplements?
    (a) SEO (b) Webinar
    (c) Influencer (d) Email

25. What instant messaging app is used for real-time Pharmaceutical communication?
    (a) Instagram (b) Facebook
    (c) WhatsApp (d) Twitter

CHAPTER

11

Data Analysis and Market Research

The Importance of Data for Pharmaceutical Marketing

The Indian pharmaceutical sector is currently experiencing a significant shift in its history, marked by a focus on accuracy and data-driven decision-making. A field that has historically been driven by scientific advancement and healthcare needs is now becoming more and more dependent on the strategic use of data. Data is not only an enabler but also a driving force in the dynamic field of marketing, which serves as a vital conduit between pharmaceutical companies and medical experts.

With its vast and varied healthcare system, India offers pharmaceutical marketers both a special opportunity and a difficult task. The nation is typified by a disjointed healthcare delivery system, a diverse illness burden across regions, and the coexistence of rural areas with limited access to healthcare services and urban areas with top-notch medical infrastructure. To navigate this complexity, one must possess a thorough understanding of the market and depend on trustworthy, actionable data to make informed decisions.

Data collection, analysis, and use in pharmaceutical marketing have been completely transformed by the introduction of new technologies and the digitisation of healthcare procedures. Data is the foundation for creating successful marketing efforts, from analysing market trends and rival strategies to comprehending prescribing habits and patient demographics. For instance, salespeople, who are frequently regarded as the industry's spokespersons when interacting with physicians and other healthcare professionals, can now use data-driven insights to tailor their messaging and engagement tactics to better meet the unique requirements and preferences of their target market.

Data serves purposes beyond only enhancing operational efficiency in pharmaceutical marketing. Data is very crucial for bridging differences in healthcare outcomes and access within a market as vast and complex as India. Pharmaceutical companies may concentrate their marketing strategies on addressing urgent healthcare needs by targeting marginalised groups or regions. This, in turn, fosters a feeling of collective value generation and societal advantage by aligning business objectives with public health priorities.

Furthermore, new avenues for data-driven innovation in marketing have been made possible by the combination of artificial intelligence, machine learning, and predictive analytics. By anticipating changes in consumer demand, predictive models assist companies in making proactive strategy adjustments. Feedback from healthcare professionals can be sentimentally analysed to improve marketing strategies and keep interaction powerful and relevant. Additionally, companies can evaluate their marketing effectiveness and make immediate course corrections when necessary thanks to real-time data tools. establish credibility and maintain long-term success, companies must handle the significant ethical, privacy, and compliance concerns that are brought up by data's continued influence on pharmaceutical marketing in India.

It's critical to comprehend the complex role that data plays in pharmaceutical marketing in India in the current environment. Marketers can investigate how data enables companies to effectively manage the intricacies of the Indian healthcare system, to public health. The pharmaceutical marketer might try to give a thorough grasp of how data has become the key to success in this crucial area by looking at real-world case studies, new trends, and ethical issues.

Types of Pharmaceutical Market Research

For pharmaceutical companies working in India's dynamic and diverse healthcare ecosystem, market research serves as the foundation for strategic decision-making. Companies must use strong market research techniques to keep ahead of the competition in the Indian pharmaceutical company, complicated regulatory frameworks, and growing healthcare demands. These techniques mostly involve primary and secondary market research, both of which are essential for obtaining useful information. Indian pharmaceutical companies may successfully manage hurdles while meeting the specific needs of patients, healthcare professionals, and other stakeholders by leveraging the most recent developments in each of these fields. Understanding the various market research techniques used by Indian pharmaceutical companies is crucial, with a focus on current trends and examples from the sector to highlight how they are applied in the field.

Primary Market Research Practices

Gathering firsthand information directly from stakeholders, including patients, chemists, distributors, and healthcare experts, is known as primary market research. The use of technology has led to a substantial evolution in primary research recently, enabling Indian pharmaceutical companies to obtain precise and comprehensive insights. The industry's main market research is being shaped by several factors.

Digital platforms for surveys are among the most notable trends. Companies are effectively gathering data from physicians, chemists, and patients through the use of mobile applications and online surveys. For example, the well-known Indian pharmaceutical company Aushadhi Plus Bharat just released a smartphone app to poll medical professionals about how they prescribe a novel antibiotic. Through the app, the company was able to collect feedback from more than 10,000 physicians in both urban and rural regions, giving them valuable information about local prescribing patterns. High response rates and precise data gathering were guaranteed by Aushadhi Plus Bharat's incorporation of gamified components and user-friendly interfaces.

The use of virtual focus groups is another trend. To overcome geographical limitations, Indian pharmaceutical companies increasingly hold focus groups with physicians and patients from various locations using video conferencing capabilities. A midsized company called Vaidyakrist Labs used online focus groups to find out how people felt about a new diabetes medication. The company successfully customised their marketing strategy by holding separate meetings with endocrinologists, general practitioners, and diabetes sufferers. The conversations uncovered geographical differences in diabetes care methods, which Vaidyakrist Labs used to inform its advertising strategies.

In primary research, real-time feedback techniques are also crucial. In medical conferences, Continuing Medical Education (CME) programmes, and product launches, companies are using tools like chatbots and real-time feedback forms. During its annual oncology summit, Jaiviksewa Solvings, a rising force in the oncology industry, used a chatbot to get immediate input from oncologists regarding its new line of cancer treatments. Jaiviksewa

Solvings was able to pinpoint communication gaps and improve its product messaging for upcoming interactions thanks to the findings.

Additionally, patient-centric research is becoming more and more important. In order to better understand patient experiences and unmet needs, Indian pharmaceutical companies are increasingly conducting observational research and direct patient interviews. To evaluate the efficacy and satisfaction levels of its inhaler product, for example, Swasthek Livio Labs conducted in-depth interviews with patients who had long-term respiratory disorders. Improvements in product design and packaging resulted from the findings, proving the importance of patient-driven insights.

Another intriguing development is ethnographic research. Researchers can better understand behaviours and difficulties by immersing themselves in the context of patients or healthcare providers. To better understand the difficulties rural doctors encounter in detecting and treating tropical diseases, Tejas Medico commissioned ethnographic studies in rural Maharashtra. Using this information, the company improved drug access in underprivileged areas and created focused awareness efforts.

Secondary Market Research Practices

Analysing pre-existing data, including public studies, government databases, and competitor analysis, is known as secondary market research. Pharmaceutical firms benefit from a wider view of market trends, industry standards, and regulatory advancements thanks to this approach. To obtain relevant insights, the Indian pharmaceutical industry has adopted innovative techniques and practices for secondary research.

The application of big data analytics is a significant trend in secondary research. Indian pharmaceutical companies are using advanced analytics to find patterns and trends in large datasets. For instance, SuryaPharm Analytics, a division of Surya Aushadhi, analyses prescription data, sales numbers, and patient demographics using big data methods. The company maximises its marketing efforts and guarantees timely drug availability by charting disease prevalence and treatment trends across states.

Another trend that is transforming secondary research is the incorporation of social listening techniques. Feedback from patients and medical professionals can now be found in abundance on social media sites and online discussion boards. A highly regarded digital marketing agency for Indian pharmaceutical companies uses social listening techniques to monitor discussions about their clients' goods and competitors. Subhupchar Solutions, one of its clients, saw an increase in patient anxiety regarding adverse effects from a rival painkiller. Using these insights, Subhupchar Solutions was able to grow its market share by emphasising the safety profile of its substitute product in later marketing campaigns.

Syndicated research studies and market intelligence reports are also essential for secondary research. To obtain comprehensive evaluations of disease patterns, market projections, and competitive environments, Indian companies usually work with market research consultancies. For example, Ujjwal Vaidh purchased a syndicated study on cardiovascular illnesses in India from a global research organisation. The analysis assisted Ujjwal Vaidh in identifying gaps in the market for fixed-dose combinations and offered insightful information on new treatment preferences.

An additional crucial component of secondary research is regulatory intelligence. Due to the intricate regulatory landscape in India, pharmaceutical companies closely monitor developments from organisations such as the Central Drugs Standard Control Organisation (CDSCO). JivanCare Biotech established a regulatory intelligence platform to track changes in medication approval procedures and compliance standards. By proactively agreeing with the amended rules early on, the company was able to speed the approval of its new biosimilar medication.

As companies look to stand out in a crowded market, competitor analysis has become more popular. Using publicly accessible data, Indian companies examine the product introductions, pricing policies, and advertising efforts of their rivals. For instance, ParamVaidh Labs researched the marketing tactics used by competitors in the dermatology market. After the investigation indicated that digital channels were not being used enough to raise awareness about skincare, ParamVaidh Labs started an informative social media campaign that appealed to younger audiences.

Lastly, investigations on healthcare affordability and accessibility are becoming more and more the focus of secondary research. To inform their marketing tactics, companies are looking at information on insurance coverage, patient affordability, and healthcare infrastructure. In research on rural healthcare access, Aashray Aushadhi identified districts where diabetic drugs were not readily available. The company increased its market presence and met a public health need by collaborating with regional distributors to guarantee a sufficient medicine supply in certain areas.

Real-World Impact of Combined Research Strategies

Indian pharmaceutical companies can make well-rounded, data-driven judgements by combining primary and secondary research. For instance, the pharmaceutical company Jivikaushadhi Remedies successfully launched a novel hypertension medication by combining insights from primary patient interviews and secondary analysis of prescription data. While secondary data indicated an increasing demand for combination therapy, the primary study revealed patient concerns over adverse effects. The drug's dual-action benefits and low side-effect profile were highlighted in Jivikaushadhi Remedies' marketing approach, which led to a successful product rollout in both urban and rural markets.

Additionally, this kind of connection enables companies to more successfully address treatment accessibility barriers. Companies like Tejas Medico and Aashray Aushadhi develop focused tactics, such as regional collaborations and educational programs, by combining secondary data on healthcare infrastructure with primary research findings on patient concerns. In addition to helping the companies, these initiatives also improve the state of healthcare in India.

To handle the complexity of the healthcare environment, Indian pharmaceutical companies are using cutting-edge primary and secondary market research techniques. These companies are improving their marketing tactics and helping patients in India receive better healthcare outcomes by embracing technology, concentrating on stakeholder involvement, and attending to ethical issues. The incorporation of real-world examples highlights how data-driven research has the ability to revolutionise the sector and influence its future.

Analysis of Sales Data for Pharmaceutical Marketing

Analysis of sales data has become an essential part of strategic decision-making in the fiercely competitive and complex Indian pharmaceutical company. Companies may improve customer interaction, spot market trends, and streamline operations by having the capacity to efficiently gather and analyse sales data. The way pharmaceutical companies obtain insights has changed as a result of technical improvements and the growth of data collection methods. By highlighting strategies used by Indian companies and providing pertinent instances, the market researchers consistently attempt to investigate the most recent developments in the gathering of sales data.

Sales Data Collection Methods

- **Digital Sales Platforms and CRM Systems:** These two innovations have completely changed how sales data is gathered in India. Pharmaceutical companies may follow the activity of their sales reps, record transactional data, and keep an eye on real-time contacts with healthcare professionals thanks to CRM systems. For example, during field visits, Vaidisewa Solutions' sales staff can record prescription data and physician feedback thanks to the implementation of an innovative CRM system. Representatives can enter information immediately into the system using mobile devices, guaranteeing data accuracy and timely availability for analysis. In order to help regional sales managers make well-informed decisions, the CRM system also gives them dashboards to monitor performance indicators.

- **Point-of-Sale (POS) Data Integration:** To gather POS data, which represents stock levels, buying patterns, and consumer preferences, pharmaceutical companies are working more and more with retail pharmacy chains. This approach enables companies to efficiently estimate demand and track sales trends. For instance, Ayurkshetra Bharat obtained daily POS statistics through a partnership with a large pharmacy chain. The company was able to pinpoint its top-selling items, modify manufacturing plans, and fortify distribution plans in weak areas thanks to this information.
- **Prescription Audit Reports:** To ascertain consumer demand and product preferences, prescription audits examine how doctors prescribe. Third-party organisations that specialise in gathering and compiling prescription data frequently help this approach. Prescription audits were used by the expanding pharmaceutical company Jaiviksewa Solvings to determine the market share of its cardiovascular medications. The company was able to improve its marketing efforts by analysing prescription trends and learning how its products were being prescribed in comparison to those of its rivals.
- **Mobile App-Based Data Collection:** Particularly in the pharmaceutical industry, mobile applications have become a practical and effective instrument for data collection. Apps are used by sales staff to record sales data, obtain market intelligence, and provide immediate pharmacy feedback. An unique software created by Jivaushadhi Ltd. that enables its sales professionals to provide thorough field reports and geo-tag their visits. The team can offer real-time insights regarding rival products and market dynamics thanks to the app's competition analysis features.
- **Social Media and E-Pharmacy Data Mining:** The emergence of social media platforms and e-pharmacies has opened up new avenues for data gathering. Companies might find new trends and preferences by evaluating client feedback and online sales data. For example, Swasthsampark Ltd. worked with an online pharmacy to research how people buy its dietary supplements. A new line of herbal supplements was introduced by the company in response to the increased demand for plant-based products.

- **IoT for Real-Time Monitoring:** Real-time stock movement and sales tracking is now feasible thanks to Internet of Things (IoT) devices. Data about product deliveries, inventory levels, and returns is gathered by sensors placed in warehouses and distribution centres. IoT technology was used by Sewaushadhi Bharat to monitor the effectiveness of its cold-chain medication supply chain, guaranteeing prompt restocking and low waste. The company increased the effectiveness of its distribution network by studying the data collected by IoT devices.
- **Telematics for Field Force Optimization:** Telematics is the use of GPS-enabled devices to track sales people' whereabouts and activity. Companies with sizable field forces dispersed over several regions will find this data collection strategy especially beneficial. Telematics was used by LakshmiMed Pharmaceuticals to monitor the coverage habits and appointment compliance of its representatives. The organisation was able to eliminate operational redundancies and optimise territory distribution thanks to the findings.
- **Digital Survey Platforms:** Companies can effectively collect patient and healthcare professional feedback by using digital surveys delivered via mobile apps or internet platforms. These questionnaires ask on product satisfaction, prescribing practices, and knowledge about novel treatments. To gather information from endocrinologists about their diabetes treatment products, AyurNetra India employed a digital survey platform. The organisation launched focused awareness efforts after using the survey results to identify physician education gaps.
- **Wearable Technology for Patient Insights:** Pharmaceutical companies are starting to gather patient health data for product analysis and sales via wearable technology. For instance, to collect information on patient adherence to prescription regimens, AyuMed Pharma teamed up with a wearable technology company. The organisation was able to create interventions that increased patient compliance thanks to the insightful information this data gave about the efficacy of its treatment plans.
- **AI-Driven Chatbots for Feedback Collection:** During conferences and promotional events, AI-driven chatbots have gained popularity as a means of getting immediate feedback from medical experts. MumSafe India used a chatbot to collect feedback on a new oncology solution during a national medical conference. The chatbot conversed with oncologists, posing targeted queries regarding the effectiveness of the medication and the offered promotional materials. Future marketing tactics were improved by analysing the input gathered by the chatbot.

- **Collaborations with Healthcare Providers:** In order to obtain anonymised patient data, pharmaceutical companies are increasingly working with clinics and hospitals. In addition to offering information into prescription trends and treatment outcomes, this collaborative strategy guarantees ethical compliance. To investigate how its anti-inflammatory medications are used, CottaMeds Pvt. Ltd. teamed up with a network of hospitals. The company discovered tendencies that affected its marketing strategies by combining data from several institutions.
- **Sentiment Analysis for Market Perception:** Sentiment analysis uses internet reviews and social media to assess consumer comments and market sentiment. Sentiment analysis was used by KhushiCare Pharma to investigate patient perceptions of its over-the-counter pain reliever gel. After the data showed that customers were consistently unhappy with the product's scent, the company decided to launch a fragrance-free version, which was warmly appreciated by customers.

Industry Implications and Examples

The practices of Indian pharmaceutical companies such as Vaidisewa Solutions, Swasthsampark Ltd., and Sewaushadhi Bharat highlight the tremendous influence of novel data collection methods. These illustrations highlight how crucial it is to adjust to new trends and technological advancements. Companies are improving their capacity to satisfy changing healthcare demands while simultaneously increasing their sales success by utilising digital platforms, IoT devices, prescription audits, and partnerships.

For example, by employing data collection via mobile apps to pinpoint high-potential areas, Jivaushadhi Ltd was able to effectively increase its market presence. Targeted initiatives were implemented by the organisation thanks to the app's detailed insights into pharmacy performance and rival activity. In a similar vein, Swasthsampark Ltd successfully launched its herbal product line by taking advantage of consumer preferences for plant-based nutritional supplements.

In the Indian pharmaceutical sector, the process of gathering sales data has grown more complex. To obtain relevant information, companies are implementing cutting-edge techniques fuelled by partnerships, technology, and patient-centric approaches. In addition to improving operational efficiency, these techniques put companies in a position to successfully address public health issues and market demands. Indian pharmaceutical companies are in a position to reshape the nation's healthcare system as data collection techniques advance.

Analytical Tools and Techniques

- **Big Data Analytics for Comprehensive Insights**

  Big data analytics has transformed the interpretation of sales data by allowing companies to evaluate enormous volumes of data from numerous sources at once. Tools like Hadoop and Apache Spark process large datasets, enabling the discovery of correlations, trends, and patterns. For instance, the mid-sized pharmaceutical company Suryavaidha Pharmaceuticals integrates data from retail sales reports, prescription checks, and CRM systems using big data analytics. This strategy enables the company to identify high-demand items, track prescription trends geographically, and effectively allocate resources. Suryavaidha Pharmaceuticals found an unexplored market for their dermatology treatments by examining data from Tier-2 cities, and it was able to successfully increase its presence there.

- **Artificial Intelligence (AI) and Machine Learning (ML) for Predictive Analysis**

  With their ability to automate tasks and provide predictive insights, AI and ML tools have become invaluable friends in the study of sales data. These technologies assist companies in responding to changing market demands by spotting trends and projecting future sales patterns. Based on past data, seasonal variances, and the introduction of competing products, Tantridawa Bharat created an ML-based system to forecast changes in sales for its neurological medications. The company was able to improve distribution planning, minimise stockouts, and optimise inventory levels thanks to the algorithm.

- **Real-Time Dashboard Tools for Data Visualization**

  Interactive dashboards that show important sales metrics in real time are frequently created using data visualisation technologies like Tableau, Power BI, and QlikView. These dashboards enable managers to scrutinise the contributions of individual sales agents, monitor regional sales performance, and identify any discrepancies. Nayanraksha Solutions implemented a Tableau-based dashboard to track sales trends for its diabetes portfolio. Sales significantly increased as a result of the company deploying more resources and launching focused marketing efforts after the tool identified underperformance in particular regions.

- **Sentiment Analysis for Customer Feedback**

  Sentiment analysis interprets consumer attitudes from surveys, online reviews, and social media using natural language processing (NLP). Pharmaceutical companies can improve their plans and assess market views with the use of this technique. Haritpatra Biotech conducted a sentiment analysis of social media discussions surrounding its herbal cough syrup. The results showed both concerns regarding the box design and positive remarks regarding the product's efficacy. In response, the business redesigned its packaging, which increased product sales and customer satisfaction.

- **Predictive Analytics for Market Forecasting**

  To predict market trends and sales prospects, predictive analytics uses statistical models and algorithms. Pharmaceutical companies can use this method to anticipate demand and make proactive decisions. During a nationwide heart health promotion, Hridayswasth Labs employed predictive analytics to predict spikes in demand for its cardiovascular medication. With the help of the insights, the company was able to increase production and acquire more inventory, guaranteeing a smooth supply for medical professionals throughout the campaign.

- **Market Basket Analysis for Product Bundling**

  Navjeevan Remedico uses a data mining method known as market basket analysis (MBA) to identify potential product bundling and buying patterns. By studying sales data, companies can identify the items that customers frequently buy together. To assess consumer preferences for its respiratory care products, Navjeevan Remedico hired an MBA. As a result of the findings, combination packs comprising nebuliser solutions and inhalers were introduced, increasing sales in both urban and rural areas.

- **Geo-Spatial Analysis for Regional Strategies**

  To find regional patterns and possibilities, geospatial analysis integrates sales data with geographic information. Pharmaceutical companies use this method to map market performance and improve regional strategies. We conducted a geospatial analysis of sales data for DawaiPrithivi Bharat's paediatric nutrition products during monsoon seasons. Flood-prone areas had higher demand, according to the data; therefore, the company decided to expand stock availability there and boost customer happiness.

- **AI-Driven Chatbots for Instant Data Collection**

  An increasingly common method for gathering and assessing sales data is the use of AI chatbots. By interacting with chemists and medical professionals, these bots instantly discover patterns and collect feedback. During a product launch event, AyurSutra Care used an AI chatbot to get doctors' feedback on their new antibiotic. After analysing the comments, the chatbot made recommendations that the company's marketing staff might implement.

- **Blockchain for Transparency and Security**

  Pharmaceutical companies are investigating blockchain technology to improve the security and transparency of sales data. Companies may guarantee data authenticity and avoid inconsistencies by putting blockchain-based technologies into place. To manage its sales transactions and provide a safe and open environment for all parties involved, Varnaushadhi Bharat India piloted a blockchain platform. In addition to enhancing data integrity, the system increased distributors' and healthcare providers' confidence.

- **CRM Analytics for Customer Insights**

  CRM analytics helps companies better understand the preferences and behaviours of their customers by using data analysis techniques on CRM data. In order to monitor the prescribing habits of general practitioners as opposed to specialists, JeevanCare Solutions examined CRM data. The findings showed that experts were more likely to recommend the company's sophisticated formulas, which prompted the creation of specialised plans for every demographic.

- **Automated Reporting Tools for Efficiency**

  Pharmaceutical companies can provide comprehensive sales reports with little administrative intervention thanks to automated reporting solutions. These tools are very helpful for monitoring KPIs and assessing the effectiveness of campaigns. NavaSewa Bharat implemented an automated reporting system to gather data from diverse sources and furnish regional managers with valuable insights. The approach increased the effectiveness of decision-making and cut down on reporting time by 40%.

- **Ethical and Compliance Analytics**

  Tools for compliance Analytics assist in making sure salespeople follow moral principles and legal requirements. Pharmaceutical companies use these technologies to monitor promotional activities and detect any deviations. An analytics tool that monitors sales representatives' interactions with medical professionals was created by Jevaraksha Inc. By pointing out disparities and offering suggestions for remedial measures, the system promotes compliance and confidence.

Industry Integration of Analytical Tools

For Indian pharmaceutical companies, the incorporation of these instruments and processes has been revolutionary. Suryavaidha Pharmaceuticals, for instance, leveraged big data analytics to identify underserved rural areas and optimise their distribution networks. In a similar vein, JeevanCare Solutions improved its product positioning by studying CRM data, while AyurSutra Care obtained useful marketing insights from its AI chatbot venture.

These procedures emphasise how crucial it is to use analytical methods and instruments to successfully handle market difficulties. Indian pharmaceutical companies are improving their operational efficiency and helping to enhance healthcare results nationwide by implementing state-of-the-art technologies and encouraging data-driven tactics.

Use of Data for Developing Marketing Strategies

With a dynamic healthcare landscape, strict regulatory frameworks, and a wide range of client needs, the Indian pharmaceutical company operates in a highly competitive and quickly changing market. Pharmaceutical companies are depending more and more on sophisticated data-driven techniques to develop and improve their marketing strategies to stay ahead of the competition. Among these are contemporary decision-making methods and predictive analytics, which are revolutionising how pharmaceutical companies handle the intricacies of the industry. These approaches, which are based on state-of-the-art technology, enable companies to predict trends, allocate resources as efficiently as possible, and create focused advertising campaigns. This essay explores the most recent developments in predictive analytics and decision-making methods used by Indian pharmaceutical companies, demonstrating their significant influence on marketing strategies with examples from the industry.

Predictive Analytics in Pharmaceutical Marketing

In the Indian pharmaceutical industry, the use of predictive analytics to develop marketing strategies has increased dramatically, changing how companies foresee trends, satisfy customer needs, and interact with healthcare stakeholders. With different geographical demands, varying illness burdens, and quickly changing consumer behaviours, the Indian pharmaceutical company operates in a competitive and diverse environment. In order to forecast results and direct decision-making processes, predictive analytics combines enormous amounts of historical and real-time data with sophisticated algorithms and machine learning models. Indian pharmaceutical companies are enhancing their market presence, increasing efficiency, and focusing on the appropriate consumers by implementing predictive analytics. This paper explores the most recent developments in predictive analytics for developing marketing strategies, illustrating their uses with real-world examples.

- **Demand Forecasting**

  Demand forecasting is one of the most well-known applications of predictive analytics, where companies forecast product demand across geographies, seasons, and clientele. Pharmaceutical companies use machine learning algorithms to better predict demand swings by analysing past sales trends, seasonal illnesses, and other external events, like festivals or monsoons. To anticipate the seasonal need for antibiotics and antipyretics during the monsoon season, JivaSafe Pharmaceuticals put in place a machine learning-based demand forecasting system. The company discovered particular trends of demand spikes by examining past data on monsoon-related illnesses in areas like West Bengal and Maharashtra. The system greatly decreased stockouts and improved patient satisfaction by enabling JivaSafe Pharmaceuticals to proactively boost inventory and modify marketing initiatives to guarantee availability during crucial times.

- **Market Segmentation**

  Another important use of predictive analytics is when companies separate their clientele into discrete groups according to characteristics, preferences, or conduct. To create marketing strategies that are relevant to each demographic, pharmaceutical company employ segmentation. NavTantri Care divided psychiatrists and neurologists into groups according to antidepressant prescription trends using predictive analytics. Through extensive data analysis, the company discovered that rural neurologists tended to use well-established formulations of SSRIs (selective serotonin reuptake inhibitors), whereas urban psychiatrists preferred the latest models. Equipped with these data, NavTantri Care initiated a dual marketing strategy that prioritised dependability for rural practitioners and innovation for urban physicians. Its market share for its antidepressant range expanded dramatically as a result of this precision-driven strategy.

- **Geo-Spatial Predictive Modelling**

  It has become a potent instrument for optimising regional marketing initiatives. This method predicts regions with strong demand and effectively allocates resources by superimposing sales data with geographic information. The demand for asthma medications in polluted areas like Delhi and Kanpur was predicted using geospatial algorithms by PrithiviMed, a pharmaceutical company that specialises in respiratory medications. The model determined times of peak demand by examining weather, hospital admission records, and air quality data. PrithiviMed gained a competitive edge in the respiratory market by launching targeted marketing in high-risk areas and making sure that its asthma inhalers were promptly available in neighbourhood pharmacies.

- **Prescription Behaviour Analysis**

  Prescription behaviour analysis, in which companies forecast prescribing trends based on historical behaviours and outside variables, is another area where predictive analytics is being utilised more and more. This enables companies to interact with physicians more successfully by learning about their preferences and adjusting their marketing messaging accordingly. Sewanek Remedies created a predictive algorithm to examine the antihypertensive medication prescription patterns of cardiologists. The model showed that after attending medical conferences, physicians were more inclined to prescribe newer formulations. Sewanek Remedies boosted the adoption rates of its novel antihypertensive medicine by strategically increasing its presence at cardiology conferences and optimising its follow-up marketing activities.

- **Patient Behaviour Prediction**

  Predictive analytics is essential for predicting patient behaviour in the consumer-facing arena, especially when it comes to understanding medication adherence. An e-pharmacy platform and Swasthshetra Biotech worked together to examine patient purchasing patterns for drugs used to treat chronic illnesses. The company started educational efforts, emphasising the value of adherence by identifying patients who were likely to stop taking their medications based on demographic information and purchase frequency. In addition to improving health outcomes, the project raised the number of repeat prescriptions for its main diabetic medication.

- **Sentiment Analysis**

  Pharmaceutical companies may now measure how consumers and medical professionals feel about their products thanks to this noteworthy trend in predictive analytics. Companies can find hidden beliefs and attitudes by studying text data from internet forums, social media, and survey replies. To find out how the general population felt about its natural pain reliever, Haritkushal Labs used sentiment analysis. In addition to highlighting unfavourable remarks concerning the product's smell, the researchers also found consistent favourable responses regarding its efficacy. In light of this realisation, Haritkushal Labs redesigned the gel with a softer scent and started a targeted digital marketing effort to relaunch the enhanced product, which led to a 15% rise in sales.

- **Predictive Pricing Models**

  Pharmaceutical companies also use predictive pricing models to determine the most effective pricing strategies for their products. These models suggest pricing levels that optimise accessibility and income by examining market elasticity, patient affordability, and competitors' prices. To determine the cost of their novel cancer medication, Navruta Solutions used a predictive pricing algorithm. According to the plan, hospitals in urban regions would charge more, while those in rural areas would charge less. This tactic guaranteed broad adoption and strengthened the company's standing as a patient-centred organisation.

- **Social Determinants of Health (SDOH)**

  In the Indian pharmaceutical industry, incorporating SDOH with predictive analytics is a revolutionary development. Companies can gain a deeper understanding of patient demands and obstacles by taking into account variables like education, access to healthcare facilities, and income levels. To forecast demand for their vitamin supplements in underprivileged areas of Uttar Pradesh, JeevanPlus Pharma used SDOH data. According to the data, there were more vitamin deficiencies in communities with lower healthcare access and literacy rates. To solve this, JeevanPlus Pharma started awareness campaigns and produced reasonably priced supplement packs specifically for these areas, which had a positive social impact and increased market share.

- **Campaign Performance Forecasting**

  It is yet another innovative use of predictive analytics. Companies use data from past marketing initiatives to forecast future campaign success and make data-driven decisions. To assess the effectiveness of its digital promotion for a new dermatology product, Nayanraksha Solutions employed predictive analytics. According to the data, young consumers would be more engaged if influencer partnerships were conducted more frequently. The company saw a 25% increase in campaign performance after putting this advice into practice.

- **Inventory Optimization Models**

  Predictive analytics powers these models, ensuring that supply chain planning aligns with marketing initiatives. To align its marketing initiatives with inventory control, Aashray Aushadhi deployed a machine learning model. For instance, the model forecasted a surge in demand in southern India during the introduction of its over-the-counter cold and flu drug because of an unseasonal viral outbreak. During the crucial time, Aashray Aushadhi prevented stockouts and gained a sizable market share by coordinating marketing initiatives with inventory replenishment.

Indian pharmaceutical companies' use of predictive analytics demonstrates their dedication to innovation and customer-centricity. These cutting-edge methods, which range from geospatial modelling and sentiment analysis to demand forecasting and market segmentation, are helping companies create marketing plans that are accurate, effective, and memorable. A data-driven future is being ushered in by companies like JivaSafe Pharmaceuticals, NavTantri Care, and Haritkushal Labs, which are using predictive analytics to maximise their marketing campaigns. The Indian pharmaceutical sector continues to establish standards for using data to improve healthcare outcomes and financial performance by fusing technology and human skills.

Decision-Making Processes

The Indian pharmaceutical sector functions within a multifaceted, rapidly changing landscape, where data-informed decision-making is essential for developing effective marketing strategies. Indian pharmaceutical companies, as major global makers of generic medications, must manoeuvre through a market marked by varied patient demographics, geographical inequalities, fierce competition, and constant regulatory modifications. Effectively harnessing data enables these organisations to refine their strategies, enhance engagement with healthcare professionals, and eventually achieve superior patient results. Recent breakthroughs in data analytics have led Indian pharmaceutical companies to embrace sophisticated decision-making tools to enhance their marketing strategies.

- **Real-Time Decision-Making Platforms**

  One of the most notable developments in decision-making is the use of these platforms, which amalgamate data from many sources, including sales numbers, market intelligence reports, and consumer feedback.

These tools enable organisations to track their marketing successes in real time and implement modifications based on actionable findings. Nayanraksha Solutions created a real-time decision-making dashboard to monitor the performance of their new respiratory care product line. The software discovered weak locations in certain Tier-2 cities by assessing sales data and physician engagement measures in real time. This revelation led the company to assign extra field workers to these areas and initiate focused marketing, resulting in a significant increase in revenue within less than two months.

- **Predictive Decision-Making Frameworks**

  These frameworks have gained traction among Indian pharmaceutical companies, allowing them to predict outcomes and formulate proactive marketing campaigns. These frameworks use historical data, machine learning algorithms, and scenario-based simulations. JivaSafe Pharmaceuticals employed predictive decision-making to assess the sales potential of its newly produced diabetes medication. Through the analysis of prescription trends, healthcare infrastructure, and illness prevalence across different states, the company strategically focused its marketing initiatives in regions like Gujarat and Tamil Nadu, where the need for diabetes management solutions was anticipated to increase. The predictive methodology optimised resource allocation and enabled a successful product launch.

- **Collaborative Decision-Making Models**

  A significant trend is the use of collaborative decision-making models that prioritise cross-functional teams in strategic development. Involving stakeholders in marketing, sales, medical affairs, and regulatory departments enables organisations to achieve organisational alignment. HaritVaidh Bharat adopted a collaborative decision-making strategy for the introduction of its innovative oncology therapy. The regulatory team integrated sales representatives' insights on oncologists' preferences with their feedback on compliance needs, resulting in a comprehensive plan. This collaboration resulted in a comprehensive campaign that adeptly met market expectations and regulatory requirements.

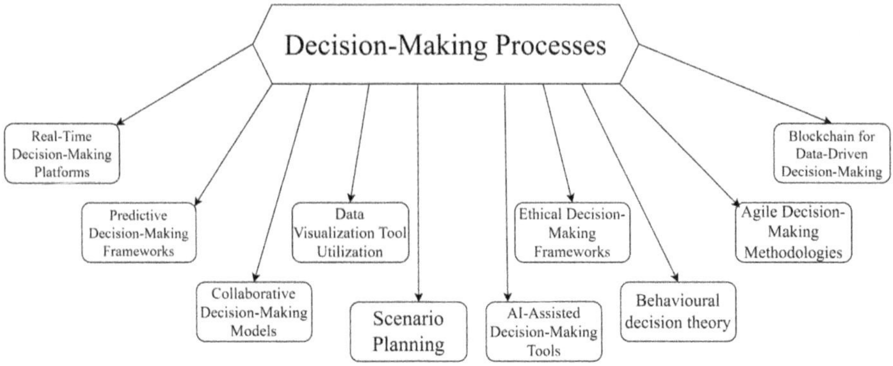

Fig. 11.1 Decision-Making Processes.

- **Data Visualization Tool Utilization**

  In the age of big data, these tools have become essential for decision-making. Platforms like Tableau and Power BI enable pharmaceutical organisations to display intricate data in intuitive visual representations, facilitating rapid and informed decision-making. Jiviruta Bharat India implemented Power BI dashboards to monitor the performance of its cardiovascular medications across several regions. One visualisation indicated that prescriptions in rural areas significantly trailed those in urban locations. This discovery prompted the enhancement of physician education programmes in rural areas, resulting in increased brand awareness and prescription rates.

- **Scenario planning**

  This is a vital decision-making method extensively used in the Indian pharmaceutical sector. This entails simulating diverse situations to assess the possible effects of various marketing methods. Sewanek Remedies engaged in scenario planning to ascertain the most effective pricing strategy for its antihypertensive medication. The simulations accounted for variables including competitor pricing, patient affordability, and hospital procurement policies. In response to the results, the company implemented a tiered pricing plan to maintain accessibility for economically disadvantaged groups while preserving profitability.

- **AI-Assisted Decision-Making Tools**

  The utilisation of these technologies has significantly improved the accuracy and effectiveness of marketing plan formulations. By automating data analysis and delivering actionable recommendations, these technologies enable marketing teams to make prompt, data-driven decisions. Tantrishetra Care included an AI technology in its marketing campaign for a neurodegenerative illness medication. The algorithm evaluated physician prescribing patterns, patient demographics, and competitor actions to suggest the most effective promotional channels. The AI-generated insights allowed the company to concentrate on digital interactions with neurologists, resulting in increased prescription rates in urban regions.

- **Ethical Decision-Making Frameworks**

  A burgeoning trend is the use of ethical decision-making frameworks, which assist companies in manoeuvring through the complex regulatory landscape of the pharmaceutical industry. By integrating compliance analytics, these frameworks guarantee that marketing initiatives conform to ethical standards and regulatory guidelines. Shubhjeevan Solutions created a compliance-orientated decision-making instrument that identified promotional activity diverging from sanctioned standards. This pre-emptive strategy enabled the company to preserve trust with healthcare providers while circumventing any legal issues.

- **Behavioural decision theory**

  This theory has gained prominence recently, concentrating on the determinants that affect physician and patient decision-making. Nao Vaidh Bharat utilised behavioural studies to analyse physicians' perceptions of clinical trial data for a novel oncology medication. The results indicated that oncologists were more inclined to administer the medication when confronted with enhancements in survival rates, rather than technical efficacy information. NaoVaidh Bharat substantially enhanced product acceptance by customising its marketing materials to highlight patient results.

- **Agile Decision-Making Methodologies**

  These techniques are transforming the responses of pharmaceutical companies to market dynamics. Agile methodologies encompass iterative planning and implementation, allowing teams to modify strategy in response to feedback and changing circumstances. Ayurkshetra Bharat implemented an agile strategy for the marketing campaign of its over-the-counter cold and flu medications. Weekly input from sales teams and distributors offers insights into campaign success, enabling the organisation to enhance its promotional materials and optimise ROI in real time.

- **Blockchain for Data-Driven Decision-Making**

  The use of blockchain for data-driven decision-making is an emerging trend that emphasises the enhancement of transparency and integrity.

Blockchain technologies offer a secure and immutable ledger of transactions, guaranteeing that marketing data used for decision-making is precise and dependable. Varnaushadhi Bharat implemented a blockchain-based marketing data management system that guaranteed the authenticity of data gathered from various channels. This boosted confidence in marketing tactics and strengthened engagement with external stakeholders, including distributors and healthcare organisations.

The application of data for formulating marketing strategies in the Indian pharmaceutical sector is seeing a significant transformation, propelled by breakthroughs in predictive analytics and novel decision-making methodologies. These approaches enable organisations to forecast market demands, customise advertising, and respond adeptly to evolving circumstances. This essay illustrates how Indian pharmaceutical companies utilise data to improve their marketing strategies and promote superior healthcare outcomes for the country using real-world examples. The amalgamation of technology and human proficiency fosters a more robust and patient-focused industry. Please inform me if you require additional clarification or particular adjustments!

Disclaimer: To ensure strict confidentiality, company names and head office locations in the examples cited in this chapter have been intentionally altered to protect confidentiality. Any resemblance to actual entities is purely coincidental.

Case Studies

Case 1: A mid-sized pharmaceutical company wanted to introduce a Type 2 diabetes fixed-dose combination medication in India's complex healthcare system. To address patient demographics, regional healthcare access gaps, and changing prescribing habits, the company used primary and secondary market research to inform its strategic marketing decisions. To gain personal insights, the organisation conducted comprehensive primary market research. This interactive smartphone survey targeted general practitioners and diabetologists in Tier 1 and Tier 2 cities and semi-urban areas. Over 12,000 physicians shared their prescribing behaviours, patient adherence issues, and fixed-dose combination opinions. Gamified survey features boosted engagement and answer accuracy. The company also held videoconferencing focus groups with patients, doctors, and chemists from different regions. These interviews indicated considerable differences in diabetes treatment awareness and cultural perceptions.

Rural patients had inadequate comprehension of long-term diabetic problems, while urban patients worried about cost and side effects. The company used digital forms and chatbots to get real-time feedback at regional medical conferences on their product communication materials' attractiveness and clarity. This direct involvement prompted immediate messaging strategy changes. The company also embedded researchers in rural clinics to monitor treatment techniques, medication storage, and counselling issues. Patients with low health literacy received visual aids and simplified instructions based on these observations. The organisation also conducted secondary market research to better understand industry trends and positioning. It mapped disease prevalence and drug usage across states using big data analytics on prescription records, sales reports, and health demographics. The investigation found underserved districts with rising diabetes rates and inadequate fixed-dose therapy access. The company used social listening technologies to monitor internet forums and patient communities and found a growing dislike of competition products due to side effects. The company used this insight to promote its product's safety. It subscribed to syndicated research on the Indian anti-diabetic medicine market for predictions, treatment preferences, and competition evaluations to support its strategy. These findings supported targeting Tier 2 and Tier 3 cities. The company also monitored CDSCO announcements with a regulatory intelligence system to ensure its marketing and labelling met changing compliance criteria. A competitive study showed established brands had minimal digital exposure, causing the company to invest extensively in social media education initiatives. Finally, healthcare affordability and access research informed the company's pricing and distribution approach. It cooperated with remote distributors to improve availability and affordability for underprivileged populations. Technology-driven data collection and careful analysis helped the organisation create a targeted marketing campaign. Within six months of debut, it penetrated unexplored markets, developed brand recognition, and met a key public health need. This case shows how integrated data-driven research might change pharmaceutical marketing in India's complex healthcare system.

Case 2: In the swiftly changing Indian pharmaceutical market, a renowned pharmaceutical company utilised sophisticated data-driven techniques to improve its marketing effectiveness in response to varied regional requirements and severe laws. By using predictive analytics, the company accurately predicted increases in treatments for respiratory illnesses during certain seasons in important states like Kerala and

Punjab, which helped them manage their inventory and target their promotions effectively. Market segmentation tactics enhanced their strategy by categorising healthcare professionals according to prescription behaviours and customising marketing messaging for metropolitan experts who like novel therapies and rural practitioners who prefer traditional formulations. To facilitate dynamic decision-making, the company implemented a real-time analytics dashboard that integrates sales, feedback, and market knowledge, thereby identifying underperforming Tier-3 regions. Agile approaches facilitated swift modifications to field strategies, enhancing engagement and sales within weeks. Furthermore, AI-driven algorithms examined prescribing trends and competitor behaviours to enhance promotional strategies by emphasising digital engagement with endocrinologists in urban regions. Ethical decision frameworks facilitated adherence to changing legislation, protecting the company's reputation. The implementation of blockchain technology ensured the integrity of marketing data, cultivating confidence among distributors and healthcare collaborators. Scenario planning simulations informed pricing methods that harmonised affordability with profitability, especially for chronic disease drugs aimed at economically vulnerable populations. Understanding how doctors behave helped shape campaign messages to focus more on patient results rather than just technical details, which improved the acceptance of new treatments. This data-driven approach optimised resource allocation and market penetration while enhancing patient-centric healthcare delivery, demonstrating the revolutionary impact of combining technology with collaborative skills in India's pharmaceutical marketing sector.

Suggestive Questions from the Chapter

1. In what ways are Indian pharmaceutical companies incorporating technology into their primary market research methodologies?
2. What is the significance of social listening in pharmaceutical secondary market research strategies?
3. In what ways does the integration of primary and secondary research enhance the efficacy of drug marketing?
4. How does ethnographic research enhance rural pharmaceutical outreach in India?
5. In what ways does CRM deployment improve the efficacy of pharmaceutical field forces in India?

6. What function does POS data serve in enhancing pharmaceutical supply chains?
7. In what ways does wearable technology enhance the analysis of pharmaceutical product performance?
8. How does sentiment analysis influence the development of products in pharmaceutical marketing?
9. In what ways does predictive analytics improve regional marketing tactics within the Indian pharmaceutical sector?
10. What is the significance of sentiment analysis in the repositioning of pharmaceutical products?

Multiple Choice Questions

1. What motivates contemporary pharmaceutical marketing?
   (a) Luck (b) Data
   (c) Guess (d) Trial
2. What facilitates communication customisation for physicians?
   (a) Gossip (b) Trends
   (c) Data (d) Ads
3. Primary research entails the collection of data from original sources.
   (a) Books (b) Stakeholders
   (c) Media (d) Reports
4. What tool facilitates real-time feedback?
   (a) Email (b) Poster
   (c) Chatbot (d) Radio
5. What underpins competitive analysis?
   (a) Survey (b) Speech
   (c) Analytics (d) Painting
6. Which technique monitors internet discourse?
   (a) Listening (b) Drawing
   (c) Preaching (d) Printing
7. What is the focus of ethnographic study?
   (a) Weather (b) Animals
   (c) Behaviour (d) Physics

8. What enhances public health objectives?
   (a) Data (b) Luck
   (c) Humour (d) Art
9. What is the primary tool for overseeing the actions of medical representatives?
   (a) IoT (b) CRM
   (c) POS (d) Telematics
10. What monitors real-time cold-chain pharmaceutical logistics?
    (a) CRM (b) Survey
    (c) IoT (d) Chatbot
11. Who supplies prescription audit data?
    (a) Retailers (b) Medical Representatives
    (c) Third-party (d) Hospitals
12. What facilitates the monitoring of patient health?
    (a) CRM (b) Telematics
    (c) Chatbot (d) Survey
13. What influences stock and consumer preferences?
    (a) POS (b) IoT
    (c) CRM (d) Wearables
14. What gathers input during conferences?
    (a) CRM (b) Survey
    (c) Chatbot (d) Wearables
15. What is the primary source of insights leveraged by predictive analytics?
    (a) Magic (b) Data
    (c) Guess (d) Luck
16. What method evaluates geographical data for marketing strategies?
    (a) Segmentation (b) Sentiment
    (c) Geospatial (d) Adherence
17. What is the type of digital content used for marketing strategies?
    (a) Pricing (b) Sentiment
    (c) Inventory (d) Demand

18. What factors facilitate adherence forecasts in chronic disease management?
    (a) Genetics (b) Behaviour
    (c) Geography (d) Surveys
19. What enhances inventory management during promotional campaigns?
    (a) Algorithms (b) Segmentation
    (c) Forecasting (d) Inventory
20. Which instrument presents intricate data in graphic representations?
    (a) Blockchain (b) Tableau
    (c) Algorithm (d) Compliance
21. Which company employed artificial intelligence for selling neuro medicines?
    (a) JivaSafe (b) HaritVaidh
    (c) Tantrishetra (d) Sewanek
22. What facilitates ethical adherence in pharmacological decision-making?
    (a) Algorithm (b) Dashboard
    (c) Blockchain (d) Framework
23. Which philosophy emphasises the decisions made by physicians and patients?
    (a) Predictive (b) Behavioural
    (c) Agile (d) Ethical
24. Which approach entails iterative planning in campaigns?
    (a) Agile (b) Static
    (c) Predictive (d) Ethical
25. Which technology guarantees data validity in pharmaceutical marketing?
    (a) Tableau (b) Blockchain
    (c) PowerBI (d) CRM

CHAPTER

12

Regulatory and Ethical Considerations

Introduction

The convergence of legislation and ethics underpins accountability and trust in industries worldwide, especially in sensitive and consequential sectors such as healthcare, pharmaceuticals, and biotechnology. Success is determined not only by innovation and commercial expansion but also by compliance with regulatory standards and ethical guidelines. Pharmaceutical product marketers must understand the regulatory and ethical considerations that influence decision-making, promote justice, and protect society's welfare.

The pharmaceutical sector establishes regulations to protect individuals, uphold quality standards, and ensure the effectiveness and safety of healthcare solutions. These frameworks, established by regulatory authorities like the FDA in the United States, are essential for supervising drug development, clinical trials, manufacturing protocols, and marketing strategies. Companies must traverse a labyrinth of intricate compliance mandates while sustaining operating efficiency and fostering innovation. Contemporary marketers must understand these regulations, as they provide a systematic framework that enables companies to ethically introduce products to the market, thereby mitigating harm and promoting transparency.

Alongside rules, ethical considerations are essential for cultivating trust among stakeholders, such as patients, healthcare professionals, regulators, and the general public. The ethics of the pharmaceutical sector include various elements, such as research integrity, patient confidentiality, equitable pricing, marketing strategies, and corporate social responsibility. Organisational decisions are frequently influenced by ethical problems, where reconciling profit goals with societal consequences present a significant challenge. Ethical violations can damage reputations, result in legal repercussions, and, most critically, lead to a loss of public trust.

A marketer must explore the relationship between regulation and ethics, illustrating their intrinsic connection. Regulations establish enforced standards, whereas ethics function as an unseen guide, directing actions that reflect values, ideals, and the collective welfare. Organisations that perceive ethical compliance as an opportunity instead of a limitation frequently position themselves at the front of innovation and societal advancement. Instances of organisations that adopt this symbiotic relationship demonstrate the transformative capacity of linking regulatory compliance with ethical behaviour.

A pharmaceutical marketer can of regulatory infractions and ethical breaches in the pharmaceutical industry. These real-world instances act as cautionary narratives, of compliance with both obligatory regulations and ethical principles. Conversely, marketers can investigate the success narratives of organisations that demonstrate regulatory excellence and ethical stewardship, establishing benchmarks for the sector.

Artificial intelligence, evolving ethical standards and the fluidity of rules are all contributing factors. Emerging technologies have created new challenges in data privacy, algorithmic bias, and digital healthcare delivery, necessitating heightened regulatory adaptation and ethical vigilance. We must establish policies and foster a culture of accountability.

By integrating theoretical insights on regulation with the actual application of ethics, the pharmaceutical marketer might strive for a holistic perspective in addressing these factors. It provides them with insights to conform and lead with integrity in a progressively regulated and ethically aware environment.

Understanding Pharmaceutical Regulations

The pharmaceutical sector in India functions within a highly intricate and rigorously regulated market, propelled by strict standards designed to guarantee the safety, efficacy, and accessibility of healthcare products. Indian regulations aim to balance the promotion of innovation, the protection of public health, and the facilitation of sustainable growth in the pharmaceutical industry. Understanding the influence of regulatory organisations and compliance systems on the Indian pharmaceutical industry is essential, as illustrated by pertinent instances.

Key Pharmaceutical Regulatory Bodies

Comprehending pharmaceutical laws in the Indian market necessitates an in-depth examination of the legal framework overseen by principal regulatory authorities that maintain standards for medicine safety, efficacy, quality, and accessibility. The Indian pharmaceutical sector, recognised as one of the foremost makers of generic medications worldwide, operates under a rigorously regulated framework to satisfy both domestic and international requirements. The regulatory structure comprises central, state, and supplementary entities collaborating to ensure pharmaceutical products adhere to rigorous quality standards while fulfilling public healthcare requirements. These regulatory agencies protect public health and foster an environment conducive to innovation and ethical standards within the sector. By examining the roles, responsibilities, and effects of various regulatory agencies, we may gain a clearer understanding of the structure governing the Indian pharmaceutical market, illustrated by industrial examples.

Central Drugs Standard Control Organization (CDSCO)

The Central Drugs Standard Control Organisation (CDSCO) is the principal regulatory authority in India, overseeing drug approvals, clinical trials, and adherence to Good Manufacturing Practices (GMP). The CDSCO operates under the Directorate General of Health Services under the Ministry of Health and Family Welfare, playing a crucial role in guaranteeing the safety, efficacy, and quality of drugs at the national level. The organisation implements the stipulations of the Drugs and Cosmetics Act of 1940 and its related regulations, which provide the basis of India's pharmaceutical legislative framework. Chikur Biotech, a prominent entity in vaccine development, obtained CDSCO approval for its domestic COVID-19 vaccine following a thorough assessment of clinical trial data. This endorsement emphasised the organization's essential role in evaluating new medication applications and safeguarding public health interests.

In addition to drug approvals, the CDSCO regulates clinical trials, a field that requires compliance with rigorous regulations to guarantee patient safety and scientific integrity. Regulations governing clinical trials in India were substantially reinforced following international apprehensions about ethical breaches in the early 2000s. Navita Aarogya exemplifies compliance with these standards; the company executed a randomised, controlled trial for its diabetes medication, fulfilling the CDSCO's criteria for ethical clearances, patient consent, and data oversight. This rigorous control enhances public confidence in the research process and strengthens India's reputation as a centre for clinical trials.

State Drug Regulatory Authorities

The state drug regulatory bodies oversee the manufacturing, distribution, and sale of pharmaceuticals at the local level, complementing the efforts of the CDSCO. Every Indian state possesses a regulatory authority responsible for ensuring that pharmaceutical enterprises under their jurisdiction adhere to legal requirements. Harigol Labs, a midsized producer located in Himachal Pradesh, faced a stringent evaluation by the state's drug control authorities to secure a manufacturing licence. The inspection concentrated on adherence to GMP, hygiene requirements, and equipment validation, confirming that the production facility complied with quality regulations. This layered regulatory framework improves accountability while addressing the varied and decentralised characteristics of India's pharmaceutical sector.

National Pharmaceutical Pricing Authority (NPPA)

The National Pharmaceutical Pricing Authority (NPPA) is a significant regulatory body that oversees medicine pricing to guarantee affordability and avert market exploitation. Formed under the Department of Pharmaceuticals, the NPPA implements the Drug Price Control Order (DPCO), 2013, which establishes maximum pricing for essential medications included in the National List of Essential Medicines (NLEM). For example, Jeevseva Aushadhi received a direction from the NPPA to adjust the pricing of its cardiovascular medication to comply with the ceiling price established under the DPCO. The choice impacted short-term profits but strengthened the company's dedication to offering inexpensive healthcare options. The NPPA's measures guarantee that essential medications remain available, especially to economically disadvantaged groups.

Indian Council of Medical Research (ICMR)

The Indian Council of Medical Research (ICMR) plays a crucial role, especially in formulating ethical guidelines for clinical research. As India emerges as a favoured location for clinical trials, ethical considerations become paramount to avert exploitation and guarantee the safety of trial participants. Jeevol Bharat, a firm focused on oncology pharmaceuticals, partnered with ICMR to develop a multi-center clinical study for their innovative cancer treatment. The experiment complied with ICMR's principles for informed consent, equitable participant selection, and data confidentiality, emphasising the importance of ethical frameworks in the responsible advancement of medical science.

BIS and FSSAI

Alongside regulatory agencies directly supervising pharmaceutical operations, auxiliary organisations, such as the Bureau of Indian Standards (BIS) and the Food Safety and Standards Authority of India (FSSAI), provide indirect support to the sector. The Bureau of Indian Standards (BIS) formulates standards for pharmaceutical apparatus, packaging, and testing methodologies, whereas the Food Safety and Standards Authority of India (FSSAI) regulates nutraceuticals and health supplements that frequently intersect with pharmaceutical products. Swasplus Biotech, a nutritional supplement producer, has confirmed its production procedures to FSSAI requirements to introduce a new line of immunity-enhancing products. This partnership among regulatory bodies guarantees that even marginal sectors of the pharmaceutical industry function within a regulated and uniform framework.

Department of Pharmaceuticals (DoP)

The Department of Pharmaceuticals (DoP), part of the Ministry of Chemicals and Fertilisers, supervises the advancement of the pharmaceutical sector via policy initiatives and incentives. The Production Linked Incentive (PLI) scheme initiated by the Department of Pharmaceuticals (DoP) seeks to enhance domestic manufacturing of active pharmaceutical ingredients (APIs) and diminish reliance on imports. Navgen Vaidyak, a recipient of the PLI scheme, developed a sophisticated API manufacturing facility in Andhra Pradesh, in accordance with the government's objective of self-sufficiency in essential pharmaceutical components.

PharmEXCIL

The pharmaceutical regulatory framework of India also encompasses the worldwide aspect of the sector. Entities like PharmEXCIL (Pharmaceuticals Export Promotion Council of India) aid enterprises in complying with international regulatory norms and penetrating global markets. Dharmeds Ltd, a generic medication exporter, partnered with PharmEXCIL to obtain regulatory licenses from the USFDA and the European Medicines Agency (EMA). This collaboration highlights the interdependence of domestic and foreign regulatory frameworks in influencing the Indian pharmaceutical sector.

The evolving landscape of pharmaceutical regulations in India necessitates that enterprises remain adaptable and aggressive. The emergence of technology and digital healthcare has presented new concerns, including data privacy, cybersecurity, and the application of artificial intelligence in medication development. Regulatory authorities are adjusting to these developments by implementing standards that tackle developing concerns. The CDSCO has released draft regulations for digital health interventions, facilitating a more systematic integration of technology in healthcare.

Compliance Requirements for the Indian Pharmaceutical Companies

Compliance mandates in the Indian pharmaceutical sector are fundamental to guaranteeing medicine safety, efficacy, and ethical marketing practices. The sector functions under a rigorous regulatory framework, motivated by the necessity to maintain public health and comply with international standards. Indian pharmaceutical companies are required to comply with comprehensive duties related to both manufacturing and marketing, as dictated by the Drugs and Cosmetics Act of 1940, the Drugs and Cosmetics Rules, and other instructions from regulatory authorities. These needs span from the production line to the marketplace, covering all stages of the pharmaceutical lifecycle. Analysing compliance in production and marketing through industry examples with fake names enhances our comprehension of the operational and legal framework supporting the Indian pharmaceutical sector.

Compliance Requirements for Manufacturing Activities

Good Manufacturing Practices (GMP)

Compliance in the Indian pharmaceutical manufacturing sector is predominantly regulated by Best Manufacturing Practices (GMP), as specified in Schedule M of the Drugs and Cosmetics Rules. Pharmaceutical Manufacturing Practice (GMP) guarantees that pharmaceuticals are uniformly manufactured and regulated to adhere to quality standards. Companies must adhere to stringent hygiene regulations, validate equipment, establish comprehensive quality assurance systems, and rigorously document manufacturing operations.

For instance, Navita Aarogya, a medium-sized producer of sterile injectables, experienced a CDSCO inspection that uncovered deficiencies in its air filtration systems and insufficient cleaning methods for its manufacturing areas. To resolve these challenges, Navita Aarogya invested in sophisticated cleanroom technologies, enhanced its filtration systems, and retrained its personnel on hygiene best practices. After demonstrating adherence to GMP standards, the company obtained fresh production licenses, allowing it to resume operations without jeopardising product quality.

Compliance for Active Pharmaceutical Ingredients (APIs)

Manufacturers must adhere to compliance regulations for active pharmaceutical ingredients (APIs). The Indian government incentivises domestic API production through measures such as the Production Linked Incentive (PLI) scheme to diminish dependence on imports. Harimed Aushadhi employed the PLI scheme to develop an API manufacturing facility compliant with environmental standards set forth by the Air (Prevention and Control of Pollution) Act, 1981. This investment not only conformed to manufacturing regulations but also enhanced self-sufficiency in essential pharmaceutical components.

Quality Control and Pharmacovigilance

Quality control and pharmacovigilance reinforce compliance in production. Companies must perform thorough testing of raw materials, intermediates, and finished goods to guarantee uniformity and safety. Manufacturers must initiate product recalls and report findings to the CDSCO when adverse events associated with a product arise. Sevagol Remedies demonstrated exemplary pharmacovigilance by withdrawing a batch of anti-infective tablets after reports of atypical side effects. The prompt response exemplified the company's dedication to patient safety and compliance with regulations.

Compliance Requirements for Marketing Activities

Marketing compliance within the Indian pharmaceutical sector includes ethical promotional methods, precise labelling, adherence to drug pricing regulations, and regulatory approval for new drugs. These compliance requirements attempt to avert deceptive claims and guarantee the responsible marketing of pharmaceutical products.

Uniform Code of Pharmaceutical Marketing Practices (UCPMP)

Ethical marketing techniques are regulated by the Uniform Code of Pharmaceutical Marketing Techniques (UCPMP), which forbids companies from providing inappropriate incentives to healthcare practitioners or making inflated assertions regarding product effectiveness. For example, Jeevecare Biotech, a producer of anti-inflammatory pharmaceuticals, instructed its medical professionals to refrain from unethical activities in the promotion of its goods. By complying with UCPMP requirements, the company preserved trust among healthcare professionals and evaded regulatory scrutiny.

Labelling Compliance

This is another essential facet of marketing regulations. Labels must provide precise information regarding the drug's formulation, dosage guidelines, and cautions concerning possible adverse effects. Chikgol Solutions received a CDSCO mandate to revise the labelling of its paediatric pain relief syrup following an inspection that uncovered inadequate warnings regarding overdose risks. The company revised its labels to include explicit dosing instructions, underscoring its dedication to consumer safety and regulatory adherence.

Drug Pricing Regulations

The Drug Price Control Order (DPCO) mandates that companies limit the prices of essential medications included in the National List of Essential Medicines (NLEM). The National Pharmaceutical Pricing Authority (NPPA) implements these pricing ceilings to guarantee affordability and accessibility. Navcur Ltd. adjusted the pricing of its cardiovascular medication in accordance with an NPPA directive, reconciling profitability with accessibility. The choice adversely affected short-term income but enhanced the company's image by prioritising public health.

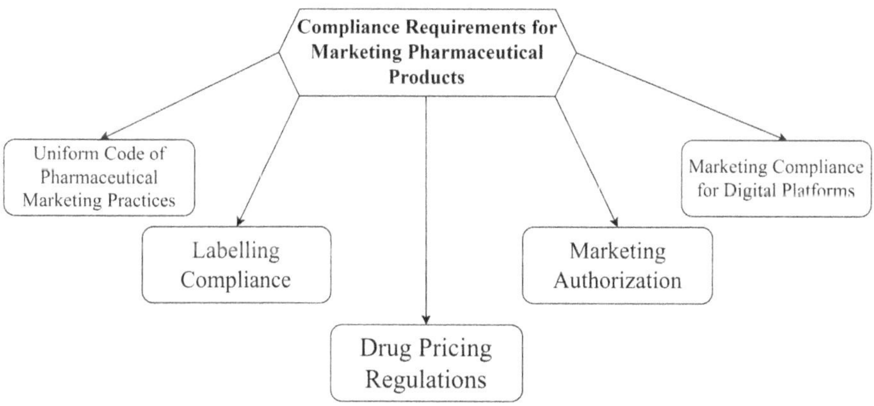

Fig. 12.1 Compliance requirements for Marketing Pharmaceutical Products.

Marketing Authorization

Obtaining authorisation from the CDSCO is essential for marketing pharmaceutical products in India. Companies are required to furnish data regarding the drug's safety, efficacy, and quality via clinical trials or bioequivalence studies. Dharmeds Ltd. received CDSCO approval for its anti-diabetic formulation following the submission of comprehensive clinical trial data evidencing the drug's efficacy. This authorisation facilitated successful product launches in Indian markets.

Marketing Compliance for Digital Platforms

Marketing compliance is mandated for digital platforms and consumer-facing communications related to the promotion of pharmaceutical products via digital channels. Companies must guarantee that advertisements, whether online or offline, comply with ethical standards and refrain from deceptive assertions. The Advertising Standards Council of India (ASCI) exercises regulatory authority in this sector. Harigol Labs faced involvement from the ASCI due to its television advertisement promoting a herbal cough medication as a "guaranteed cure" for respiratory diseases. The company then amended its advertising content to comply with regulatory guidelines, safeguarding its brand reputation.

Challenges and Integration of Compliance

The amalgamation of manufacturing and marketing compliance is essential for the comprehensive success of pharmaceutical companies in India. Noncompliance with regulatory mandates may result in sanctions, product prohibitions, and erosion of consumer confidence. Nonetheless, traversing the intricacies of compliance systems presents difficulties, especially for smaller companies with constrained resources.

Technological innovations, including blockchain for data integrity and AI-driven solutions for pharmacovigilance, are assisting companies in addressing these difficulties. Prismed Bharat established a blockchain-based system to securely handle industrial records, thereby providing transparency and traceability. Utcare Solutions similarly implemented AI techniques to monitor adverse drug reactions in real time, thereby augmenting its pharmacovigilance skills.

Compliance obligations for Indian pharmaceutical companies are complex, encompassing both production processes and marketing operations. Compliance with GMP standards and environmental legislation, together with the promotion of ethical marketing and precise labelling, protects public health and stimulates industry growth. Examples from the industry, such as Navita Aarogya, Harimed Aushadhi, and Jeevecare Biotech, underscore the significance of compliance in preserving confidence and achieving operational excellence. As the pharmaceutical sector progresses, companies must proactively implement innovative solutions and comply with regulatory frameworks to overcome hurdles and succeed in the Indian market.

Comprehending pharmaceutical regulations in India necessitates a thorough understanding of the functions of principal regulatory authorities and the rigorous compliance obligations that companies must meet. Key regulatory agencies, including CDSCO, NPPA, and ICMR, fulfil unique but interrelated functions, establishing a comprehensive framework for compliance and innovation. Regulations governing manufacturing standards and ethical marketing activities guarantee the safety and accessibility of healthcare products. Industry examples illustrate how Indian enterprises manoeuvre through a complicated regulatory framework to maintain operational excellence and efficiently serve the public. The on-going evolution of the industry will ensure that the relationship between rules and compliance remains pivotal for attaining sustainable growth and enhancing healthcare outcomes throughout India. Compliance with regulatory requirements not only safeguards public health but also bolsters the credibility and competitiveness of Indian pharmaceutical companies. As the industry adapts to emerging challenges and opportunities, the regulatory framework will remain fundamental to its success, ensuring that India retains its position as a global leader in pharmaceutical innovation and accessibility.

Ethical Marketing Practices of Pharmaceutical Products

Ethical marketing techniques are fundamental to fostering trust, transparency, and responsibility within the Indian pharmaceutical sector, especially regarding the sale and advertising of prescription medications. India, being one of the major pharmaceutical markets, presents ethical problems in marketing, compelling companies to reconcile competitive expansion with social responsibility. Ethical issues predominantly stem from behaviours, including inappropriate influence on prescribing, deceptive marketing, and conflicts of interest between pharmaceutical companies and healthcare professionals. Companies are required to implement a strict code of conduct for their medical representatives, emphasising professionalism, ethics, and compliance with regulatory and ethical norms. This essay examines the ethical dilemmas in pharmaceutical sales and underscores the necessity of a well-articulated code of conduct for medical representatives, shown by industry examples.

Ethical Issues in Pharmaceutical Sales and Marketing

Ethical marketing techniques in the Indian pharmaceutical sector are crucial for upholding trust, transparency, and accountability in the promotion and sale of prescription medications. Considering the pivotal significance of prescription medications in public health, unethical marketing techniques can have extensive repercussions, impacting both patient well-being and the integrity of the healthcare system. The Indian pharmaceutical market, among the largest market worldwide, faces distinct problems, including fierce competition, a fragmented healthcare system, and a heterogeneous customer demographic. These characteristics frequently engender ethical dilemmas in pharmaceutical sales and marketing, especially with the distribution of prescription medications. This essay examines prominent ethical difficulties in this field, shown by industrial examples using fictional firm names, and underscores the necessity for accountability to maintain the integrity of pharmaceutical marketing methods.

Polypharmacy

A major ethical concern in the marketing of prescription medications is the inappropriate effect pharmaceutical companies have on prescribing behaviours. Sales and marketing teams frequently employ incentives, including gifts, sponsorships, or monetary rewards, to influence physicians' prescribing choices. These incentives can undermine physicians' autonomy and lead to polypharmacy, involving the overprescription of medications that may not serve the patients' best interests. Navmedi Aushadhi faced significant criticism for hosting an all-expenses-paid luxury symposium for cardiologists to promote its cholesterol-lowering medication. Although these marketing strategies may enhance immediate sales, they prompt enquiries over whether the drug was given due to clinical validity or marketing persuasion. This approach, while not unlawful under existing voluntary norms, raises ethical concerns because it may prioritise profit over patient well-being.

Exaggeration of Product Efficacy

Deceptive marketing assertions represent a considerable ethical dilemma within the pharmaceutical sector. Companies occasionally amplify the effectiveness of their products or minimise any adverse effects in order to secure a competitive advantage in the marketplace. Harigol Labs encountered regulatory repercussions after advertising its herbal diabetic pill as a "clinically proven cure" for diabetes. A further inquiry disclosed that the product lacked adequate proof to validate these assertions. Misleading marketing not only misleads patients but also undermines public trust in pharmaceutical companies. Ethical marketing techniques necessitate that assertions regarding a drug's advantages or hazards be substantiated by robust scientific evidence, enabling patients and healthcare practitioners to make educated choices.

Aggressive Sales Targets

A significant ethical concern is the pressure exerted on medical personnel to achieve stringent sales targets. This pressure may compel representatives to prioritise income over ethical considerations, prompting physicians to prescribe drugs inappropriately or at excessive doses. Pramsev Dawai reportedly established a performance-based incentive system for its sales force, leading representatives to provide discounts and complimentary samples to physicians who agreed to prescribe their pain-management medication. This method may improve sales success but can result in polypharmacy, abuse, and potential patient reliance on prescriptions, particularly with addictive chemicals.

Conflict of Interest

The absence of openness in financial affiliations between pharmaceutical companies and healthcare personnel exacerbates the ethical situation. Physicians often conceal the compensation they receive for participation in corporate advisory boards, speaking engagements, or clinical trials, potentially creating a conflict of interest. Navgen Vaidyak faced criticism for providing significant honorariums to Key Opinion Leaders (KOLs) in return for promoting their new antidepressant product. These endorsements, framed as impartial expert assessments, may improperly sway the prescribing behaviours of other physicians and undermine the principle of evidence-based care.

Lack of Transparency in Promoting Prescription Drugs

Unethical marketing methods for prescription medications may also involve targeting vulnerable patient populations. Some companies promote prescription medications directly to patients through marketing strategies that exaggerate their benefits and minimise hazards. Swasplus Biotech conducted a social media campaign urging individuals to enquire with their physicians about a particular arthritic medicine, asserting it may "restore full mobility in merely weeks." Nevertheless, the advertisement neglected to disclose significant potential adverse effects, resulting in criticism from patient advocacy organisations. Although patient education is essential, such initiatives must be clear and equitable to prevent the establishment of unrealistic expectations.

Post-Marketing Surveillance and Pharmacovigilance

Pharmaceutical companies have ethical dilemmas in overseeing post-marketing surveillance and pharmacovigilance. Upon the launch of pharmaceuticals, companies are accountable for overseeing their safety and managing any adverse effects. Nevertheless, certain organisations neglect to prioritise this essential issue, leading to delayed actions that may adversely affect patients. Dharmacure Dawai received criticism for postponing the recall of a batch of blood-pressure medication associated with severe allergic reactions. Ethical marketing practices necessitate that organisations respond swiftly and honestly to emerging difficulties, showcasing their commitment to patient safety as a priority.

Uniform Code of Pharmaceutical Marketing Practices (UCPMP)

The Uniform Code of Pharmaceutical Marketing Practices (UCPMP) was established as a voluntary framework to promote ethical marketing in India, addressing these difficulties. The UCPMP emphasises the value of honest advertising, the ban on inappropriate incentives, and the preservation of transparency in the ties between companies and physicians. Nonetheless, its voluntary nature constrains its efficacy, as adherence predominantly relies on the individual enterprises' dedication to ethical standards. For instance, Chivita Vaidyak has diligently implemented UCPMP requirements by guaranteeing the accuracy of its promotional materials and training its medical personnel in ethical practices, whilst other companies have been sluggish in conforming to these standards.

The sales and marketing of prescription pharmaceuticals in India provide considerable ethical concerns for the pharmaceutical sector. Undue influence on prescribing patterns, deceptive claims, lack of transparency, and inadequate pharmacovigilance erode the confidence essential to healthcare. Case studies, like Navmedi Aushadhi, Harigol Labs, and Swasplus Biotech, highlight the pressing necessity for enhanced enforcement of ethical standards and a transition towards accountability and responsibility in marketing tactics. By adopting ethical marketing principles, pharmaceutical companies can strengthen their credibility and significantly contribute to patient well-being and the integrity of the healthcare system. As the industry progresses, cultivating a culture of ethical marketing will be essential for tackling these challenges and establishing a more reliable pharmaceutical ecosystem.

Ethical Code of Conduct for Medical Representatives

In the Indian pharmaceutical industry, ethical marketing practices for prescription drugs are crucial for upholding the integrity of the healthcare system and safeguarding patient welfare. A fundamental aspect of ethical marketing is adherence to a code of behaviour for medical representatives, who are pivotal in linking pharmaceutical companies with healthcare practitioners. These individuals act as public representatives of pharmaceutical organisations and are responsible for promoting medications to healthcare professionals. Emphasising ethical conduct is essential, especially in India's dynamic and competitive market, where aggressive sales strategies may sometimes hide moral responsibility. A code of conduct outlines certain standards for professional behaviour, truthful communication, and ethical engagement to maintain confidence and transparency. A pharmaceutical marketer must examine the significance of a code of conduct for pharmaceutical medical representatives in India, supported by pertinent industry examples.

Code of Conduct for Medical Representatives in India

Medical advocates play a crucial role in promoting medications to physicians and influencing prescription patterns. However, we expect their conduct to conform to ethical standards that promote fair competition and prioritise patient care over sales incentives. Medical representatives must prioritise scientific communication by providing accurate and evidence-based information to physicians. Let us analyse the situation of a medical representative working for an Indian pharmaceutical company, Turheal Labs. Unlike many of his peers who used aggressive marketing tactics, Rahul strictly adhered to ethical principles. In advocating for a newly launched antibiotic, he emphasised the delivery of scientific material, clinical trial data, and adverse effect information to clinicians instead of employing unethical incentives. His ethical stance earned him lasting esteem among physicians and senior doctors in Mumbai. The physicians valued the scientific discussion and prescribed the Turheal Labs drug exclusively after confirming its efficacy. This scenario demonstrates how ethical marketing may cultivate trust and enduring business relationships. Conversely, unethical practices persist in specific sections of the industry. A case inspired by the industry features a medical representative from Hariswas Aarogya. To market a newly introduced hypertension drug, the medical representative sent extravagant gifts and funded a family vacation for a distinguished cardiologist in Delhi. While these techniques were formerly common, they are currently under increased scrutiny by regulatory agencies and medical organisations. Subsequent to a whistleblower report, Hariswas Aarogya was subjected to an investigation, culminating in a warning issued to the involved cardiologist by the Medical Council of India (MCI), underscoring the heightened enforcement of ethical standards.

Truthful and Evidence-Based Promotion

An essential component outlined in every code of conduct is the requirement for truthful and evidence-supported marketing of pharmaceutical products. Medical representatives must provide accurate and scientifically substantiated information about the drugs they promote, including benefits, risks, and appropriate usage. Navmedi Aushadhi, a prominent firm in cardiovascular pharmaceuticals, ensures that its medical personnel are equipped with comprehensive clinical trial data while promoting a novel cardiac therapy. During dialogues with cardiologists, Navmedi Aushadhi's medical staff emphasises empirical evidence without overstating the drug's efficacy or downplaying its side effects. This approach fosters informed decision-making among physicians and enhances trust between the organisation and the healthcare sector.

Prohibition of Unethical Inducements

A crucial element of the code of conduct is the prohibition of unethical incentives offered to healthcare providers. Ethics standards specifically forbid the use of gifts, financial inducements, or lavish hospitality to influence prescribing behaviours. Nevertheless, some companies succumb to competitive pressures and engage in such techniques, leading to a significant ethical dilemma. In response, Sevagol Remedies instituted a zero-tolerance policy regarding inducements. Medical representatives are restricted from offering anything beyond low-cost educational materials, such as drug monographs or medical literature. Sevagol Remedies emphasises value-driven interactions, highlighting the need for professionalism and respect for doctors' clinical autonomy.

Professional Independence for Doctors and Physicians

Preserving the professional autonomy of healthcare practitioners is a fundamental principle of the ethical code for medical representatives. Pharmaceutical businesses must guarantee that their representatives interact with healthcare professionals in a manner that respects their experience and clinical judgement. For example, Jeegol Aushadhi instructs its representatives to prioritise comprehending the distinct requirements of doctors, physicians, and their patients and customise their dialogues to offer solutions without imposing excessive pressure. His strategy eschews coercive strategies, such as imposing monthly prescription quotas or providing conditional incentives, which may compromise the ethical demarcation between healthcare practitioners and pharmaceutical companies.

Uniform Code of Pharmaceutical Marketing Practices (UCPMP)

Notwithstanding the presence of ethical rules, compliance continues to pose a difficulty in a fiercely competitive industry. Certain companies prioritise sales objectives over ethical standards, creating an environment in which medical professionals may feel compelled to engage in dubious practices. The Uniform Code of Pharmaceutical Marketing Practices (UCPMP) functions as a voluntary framework to promote ethical marketing within the industry. Nonetheless, its nonbinding character restricts its enforceability, necessitating that individual enterprises accept and internalise these values.

Regular Training Programs

Education and training are essential for enabling medical representatives to internalise the concepts of ethical marketing. Pharmaceutical businesses are progressively allocating resources towards on-going training programs aimed at instructing their medical representatives on legal and ethical standards, product expertise, and proficient communication skills. Navmed Solutions conducts monthly workshops for its sales teams, addressing subjects such as adherence to the Uniform Code of Pharmaceutical Marketing Practices (UCPMP) and ensuring transparency in their engagements with healthcare professionals (HCPs). These training sessions not only augment the proficiency of representatives but also strengthen a culture of ethical awareness within the organisation.

Ethical Standards for Continuing Medical Education (CME) Sponsorships

Pharmaceutical companies frequently provide Continuing Medical Education (CME) seminars to inform physicians about the newest breakthroughs in medicine. While these events serve an educational purpose, ethical issues arise when they serve as a front for lavish sponsorships and hidden marketing tactics. An exemplary instance is Jeeplus Raambaan, which conducted a Continuing Medical Education (CME) event in Bengaluru with esteemed medical professionals who deliberated on recent advancements in cardiology. The program was devoid of product endorsements and concentrated exclusively on scientific education. BiswaSewa Solutions conducted a comparable event in Goa, providing doctors with all-expense-paid luxury accommodations, which has elicited concerns regarding ethical breaches. Regulatory authorities are progressively scrutinising CME events to ensure adherence to ethical norms.

Monitoring and Accountability Mechanisms

Monitoring and accountability measures are essential for enforcing the code of conduct and rectifying departures from ethical standards. Organisations frequently create compliance committees or appoint special ethical officers to supervise medical representatives' actions. For instance, Jeewell Dawai established a whistleblower policy that promotes the reporting of unethical conduct by employees without the apprehension of retaliation. The organisation employs digital tracking techniques to assess the frequency, content, and results of medical representatives' visits to physicians. These procedures guarantee that interactions conform to ethical standards and regulatory obligations.

Transparency in Drug Pricing and Sample Distribution

A crucial element of ethical marketing is transparency in pharmaceutical pricing and the dissemination of complimentary samples. The Indian pharmaceutical business frequently encounters pricing disputes, as certain companies maintain artificially elevated medicine prices while providing substantial discounts to physicians, resulting in opaque pricing practices. A medical representative from Chikvish Vaidyak adhered to ethical standards while providing complimentary samples. The medical representative strictly adhered to the strategy of supplying minimal samples for physicians to evaluate drug efficacy rather than distributing excessive quantities to sway prescriptions. Conversely, a medical representative from the rival firm Jeevecare Biotech consistently supplied bulk samples to clinics, so facilitating the endorsement of his company's product by physicians over alternatives. Ethical marketing standards admonish these practices, despite their prevalence.

Ethical Practices in Digital and Social Media Promotions

The pharmaceutical industry's adoption of digital transformation has led to an expansion of the ethical code for medical representatives, incorporating requirements for digital engagement. Pharmaceutical companies are employing ethical online marketing to educate physicians and patients, facilitated by the emergence of digital platforms. Medical personnel are now required to engage in virtual conversations with the same degree of professionalism and transparency as in-person meetings. Harigol Remedies has a digital marketing policy mandating its sales team to maintain honesty and balance in online promotional materials, refraining from dramatic claims or targeting susceptible patient demographics. Harigol Remedies retains its reputation in a progressively technology-orientated business by incorporating ethical ideals into its digital strategies. Social media, webinars, and mobile applications have emerged as indispensable instruments for ethical pharmaceutical advertising. Kalyur Bharat initiated an educational effort on LinkedIn and Twitter, disseminating validated research and expert insights on diabetes care. The campaign emphasised disease awareness more than direct product advertising, thereby ensuring compliance with ethical rules. Despite India's prohibition on direct-to-consumer (DTC) prescription medication promotion, several companies continue to exploit digital networks for this purpose. A significant example concerned Swaspram Remedies, which encountered regulatory punishment for advertising a prescription-only antibiotic on Facebook, contravening ethical marketing standards.

Pharmacovigilance Efforts

Medical personnel contribute to pharmacovigilance initiatives by monitoring and reporting Adverse Drug Reactions (ADRs). Ethical rules underscore the obligation of representatives to communicate any input from doctors, physicians, or patients concerning drug safety to the company's pharmacovigilance team. Utcare Solutions prompts its medical representatives to record and escalate complaints of adverse drug reactions (ADRs) related to its products, facilitating prompt investigations and remedial measures. This practice solidifies the company's dedication to patient safety and adherence to regulations.

Ethical Relationship between Doctors and Pharmaceutical Companies

The association between physicians and pharmaceutical companies should be grounded in scientific principles and patient welfare, rather than personal gain. Ethical norms forbid companies from providing financial incentives, extravagant gifts, or vacations in return for the prescription of their medicines. Turcur Aarogya exemplifies success by fostering robust interactions with physicians through scientific discourse, medical conferences, and research partnerships. They supported autonomous research endeavours instead of swaying physicians with unethical inducements. Conversely, a judicial examination found Swagol Labs culpable for providing costly electronic devices to physicians who met a specific prescription threshold.

Regulatory Bodies and the Future of Ethical Pharmaceutical Marketing in India

Regulatory agencies such as the National Pharmaceutical Pricing Authority (NPPA), the Central Drug Standard Control Organisation (CDSCO), and the Medical Council of India (MCI) are intensifying enforcement against unethical pharmaceutical marketing activities. Although currently voluntary, we anticipate that the UCPMP will become legally obligatory, thereby enforcing stricter adherence.

Adhering to a rigorous code of conduct provides benefits that extend beyond simple compliance; it promotes the sustained success of pharmaceutical companies. Organisations that prioritise ethical marketing foster strong alliances with medical experts, enhance their brand reputations, and mitigate their legal obligations. Harigol Labs' commitment to ethical standards has positioned the company as a trustworthy collaborator for physicians and healthcare institutions, leading to sustained market growth despite fierce competition.

Ethical marketing methods are essential for tackling the difficulties related to the sale and promotion of prescription medications in the Indian pharmaceutical sector. Pharmaceutical companies are essential in maintaining integrity and accountability by addressing concerns including undue influence and deceptive claims, as well as establishing complete rules of conduct for medical representatives. The code of conduct for pharmaceutical medical representatives is essential in fostering ethical marketing practices within the

Indian pharmaceutical sector. By prioritising honest marketing, forbidding unethical incentives, honouring the autonomy of physicians, and encouraging transparency, these rules guarantee that the interests of patients and healthcare professionals are paramount. Industry examples demonstrate how organisations can effectively incorporate ethical values in their sales and marketing practices. As the business evolves, the implementation of comprehensive ethical norms and stringent enforcement procedures will be essential for fostering confidence, enhancing patient care, and maintaining the sustainability of the pharmaceutical sector in India.

Disclaimer: To ensure strict confidentiality, company names and head office locations in the examples cited in this chapter have been intentionally altered to protect confidentiality. Any resemblance to actual entities is purely coincidental

Case Studies

Case 1: In the heavily regulated Indian pharmaceutical market, companies must manoeuvre a complicated framework of compliance standards overseen by various regulatory authorities to guarantee the safety, efficacy, and accessibility of their medicines. An exemplary case is Sankalp Therapeutics, a mid-sized pharmaceutical company located in Gujarat that produces both generic medications and nutraceuticals. The company commenced the expansion of its operations by constructing a new sterile injectable facility, for which it requested authorisation from the Central Drugs Standard Control Organisation (CDSCO). An exhaustive examination uncovered deficiencies in the documentation of sanitation procedures and air management systems. Sankalp promptly enhanced its HVAC systems, digitised standard operating procedure documentation, and strengthened staff training, ultimately obtaining CDSCO accreditation in accordance with Schedule M Good Manufacturing Practices (GMP). Simultaneously, to diminish its reliance on imports, the company created an internal Active Pharmaceutical Ingredient (API) manufacturing facility. It enrolled in the Production Linked Incentive (PLI) system under the Department of Pharmaceuticals, necessitating compliance with particular environmental requirements and local sourcing regulations. The state drug control authority evaluated the facility for a license, emphasising hygiene, batch record management, and equipment validation. Sankalp simultaneously introduced a new heart medication and adjusted its pricing in accordance with a direction from the National Pharmaceutical Pricing Authority (NPPA) under the Drug Price Control Order (DPCO), thereby affecting its pricing strategy while enhancing patient affordability. The company collaborated with the Indian Council of Medical Research (ICMR) to conduct an ethically compliant clinical trial, following protocols for informed consent and data privacy. In anticipation of future export endeavours, Sankalp partnered with PharmEXCIL to conform to international standards, including those set by the USFDA. This case demonstrates how adherence to regulatory, ethical, and manufacturing standards can facilitate operational expansion while fulfilling public health objectives.

Case 2: In the rapidly evolving and competitive Indian pharmaceutical sector, Pratham Therapeutics, a midsize pharmaceutical manufacturing company located in Ahmedabad, implemented an innovative ethical marketing campaign that revolutionised its field force culture. The company implemented a compulsory "Ethical Interaction Protocol" (EIP) for all medical representatives (MRs), highlighting scientific discourse, the prohibition of incentives, and transparent communication. An MR named Meera Srivastava, operating in the cancer healthcare market in Pune, embodied these principles during her regular visits to doctors. Instead of emphasising promotional objectives or providing incentives, Meera constantly disseminated peer-reviewed journal data, pharmacoeconomic evaluations, and real-world safety information regarding Pratham's novel oral chemotherapy medication. She established a reputation as a trustworthy provider of impartial scientific knowledge. Her ethical methodology resulted in heightened acceptance among oncologists, who valued her deference to their clinical judgement. Simultaneously, the company allocated resources to on-going training sessions centred on the Uniform Code of Pharmaceutical Marketing Practices (UCPMP), guaranteeing that all field personnel understood the limits of permissible behaviour. Pratham created a computerised visit tracking system that identified discrepancies between sanctioned interaction guidelines. Consequently, the company experienced a consistent increase in prescription volume for their new medication, achieved not through inducement but through established confidence. Regulatory audits revealed no compliance violations, and the firm was commended by a regional medical ethics organisation. This case demonstrates how strong ethical frameworks, personnel training, and monitoring systems can establish a corporation as a reliable partner in healthcare, thereby improving both reputation and performance while safeguarding patient welfare and professional integrity.

Suggestive Questions from the Chapter

1. In what manner do Indian regulatory authorities balance innovation and public safety within the pharmaceutical sector?
2. How does ethical compliance affect the reputations of pharmaceutical marketers and their organisations?
3. In what manner do CDSCO and NPPA together ensure drug safety, accessibility, and affordability in India?
4. In what ways do regulatory frameworks affect the operational strategy of Indian pharmaceutical companies in production and marketing?
5. What obstacles do smaller pharmaceutical companies encounter in adhering to India's rigorous compliance regulations?
6. In what ways are technological developments enhancing compliance and pharmacovigilance within the Indian pharmaceutical sector?
7. What is the impact of aggressive pharmaceutical marketing on physicians' prescribing practices and patient treatment results in India?
8. In what manner do conflicts of interest between physicians and companies influence evidence-based healthcare decision-making processes?
9. In what manner does the ethical behaviour of medical representatives affect enduring trust between physicians and pharmaceutical companies?
10. How can digital promotions conform to ethical requirements within India's pharmaceutical marketing sector?

Multiple Choice Questions

1. Which authority oversees drug approvals and clinical trials at the national Indian level?
   (a) WHO (b) CDSCO
   (c) NITI Aayog (d) FDA
2. What is the primary concern of regulations enforced during pharmaceutical clinical trials?
   (a) Cost (b) Innovation
   (c) Safety (d) Branding

3. What law serves as the backbone of India's pharmaceutical legislative framework?
   (a) Patent (b) Tax
   (c) Drugs (d) Copyright
4. Which company conducted trials adhering to ethical standards for diabetes drug approval?
   (a) Zydus (b) Cipla
   (c) Navita (d) Lupin
5. What must companies like Harigol Labs comply with to secure manufacturing licenses?
   (a) HACCP (b) GDP
   (c) GMP (d) CSR
6. Who implements the ceiling prices under the Drug Price Control Order (DPCO), 2013?
   (a) ICMR (b) CDSCO
   (c) NPPA (d) PharmEXCIL
7. Which organization regulates clinical research ethics in the Indian pharmaceutical industry?
   (a) FSSAI (b) ICMR
   (c) BIS (d) DoP
8. What regulates manufacturing standards under Schedule M of Drugs and Cosmetics Rules?
   (a) GMP (b) UCPMP
   (c) FSSAI (d) ASCI
9. Who supervises the Production Linked Incentive (PLI) scheme for pharmaceutical growth?
   (a) BIS (b) NPPA
   (c) DoP (d) CDSCO
10. Which council helps Indian pharmaceutical companies obtain international regulatory approvals?
    (a) ICMR (b) NPPA
    (c) PharmEXCIL (d) ASCI

11. Which organization established blockchain to enhance transparency in pharmaceutical industrial record-keeping?
    (a) Utcare (b) Navita
    (c) Prismed (d) Swasplus
12. What marketing issue involves overstating a drug's benefits while ignoring possible risks?
    (a) Polypharmacy (b) Transparency
    (c) Exaggeration (d) Pharmacovigilance
13. Which voluntary framework encourages ethical pharmaceutical marketing in India?
    (a) NPPA (b) ICMR
    (c) CDSCO (d) UCPMP
14. Who ensures ethical promotion of medications and maintains scientific dialogue with doctors?
    (a) Advertisers (b) Chemists
    (c) Representatives (d) Manufacturers
15. Which fictional company funded a physician's luxury vacation, raising ethical concerns?
    (a) Harigol (b) Turheal
    (c) Hariswas (d) Jeevecare
16. What ensures marketing claims about drugs are scientifically valid and responsibly communicated?
    (a) Fiction (b) Evidence
    (c) Opinion (d) Speculation
17. What type of incentives is strictly forbidden in ethical pharmaceutical marketing practices?
    (a) Gifts (b) Surveys
    (c) Posters (d) Samples
18. What principle protects doctors from pressure in prescribing decisions by companies?
    (a) Coercion (b) Manipulation
    (c) Independence (d) Quota

19. What nonbinding framework guides ethical promotion in the pharmaceutical industry?
    (a) WHO (b) FDA
    (c) UCPMP (d) IMA
20. What promotes internal awareness about ethics through regular company-conducted workshops?
    (a) Lectures (b) Retreats
    (c) Training (d) Bonuses
21. Which platform did Kalyur Bharat use for educational diabetes awareness campaign in India?
    (a) YouTube (b) Instagram
    (c) LinkedIn (d) Pinterest
22. What kind of drug was Swaspram Remedies penalised for advertising on Facebook?
    (a) Vitamin (b) Antibiotic
    (c) Analgesic (d) Antacid
23. What do medical representatives report as part of pharmacovigilance activities?
    (a) Discounts (b) Sales
    (c) Complaints (d) Reactions
24. What type of gifts is considered unethical in pharma-doctor relationships?
    (a) Pens (b) Books
    (c) Vacations (d) Samples
25. Which body may make UCPMP legally binding for pharmaceutical marketing in India?
    (a) MCI (b) WHO
    (c) FDA (d) CPCB

CHAPTER 13

Future Trends and Innovations in Field Marketing

Introduction

The pharmaceutical sector in India is seeing swift upheaval, driven by technical developments, changing customer expectations, and regulatory reforms. India, a leading manufacturer of generic medications and a prominent participant in global pharmaceutical exports, is positioned for substantial innovation in its prescription medicine market. Due to changing healthcare demands, increasing regulatory restrictions, and a difficulties and opportunities. In this dynamic context, sales and marketing tactics for prescription medications are undergoing extraordinary transformations. The sales and marketing landscape of prescription medications is undergoing. The era of traditional marketing channels is ended; contemporary methods based on data-driven decision-making, patient-centricity, and digital engagements are transforming the market introduction of prescription medications. The advent of data-driven decision-making, telemedicine, and patient-centric marketing techniques is transforming the interaction between pharmaceutical corporations, healthcare professionals (HCPs), and patients. The pharmaceutical marketer must comprehend the rising trends and disruptive ideas that are transforming this vital company.

For decades, the Indian pharmaceutical industry mostly depended on traditional marketing strategies, chiefly involving medical representatives engaging with physicians. The rising costs of healthcare and value-based healthcare strategies. This necessitates a more advanced and customer-centric approach to sales and marketing. A prominent trend in pharmaceutical sales is the integration of digital and omnichannel marketing with Artificial Intelligence (AI), Machine Learning (ML), and Big Data analytics. These have completely revolutionised the functioning of pharmaceutical sales and marketing teams. Pharmaceutical companies collaborate with physicians and clinicians. Predictive analytics and AI-generated customer insights facilitate demographic analysis with remarkable precision, while machine learning algorithms enhance resource allocation for increased marketing efficiency. AI-driven chatbots, automated CRM systems, and big data analytics are enabling pharmaceutical companies to enhance their marketing strategies, ensuring that the relevant content reaches the proper audience at the ideal moment.

In conjunction with technical advancements, demographic and India's population significantly influence the marketing landscape. Pharmaceutical marketers must comprehend the influence of data-driven decision-making and investigate how pharmaceutical real-world evidence and predictive analytics to enhance their sales and marketing strategies. Telemedicine and e-pharmacies are transforming the sales and distribution of prescription medications. As online consultations and digital prescriptions gain acceptance, pharmaceutical companies are investigating direct-to-consumer (DTC) marketing strategies. With the expansion of urbanisation and the deepening of internet penetration, people are increasingly aware and engaged in maintaining their health. Digital platforms, such as telemedicine, e-commerce, and social media, have become essential avenues for pharmaceutical marketing. This transformation in market dynamics is promoting a more transparent and patient-centred methodology, wherein patients have enhanced access to pharmaceutical information and treatment alternatives. Moreover, the emergence of mobile health (mHealth) applications presents pharmaceutical companies with opportunities to engage directly with patients and oversee their compliance with prescribed treatments. The market's revolutionary development presents regulatory issues, as India's pharmaceutical industry must reconcile innovation with compliance to uphold ethical marketing practices.

The legal framework in India regarding drug promotion is getting more rigorous, necessitating enhanced transparency and ethical adherence. This trend requires marketers to devise innovative techniques that reconcile regulatory compliance with effective messaging. A significant domain of innovation is precision medicine and the influence of genetics in pharmaceutical marketing. Biotechnology advancements are facilitating pharmaceutical corporations in creating targeted medicines informed by genetic profiles. Contemporary pharmaceutical marketers must examine the problems and opportunities inherent in this intricate regulatory landscape, highlighting the necessity for ethical and responsible marketing strategies.

Emerging trends in prescription medicine marketing underscore the increasing significance of sustainability and social responsibility. The function of medical representatives is also transforming due to these technological improvements. Although in-person connections are essential, the hybrid paradigm of digital and physical engagement is becoming increasingly significant. Although direct encounters are essential, the hybrid approach of digital and physical engagement is becoming increasingly significant. Medical reps are now equipped with AI-driven tools, digital dashboards, and e-detailing platforms that augment their capacity to provide data-driven insights to physicians. The future of pharmaceutical sales in India will certainly be influenced by technology, regulation, and changing stakeholder expectations. Through the analysis of technology instruments and strategic frameworks, contemporary pharmaceutical marketers can identify the opportunities and difficulties confronting industry participants in this dynamic environment. The Indian pharmaceutical market adjusts to these changes; companies that embrace innovation and implement a multi-channel marketing strategy will secure a competitive advantage. The emphasis is on recognising sustainable and ethical approaches that prioritise patient welfare and enhance healthcare progress in India.

Emerging Technologies for Pharmaceutical Sales

India's pharmaceutical market is a dynamic sector where emerging technologies are transforming the marketing, distribution, and alignment of prescription pharmaceuticals with patient needs. Emerging technologies, including artificial intelligence (AI), machine learning (ML), e-commerce and logistics developments, and big data-driven patient analytics, are essential for optimising pharmaceutical product sales. The amalgamation of these technologies transcends mere technological sophistication; it involves devising customised solutions for the distinctive and extensive requirements of India's populace. Numerous industrial examples illustrate this transition in India, highlighting how digital innovations are optimising processes and closing gaps in the healthcare ecosystem. The sales of prescription medications, an essential sector, are undergoing a transformation propelled by artificial intelligence, e-commerce, and big data analytics.

AI and Machine Learning for Pharmaceuticals Sales

Emerging technologies, especially artificial intelligence (AI) and machine learning (ML), are transforming the sale of prescription medications in the Indian pharmaceutical sector, facilitating improved efficiency, personalisation, and accuracy in targeting healthcare professionals and patients. As the demand for prescription medications escalates, pharmaceutical companies are progressively utilising these technologies to refine sales strategies, optimise operations, and increase patient outcomes. Historically, pharmaceutical sales in India have depended significantly on medical representatives consulting physicians, a practice that, although effective, is resource-intensive and frequently lacks detailed data analysis. These technologies have profoundly influenced the sales of prescription medications in India, as corporations implement AI-driven solutions to enhance sales force efficacy, forecast market trends, and engage healthcare professionals more effectively. AI-driven platforms can transform this methodology by evaluating extensive information, encompassing physician prescription trends, patient demographics, regional disease prevalence, and social media sentiment, to yield actionable insights.

Identifying High Potential Customers by AI

A significant domain where AI is exerting influence is in the analysis of prescribing trends and the identification of high-potential clients. Pharmaceutical companies can mitigate stagnant sales in semi-urban or rural areas by implementing AI-driven sales platforms. This technology may examine historical sales data, patient demographics, and regional disease frequency patterns to determine clusters of physicians most likely to prescribe medications. The system may classify physicians based on their prescribed behaviours—general practitioners, specialists, and key opinion leaders—allowing the corporation to customise its outreach strategy. The sales team, equipped with AI-driven insights, approaches this cluster with personalised instructional materials, clinical trial data, and customised engagement strategies. This can result in substantial growth in prescription numbers for its main antibiotic.

Enhancing Customer Relationship Management

Improving medical salespeople's customer relationship management (CRM) systems is a major application of AI and ML. Let us examine a pharmaceutical company that manufactures respiratory medications. Acknowledging that medical representatives may allocate unnecessary time to plan organisation and reporting, the organisation might implement an AI-integrated CRM system. The system's predictive functionalities will recommend appropriate visitation patterns, considering each physician's availability, recent interactions, and prescribing potential. The CRM can deliver comprehensive, real-time updates on competitors' pharmaceuticals and industry trends, allowing medical professionals to effectively communicate competitive advantages. Medical professionals can use the method to obtain a prescription commitment from a single hospital by demonstrating how their company's product exceeds competitors' safety metrics. It would not only enhance the efficiency of the medical representative but also lead to a boom in sales.

AI Integration in Digital Marketing

The role of AI in targeting digital marketing channels can be transformational. Pharmaceutical companies can use machine learning algorithms to analyse patient behaviours online. Through the analysis of questions about symptoms and medications on platforms like Google-powered health forums, companies can gain valuable insights. Companies can discern trends in demand for their product line. Pharmaceutical companies can leverage these insights to develop precisely targeted digital marketing that furnishes patients with educational content and encourages them to contact qualified physicians. Companies can design a campaign with interactive features like virtual symptom checkers and mental health resource guides for patients to explore. Consequently, the companies can observe a significant rise in prescription rates.

Digital Engagement Through AI and ML

Artificial intelligence and machine learning have enhanced digital engagement methods within the Indian pharmaceutical sector. As telemedicine and e-pharmacy proliferate, pharmaceutical companies can utilise AI-driven digital platforms to engage with physicians and patients. Companies may collaborate with prominent telemedicine platforms to advertise their prescription medications using AI-generated content recommendations. During online consultations, the platform can recommend pertinent medications based on AI analysis of patient symptoms and treatment history. This connection will enable pharmaceutical companies to expand their audience, hence enhancing accessibility to prescription pharmaceuticals.

AI-Driven Chatbots

Chatbots and virtual assistants may serve as formidable instruments in pharmaceutical sales and post-sales support. These AI-driven tools can aid medical reps in delivering immediate information to physicians and chemists regarding new pharmaceuticals, dosage protocols, and clinical trial data. Firms can create pharmaceutical chatbots to interact with physicians via WhatsApp and mobile applications. Chatbots generally deliver real-time updates regarding new prescription medications, dosages, clinical trial outcomes, drug efficacy, promotional offers, and regulatory modifications. The chatbot can facilitate order placement and shipment tracking, thereby alleviating the strain on medical representatives and improving drug wholesalers' satisfaction. Integrating AI-powered chatbots enables pharmaceutical companies to facilitate effective contact with healthcare experts, resulting in enhanced sales performance.

Enhancing Pharmaceutical Marketing Campaigns

Furthermore, AI can improve the efficacy of pharmaceutical marketing initiatives. Historically, marketing strategies have frequently depended on generic messages that may not connect with all physicians or patients. AI-driven systems can evaluate physician profiles and patient preferences to tailor marketing communications, guaranteeing their relevance and engagement. Companies can utilise AI to assist doctors and clinicians engaged in rare illness treatments and research. Consequently, companies can provide promotional materials and research data pertaining to their R&D on the newest clinical trial findings and research publications. This focused strategy can enhance the probability of physicians' dependence on the companies and their offerings.

Facilitating Remote Patient Monitoring And Adherence

AI-driven technologies can enhance remote patient monitoring and compliance. This is especially pertinent in the management of chronic conditions such as diabetes and hypertension, where patient compliance with drug protocols is essential. Pharmaceutical start-ups can create mobile applications that use AI to monitor patients' medication adherence, measure vital signs, and deliver personalised reminders. The application could facilitate connections between patients and medical professionals for remote consultations and assistance.

AI Driven Sales Forecasting

AI-assisted sales forecasting is a transformational breakthrough in the Indian pharmaceutical sector. Conventional forecasting techniques often depend on past sales data; however, artificial intelligence can augment this process by integrating external variables such as seasonal illnesses, economic trends, and regulatory modifications. Organisations can use AI-driven forecasting instruments to anticipate the sales success of pharmaceuticals. The AI technologies can leverage real-time data from hospitals, governmental health programs, and meteorological patterns to predict seasonal diseases. Such prediction allows pharmaceutical companies to modify production schedules, enhance inventory management, and strategically allocate sales teams.

Integrating AI in Field Force Management

The incorporation of AI into field force management can augment the productivity of medical representatives. AI-driven smartphone applications can assist sales teams with scheduling visits, analysing physician preferences, and monitoring their effectiveness. Pharmaceutical companies can provide their medical representatives with an AI-enabled mobile application that recommends the most effective routes for physician appointments, thereby assuring optimal time management. These applications can also offer instantaneous feedback on sales presentations, enabling representatives to enhance their strategies based on physician reactions. AI-driven solutions for managing field forces can enhance the efficiency of medical representatives, resulting in increased prescription medicine sales.

Integrating AI in Pharmaceutical Sales Training

Moreover, AI has enhanced the effectiveness of pharmaceutical sales training programs. Educating medical personnel is essential for the proper promotion of prescription drugs, and AI-driven e-learning platforms have revolutionised this process. TrainPharm Academy, an AI-based pharmaceutical training institution in Mumbai, provides customised learning courses for salespeople. The AI system evaluates personal performance, detects knowledge deficiencies, and recommends tailored training materials. This strategy guarantees that sales staff remains educated about the most recent medical innovations and regulatory modifications, which facilitates more knowledgeable engagements with physicians.

Predictive Analytics for Optimizing Inventory and Supply Chain Management

Given India's extensive geography and diverse supply chain infrastructure, the timely delivery of prescription medications is essential. Machine learning algorithms can forecast demand variations by analysing historical sales data, seasonal patterns, and epidemiological trends. Pharmaceutical firms can use predictive analytics, a branch of AI, to enhance inventory and supply chain management. Let us examine a real-world scenario in which a pharmaceutical company encounters substantial difficulties in guaranteeing prompt deliveries to remote regions, particularly during festive seasons when demand frequently escalates unpredictably. By implementing a machine learning-based predictive inventory management system, the company can examine previous sales trends, holiday dates, and seasonal illnesses to correctly forecast supply needs.

This proactive strategy can mitigate stockouts in different locations of the country, substantially decreasing revenue losses. Artificial intelligence can optimise the order fulfilment process by minimising errors and delays. AI-driven chatbots can be incorporated into a pharmaceutical distributor's online portal to address customer enquiries, facilitate order processing, and monitor shipments, thereby alleviating the burden on medical personnel. This capability is especially vital in rural regions where access to medical professionals is restricted, and the prompt provision of needed pharmaceuticals is critical.

Pharmacovigilance through AI

Drug safety monitoring is another area where AI is proving to be transformative. An AI technology can track adverse drug reactions (ADRs) reported by patients and healthcare professionals. These machine learning algorithm-based solutions can analyse electronic health data and social media platforms to identify pharmacological adverse effects. Consequently, these technologies can assist pharmaceutical companies in making strategic decisions regarding their marketing campaigns, by emphasising clearer dosage directions and warnings. Consequently, these AI tools can significantly aid in risk reduction more expeditiously.

Detection and Prevention of Counterfeit Drugs

Artificial intelligence systems can aid in the identification and prevention of counterfeit pharmaceuticals, a critical issue in the Indian drug business. Machine learning algorithms can examine the chemical makeup and packaging of pharmaceuticals to detect counterfeit items. Regulatory authorities can employ an AI-driven system to examine and analyse pharmaceutical samples obtained from pharmacies and hospitals nationwide. This device can swiftly detect counterfeit medications and notify authorities, so it prevents them from reaching patients. This capability is essential for guaranteeing the safety and effectiveness of prescribed medications.

As these technologies advance, their integration will undoubtedly intensify, promoting collaborations among pharmaceutical companies, technology providers, and healthcare stakeholders. Despite problems including data privacy, algorithm transparency, and equal access, the future holds significant potential. Nonetheless, with on-going technological progress and increasing investments in AI-driven solutions, the Indian pharmaceutical business is set for further transformation. Organisations that adopt AI and ML will secure a competitive advantage, facilitate efficient prescription medicine sales, and enhance patient outcomes.

E Commerce and Logistics in Pharmaceutical Marketing

Innovations in e-commerce and sophisticated logistics are driving a digital transformation in the Indian pharmaceutical market. The amalgamation of these technologies has the potential to transform the prescription drug sales framework, enhancing its efficiency, transparency, and patient orientation. The integration of e-commerce and advanced logistics for pharmaceutical companies has the potential to revolutionise prescription drug sales in the Indian market. India, as the preeminent supplier of generics and with a swiftly expanding domestic healthcare sector, presents a conducive environment for innovation in this domain. Should pharmaceutical firms use innovative e-commerce solutions and cutting-edge logistics technologies, they are likely to experience numerous advantages, including enhanced market reach, optimised operations, improved patient outcomes, and strengthened regulatory compliance. The seamless incorporation of e-commerce would enable patients in rural areas of the country, who were previously underserved, to obtain crucial pharmaceuticals with unparalleled convenience. The direct-to-consumer strategy will significantly diminish dependence on middlemen, optimise the supply chain, and guarantee prompt delivery, thereby enhancing patient adherence and health outcomes.

Enhancing Accessibility of Drugs through E-Commerce

In a future when e-commerce platforms are essential to pharmaceutical distribution, companies can markedly improve the accessibility of prescription medications throughout India's extensive and varied landscape. Conventional brick-and-mortar pharmacies frequently do not reach remote rural regions, resulting in millions lacking prompt access to vital prescriptions. Through the use of e-commerce, pharmaceutical companies can create virtual pharmacies, enabling patients to submit prescriptions online and obtain home delivery of their medicines. The growing prevalence of internet access and smartphone usage positions e-commerce platforms as transformational for pharmaceutical companies. By creating online prescription drug marketplaces, companies can expand their reach to tier-2 and tier-3 cities, as well as rural regions where access to quality medications is frequently constrained. Companies embracing e-commerce will facilitate the implementation of digital prescription fulfilment models, ensuring patients obtain their medications without undue delays. Moreover, the use of AI-driven recommendation systems in e-commerce platforms might provide patients with tailored choices for related products, such as wellness supplements or appropriate medicines, thereby improving consumer happiness and loyalty.

Developing Pharmaceutical Logistics with IoT

The successful operation of e-commerce in pharmaceutical sales hinges on the capacity to supply prescription medications securely, efficiently, and in accordance with regulatory standards. Premium logistics may function as the foundation of the e-commerce ecosystem, guaranteeing the efficient, safe, and compliant delivery of drugs in accordance with rigorous storage standards. We anticipate that innovations such as IoT-enabled cold chain logistics will revolutionise the transportation of temperature-sensitive pharmaceuticals, such as vaccines, insulin, and biologics. Pharmaceutical companies may minimise product spoilage during transit and preserve the integrity of their medications by utilising smart sensors to monitor conditions, such as temperature, humidity, and vibration, in real time. This skill is particularly vital for India, where environmental variability and infrastructure obstacles frequently threaten medicine quality. In the future, AI-driven demand forecasting will enable companies to anticipate the requirement for specific medicines across several geographies, ensuring effective distribution and inventory management. In the future, pharmaceutical companies may investigate the application of IoT technology to establish transparent and tamper-proof supply chains, guaranteeing that medications arrive to consumers in their original state with minimal risk.

AI and Blockchain for Prescription Verification and Fraud Prevention

A significant concern in online prescription drug sales is the threat of counterfeit medications and false prescriptions. Pharmaceutical companies can create a secure and transparent prescription verification system by integrating AI and blockchain technologies. AI-powered algorithms will examine submitted prescriptions, validate them against medical databases, and confirm their legitimacy prior to order processing. This approach will mitigate the risk of misuse and guarantee adherence to medical laws. Blockchain technology can augment security by establishing an immutable ledger of transactions. Every prescription can be documented on the blockchain, enabling parties such as physicians, chemists, and regulators to monitor the progression of medications from production to ultimate delivery. Such an approach can guarantee accountability, reduce the likelihood of counterfeit drugs infiltrating the supply chain, and foster consumer confidence in online pharmaceutical services.

Emergency Drone Delivery Distribution Systems for Pharmaceutical Products

Drone delivery systems signify ground breaking advancement in logistics, set to transform the distribution of prescription medications. Advancements in drone technology and favourable legal frameworks may enable pharmaceutical companies to use autonomous drones for medication delivery in inaccessible locales, like hilly terrain, flood-affected areas, or regions isolated by natural disasters. In the forthcoming years, drone technology will facilitate expedited and contactless delivery of prescription medications, particularly in remote and rural regions where conventional logistical networks encounter difficulties. Drones can enhance delivery efficiency and guarantee the continuous availability of essential medications by diminishing dependence on traditional transportation systems, especially in adverse conditions. Regulatory-sanctioned drone deliveries will markedly decrease the duration required to transport emergency pharmaceuticals, guaranteeing that vital patients obtain their prescriptions promptly, particularly in urban environments. Moreover, driverless trucks featuring intelligent storage compartments will optimise last-mile deliveries, enabling patients to retrieve their medicines from safe collection locations. This breakthrough has the potential to transform emergency response capabilities, providing a swift and dependable answer for critical medical needs.

Converging Telemedicine and E-Pharmacies for a Digital Health Ecosystem

Moreover, the future may see the integration of telemedicine and e-pharmacies, resulting in a comprehensive healthcare experience. Patients will have the capability to chat with physicians remotely, obtain electronic prescriptions, and effortlessly order their meds via linked platforms. AI-driven chatbots and virtual assistants can offer tailored pharmaceutical advising and adherence assistance, enabling patients to manage their health effectively. A patient may receive a virtual consultation from a professional, followed by automatic medication delivery to their residence, accompanied by personalised reminders and educational resources. This integrated strategy can enhance patient involvement and adherence, resulting in improved health outcomes and decreased healthcare expenditures. The consolidation of patient data via e-commerce platforms can facilitate the creation of predictive analytics that reveal trends in disease prevalence and medication utilisation. Pharmaceutical companies can harness these insights to optimise marketing efforts, devise tailored interventions, and enhance patient access to important medications. A pharmaceutical corporation may use AI to discover areas with a high prevalence of diabetes and subsequently implement tailored awareness campaigns and medication distribution programs. In the future, pharmaceutical companies may partner with telemedicine platforms to establish a cohesive healthcare environment that enables patients to consult physicians, obtain digital prescriptions, and acquire medications through a unified interface. Utilising AI-driven chatbots and virtual healthcare assistants, organisations will provide immediate assistance to patients by responding to enquiries regarding medication usage, side effects, and dosage compliance. This proactive strategy can enhance illness management and elevate public health results.

Subscription-Based Medication Delivery and Immersive Technologies in Patient Care

The future of prescription medicine sales may include the rise of subscription-based medication through e-commerce platforms, serving individuals with chronic diseases. Patients may subscribe to plans for automatic monthly delivery of their medicines, guaranteeing continuous treatment and alleviating the necessity for frequent purchases. In the future, patients with hypertension may subscribe to a monthly drug delivery service, guaranteeing they never miss a dosage. Such a service can streamline drug management and enhance patient quality of life. Moreover, the use of augmented reality (AR) and virtual reality (VR) technology can improve patient education and drug compliance. Augmented reality applications will offer interactive demonstrations of medicine administration, and virtual reality simulations will assist patients in managing chronic pain and anxiety. In the near future, patients may commonly use an AR application to learn insulin injection techniques or employ VR headsets to alleviate chronic pain through guided meditation. These advanced technologies can enable people to assume an active role in their healthcare.

Robotic Automation in Pharmaceutical Warehousing

A forward-looking perspective on e-commerce within the pharmaceutical sector may include the implementation of robotic automation in warehouses to enhance order fulfilment efficiency. Automated solutions, including robotic arms, conveyor belts, and AI-driven inventory management applications, can significantly improve operational efficiency by minimising manual errors and processing durations. Pharmaceutical companies might establish intelligent warehouses outfitted with autonomous cars for intra-facility logistics, facilitating expedited and precise order fulfilment. By adopting automation, firms enhance their profitability while acquiring the agility necessary to promptly address market demands.

Transparency and Traceability through Advanced Logistics

The integration of advanced logistics technologies within the e-commerce framework can enhance the transparency and traceability of pharmaceutical shipments, thereby cultivating trust among consumers and regulatory authorities. GPS and geotagging-enabled real-time monitoring technology will allow patients to monitor the status and location of their items, ensuring a flawless delivery experience. Simultaneously, these technologies can provide pharmaceutical companies with critical operational insights, like delivery times, route optimisation opportunities, and last-mile challenges. Actively resolving these issues ensures that companies maintain high service standards while minimising distribution costs.

Regulatory Alignment and Compliance Automation

The effective execution of e-commerce and advanced logistics in prescription drug sales necessitates that pharmaceutical enterprises conform to changing regulatory frameworks. Future technologies will encompass compliance automation solutions that guarantee conformity to governmental regulations, pharmaceutical safety requirements, and ethical protocols. AI-powered compliance management systems will oversee transactions, identify anomalies, and deliver instantaneous notifications to regulatory bodies. Automated audits and digital documentation will streamline compliance reporting, alleviating the administrative burden on pharmaceutical companies and facilitating seamless operations within the legal framework.

Sustainability and Green Logistics in Pharmaceutical Distribution

With the pharmaceutical company adopting digital transformation, sustainability will become a primary focal point. Future logistics systems will integrate sustainable packaging materials, electric delivery vehicles, and AI-based route optimisations to minimise carbon footprints. Pharmaceutical companies implementing green logistics techniques will enhance environmental conservation and secure a competitive advantage by conforming to global sustainability requirements. Customers are increasingly favouring companies that exhibit dedication to environmentally sustainable methods, rendering sustainable logistics a crucial element of future pharmaceutical distribution networks.

Challenges in Adopting E-Commerce for Pharmaceutical Sales

The shift to an e-commerce-centric strategy presents several obstacles. Organisations must allocate resources towards comprehensive cybersecurity protocols to safeguard confidential patient data and adhere to data protection rules. Moreover, cultivating customer trust in e-commerce platforms necessitates reliable delivery performance, clear return policies, and prompt customer care. Pharmaceutical companies must manage the intricacies of India's regulatory system, ensuring that digital marketing and online sales comply with ethical and legal norms.

The integration of e-commerce and advanced logistics by pharmaceutical companies signifies a transformative phase of innovation and accessibility in the Indian prescription medicine sector. This can undoubtedly uncover unparalleled growth potential for pharmaceutical companies in India. These emerging technologies present a promising avenue to tackle enduring difficulties while allowing companies to realise unprecedented opportunities for growth and influence. The on-going evolution of the ecosystem will likely determine the future direction of the sector, creating a healthcare landscape that is more efficient, patient-centric, resilient, and inclusive. Utilising AI, blockchain, drones, and autonomous cars, companies will transform prescription drug sales, guaranteeing accessibility, affordability, and efficiency. Pharmaceutical companies that use these developing technologies will secure a competitive advantage and foster a healthier, more equal healthcare system for millions of Indians. The future promises a cohesive, patient-centred pharmaceutical ecosystem, wherein technology enables individuals to pursue healthier and more rewarding lifestyles.

Big Data and Patient Analytics in Pharmaceutical Marketing

In the evolving landscape of the Indian pharmaceutical sector, big data and patient analytics are crucial in reshaping the marketing, distribution, and consumption of prescription pharmaceuticals. The sector, historically reliant on interpersonal dynamics between medical representatives and physicians, now confronts escalating complexity stemming from evolving illness patterns, altering patient behaviours, stringent regulatory frameworks, and intensified rivalry. Pharmaceutical companies are progressively implementing data-driven tactics to secure a competitive advantage. By utilising extensive amounts of structured and unstructured data—e.g., electronic health records, insurance claims, prescriptions, diagnostic reports, and social media interactions—companies can extract useful insights regarding prescribing habits and patient requirements. This analytical transformation enhances operational efficiency and market targeting while facilitating the provision of more tailored healthcare solutions. Although still nascent relative to global standards, India's pharmaceutical company is progressively adopting this transition, establishing big data and patient analytics as fundamental components of contemporary pharmaceutical marketing.

Data-Driven Prescription Trend Mapping

A significant application of big data analytics in India is the discovery of prescription trends across various areas and specialities. Pharmaceutical companies can leverage data compiled by third-party prescription tracking organisations and pharmacy networks to examine prescription trends for their primary anti-diabetic medications. By analysing this data, companies can find that physicians in tier-2 cities, such as Nagpur and Coimbatore, prescribe newer- generation anti-diabetic medications at a higher rate than previously anticipated. This data can facilitate corporations in realigning their sales team and focusing their efforts on these micro-markets, potentially resulting in an increase in prescriptions. Furthermore, data indicates that endocrinologists under the age of 40 are more inclined to adopt novel compounds. Organisations can develop tailored engagement initiatives with data-driven presentations for particular populations, integrating medical education with patient case analysis.

AI-Driven Insights Boost Prescription Sales

Mid-sized pharmaceutical companies specialising in gynaecology and dermatology can partner with a health analytics start-up to develop an AI-driven patient feedback loop by evaluating electronic medical records (EMRs) in urban hospitals. Insights derived from EMR data may reveal increasing patterns in the prescription of combination hormonal therapy for PCOS patients in urban areas such as Mumbai and Hyderabad. Consequently, corporations can introduce new items designed for the urban, technologically adept female market. Furthermore, corporations can use location-specific prescription data to design tailored continuing medical education (CME) programs for gynaecologists, who may be more predisposed to investigating novel therapeutic combinations. This customised strategy, driven by big data, can guarantee the optimised allocation of sales staff and concentrated marketing initiatives, leading to a potential rise in new prescriptions.

Tailored Marketing through Prescription Analytics

A prominent application of big data in India is its capacity to examine prescribing trends across diverse demographics and regions. In the future, pharmaceutical companies may employ big data analytics to analyse prescription data from Tier 1 and Tier 2 cities, as well as rural areas of the country. Through the analysis of datasets gathered from hospitals, clinics, and pharmacies, the relevant company can ascertain that physicians in Tier 1 cities, such as Delhi and Mumbai, primarily prescribe higher-priced branded medications, while practitioners in rural areas tend to favour generics due to patients' cost sensitivity. This knowledge allows the corporation to customise its marketing methods, concentrating its premium product line in metropolitan areas while enhancing its assortment of affordable generics for rural markets.

Predictive Analytics in Pharmaceutical Product Distribution

In addition to targeting and promotional planning, big data may significantly contribute to predicting the demand for prescription medicines and enhancing inventory management throughout the extensive and intricate distribution network of the country. Companies can amalgamate prescription trend data with distributor billing data to develop predictive inventory management models. Utilising analytics, they can foresee fluctuations in prescription patterns associated with seasonal health trends (e.g., an increased prevalence of hypertension-related problems during the summer months in northern India). Utilising this predictive data, corporations may instruct their distributors across diverse regions to adequately stock their top-selling drugs, thereby minimising stockouts and enhancing prescription fulfilment rates.

Data-Driven Patient Marketing Strategies

Patient analytics, facilitated by big data, can improve the precision of marketing strategies. Through the analysis of electronic health records (EHRs) and anonymized patient data, pharmaceutical companies can discern high-risk patient populations and tailor their campaigns appropriately. In the future, companies may use analytics to identify locations with a high frequency of cardiovascular disorders, such as Tamil Nadu or possibly Gujarat. Organisations may partner with cardiologists in certain areas to conduct awareness campaigns regarding the significance of early diagnosis and prevention. Moreover, organisations can use predictive analytics to pinpoint patients susceptible to non-adherence to statin therapy, enabling the provision of tailored reminders and support services. This data-driven methodology can enhance the company's brand positioning and improve patient outcomes.

Personalized Doctor Engagement Using Analytics

Big data can enable pharmaceutical corporations to tailor physician interaction initiatives. In the future, pharmaceutical companies may develop digital doctor segmentation models by analysing extensive prescription records, which could encompass prescription frequency, molecule preferences, specialities, patient volume, and involvement in prior pharmaceutical company-sponsored programmes. Doctors can be categorised according to specific factors such as "innovators", "early adopters", "mainstreamers", and "laggards", based on the models. The corporation customised interaction accordingly—providing innovators with early access to clinical trial results, while mainstreamers may obtain traditional academic information. This tiered engagement, which utilises data analytics, can improve the efficiency of organisations' engagement and potentially enhance their prescription-to-call ratio across various states.

Data Analytics Empowering Rural Healthcare

In India's semi-urban and rural healthcare environments, where conventional market research is sometimes costly and logistically complex, data analytics can provide economical methods for monitoring physician conduct and patient outcomes. A midsized pharmaceutical company can partner with government-sponsored fair price medicine outlets and health initiatives to monitor real-time sales of its generic antibiotic, Cefuroxime Axetil 500, throughout rural India. By amalgamating sales data with patient input, likely gathered via mobile questionnaires, the corporations assess efficacy perception, prescription adherence, and adverse effects. This comprehensive perspective enables corporations to reconfigure their packaging with explicit dose recommendations in local languages and to educate their field personnel to advice patients more efficiently. These measures may enhance therapeutic adherence and foster more trust among rural physicians, ultimately augmenting prescription renewals and market share.

Big Data in Drug Safety

The improvement of drug safety in the following years will significantly rely on the strategic use of big data analytics for monitoring adverse drug reactions (ADRs) and pharmacovigilance. In response to heightened regulatory scrutiny and the escalating complexity of medication interactions, Indian pharmaceutical companies are implementing sophisticated analytical technologies to identify safety flags promptly. By amalgamating data from many sources, including digital prescription records, patient helplines, social media, and hospital databases, and employing methodologies such as natural language processing (NLP) and artificial intelligence (AI), organisations can proactively detect and mitigate probable negative effects. This data-centric methodology facilitates prompt revisions to drug labelling, focused recommendations for healthcare practitioners, and enhanced patient results. With the on-going digitisation of the Indian pharmaceutical ecosystem, Big Data will be essential for guaranteeing regulatory compliance, bolstering patient trust, and strengthening the industry's dedication to ethical and safe medical procedures.

Optimizing Sales Performance with Predictive Analytics

Predictive analytics is poised to transform pharmaceutical sales performance management by facilitating data-driven, real-time insights. Transitioning from manual reporting, sophisticated dashboards will amalgamate various data sources—encompassing call activity, travel patterns, and sales target attainment—enabling managers to proactively discern performance deficiencies and implement targeted interventions. Concurrently, AI-driven sentiment analysis will elucidate emerging patient concerns, informing the creation of targeted, culturally sensitive marketing campaigns. By utilising predictive techniques, pharmaceutical companies will improve field force efficiency and resource distribution while also cultivating stronger relationships with healthcare providers and patients. With the Indian pharmaceutical sales sector undergoing digital transformation, predictive analytics will be pivotal in developing flexible, accountable, and high-performing sales teams.

Forecasting Demand with Data Intelligence

Big data analytics will be crucial for future demand forecasting and supply chain optimisation in India's intricate pharmaceutical sector. Given the nation's extensive and varied geography, guaranteeing prompt and sufficient access to prescription medications will continue to pose a difficulty. Pharmaceutical companies may precisely forecast regional demand fluctuations by utilising advanced analytics to analyse past sales data, seasonal trends, and external factors, like weather patterns. This foresight will facilitate proactive inventory planning and more intelligent distribution tactics, mitigating the risk of stockouts and surplus inventory. Consequently, enterprises will improve supply chain efficiency, reduce revenue losses, and guarantee consistent drug availability across geographies. Incorporating predictive analytics in supply chain operations is crucial for establishing a responsive, robust, and patient-centred pharmaceutical ecosystem in India.

Dynamic Pricing Strategies Using Data

The practical applications of big data will progressively impact pricing tactics within the pharmaceutical sector. As the affordability of healthcare remains a significant issue in India, corporations will encounter increasing pressure to provide competitive and accessible pricing. By leveraging advanced analytics to analyse pricing trends across various geographies, market competitiveness, and patient demographics, companies will implement customised dynamic pricing models for different economic groups. Forward-thinking organisations will employ a data-driven methodology to establish region-specific pricing strategies that reconcile profitability with affordability. This segmentation will enable pharmaceutical companies to address patient requirements more efficiently while ensuring sustainable growth in a competitive market.

Ethical Marketing through Analytics

The promise of big data and patient analytics in the Indian pharmaceutical sector encompasses not only immediate commercial advantages but also the promotion of regulatory compliance and ethical norms. Predictive analytics methods can identify promotional materials that may contravene the Code of Pharmaceutical Marketing Practices (CPMP) in India. Organisations can utilise these instruments to guarantee that their sales personnel comply with ethical marketing standards, evading legal repercussions and fostering trust with healthcare stakeholders.

The Indian pharmaceutical sector is poised for a dramatic transition, propelled by the deliberate incorporation of big data and patient analytics into marketing and sales operations. Despite being in a nascent phase, the adoption of these technologies is swiftly accelerating, with progressive enterprises already utilising data to refine decision-making, tailor physician interactions, and improve patient outcomes. With the expansion of digital healthcare initiatives, such as Ayushman Bharat and the National Digital Health Mission, the quantity and diversity of healthcare data will increase significantly, providing enhanced insights into patient behaviour and market dynamics. Big data and patient analytics have become crucial innovations for attaining competitiveness, operational efficiency, and market response. In the dynamic realm of pharmaceutical marketing in India, these technologies will be pivotal in developing agile, efficient, and patient-centric strategies that foster sustainable growth.

Future of Sales Force Automation

The future of sales force automation (SFA) in the Indian pharmaceutical sector is poised to revolutionise the interaction between corporations and healthcare providers, optimise field operations, and enhance prescription medicine sales. Due to swift progress in Artificial Intelligence (AI), Machine Learning (ML), Big Data analytics, Natural Language Processing (NLP), and the Internet of Things (IoT), SFA systems are poised to transform from rudimentary call reporting tools into sophisticated decision-support platforms. These tools will equip medical representatives with immediate data regarding prescription trends, pharmacy inventories, and the efficacy of promotional campaigns, facilitating more strategic call planning and improved resource allocation. Customised SFA solutions will address the distinct issues faced by enterprises manufacturing broad medicinal molecules requiring high-volume distribution, as well as those operating in specialised therapeutic areas such as gynaecology, dermatology, cardiovascular health, or ophthalmology. This transition to digital empowerment and tailored involvement would enhance efficiency and collaboration while aligning with the increasing demand for patient-centric methodologies in India's evolving pharmaceutical sector. Conventional, paper-based approaches will soon be supplanted by intuitive, AI-driven technologies that transform sales force productivity.

AI-Driven Sales Optimization in Pharmaceutical Marketing

Pharmaceutical companies producing generic drug molecules in highly competitive, volume-orientated marketplaces are likely to be early adopters of AI-enhanced Sales Force Automation (SFA) solutions. These companies, with extensive MR networks across several regions, can use AI for dynamic territory optimization—designing daily routes based not only on geography but also on physician engagement patterns, prescription possibilities, and seasonal disease trends. For instance, MRs may obtain itineraries ranked by the probability of securing prescriptions, thereby minimising unproductive calls and improving physician coverage. Predictive analytics in SFA systems can discern regional prescribing patterns for generics such as antibiotics or antipyretics, facilitating resource allocation in anticipation of increased demand. This facilitates targeted interaction with high-prescribing healthcare professionals while ensuring regular communication with remote clinics. Moreover, conversational AI systems like voice-activated reporting and chatbots could supplant manual data entry, facilitating real-time field updates and reducing errors. AI-driven SFA tools provide a data-centric methodology to enhance sales strategies, increase operational efficiency, and bolster outreach in competitive pharmaceutical markets.

Specific Pharmaceutical Sales Strategies Based on AI

Pharmaceutical companies focused on producing gynaecological or dermatological medications, which address specific and delicate therapeutic domains, may gain advantages from enhanced and content-rich SFA systems. In the foreseeable future, these corporations may use sophisticated SFA systems that suggest product messages and digital visual aids tailored to a physician's profile, prior encounters, and clinical inclinations. A dermatology-focused MR could be directed by the system to recommend a specific acne treatment product to a dermatologist who specialises in adolescent patients while proposing an alternative formulation for a physician with a predominantly geriatric patient demographic. Furthermore, these specialised organisations may implement systems that integrate with electronic health records (EHRs) to provide real-time insights about common dermatological or gynaecological problems in certain locations, helping sales teams promote pertinent medications. Companies may utilise virtual reality (VR) modules integrated into SFA applications to deliver immersive product demos, particularly those appealing to younger professionals operating in metropolitan India.

AI Helping the Pharmaceutical Companies to Improve Patient Care

Artificial intelligence is revolutionising patient care within the pharmaceutical sector, especially for chronic and cardiovascular ailments, by empowering medical representatives to utilise patient-focused automation tools for sales linked with adherence analytics. These technologies monitor prescription renewals, refill discrepancies, and patient outcomes, initiating automatic follow-ups for prompt treatments. Integration with wearable health technology and IoT-enabled devices, such as connected blood pressure monitors, facilitates remote monitoring and data sharing with healthcare professionals (HCPs) via CRMs. Aggregated data facilitates the personalisation of communications and marketing initiatives while safeguarding privacy. This innovation transforms pharmaceutical sales personnel from mere product promoters to comprehensive healthcare partners, thereby promoting treatment compliance, improving long-term results, and fostering proactive, patient-centered engagement.

Improving Pharmaceutical Supply Chain Using AI

Artificial intelligence is revolutionising pharmaceutical organisations by facilitating the seamless integration of sales automation tools with essential activities such as supply chain management, regulatory compliance, and pharmacovigilance. This networked ecosystem facilitates real-time feedback from medical representatives (MRs) regarding stock availability, physician preferences, and regional health trends for both general and specialised drug categories. The increasing need for hormonal therapy in gynaecology may necessitate urgent inventory modifications. A medical representative can promptly verify stockists' availability to fulfil a physician's request, while specialised pharmaceutical companies can safely disseminate real-world proof alongside research and development. This AI-driven integration mitigates stock-outs, diminishes waste, guarantees regulatory compliance, and expedites innovation—ultimately enhancing patient care through more accurate demand forecasts and expedited responses throughout the pharmaceutical value chain.

Companies for AI-enabled Proactive Doctor-Patient Relationships

Focused pharmaceutical companies in India are progressively utilising AI-driven sales force automation (SFA) systems to cultivate personalised, proactive connections with physicians, especially in Tier-2 and Tier-3 locations. These solutions amalgamate teleconsultation data, regional disease trends, and physician attitude analysis to facilitate micro-targeted outreach, while technology such as facial recognition authenticates remote MR-doctor contacts. Intelligent CRM-enabled SFA systems facilitate the dissemination of tailored content—such as effectiveness studies, biomarker dashboards, and AI-generated product performance reports enhanced with real-world evidence (RWE)—thereby augmenting clinical discussions, particularly in post-operative care. These technologies provide multichannel interaction through in-person visits, telephonic communications, WhatsApp, and webinars customised to physicians' preferences while automating intelligent follow-ups such as thank-you messages and the dissemination of scientific knowledge to cultivate trust. To address India's linguistic and geographic variety, forthcoming SFA solutions are anticipated to provide multilingual and GPS-enabled assistance, facilitating medical representatives' access to materials in local languages and enabling efficient outreach to healthcare professionals. This is essential for both general and specialised drug molecule makers seeking to broaden their market presence. Remote engagement strategies—such as tele-detailing, virtual meetings, and webinars—will enable corporations to connect with physicians and key opinion leaders nationwide, thereby improving patient care through more intelligent, digitally facilitated interactions.

AI Helping Pharmaceutical Companies Follow Regulatory Compliance

Additionally, voice biometrics, electronic signature verification, and real-time geotagging may become standard in SFA technologies, assisting pharmaceutical companies in improving compliance with regulatory requirements and internal audit procedures. In regulated markets such as Maharashtra or Delhi, sales calls may necessitate obtaining e-consent from the physician, documented via the app and thereafter stored on a secure cloud platform. These elements can protect organisations from accusations of unethical conduct and enhance their openness.

AI Helping the Pharmaceutical Companies for Data Safety and Security

Data privacy and cybersecurity are likely to be fundamental components of future SFA systems. Companies, particularly those involved in sensitive therapeutic areas like psychiatric or sexual health treatments, may use blockchain-enabled data storage systems in their SFA tools to guarantee secure sharing of promotional materials and confidential patient result data. Both general and speciality pharmaceutical companies may interface their SFA systems with national health data platforms, such as the National Digital Health Mission (NDHM), facilitating better alignment with governmental health programs and enhanced access to real-time epidemiological data.

AI Helping the Pharmaceutical Sales Teams in Training and Evaluation

Artificial intelligence is revolutionising the training and assessment of pharmaceutical sales teams with novel instruments, such as gamification, virtual reality courses, and instantaneous AI-generated feedback. Future SFA systems will monitor call volumes, assess the quality of physician interactions, evaluate digital engagement ratings, analyse content utilisation, and measure patient outcomes. Specialised pharmaceutical sectors, such as dermatology, may implement scenario-based, AI-driven training that replicates real-world obstacles, focussing on patient-specific issues, such as skin sensitivity. This evolution guarantees the on-going enhancement of medical representatives' skills, allowing them to instruct healthcare professionals more efficiently. With the expansion of the Indian pharmaceutical market, advanced training and performance models will enable sales teams to address the varied and evolving requirements of the healthcare ecosystem.

Smarter Pharmaceutical Sales Teamwork by AI

Future SFA systems may integrate AI-driven digital assistants to assist MRs in their daily interactions. These virtual assistants can assess previous conversations and provide customised recommendations for engaging healthcare professionals, including scheduling meetings, disseminating targeted training content, or addressing intricate product queries in real time. This breakthrough may especially advantage organisations focused on ophthalmology and dermatology, where intricate formulations frequently require comprehensive elucidation of active components or innovative drug delivery systems. By alleviating the cognitive load on MRs, such solutions can liberate critical time for strategic relationship-building initiatives.

Educating Doctors and Physicians about Drug Molecules through AI

The integration of augmented reality (AR) and virtual reality (VR) functionalities into SFA platforms could revolutionise the way pharmaceutical companies inform healthcare professionals (HCPs) about their products. Companies producing specialised pharmaceutical compounds, such as oncology therapies or ophthalmic breakthroughs, may employ AR/VR technologies to deliver immersive demonstrations of medication mechanisms, granting healthcare professionals greater tactile comprehension without the need for actual samples. By utilising these methods, MRs can foster memorable interactions, especially in competitive therapeutic categories, thereby improving the memory value of their goods.

Data Driven Decision Making in Pharmaceutical Industry through AI

A significant advancement that could influence the future of SFA in the Indian pharmaceutical sector is the incorporation of big data and analytics into sales methodologies. Pharmaceutical companies may use these capabilities to evaluate extensive databases of prescription trends, market shares, and sales performance measures to forecast upcoming market opportunities. Conversely, specialised pharmaceutical makers may concentrate on detailed insights—such as patient adherence metrics or treatment outcomes—to optimise their healthcare professionals' engagement initiatives. Advanced SFA systems can consolidate these facts into a singular, user-friendly interface, allowing decision-makers to assess sales efficiency across regions, product lines, and individual representatives instantaneously.

AI Guiding Pharmaceutical towards Ethical Balance

Ethical considerations and compliance will likely continue to be essential in the implementation of future SFA systems. In India, where pharmaceutical marketing is governed by changing legislation, sophisticated SFA solutions may incorporate real-time compliance checkers to guarantee that all marketing activities conform to the Code of Pharmaceutical Marketing Practices (CPMP). Specialised pharmaceutical manufacturers particularly benefit from this function, as their marketing materials often delve into intricate technical details that require accurate communication. By alleviating risks of noncompliance, companies may protect their reputations while cultivating confidence among healthcare professionals.

AI-Based Trend Prediction and Safety Improvement in Pharmaceuticals

Artificial intelligence (AI) and machine learning (ML) can be intricately integrated into future SFA platforms. Envision AI-driven virtual assistants capable of proactively recommending the most pertinent content for a sales call, informed by the physician's previous interactions and accessible medical literature. These assistants can evaluate extensive databases to detect emerging prescribing trends or probable adverse occurrences, offering early warnings and facilitating proactive actions. The predictive capabilities of organisations that manufacture both general and specialised drug molecules can enhance sales tactics and improve patient safety outcomes.

The future of sales force automation (SFA) in the Indian pharmaceutical sector possesses significant potential to revolutionise the interaction between corporations, healthcare providers, and patients. Utilising technologies such as AI, ML, big data, IoT, and multilingual platforms, SFA can enhance intelligence, efficiency, and personalisation in both general and specialised pharmaceutical sectors, including gynaecology, dermatology, and cardiovascular care. These solutions will enable sales teams to optimise operations, improve remote interactions, and satisfy the increasing demand for patient-centricity. Although the transition may necessitate investment and cultural adjustment, the long-term advantages—enhanced collaboration, superior patient outcomes, and a sustainable, digitally empowered sales ecosystem—are significant.

Changing Drug Regulatory Landscape

One of the most awaited modifications in the Indian drug regulatory framework is the digitisation of regulatory submissions and approvals. The Central Drugs Standard Control Organisation (CDSCO) is advancing online applications for licenses, suggesting that future medication approval and post-marketing surveillance processes will be entirely consolidated into a centralised digital platform. This digital transition may compel pharmaceutical companies, especially those producing generic medication molecules such as antibiotics, antipyretics, and anti-allergies, to synchronise their field operations using Future Sales Force Automation (SFA) technologies. These systems can automatically synchronise regulatory changes, sanctioned product claims, and updated marketing materials to the mobile devices of Medical Representatives (MRs), ensuring immediate compliance during physician visits. A company manufacturing generic analgesics may implement an SFA platform that prohibits MRs from utilising obsolete promotional materials following the issuance of fresh regulatory recommendations.

Digitization and Compliance in Pharmaceutical Field Operations

Pharmaceutical companies, particularly in cardiology, gynaecology, and dermatology, can gain advantages by incorporating pharmacovigilance into their sales tactics. With the growing focus of Indian rules on real-world evidence and adverse event reporting, SFA platforms are adapting to incorporate mechanisms for capturing patient-reported outcomes. For example, dermatology medical representatives may utilise mobile applications that allow physicians to document post-prescription dermatological reactions, so enhancing trust and ensuring regulatory compliance. The increasing emphasis on ethical marketing and transparency is compelling organisations to implement digital detailing, e-sampling, and compliance-integrated sales force automation workflows. These technologies boost data accuracy and regulatory compliance while establishing centralised systems that contribute to regulatory databases, fostering a culture of accountability in specialised pharmaceutical sales.

Pharmacovigilance Integration in Specialized Pharmaceutical Sales

The emergence of personalised medicine and targeted medicines is transforming pharmaceutical sales techniques, particularly for specialised medications in ophthalmology, cancer, dermatology, and gynaecology. Regulatory systems are anticipated to require more precise depiction of patient eligibility, dosage personalisation, and outcomes. In response, corporations are implementing AI-driven SFA tools that generate tailored presentations for physicians based on their prescribing patterns and compliance standards. Field representatives may utilise augmented reality applications that simulate treatment outcomes or digital dashboards that incorporate clinical trial data to provide visually engaging, evidence-supported advertising. These hyper-personalized solutions can dynamically produce region-specific information, assisting specialists in making educated decisions while ensuring regulatory compliance and augmenting the overall efficacy of pharmaceutical communication.

Personalized Strategies in Automated Pharmaceutical Sales

The emergence of personalised medicine and targeted medicines is transforming pharmaceutical sales techniques, particularly for specialised medications in ophthalmology, cancer, dermatology, and gynaecology.

Regulatory systems are anticipated to require more precise depiction of patient eligibility, dosage personalisation, and outcomes. In response, corporations are implementing AI-driven SFA tools that generate tailored presentations for physicians based on their prescribing patterns and compliance standards. Field representatives may utilise augmented reality applications that simulate treatment outcomes or digital dashboards that incorporate clinical trial data to provide visually engaging, evidence-supported advertising. These hyper-personalized solutions can dynamically produce region-specific information, assisting specialists in making educated decisions while ensuring regulatory compliance and augmenting the overall efficacy of pharmaceutical communication.

Ethical Compliance in Pharmaceutical Marketing

Furthermore, the growing focus on ethical marketing and openness by Indian regulators may result in more stringent oversight of field force operations. To verify compliance with established guidelines and prevent unethical inducements, general medication makers may incorporate geo-tagging, time-stamping, and AI-driven audit trails into their SFA platforms. The compliance modules in these systems may incorporate auto-generated disclosures regarding pharmacological benefits and adverse effects, especially for high-volume prescribers. These techniques may prove crucial when authorities implement more stringent standards akin to the Uniform Code for Pharmaceuticals Marketing Practices (UCPMP), which may soon attain legal enforceability.

Outcome-Based Regulations and SFA Integration Trends

A prospective trend in the Indian regulatory landscape is the potential transition towards outcome-based drug clearance and payment systems, particularly within public health initiatives. This transition may prompt pharmaceutical companies, especially those involved in chronic and lifestyle illness sectors such as cardiovascular or diabetic medications, to prioritise patient adherence, follow-ups, and treatment results. Consequently, field marketing campaigns may incorporate patient education capabilities within the SFA platforms. Representatives may be educated not only in brand advocacy but also in advising physicians on outcome-tracking instruments or digital health integrations. A firm developing a novel cardiovascular drug may grant medical representatives access to a patient monitoring dashboard displaying aggregated, anonymized data from wearable devices, thus enabling better informed and regulation-compliant discussions with cardiologists.

Digital Health Integration in Pharmaceutical Marketing

Regulatory reforms in India are fostering more integration between pharmaceutical companies and the nation's burgeoning digital health infrastructure, exemplified as the Ayushman Bharat Digital Mission (ABDM). Future sales force automation (SFA) solutions may integrate with government databases to obtain epidemiological information, allowing field reps to address region-specific disease loads with physicians. A gynaecology-focused corporation may utilise district-level anaemia data to bolster iron supplement advertisements. Furthermore, regulatory frameworks may need cooperation with telemedicine platforms to guarantee ethical and accessible pharmaceutical marketing. Dermatology-centric enterprises could implement integrated marketing platforms to disseminate promotional content digitally to Healthcare Professionals. This digital alignment improves regulatory compliance, facilitates data-driven marketing, and accommodates changing physician preferences for convenience and virtual interaction.

Pharmaceutical Marketing: Digital & Regulatory Compliance

The pharmaceutical marketing environment in India is progressively evolving due to the use of digital tools and adherence to regulatory compliance methods. Conventional promotional materials are being supplanted by QR-coded digital resources, enabling medical representatives to provide healthcare professionals with immediate access to drug monographs, safety alerts, and CDSCO notifications within a secure digital framework. This transition not only improves efficiency but also conforms to environmental sustainability objectives. Simultaneously, Artificial Intelligence (AI)-driven Sales Force Automation (SFA) solutions are increasingly crucial for compliance with the Code of Pharmaceutical Marketing Practices (CPMP). These technologies can monitor promotional materials in real-time and identify non-compliant content prior to its dissemination to physicians. In preparation for rules such to the Sunshine Act that require public disclosure of pharmaceutical interactions with healthcare professionals, companies are integrating transparency modules into their SFA platforms to monitor sponsorships, samples, and promotional spending. For makers of high-value speciality pharmaceuticals, AI-driven predictive compliance systems provide insight into changing regulations, enhancing ethical and proactive marketing strategies.

Enhancing Drug Traceability through Emerging Technologies

A projected regulatory trend may emphasise enhanced traceability of pharmaceuticals from manufacturing to dispensation. Pharmaceutical companies in both general and specialised sectors may utilise IoT-enabled devices and blockchain technology to attain comprehensive traceability. Field marketing teams can utilise this data to reassure healthcare professionals on the authenticity and quality of their products. Manufacturers of cardiovascular drugs may employ blockchain technology to demonstrate the integrity of their cold chain logistics, highlighting the secure delivery of delicate medical. This transparency may foster trust, especially in therapeutic domains where drug quality directly influences patient outcomes.

Patient-Centricity and Regulatory Impact in Pharmaceuticals

Furthermore, patient-centricity is anticipated to significantly influence regulatory standards in India. Pharmaceutical companies producing generic medication molecules may utilise patient analytics to synchronise their field marketing strategies with legislation prioritising personalised treatment. Future SFA systems may furnish field marketers with anonymized patient adherence data, allowing them to create campaigns that target deficiencies in treatment compliance. Specialised pharmaceutical companies, especially those focused on gynaecological treatments, may utilise these data to initiate targeted educational initiatives on maternal health or adherence to hormone therapy.

Digital Transformation of Field Marketing in Pharmaceutical Sales

The digital transformation of field marketing in pharmaceutical sales is driven by Big Data, artificial intelligence, and Sales Force Automation tools. Companies, regardless of their focus on general or specialised pharmaceuticals, are utilising modern analytics to comprehend regulatory trends, enhance promotional methods, and guarantee compliance across several places. Predictive tools facilitate the anticipation of changes in prescribing behaviour, whereas SFA systems produce actionable insights derived from physician interactions and prescription trends. AI-driven technologies augment efficiency by automating operations such as appointment scheduling and tailoring material according to specific physician profiles. For example, dermatological or cardiovascular-focused companies can customise advertisements utilising region-specific data. In India's distinctive high-volume, price-sensitive environment, AI-integrated SFA solutions can pinpoint primary prescribers, optimise order placements, and oversee inventories in real-time. These advances enable medical representatives to engage more strategically, decrease operating expenses, and enhance impact, signifying a substantial transition towards data-driven, flexible, and personalised field marketing within the pharmaceutical sector.

Future Trends in Sustainable Specialized Pharmaceutical Marketing

Future field marketing in specialised pharmaceutical markets, including ophthalmology, oncology, gynaecology, dermatology, and cardiovascular care, is set to adopt virtual engagement solutions in accordance with sustainability-oriented laws. Organisations are expected to implement augmented reality (AR) and virtual reality (VR) technologies to instruct healthcare professionals (HCPs) on intricate medication mechanisms, hence diminishing reliance on physical samples and written resources. Advanced Sales Force Automation (SFA) technologies will facilitate personalised digital details, allowing medical personnel to present interactive, scientifically-based content on tablets. These technologies not only improve communication but also encourage sustainable practices. Moreover, SFA tools will enhance Key Opinion Leader (KOL) participation via virtual meetings, instantaneous data sharing, and engagement monitoring. This strategic transition will promote effective, compliant, and low-impact marketing in specialised therapeutic domains, advancing both innovation and sustainability.

Digital Health and Telemedicine in Field Marketing

Moreover, the emergence of digital health and telemedicine in India can generate new opportunities for field marketing. Medical representatives may transition into "digital engagement specialists," utilising virtual platforms to communicate with healthcare professionals in remote locations or during periods when in-person visits are limited. SFA systems can link with telemedicine platforms, offering MRs a comprehensive perspective on a healthcare professional's digital activities and preferences, hence facilitating more personalised and pertinent engagements. Companies producing specialised drugs for chronic diseases may significantly benefit from this trend by providing on-going support and information to patients and physicians through integrated digital channels handled by their SFA systems.

As India's medication regulatory framework evolves towards enhanced digitisation, transparency, and patient focus, the future of pharmaceutical field marketing will be characterised by astute adaptability and technological integration. Sales Force Automation (SFA) technologies are anticipated to transform into dynamic, compliance-oriented platforms that not only optimise sales operations but also guarantee ethical engagement and regulatory conformity across various regions. Conventional pharmaceutical manufacturers may utilise these systems to improve efficiency and broaden their market presence, whereas specialised drug producers are expected to implement advanced technologies—such as AI-driven analytics, blockchain, augmented reality/virtual reality detailing, and predictive dashboards—to provide more personalised and value-oriented engagements with healthcare professionals. The conventional function of the medical representative is set to evolve into a technologically empowered, strategically focused professional, adept at managing intricate compliance requirements and providing customised, data-driven communication. Organisations that actively adopt these forward-thinking ideas will spearhead the development of ethical, impactful, and regulation-compliant field marketing tactics within India's transforming pharmaceutical ecosystem.

Predictive and Prescriptive Analytics

In the developing Indian pharmaceutical market, predictive and prescriptive analytics are poised to transform the formulation and execution of product marketing strategies. With data becoming essential for decision-making, pharmaceutical companies—whether manufacturing general drug molecules such as antibiotics, antipyretics, and analgesics, or focussing on specialised areas like gynaecology, dermatology, cardiovascular health, and ophthalmology—are increasingly utilising advanced analytics to enhance precision in field marketing. Predictive analytics allows companies to foresee seasonal demand fluctuations and regional illness trends, facilitating proactive inventory management and strategic allocation of field personnel. Identifying flu-prone months in North India can facilitate prompt consultations with healthcare professionals and pharmacies, hence reducing stockouts and optimising market penetration. In addition, prescriptive analytics advises on the most effective activities by simulating results and optimising decisions, encompassing territory planning and customised communication tactics. With the integration of advanced Sales Force Automation (SFA) technology, pharmaceutical marketing in India is set to become increasingly data-driven, personalised, and outcome-oriented.

Optimizing Doctor Engagement with Advanced Analytics

In the future, enhancing physician interaction through sophisticated analytics will be pivotal to pharmaceutical strategy, particularly via hyper-personalized, AI-driven insights. Specialised companies in fields such as gynaecology or dermatology may employ prescriptive analytics to customise interaction by determining which physicians choose in-clinic visits, webinars, or case-based talks. Cardiovascular and ophthalmology companies might amalgamate wearable health data to develop therapy-specific initiatives, disseminating anonymised patient patterns to physicians to bolster product credibility. Concurrently, large-scale pharmaceutical manufacturers may use AI-driven Sales Force Automation (SFA) solutions customised for the Indian market, facilitating real-time prescription analysis, effective medical representative deployment, streamlined order processing, and sales monitoring. This data-centric methodology aims to enhance physician engagement, augment brand recognition, and optimise sales efficacy.

Prescriptive Analytics for Optimized Pharmaceutical Product Marketing

Prescriptive analytics is set to transform pharmaceutical product marketing by facilitating forward-looking, data-driven tactics. Manufacturers of general medicinal compounds can enhance inventory optimisation and field targeting by incorporating predicted insights, like seasonal disease trends and regional demand patterns, into prescriptive models. During the monsoon, a surge in antipyretic demand in Maharashtra or Kerala can be predicted and pre-emptively addressed. Prescriptive analytics will additionally suggest region-specific resource distribution, pricing methods informed by competitor actions, and optimal communication channels tailored to diverse physician profiles. For specialised pharmaceutical manufacturers, it will direct hyper-personalized marketing, instructing sales teams on specific messaging customised to the interests and digital preferences of individual physicians. As Sales Force Automation (SFA) technologies advance, they will progressively provide actionable, real-time recommendations, enabling pharmaceutical companies to not only satisfy demand but also optimise engagement and marketing efficacy throughout India's varied healthcare environment.

Real-Time Predictive Analytics in Pharmaceutical Product Marketing

In the imminent future, predictive analytics in field marketing will be effortlessly amalgamated with real-time data streams, encompassing live prescription trends, patient adherence patterns, and social media sentiment. Pharmaceutical companies will utilise these dynamic inputs to rapidly identify developing trends, such as an increase in demand for immune-boosting medications amid public health crises. Advanced prescriptive analytics will provide immediate, data-driven recommendations to adjust marketing strategies, divert field force activities, or reallocate resources accurately. This adaptable strategy will enable pharmaceutical marketers to stay nimble, proactive, and highly responsive to changing market conditions, assuring optimal impact and competitiveness in a rapidly shifting healthcare environment.

AI-Driven Future of Sales Force Automation

In the near future, sophisticated Sales Force Automation (SFA) systems will transform into intelligent command centres, seamlessly integrating predictive insights—such as high-prescription probability areas, competitor activities, and physician responsiveness metrics—with prescriptive recommendations including optimal visit timings, customised messaging, and ideal engagement frequency. Pharmaceutical companies will implement AI-driven smart scheduling systems that autonomously optimise the routes and priorities of medical representatives, significantly improving productivity. Specialised companies, particularly in dermatology, will aim at physicians by utilising dynamic data, including local weather patterns and anticipated skin disease prevalence. Mobile-based SFA platforms, integrated with real-time AI guidance, will equip medical representatives with immediate prompts regarding pitch strategies, anticipated objections, and the most recent clinical data—all provided at the moment of interaction, converting each doctor visit into a meticulously executed, data-driven opportunity for optimal impact.

In the future, predictive and prescriptive analytics will significantly revolutionise pharmaceutical product marketing in India. Organisations that include these technologies into their operational plans can forecast market trends, tailor healthcare professional (HCP) involvement, and enhance resource allocation—establishing themselves as leaders in the sector. As healthcare transitions to patient-centered and digital paradigms, sophisticated analytics integrated inside Sales Force Automation (SFA) systems will reconcile pharmaceutical science, physician anticipations, and field implementation. Upcoming developments, including AI-driven chatbots, VR/AR-enhanced detailed tools, and wearable technology for real-time performance monitoring, will significantly improve marketing accuracy. This transformation will transition field sales from a transactional function to a strategic one, facilitating flexible, intelligent, and personalised interactions that enhance patient outcomes and augment the overall efficacy of pharmaceutical marketing in a complicated and competitive environment.

Evolving Market Dynamics

The Indian pharmaceutical market is undergoing a dynamic transformation, with field marketing set for substantial modification due to digital disruption, regulatory developments, and a transition towards patient-centric and value-based care. Companies producing both general and specialised pharmaceutical compounds—particularly gynaecology, dermatology, cardiovascular health, and ophthalmology—are anticipated to adopt hybrid marketing approaches that integrate face-to-face interactions with digital technologies, data analytics, and AI-driven strategies. Due to escalating rivalry and cost constraints, particularly among general pharmaceutical makers, the sector may increasingly depend on predictive analytics to discern regional prescription trends and enhance resource allocation. AI-generated insights may inform strategic initiatives in rapidly developing states, such as Uttar Pradesh and Bihar, where the need for anti-infectives and anti-diabetics is anticipated to increase due to urbanisation and lifestyle changes. Moreover, legislative modifications within India's developing healthcare framework may encourage ethical, transparent, and technologically compatible marketing methods. Companies may investigate virtual detailing, digital content distribution, e-pharmacy partnerships, and direct-to-consumer contact to expand their market reach. As India evolves into a global centre for cost-effective, high-quality pharmaceuticals, pharmaceutical companies must implement new and adaptive field marketing tactics to maintain competitiveness in a progressively technologically orientated and patient-conscious environment.

Precision Marketing for Specialized Pharmaceutical Products

In the future, specialised pharmaceutical firms will spearhead innovations in field marketing through the integration of real-time data analytics and targeted physician involvement. Gynaecology, dermatology, cardiovascular, and ophthalmology enterprises will use modern technology, such as digital health records, augmented reality (AR), and AI-driven diagnostic tools, to tailor marketing strategies. Organisations will utilise patient data and predictive analytics to categorise physicians according to treatment inclinations, while field representatives will illustrate therapeutic effects through graphical treatment results and digital kits. Precision marketing will incorporate genomic and biomarker data to identify patient subpopulations most likely to benefit from medicines, hence enhancing interactions with healthcare providers. AI-powered Sales Force Automation (SFA) tools will propose customised engagement tactics, including virtual roundtables and expert panels, ensuring that each encounter is clinically pertinent and data-supported, thus improving physician relationships and treatment results.

Omnichannel Strategies in Pharmaceutical Field Marketing

In the transforming realm of Indian pharmaceutical field marketing, omnichannel engagement tactics are set to become standard practice. Manufacturers of general medicine, particularly those specialising in high-volume generics, are expected to use email campaigns, WhatsApp messaging, AI-powered chatbots, and virtual medical conferences to maintain uninterrupted connections. This digital-first strategy will diminish dependence on the conventional "boots on the street" model, facilitating broader physician outreach without increasing field personnel. Specialised pharmaceutical sectors, including ophthalmology and oncology, are anticipated to adopt remote sampling and e-detail models, especially in metropolitan and urban clinics, where time-pressed specialists may prefer succinct digital interactions to traditional in-person meetings, thereby transforming the dynamics of pharmaceutical relationships.

Patient Inclusive Compliant Field Marketing Strategies & Analytics

In the future, patient-centric and compliant field marketing techniques will be pivotal to pharmaceutical outreach, particularly in dermatology, gynaecology, and general medicine. Medical representatives may collaborate to create campaigns that include digital surveys, patient feedback mechanisms, and referrals for support programs during clinic visits. Within India's developing regulatory framework, particularly the National Digital Health Mission (NDHM), pharmaceutical companies are expected to instruct their medical representatives to use e-consent technologies, disseminate scientific information digitally, and record actions through mobile applications for enhanced transparency. Moreover, pharmaceutical producers may use AI and predictive analytics to monitor regional health trends—such as monsoon-related diseases in Maharashtra or Kerala—to facilitate targeted, region-specific marketing and proactive interaction with healthcare professionals (HCPs).

Leveraging Digital Health for Pharmaceutical Marketing

In the future, digital healthcare solutions will be essential for revolutionising field marketing techniques. As internet access expands and telemedicine becomes prevalent in India, pharmaceutical companies are anticipated to include these platforms in focused outreach strategies. Dermatology-centric companies may leverage real-time telemedicine data to discern prescribing trends for chronic ailments such as eczema or acne. Armed with these insights, field marketers will provide tailored product information and evidence-based assistance directly via digital channels. This transition will enhance the accuracy and relevance of interactions, fostering stronger relationships with healthcare professionals while aligning marketing strategies with the evolving digital healthcare landscape and patient-centred demands.

Blockchain for Transparency in Pharmaceutical Marketing

In the forthcoming years, changing market dynamics will probably generate a significant need for transparency and traceability in pharmaceutical supply chains, creating new opportunities for field marketing innovation. Organisations in both the general and specialised pharmaceutical sectors are anticipated to implement blockchain-based systems to authenticate, assess quality, and track the distribution of drugs. Manufacturers specialising in gynaecology may utilise these technologies to guarantee the safety and verified origins of hormonal medicines for healthcare providers and patients. Field marketers will be essential in conveying these developments, utilising digital tools to emphasise traceability during clinic visits. This forward-thinking strategy will cultivate enhanced trust and sustained engagement with healthcare providers.

Innovative Tools for Ethical Pharmaceutical Marketing

Future regulatory frameworks that prioritise ethical marketing practices are expected to expedite the integration of new technologies in field marketing. Pharmaceutical companies, especially those manufacturing ophthalmic medications, may increasingly employ augmented reality (AR) and virtual reality (VR) to provide realistic, scientifically substantiated demonstrations of therapeutic efficacy, therefore reducing dependence on physical samples. These advanced tools are anticipated to conform to more stringent compliance standards while improving interaction with healthcare practitioners. Furthermore, they will provide environmentally sustainable and economically viable alternatives to conventional promotional strategies, enhancing field marketing's participatory, accountable, and sustainable nature within a digitally regulated healthcare landscape characterised by innovation and transparency.

The future of pharmaceutical product marketing in India will be influenced by a dynamic amalgamation of personalisation, digital innovation, regulatory compliance, and value-driven engagement. As the healthcare landscape evolves, both general and speciality pharmaceutical companies must adapt by adopting new technology, data-driven insights, and tools that facilitate ethical incompliant marketing. Field marketing methods are expected to transition from volume-oriented promotions to personalised, patient-centric methodologies that emphasise therapeutic and economic benefit. Investments in health economics and outcomes research (HEOR), integration with digital therapies, and partnerships with technology companies will be important. Medical representatives can evolve into digitally empowered medical science liaisons, cultivating stronger, value-orientated connections with healthcare professionals in a competitive and regulated landscape.

Evolving Customer Expectations

The Indian pharmaceutical market is seeing a swift shift, propelled by increased digital literacy and an escalating desire for personalised, outcome-focused care among healthcare professionals, patients, carers, and institutional purchasers. As consumers grow more knowledgeable, connected, and discerning regarding value, pharmaceutical companies—whether producing high-volume generic medications or specialised treatments in fields such as gynaecology, dermatology, cardiovascular health, and ophthalmology—must re-evaluate their conventional field marketing approaches. The future of pharmaceutical marketing in India will require a transition to multi-faceted, ethically based strategies that incorporate technology, real-time data, and patient-focused involvement. Companies will likely need to implement virtual detailing, expert-led webinars, AI-driven support systems, and transparent pricing to meet expectations for accessible, evidence-based, and personalised healthcare communication.

Evolving Marketing Strategies in General Drug Segment

Future marketing techniques in the general pharmaceutical sector—encompassing antipyretics, antibiotics, and analgesics—will transition towards value-added services that extend beyond mere product efficacy. As patient expectations change, particularly among elderly demographics in both rural and urban settings, pharmaceutical companies may use digital tools such as applications and chatbots for dosage reminders, side effect monitoring, and food advice. Field personnel will advocate for pharmaceuticals and exhibit these tools to enhance adherence. AI-driven sales force automation solutions (SFA) will facilitate real-time, geo-targeted health data analysis, enabling marketers to customise messages according to local prescription patterns. Proactive, data-informed initiatives during seasonal epidemics and the delivery of orientated instructional tools will facilitate the anticipation of demands, strengthen customer connections, and guarantee the prompt availability of vital drugs.

Hyper-Personalized Strategies in Specialist Drug Marketing

In the future, corporations that produce specialised medication molecules in therapeutic fields such as gynaecology, dermatology, cardiovascular health, and ophthalmology will progressively implement hyper-personalized marketing techniques to address the specific demands of expert physicians. Healthcare workers will require real-time, evidence-based information—encompassing region-specific patient outcomes and AI-driven risk assessment tools—provided via both physical and virtual platforms. Gynaecologists may request data comparing hormonal therapy across various age groups, while dermatologists may need digital dashboards illustrating treatment efficacy for different populations. Dermatology brands, propelled by increasing cosmetic demands, may incorporate influencer marketing and patient testimonial videos to bolster trust and relatability. Advanced SFA platforms with integrated analytics will enable medical professionals to deliver personalised case studies, augmented reality product demos, and remote consultation tools. Moreover, corporations can assist specialist physicians and patients through telemedicine systems, patient education, and virtual partnerships with international experts. These highly personalised techniques will establish pharmaceutical companies as essential collaborators in providing precise, patient-centred healthcare solutions.

Data-Driven Marketing in Cardiovascular Pharmaceutical Sales

In the realm of speciality drug marketing, cardiovascular pharmaceutical companies are expected to implement hybrid field marketing models, wherein representatives possess extensive product knowledge and the capability to analyse and convey real-time, longitudinal patient data. As precision medicine and evidence-based outcomes become pivotal to cardiologists' expectations, medical representatives may use wearable health data and interactive dashboards to model patient-specific treatment results. Predictive analytics and prescriptive tools will assist marketers in pinpointing target prescribers and enhancing engagement methods. By visualising the effects of drugs on biomarkers, such as blood pressure or cholesterol, corporations may provide highly personalised, data-driven narratives, thereby improving decision-making and cultivating confidence among healthcare professionals in the management of chronic diseases.

Evolving Marketing Strategies in Ophthalmic Pharmaceuticals

In the future of evolving marketing strategies in ophthalmic pharmaceuticals, corporations will transcend conventional product promotion to provide precision-driven, comprehensive eye care solutions. As increased screen time affects ocular health across many demographics, marketers will emphasise innovation by integrating treatments with diagnostic and preventive services. Pharmaceutical companies are expected to collaborate with optometry start-ups and digital health platforms to implement mobile screening units, facilitating outreach in Tier-2 and Tier-3 cities. Field staff will provide integrated solutions—merging drugs, diagnostics, and digital tools—to address the increasing demand for comprehensive eye health. This value-added strategy will enhance confidence with ophthalmologists and establish corporations as collaborators in long-term patient care, rather than merely suppliers of ocular drugs.

Patient Influence in Pharmaceutical Marketing Strategies

In the future, patients will assume a more significant role in influencing pharmaceutical marketing techniques. As access to digital health information increases, patients will seek enhanced transparency, tailored support, and proactive involvement from pharmaceutical companies. We anticipate that enterprises in both general and speciality sectors will incorporate patient adherence information into their field marketing strategies. Medical representative may showcase real-time adherence trends and undertake collaborative educational campaigns with healthcare professionals to emphasise the need for long-term care. Gynaecology-focused companies may collaborate with healthcare professionals to create digital awareness initiatives that promote adherence to hormone therapy or improve maternal health, emphasising patient-centred outcomes in their promotional strategies. This transition will re-establish patient influence as a fundamental element in drug engagement initiatives.

Telemedicine-Driven Marketing in Pharmaceutical Engagement

In the imminent future, digital health solutions will emerge as a primary conduit for pharmaceutical involvement, transforming expectations for accessibility and response. Manufacturers of dermatological and ophthalmological pharmaceuticals are expected to incorporate telemedicine data into their marketing strategy, equipping field marketers with insights about digital prescription patterns. Marketers will progressively involve healthcare professionals that utilise telemedicine platforms, providing tailored, context-sensitive promotional content that integrates with their digital workflows. This strategy will improve the pertinence of marketing engagements and fortify ties with technologically adept professionals. As telemedicine advances, it will promote more flexible, efficient, and focused drug interaction tactics.

Enhancing Ethical Practices in Pharmaceutical Field Marketing

In the future, escalating demands from healthcare professionals, regulators, and patients will compel pharmaceutical corporations to embrace more open and ethically principled field marketing strategies. Companies, particularly in the cancer and cardiology sectors, are expected to adopt blockchain-based systems to guarantee drug authenticity and maintain supply chain integrity. These technologies will enable field marketers to exhibit traceability and cultivate trust with stakeholders. Ethical training and compliance instruments will become normal for sales teams, connecting daily operations with regulatory standards. By emphasising responsibility and sustainability, enterprises will fulfil future compliance requirements and enhance their reputation as responsible, forward-thinking organisations dedicated to ethical healthcare provision.

Collaborative Engagement in Pharmaceutical Interactions

In the future, interactions between pharmaceutical customers will likely transform into collaborative ecosystems, transcending conventional product-centric discussions. Specialist drug makers, especially in fields such as gynaecology, are anticipated to spearhead initiatives by organising multi-stakeholder forums that bring healthcare professionals, patients, and advocacy organisations together to tackle real-world healthcare issues. Field marketers will be important in supporting these engagements, offering forums for the co-development of instructional campaigns, treatment procedures, and awareness activities. This transition towards inclusive, object-oriented cooperation will convert drug engagement into a partnership model founded on shared value and reciprocal empowerment—where customers evolve into contributors to solutions rather than mere recipients of products or services.

Integrating AR/VR in Pharmaceutical Field Marketing

In the near future, pharmaceutical field marketing is expected to adopt immersive technologies like augmented reality (AR) and virtual reality (VR) to satisfy increasing demands from healthcare professionals (HCPs). Companies engaged in the development of specialised medication compounds are anticipated to use AR and VR tools to provide more profound and immersive views of complex drug mechanisms. Medical representatives in field may provide interactive demonstrations that graphically represent drug interactions within the human body, such as illustrating how ophthalmic drugs interact with ocular tissues, thereby improving healthcare professionals' comprehension and memory. These technologies will facilitate more personalised, memorable, and informative interactions, converting conventional product presentations into immersive learning experiences and underscoring the scientific significance of breakthrough cures.

The future of pharmaceutical product marketing in India will be increasingly influenced by changing customer expectations, necessitating a transition from conventional sales strategies to more empathic, data-informed, and transparent engagement models. We anticipate that healthcare professionals, patients, and other stakeholders will reject generic proposals in favour of personalised, morally sound, and scientifically rigorous communications. Transparency in pharmaceutical pricing, clinical trial documentation, sustainable packaging, and post-marketing surveillance will undoubtedly become essential requirements. Consequently, field agents must transform into hybrid consultants—professionals who adeptly integrate emotional intelligence with technology expertise, providing value that are beyond mere product marketing. Companies should invest in extensive training programs that focus on omni-channel communication, compliance awareness, AI integration, and ethical digital engagement.

We expect producers of both generic and specialised drug molecules to implement marketing tactics based on predictive analytics, immersive technology, and digital health integration. These innovations will address the informational requirements of healthcare professionals while simultaneously improving patient involvement through accessible formats, including films, infographics, and user-friendly summaries. Moreover, with the proliferation of social media and digital health communities, pharmaceutical companies are compelled to interact in a responsible and transparent manner, frequently partnering with patient advocacy organisations and influential opinion leaders to collectively produce credible material. Success in Indian pharmaceutical marketing will ultimately hinge on a company's capacity to foresee market changes, adopt innovation, and maintain a genuine dedication to patient-centricity, thus redefining its position as a trustworthy and progressive healthcare partner in a rapidly evolving environment.

Case Studies

Case 1: Arogyam Biolabs, a pioneering Indian pharmaceutical company located in Ahmedabad, revolutionised its marketing and sales strategy for prescription medications by utilising new technologies, including artificial intelligence, machine learning, and big data analytics. The company noticed inefficiencies in traditional medical representative-centric outreach and created an AI-integrated CRM solution that evaluated regional disease prevalence and prescription patterns. This solution allowed the sales team to pinpoint high-potential physicians in tier-2 cities such as Indore and Nagpur and interact with them through customised digital details and clinical insights. The respiratory medicine section employed machine learning algorithms to enhance visit scheduling and identify the most efficient times and techniques for engaging each clinician. The marketing team concurrently initiated an AI-driven campaign aimed at individuals enquiring about asthma symptoms on health forums, directing them to teleconsultation platforms associated with Arogyam. During these meetings, the system independently suggested Arogyam's prescriptions based on AI analysis of patient characteristics. Moreover, WhatsApp-based chatbots delivered instantaneous product updates and order support to chemists and healthcare practitioners. The amalgamation of these technologies resulted in a 37% augmentation in prescription rates within six months, notable growth in semi-urban regions, and enhanced adherence to India's increasing regulatory norms. Arogyam Biolabs illustrated the capacity of Indian pharmaceutical companies to effectively amalgamate innovation, ethics, and technology to transform patient involvement and physician outreach in the digital era.

Case 2: Bharat Swasthya Pharmaceuticals, an emerging pharmaceutical company in India's pharmaceutical industry, revolutionised its marketing strategy by effectively utilising big data and patient analytics. Historically reliant on physician representatives and personal selling, the company changed its operations following observed stasis in prescription growth within critical therapeutic sectors. BharatSwasthya collaborated with a health analytics start-up to consolidate electronic medical records (EMRs), prescription trend data, social media feedback, and distributor billing information on a centralised AI-driven analytics platform. Such collaboration allowed the corporation to reveal an unexpected increase in demand for newer-generation anti-diabetic medications in Tier-2 cities like Indore and Surat. Strategic reallocation of the sales team and tailored continuing medical education programs for younger endocrinologists in these areas increased prescriptions by 27% over the past two quarters. The dermatology section used predictive analytics to examine urban electronic medical records, uncovering an increased demand for hormone therapy among PCOS patients in metropolitan areas like Bengaluru and Chennai. A novel product line designed for this urban audience, coupled with location-specific digital ads, resulted in a 35% rise in market share. BharatSwasthya employed NLP algorithms to track adverse drug reactions using social media and helpline data, facilitating real-time revisions to drug safety labels and promoting compliance. The company implemented dynamic pricing models that utilised patient income data and prescription affordability to provide varied pricing for branded medications in urban and rural areas. Rural analytics, utilising sales data from fair pricing retailers and mobile-based patient feedback, enhanced the dosage directions in local languages, hence enhancing adherence. Sales success was monitored by predictive dashboards that combined call data and trip indicators, facilitating prompt adjustments. By 2029, BharatSwasthya Pharmaceuticals is targeting to establish itself as a data-driven leader, harmonising profitability with patient welfare. The innovative application of analytics transformed pharmaceutical marketing in India, demonstrating that ethical, intelligent, and adaptive techniques might change the future of healthcare.

Suggestive Questions from the Chapter

1. In what ways do AI and ML enhance pharmaceutical sales techniques and client targeting in India?
2. What effect do developing technologies exert on the functions of medical representatives in India?
3. In what ways might predictive analytics and IoT enhance the efficiency of pharmaceutical inventory management and cold chain logistics?
4. What is the function of AI in verifying the authenticity of prescription drugs and combating the online distribution of counterfeit medications?
5. In what ways may data-driven insights from electronic medical records enhance new product launches in targeted urban markets?
6. What obstacles may emerge from the integration of AI-driven compliance with India's developing regulatory frameworks?
7. In what ways can AI-driven predictive analytics revolutionise physician engagement tactics for pharmaceutical corporations in rural Indian markets?
8. What ethical dilemmas arise from the implementation of dynamic pricing models that utilise big data analytics in pharmaceutical marketing?
9. In what ways may blockchain improve transparency and trust in marketing strategies for specialised medicinal products in India?
10. What effect would hyper-personalised methods have on physician engagement in specialised therapeutic pharmaceutical segments?

Multiple Choice Questions

1. Which technology facilitates predictive analytics in pharmaceutical marketing and sales strategies?
   (a) Blockchain (b) Robotics
   (c) AI (d) Printing
2. Which platform facilitates direct-to-consumer marketing of prescription medications for pharmaceutical companies?
   (a) Email (b) Telemedicine
   (c) Billboard (d) Television

3. What principle guarantees that marketing adheres to ethical and legal requirements in the pharmaceutical industry?
   (a) Creativity (b) Innovation
   (c) Compliance (d) Popularity
4. What characteristics aid AI in the classification of physicians in sales planning?
   (a) Emotion (b) Clusters
   (c) Memory (d) Surveys
5. What is altering the engagement strategies between pharmaceutical companies and patients?
   (a) Literature (b) Sculpture
   (c) Technology (d) Hypnosis
6. Predictive analytics enhances pharmaceutical distribution by anticipating drug demand and minimising stockouts.
   (a) Diagnosis (b) Distribution
   (c) Innovation (d) Regulation
7. Cardiovascular awareness initiatives are enhanced by regional patient data analytics and risk prediction insights.
   (a) Seasonal (b) Regional
   (c) Generic (d) Digital
8. Analytics classifies physicians based on prescription data as "Digital Engagement Models."
   (a) Therapy (b) Outreach
   (c) Engagement (d) Research
9. Adverse reaction monitoring employs artificial intelligence and social data for early safety identification.
   (a) Clinical (b) Pricing
   (c) Predictive (d) Social
10. Region-specific pricing strategies depend on comprehensive demographic and economic patient data.
    (a) Clinical (b) Predictive
    (c) Demographic (d) Logistics

11. Which technology converts SFA from mere reporting to decision support systems?
    (a) AI (b) CRM
    (c) ERP (d) GPS
12. Which system facilitates monitoring patient outcomes in speciality pharmaceutical sales?
    (a) CRM (b) SFA
    (c) HER (d) CMS
13. Which technology in SFA provides immersive product demos for physicians?
    (a) VR (b) ML
    (c) IoT (d) NLP
14. Which integration assists pharmaceutical businesses in monitoring real-time stock availability?
    (a) SFA (b) CRM
    (c) ERP (d) HRIS
15. What guarantees adherence to marketing ethics through the use of geo-tagging in Sales Force Automation (SFA)?
    (a) Audit (b) Review
    (c) Policy (d) Manual
16. CDSCO digitisation seeks to unify medication approval inside a singular ______ platform.
    (a) Physical (b) Digital
    (c) Manual (d) Paper
17. SFA assists MRs by synchronising new marketing content to their ______ devices.
    (a) Office (b) Mobile
    (c) Home (d) Personal
18. AI-driven SFA solutions produce customised presentations for physicians depending on their ______.
    (a) Eating (b) Sleeping
    (c) Prescribing (d) Reading

19. Patient-centric rules may facilitate field marketing utilising patient ______ data.
    (a) Travel (b) Adherence
    (c) Financial (d) Social
20. Augmented reality helps HCPs understand complex pharmaceutical mechanics, decreasing physical ______ use.
    (a) Samples (b) Doctors
    (c) Patients (d) Hospitals
21. What technique improves engagement with professionals through immersive demonstration of pharmaceutical tools?
    (a) Genetics (b) Telepathy
    (c) AR/VR (d) Metaverse
22. What facilitates ethical adherence and openness in the supply chains of cancer pharmaceuticals?
    (a) Blockchain (b) Marketing
    (c) Robotics (d) Chatbots
23. Which technology facilitates the analysis of prescription patterns for targeted pharmaceutical engagement?
    (a) Animation (b) Analytics
    (c) Fluorescence (d) Telephony
24. In which sector is there a growing integration of marketing through beauty influencer engagement?
    (a) Oncology (b) Dermatology
    (c) Endocrinology (d) Psychiatry
25. What will future field agents integrate with emotional intelligence for engagement?
    (a) Agriculture (b) Technology
    (c) Linguistics (d) Cartography

Glossary

ABDM: Ayushman Bharat Digital Mission
Accessibility: Easy reach to medicines
Accountability: Being responsible for actions
Acumen: Sharp business and sales insight
Adaptability: Ability to adjust strategies
Adherence: Patient follows prescribed medication
Adherence Analytics: Monitoring patient medication compliance
ADR: Adverse Drug Reactions
Adverse Drug Reactions: Bad side effects from medicines
Adverse Event Reporting: Recording drug side effects
Advisory Board Meetings: Product guidance by Expert groups
Affordability: Cost-effectiveness of medical treatments
Agents: Intermediary service providers
Agile Decision-Making: Quick adaptable strategic changes
AI: Artificial Intelligence
AI-Assisted Decision: Making Automated Decision Making
AI-driven Analytics: Artificial intelligence powered data analysis
AI-Driven Chatbots: Auto conversational tool for customer query
AI-driven Digital Assistants: Virtual support for sales
AI-Driven Insights: Artificial intelligence based analytics

Allergies: Adverse immune system reactions
Allocation: Distribution of sales territories
Analgesics: Pain relieving medications
Analytical: Data examination and interpretation skills
Analytical Tools: Software used to study data patterns
Analytics: Data analysis for insights
Angioplasty: Heart procedure opening arteries
Antacids: Neutralize excess stomach acid
Anti:inflammatory: Reduce inflammation and swelling
Antibiotics: Bacterial infection fighting drugs
Antidepressants: Treat depression and anxiety
Anti-diabetic: Manage blood sugar levels
Antifungals: Combat fungal infection diseases
Antihistamines: Allergy symptom treatment medicines
Antihypertensives: Control high blood pressure
Antiparasitics: Eliminate parasitic disease organisms
Antipsychotics: Manage severe mental illnesses
Antipyretics: Reduce fever and temperature
Antivirals: Viral infection treatment drugs
Anxiolytics: Relieve anxiety and panic
API: Active Pharmaceutical Ingredient
Appointment: Scheduled meeting with Doctors
Appraisal: Formal evaluation of employee work performance
Approval: Regulatory permission for drug marketing
AR: Augmented Reality
Arbitrating: Settling disputes through neutral parties
Artificial Intelligence: Computer systems that mimic human thinking
Assessment: Evaluation of candidate skills
Attrition: Employee turnover and departure
Aurobindo: Major Indian pharmaceutical company
Authorization: Official permission
Automated Resume Screening: Digital filtering of job applications
Autonomy: Independence in decision making
Availability: Presence of medicines everywhere

Awareness Campaigns: Activities to inform target audiences
Ayushman Bharat: Government health insurance scheme
B.Pharm: Bachelor of Pharmacy degree
Background: Previous experience and history
Background Verification: Confirming candidate credentials authenticity
BAMS: Bachelor Ayurvedic Medicine Surgery
BARS: Behaviourally Anchored Rating Scales
Behavioural: Relating to conduct patterns
Behavioural Decision Theory: Understanding how people make choices
Behavioural Interviews: Assessing personality and attitudes
BHMS: Bachelor Homeopathic Medicine Surgery
Bias: Unfair preference in selection
Big Data: Large complex healthcare datasets
Big Data Analytics: Large-scale data pattern analysis
Bioavailability: Amount of drug entering bloodstream
Biocon: Leading Global Biotechnology Company from India
Bioequivalence: Same medicine effect comparison
Biologics: Living organism derived medicines
Biomarker Dashboards: Medical indicator tracking systems
Biopharmaceuticals: Medicines from biological sources
Biosimilars: Generic versions of biologic medicines
Biotechnology: Science using living organisms therapeutically
Blister Packs: Protective medicine packaging
Blockchain: Secure digital record keeping system
Blockchain Technology: Secure distributed transaction ledger
Blockchain-enabled Data Storage: Secure distributed ledger technology
Bonuses: Additional monetary performance rewards
Brand Awareness: Recognition of product by customers
Brand Credibility: Trust customers have in product
Brand Identity: Unique name and image recognition
Brand Positioning: Strategic product market positioning
Brand Reputation: Company's public image standing
Brand Visibility: How well known product is
Branded: Company specific product names

Brochures: Printed materials for product information
Bronchodilators: Airway opening respiratory medicines
Budget: Financial plan for expected income expenses
Budgeting: Financial planning and allocation
Bulk: Large quantity purchases
Bulk Purchasing Incentives: Discounts for buying large quantities
Bypass: Surgery redirecting blood flow
Call Planning: Strategic sales visit organization
Campaign Performance Forecasting: Predicting how well advertisements work
Candidates: Job applicants seeking positions
Cardiologists: Heart disease specialist doctors
Cardiovascular: Heart and blood vessels
Cardiovascular Health: Heart and circulation medicine
CDSCO: Central Drugs Standard Control Organisation
Certification: Professional qualification or training
CFAs: Carrying and Forwarding Agents
Chain: Connected pharmacy network
Chatbots: Automated conversational AI systems
Chemist: Licensed medicine dispenser
Chemotherapy: Cancer treatment using drugs
Cipla: Prominent Indian pharmaceutical company
Clinical: Medical practice and research
Clinical Trials: Clinical trial under supervision
CME: Continuing Medical Education
Co-branded Marketing: Two companies promoting together
Cold Chain Logistics: Temperature-controlled supply chain management
Collaborative Decision-Making: Teams working together on choices
Collaborative Engagement: Multi-stakeholder partnership marketing approach
Combination Therapy: Using multiple drugs together
Communication: Information exchange and presentation
Communication Skills: Effective verbal presentation abilities
Community Engagement: Building trust with local people

Company-organized Meets: Business events hosted by companies
Competency: Skills and knowledge capability
Competitive: Rival products and market
Competitive Analysis: Studying rival companies and products
Competitive Environment: Market conditions with rival companies
Competitor Analysis: Study of rival companies' strategies
Compliance: Following regulatory rules and guidelines
Compliance Adherence: Following rules and ethical business standards
Compliance Analytics: Checking if rules are followed
Compliance Automation: Automated adherence to regulatory requirements
Compliance Checkers: Regulatory adherence monitoring tools
Composition: Active ingredients in medicines
Conflict of Interest: Personal gain influencing decisions
Consultants: Specialist advisory medical doctors
Consumer Behaviour: How patients make buying decisions
Content Strategy: Plan for creating marketing messages
Contractual: Related to legal binding agreements
Contraindications: Medical reasons avoiding treatment
Conversational AI Systems: Interactive automated communication platforms
Coordination: Organized teamwork and planning
Corticosteroids: Anti:inflammatory hormone medications
Cosmetics: Beauty products regulatory category
Cost Efficiency: Achieving goals while minimizing spending costs
Counselling: Providing guidance and medical advice
Counterfeit: Fake or duplicate medicines
Counterfeit Drug Detection: Identification and prevention of fake medications
Coverage: Territory visit frequency management
CPD: Continuous Professional Development
CPMP: Code of Pharmaceutical Marketing Practices
Credibility: Trustworthiness and professional reputation
Credit: Extended payment terms arrangement
Creditworthiness: Ability to repay borrowed money
CRM: Customer Relationship Management

CRO: Clinical Research Organisation
Cultural Fit Assessment: Organizational values alignment evaluation
Customer Insights: Understanding of customer needs and behaviours
Customer Retention: Keeping existing clients from leaving
Customer Satisfaction: How happy clients are with service
Customer Segmentation: Dividing clients into specific groups
Cybersecurity: Protection of digital systems and patient data
Data Collection: Gathering information for business decisions
Data Mining: Finding patterns in large databases
Data Visualization: Showing data through charts and graphs
Data-centric Methodology: Information-driven strategic approach systems
Data-Driven Decision Making: Strategic choices based on analytical insights
DCGI: Drug Controller General India
Decision-Making Processes: Steps taken to make choices
Decision-support Platforms: AI-powered business intelligence tools
Delivery: Transportation of medicines
Demand **Forecasting:** Predicting future customer wants/needs
Dermatology: Skin condition medical specialty
Detailing: Product presentation to doctors
Development: Professional skill enhancement programs
Diabetes: Blood sugar metabolism disorder
Diagnosis: Medical condition identification process
Digital Detailing: Electronic product presentations to physicians
Digital Divide: Technology access limitations
Digital Empowerment: Technology-enabled capability enhancement
Digital Engagement: Online interaction strategies with stakeholders
Digital Health Integration: Technology-enabled healthcare marketing solutions
Digital Integration: Using technology in marketing plans
Digital Marketing: Promotional activities through digital channels
Digital Platforms: Online tools and websites
Digital Prescriptions: Electronic prescription generation
Digital Transformation: Converting to technology-based processes
Digital Visual Aids: Electronic presentation support tools

Direct Sales: Selling products face-to-face
Direct-to-Consumer: Selling Promoting directly to End users
Distribution: Process of delivering pharmaceutical products
Distribution Network: System delivering products to customers
Distribution Reach: Geographic areas where products are available
Distributor: Wholesale medicine supplier
Distributors: Wholesale pharmaceutical product suppliers
Diuretics: Water removing blood medications
Diversity: Variety in workforce composition
Doctor Calls: Sales Visits to Doctors
Doctor Coverage: Number of physicians contacted by sales
Doctors: Healthcare professionals prescribing medicines
Document Verification: Confirming candidate credentials
Documentation: Record keeping and reporting
Dosage: Prescribed medicine amount quantity
DPCO: Drug Price Control Order
DPP-4 Inhibitor: Type of diabetes medicine
Drone Delivery: Unmanned aerial vehicles for medicine transport
Drug Approval Process: Steps to get medicine legally sold
Drugs: Medicinal chemical substances
DTC: Direct-to-Consumer
Dynamic Pricing: Flexible pricing
Dynamic Territory Optimization: Adaptive sales region management
E:commerce: Online medicine Sales
E:detailing: Online presentations to doctors
E:marketing: Promoting products through internet
E:Pharmacy: Online pharmaceutical retail platform
E:Pharmacy Partnerships: Online pharmacy collaboration strategies
E:sampling: Electronic drug sample distribution
Ecosystem: Healthcare industry environment
Effectiveness: Achieving desired performance results
Efficacy: Medicine's therapeutic effectiveness
EHR: Electronic Health Records
EMA: European Medicines Agency regulatory body

Email Campaigns: Marketing messages sent via email
Empowerment: Granting authority and responsibility
EMR: Electronic Medical Record
Engagement: Healthcare professional interaction quality
Engagement Platform: Technology connecting companies with customers
Enzymes: Biological catalysts for reactions
Epilepsy: Neurological seizure brain disorder
Ethical: Following moral business standards
Ethical Integrity: Maintaining professional moral standards
Ethical Marketing: Responsible promotional practices
Ethics: Right and wrong behaviour
Ethnographic Research: Studying people in their natural settings
Evaluation: Performance assessment and review
Evidence: Scientific proof supporting treatments
Evidence-Based: Proven by scientific facts
Exclusivity: Sole rights to sell products
Expense: Business cost tracking documentation
Experienced: Having relevant work background
Experienced Candidate Referral: Employee recommendation hiring process
Extrinsic Motivation Techniques: External reward driven incentives
Facial Recognition: Biometric identity verification technology
Favouritism: Unfair preference toward individuals
FDA: Food and Drug Administration
Feedback: Information about performance from various
Field Force: Sales representatives working in territory
Field Force Optimization: Making sales teams work better
Field Force Training: Teaching sales teams product knowledge
Field Marketing: Direct physician engagement strategies
Field Operations: On-ground sales activity management
Field Sales Force Management: Managing medical representative teams
Field Sales Staff: People selling outside office
Final Selection and Feedback: Concluding recruitment decisions
Fixed-dose Combination: Two medicines combined in one pill
Focus Groups: Small discussion groups for market research

Forecasting: Predicting future sales or market trends
Formulary: List of approved medicines
Formulation: Drug composition and preparation
Formulations: Medicine preparation and Composition
Fraud Prevention: Measures to prevent pharmaceutical misconduct
Fulfilment: Completing and Delivering Customer Orders
Gamification: Game-like engagement motivation techniques
Gamified: Game-based assessment methods
Generic: Non-branded version of medicine
Generic Drug Molecules: Non-branded pharmaceutical compounds
Generic Medications: Non-branded pharmaceutical products
Generics: Non-branded medicine copies
Genomic Data Integration: DNA-based personalized treatment marketing
Geography: Regional territory distribution mapping
Geo-Spatial Analysis: Study of data based on location
Geotagging: Location-based digital data marking
GIS: Geographic Information Systems
GlaxoSmithKline: Major Multinational Pharmaceutical Company
GMP: Good manufacturing practice
Goals: Specific objectives to achieve
Go-to-Market Strategy: Plan for launching products
GP: General Practitioners primary doctors
GPS: Global Positioning System
GPS Tracking: Location-based monitoring technology
Graduates: Recent academic degree holders
Green Logistics: Environmentally sustainable distribution practices
Guidelines: Standardized medical treatment protocols
Gynaecologists: Women's reproductive health specialists
Gynaecology: Women's reproductive health specialty
HAL: Hindustan Antibiotics Limited
HCP: Healthcare Professional
Healthcare: Medical treatment services
High-Potential Customers: Priority target segments for sales efforts
Hiring: Process of recruiting employees

Hiring Flow: Medical representative recruitment process
Homeopathy: Alternative diluted medicine system
Homogeneity: Lack of workforce diversity
Hormonal: Related to body hormones
Hospitals: Medical treatment facilities
Hybrid Detailed Approach: Combining in-person and online methods
Hybrid Marketing: Combination of digital and traditional marketing
Hyper-personalization: Highly customized individual targeting
Hypertension: High blood pressure condition
IDPL: Indian Drugs and Pharmaceuticals Limited
Immersive Technology: AR/VR enhanced marketing experiences
Immunizations: Vaccines preventing infectious diseases
Immunosuppressants: Suppress immune system activity
Incentive Planning: Designing rewards to motivate sales performance
Incentives: Rewards to influence behaviour
Indications: Medical reasons for treatment
Inducements: Gifts to sway decisions
Influencer Partnerships: Collaborating with popular social personalities
Infrastructure: Technology and connectivity systems
Innovation: Development of new medical treatments
Insulin: Hormone regulating blood sugar
Integrity: Honesty and ethical behaviour
Interactions: Drug combinations affecting effectiveness
Interactive Digital Sessions: Online meetings with audience participation
Interpersonal: People interaction and relationship
Interviews: Formal candidate assessment meetings
Inventory: Stock of medicines
Inventory Management: Control and optimization of stock levels
Inventory Optimization: Managing stock levels efficiently
IoT: Internet of Things
IoT Devices: Internet connected smart monitoring equipment
IoT-enabled Devices: Internet connected smart devices
IPR: Intellectual Property Right
Itinerary: Planned travel route schedule

Job Analysis: Defining role requirements clearly
Knowledge: Understanding of pharmaceutical products
KOL: Key Opinion Leaders
KPI: Key Performance Indicators
Labelling: Medicine package write up for information
Landscape: Overall industry environment structure
Launch Event: Big meeting introducing new medicine
Launch Planning: Preparing strategy for product introduction
Launch Strategy: Overall plan for product introduction
Leadership: Guiding and managing others
Live-streamed Sessions: Real-time online video broadcasts
Logistics: Medicine transportation management
Logistics Planning: Organizing medicine delivery and storage
Loyalty Programs: Rewards for repeat customers
Lupin: Established Indian pharmaceutical company
M.Pharm: Master of Pharmacy degree
Machine Learning: Computer systems that learn from data
Management: Supervision and organizational control
Manufacturers: Medicine production companies
Manufacturing: Drug production industrial processes
Market Analysis: Studying customers and competition carefully
Market Basket Analysis: Study of products bought together
Market Intelligence: Industry and competitor insights
Market Penetration: Entering and expanding in markets
Market Potential: Possible sales opportunity in area
Market Research: Study of customer needs and preferences
Market Segmentation: Dividing customers into similar groups
Market Share: Company's portion of total sales
Marketing: Product promotion and sales
Marketing Authorization: Permission to sell
Mass Media Advertising: TV, Radio, Newspaper Promotions
MBBS: Bachelor Medicine Bachelor Surgery
MBO: Management by Objectives
MCh: Master Chirurgiae surgical specialty

Mediating: Helping resolve disputes between parties
Medical: Related to medicine and healthcare
Medical Detailing: Explaining drug benefits to doctors
Medical Representatives: Company salespeople to doctors
Medical Science Liaisons: Advanced clinical knowledge representatives
Medication: Pharmaceutical drugs for treatment
Medications: Therapeutic chemical substances
Merck: Global Pharmaceutical Company
Metrics: Measurable performance indicator standards
mHealth: Mobile Health
Micro-targeted Outreach: Precision-focused communication strategies
Misinformation: False or misleading health information
ML: Machine Learning
Mobile Applications: Phone apps for business
Mobile Health Applications: Smartphone-based patient engagement tools
Monitoring: Regularly checking progress against set targets
Monoclonal: Identical antibodies from clones
Morale: Team spirit and confidence
Motivation: Drive to achieve goals
MR: Medical Representative sales role
MRs: Medical Representatives selling Pharmaceutical Products
Multi-center Trials: Testing medicine in different locations
Multichannel Interaction: Multiple communication pathway engagement
Multi-Channel Marketing: Integrated approach across various platforms
Multilingual Platforms: Multi-language technology support system
NDHM: National Digital Health Mission
Negotiation: Discussion for mutual agreement
Network: Connected distribution system
Networking: Building professional relationships
Networks: Professional relationship connections
Neurologists: Nervous system specialist doctors
Neurosurgeons: Brain spine surgery specialists
NLEM: National List of Essential Medicines
NLP: Natural Language Processing

Novartis: International Pharmaceutical Company
NPPA: National Pharmaceutical Pricing Authority
NPS: Net Promoter Score
NSAIDs: Non-steroidal anti-inflammatory drugs
Omnichannel Marketing: Seamless experience across all touchpoints
Omnichannel Strategies: Integrated multi-platform marketing approach
Oncologists: Cancer treatment specialist doctors
Oncology: Medical specialty treating cancer patients
Online Application Forms: Digital candidate submission process
Online Assessments: Digital skill evaluation tests
Online Engagement: Interacting with customers via internet
Online Screening: Digital candidate evaluation methods
Open Application Process: Public recruitment announcement system
Optimization: Improving efficiency and performance
Organizational: Structure and management skills
Orthopedic: Bone joint muscle specialists
OTC: Over-the-counter medicines
OTC Products: Over-the-counter medicines without prescription
Outcome-based Regulations: Results-focused regulatory compliance
Oversight: Supervision and management control
Overstocks: Surplus stock beyond needs
Paediatricians: Children's health specialist doctors
Patents: Legal protection for pharmaceutical inventions
Patient Analytics: Patient behaviour outcome analysis
Patient Education: Teaching patients about treatments
Patient Journey Mapping: Tracking patient's treatment experience
Patient Outcomes: Treatment result measurement metrics
Patient-Centric Marketing: Marketing approaches focused on patient needs
Patient-Centric Research: Studies focused on patient experiences
Patients: Individuals receiving medical care
PCI: Pharmacy Council of India
Penicillin: First widely used antibiotic medicine
Performance: Results achieved by individuals
Performance Appraisal: Formal review of employee work results

Performance Management: System tracking and improving work results
Performance Targets: Specific goals for sales achievement
Personal Interview: Face-to-face candidate assessment
Personalized Content: Customized messages for individuals
Personalized Marketing: Customized promotional strategies
Pfizer: Major Global Pharmaceutical Company
Pharmaceutical Marketing: Promoting medical products and drugs
Pharmaceuticals: Medicinal drug products industry
Pharmacies: Medicine retail outlets
Pharmacists: Licensed medicine experts
Pharmacodynamics: Drug effects on body
Pharmacokinetics: Body's drug processing mechanisms
Pharmacology: Study of drug effects
Pharmacovigilance: Monitoring and assessment of drug safety
Physicians: Medical doctors treating patient conditions
Pilot Testing: Small trial before full launch
PMS: Post-Marketing Surveillance
Point-of-Sale Data: Information from retail purchase transactions
Polypharmacy: Prescribing too many medicines
Pool Selling: Team approach covering larger territories
Post-Launch Activities: Actions after product introduction
Precision Marketing: Targeted specialized therapeutic approaches
Precision Medicine: Personalized treatment for individual needs
Predictive Analytics: Forecasting future trends using historical data
Predictive Pricing Model: Setting prices using data analysis
Pre-launch Activities: Actions before product launch
Prescribing: Doctor's medication recommendation process
Prescription: Doctor's medicine orders
Prescription Audit: Analysis of doctor prescribing patterns
Prescription Growth: Increase in doctor recommendations
Prescription Trend Mapping: Analysis of prescribing patterns and behaviours
Prescription Verification: Authentication of medical prescriptions
Prescription Volume: Number of medicine orders from doctors

Prescriptive Analytics: Actionable recommendation generation systems
Presentation: Product demonstration and communication
Pricing Strategy: Deciding how much to charge
Primary Market Research: Original data collected directly from sources
Process of Recruitment: Systematic hiring procedures
Products: Pharmaceutical drugs and medicines
Proficiency: Skill level and competence
Profitability: Business revenue minus expenses
Promotion: Marketing activities for pharmaceutical products
Promotional: Marketing activity expense category
Promotional Materials: Marketing tools and content
Promotionals: Marketing materials for products
Psychiatrists: Mental health specialist doctors
Psychometric: Psychological trait measurement tools
Psychotropic: Affects mind and behaviour
Psychotropics: Mental health affecting medications
QR-Coded Resources: Quick response digital content
Quality: Medicine safety standards
Quality Control: Checking medicine safety standards
R&D: Research and development
Rapport: Trust building relationship development
Real-Time Dashboard: Live display of current business data
Real-Time Data: Live market information integration
Real-time Decision-Making: Making choices using current live data
Real-time Epidemiological Data: Live disease pattern information
Real-Time Feedback: Getting immediate responses from users
Real-Time Monitoring: Continuous observation and data collection
Real-time Training: Live online education sessions
Recognition: Acknowledgment of good performance
Recombinant: Proteins from engineered DNA
Recruitment: Process of hiring employees
Reference Checks: Verifying candidate work history
Referrals: Recommendations from existing employees
Regulations: Government medicine rules

Regulatory: Government rules and oversight
Regulatory Approval: Government permission to sell medicine
Regulatory Compliance: Adherence to pharmaceutical laws and regulations
Regulatory Dossier: Complete file of medicine information
Regulatory Framework: Rules governing medicine industry
Regulatory Intelligence: Information about government rules/laws
Relationship Building: Developing healthcare professional connections
Remote Patient Monitoring: Distance-based health status tracking
Reporting: Performance data communication process
Representative: Medical sales professional role
Representatives: Sales professionals promoting company products
Research: Scientific investigation for drug development
Resilience: Ability to overcome challenges
Resource Allocation: Distributing money and staff efficiently
Respiratory: Related to breathing system
Retail: Pharmacy counter sales monitoring
Retailer Calls: Sales visits to pharmacy stores
Retailers: Final medicine sellers
Retention: Keeping employees in organization
Revenue: Income generated from sales
Robotic Automation: Use of robots for operational efficiency
ROI: Return on Investment
Role-play: Simulated scenario-based assessment
Route Optimization: Finding best paths for sales visits
Rural Marketing: Promoting products in countryside
RWE: Real-world Evidence
Safety: Drug security and protection from harmful effects
Sales: Product selling and revenue generating business activities
Sales Analytics: Data analysis for sales decisions
Sales and Negotiation Skills: Persuasion and deal-making abilities
Sales Budget: Financial plan for sales revenue expenses
Sales Data Analysis: Studying information about product sales
Sales Force Automation (SFA): Technology systems for sales management
Sales Force Deployment: Placing sales team in territories

Sales Forecasting: Prediction of future sales performance and trends
Sales Growth: Increase in sales over time period
Sales Targets: Revenue goals for teams and specific performance goals
Sales Territory: Geographic area assigned to salesperson
Sales Volume: Total amount of products sold
Samples: Free medication trial portions and product trials for physicians
Sampling: Providing free product trials
Scenario Planning: Preparing for different possible situations
Scientific Detailing: Sharing research data with doctors
Screening: Initial candidate filtering process and application filtering stage
Secondary Market Research: Analysis of existing published data
Selection: Choosing candidates for positions
Self-Appraisal: Employee evaluating their own work performance
Seminars: Educational training and workshops
Sentiment Analysis: Study of opinions and emotions from responses
SEO: Search Engine Optimization
SFA: Sales Force Automation systems
Shortlisting: Narrowing down candidate pool
SMART: Specific Measurable Achievable Relevant Time-bound goals
SMART Objectives: Specific measurable achievable relevant time-bound goals
Social Determinants of Health: Factors affecting community health
Social Listening: Monitoring social media for brand mentions
Social Media Campaigns: Marketing through Social Media
Social Media Marketing: Promotional activities on social platforms
Social Media Screening: Online profile evaluation process
Sourcing Candidates: Finding potential job applicants
Specialists: Advanced medical field experts
Specialized Pharmaceuticals: Targeted therapeutic area drugs
Stakeholder Engagement: Build key business relationships
Stakeholders: Affected people and associated parties
Statement: Financial performance summary document
Stockists: Company appointed medicine wholesalers
Stockouts: Complete depletion of product inventory

Strategy: Business planning approach method
Subscription-Based Delivery: Recurring medication delivery services
Sunshine Act: Transparency in industry payments
Supply: Medicine availability system
Supply Chain: Products move from makers to consumers
Supply Chain Optimization: Improvement of distribution networks
Surgeons: Operative medical procedure doctors
Surveillance: Post-market drug safety monitoring
Sustainability: Environmental responsibility in operations
Syndicated Research: Shared market studies sold to companies
Target Audience: Specific group of potential customers
Target Demographics: Specific groups of customers
Targeted Marketing: Focused promotional efforts on specific segments
Targeted Therapies: Specific disease treatment approaches
Targets: Specific performance goals set
Teleconsultation Data: Virtual medical consultation information
Tele-detailing: Remote pharmaceutical product presentations
Telematics: GPS tracking technology for field teams
Telemedicine: Remote healthcare consultation and delivery
Telemedicine Integration: Remote consultation marketing opportunities
Telemedicine Platforms: Online doctor consultation services
Territorial: Related to geographic selling boundaries
Territory: Sales area assigned by company
Territory Management: Organizing and controlling sales areas
Territory Optimization: Maximizing sales efficiency of sales regions
Territory Planning: Strategically organize and optimize markets
Themed Product launches: Special events introducing new products
Therapeutic: Medical treatment and disease approaches
Therapeutic Areas: Specialized medical treatment fields
Therapeutics: Medicines and methods for treatment
Tier 1/2/3 Cities: Classification of Indian cities
Tiered Pricing: Different prices for different customers
Time Management Skills: Efficient task organization abilities
Time-stamping: Recording exact activity times

Traceability: Ability to track products in supply chain
Training: Skill development and education programs
Transparency: Open honest communication practices
Transplants: Organ replacement surgical procedures
Transportation: Travel method expense category
Treatment: Medical care and therapy
Trials: Clinical testing phases for medicines
UCPMP: Uniform Code for Pharmaceuticals Marketing Practices
Unethical Practices: Wrong business behaviour methods
Unmet Medical Needs: Health problems without good solutions
USP: Unique Selling Propositions
Vaccines: Preventive and disease-fighting medicines
Value Proposition: Main benefit product offers customers
Value-Based Care: Outcome focused treatment approaches
Verification: Confirming authenticity and accuracy
Video: Digital interview screening method
Video Interviews: Remote candidate assessment sessions
Virtual Assistants: AI-powered support tools
Walk-in Interview: Immediate recruitment without appointments
Warehouse Automation: Automated systems for storage and fulfilment
Warehousing: Medicine storage facilities
Wearable Health Data: Patient monitoring device information
Wearable Health Technology: Body-worn medical monitoring devices
Wearable Technology: Health monitoring devices worn by patients
Webinars: Online educational presentations
WHO: World Health Organization
Wholesalers: Bulk medicine distributors
Wholesalers' meets: Marketing Event targeting the distributors
Workforce: Total employees in organization
Workload Balance: Equal distribution of work tasks
Workshops: Interactive learning and training

Answers

Chapter 1

1.	(b)	**5**	(a)	**9.**	(b)	**13.**	(b)	**17.**	(b)	**21.**	(b)	**25.**	(c)
2.	(b)	**6.**	(c)	**10.**	(c)	**14.**	(b)	**18.**	(b)	**22.**	(c)		
3.	(c)	**7.**	(b)	**11.**	(b)	**15.**	(c)	**19.**	(d)	**23.**	(b)		
4.	(b)	**8.**	(b)	**12.**	(b)	**16.**	(d)	**20.**	(d)	**24.**	(b)		

Chapter 2

1.	(c)	**5**	(b)	**9.**	(c)	**13.**	(b)	**17.**	(b)	**21.**	(b)	**25.**	(a)
2.	(b)	**6.**	(c)	**10.**	(a)	**14.**	(b)	**18.**	(c)	**22.**	(a)		
3.	(c)	**7.**	(b)	**11.**	(c)	**15.**	(c)	**19.**	(c)	**23.**	(a)		
4.	(c)	**8.**	(d)	**12.**	(d)	**16.**	(c)	**20.**	(a)	**24.**	(c)		

Chapter 3

1.	(b)	**5**	(b)	**9.**	(b)	**13.**	(b)	**17.**	(b)	**21.**	(c)	**25.**	(b)
2.	(d)	**6.**	(c)	**10.**	(c)	**14.**	(c)	**18.**	(b)	**22.**	(b)		
3.	(c)	**7.**	(a)	**11.**	(c)	**15.**	(a)	**19.**	(c)	**23.**	(b)		
4.	(a)	**8.**	(a)	**12.**	(a)	**16.**	(b)	**20.**	(b)	**24.**	(b)		

Chapter 4

1.	(d)	**5**	(b)	**9.**	(c)	**13.**	(a)	**17.**	(b)	**21.**	(b)	**25.**	(c)
2.	(b)	**6.**	(b)	**10.**	(a)	**14.**	(b)	**18.**	(c)	**22.**	(a)		
3.	(d)	**7.**	(a)	**11.**	(c)	**15.**	(c)	**19.**	(b)	**23.**	(d)		
4.	(c)	**8.**	(b)	**12.**	(b)	**16.**	(d)	**20.**	(b)	**24.**	(b)		

Chapter 5

1.	(a)	**5**	(c)	**9.**	(c)	**13.**	(c)	**17.**	(b)	**21.**	(b)	**25.**	(c)
2.	(c)	**6.**	(a)	**10.**	(b)	**14.**	(c)	**18.**	(c)	**22.**	(b)		
3.	(d)	**7.**	(c)	**11.**	(c)	**15.**	(b)	**19.**	(b)	**23.**	(c)		
4.	(a)	**8.**	(a)	**12.**	(d)	**16.**	(b)	**20.**	(c)	**24.**	(b)		

Chapter 6

1.	(b)	**5**	(c)	**9.**	(d)	**13.**	(a)	**17.**	(c)	**21.**	(a)	**25.**	(c)
2.	(d)	**6.**	(b)	**10.**	(b)	**14.**	(c)	**18.**	(b)	**22.**	(c)		
3.	(a)	**7.**	(c)	**11.**	(c)	**15.**	(c)	**19.**	(b)	**23.**	(d)		
4.	(a)	**8.**	(b)	**12.**	(d)	**16.**	(c)	**20.**	(b)	**24.**	(d)		

Chapter 7

1.	(b)	**5**	(a)	**9.**	(b)	**13.**	(a)	**17.**	(a)	**21.**	(c)	**25.**	(c)
2.	(a)	**6.**	(d)	**10.**	(b)	**14.**	(b)	**18.**	(b)	**22.**	(c)		
3.	(b)	**7.**	(b)	**11.**	(a)	**15.**	(d)	**19.**	(b)	**23.**	(c)		
4.	(a)	**8.**	(b)	**12.**	(b)	**16.**	(c)	**20.**	(d)	**24.**	(c)		

Chapter 8

1.	(b)	**5**	(a)	**9.**	(b)	**13.**	(a)	**17.**	(b)	**21.**	(b)	**25.**	(c)
2.	(b)	**6.**	(b)	**10.**	(a)	**14.**	(a)	**18.**	(c)	**22.**	(b)		
3.	(b)	**7.**	(a)	**11.**	(c)	**15.**	(c)	**19.**	(a)	**23.**	(a)		
4.	(b)	**8.**	(b)	**12.**	(c)	**16.**	(b)	**20.**	(b)	**24.**	(b)		

Chapter 9

1.	(b)	5	(a)	9.	(b)	13.	(b)	17.	(c)	21.	(b)	25.	(c)
2.	(b)	6.	(b)	10.	(c)	14.	(c)	18.	(a)	22.	(b)		
3.	(b)	7.	(b)	11.	(c)	15.	(b)	19.	(c)	23.	(c)		
4.	(b)	8.	(d)	12.	(b)	16.	(c)	20.	(b)	24.	(c)		

Chapter 10

1.	(b)	5	(b)	9.	(a)	13.	(b)	17.	(a)	21.	(b)	25.	(c)
2.	(c)	6.	(c)	10.	(b)	14.	(c)	18.	(b)	22.	(b)		
3.	(c)	7.	(a)	11.	(a)	15.	(d)	19.	(c)	23.	(c)		
4.	(a)	8.	(b)	12.	(c)	16.	(b)	20.	(c)	24.	(c)		

Chapter 11

1.	(b)	5	(c)	9.	(b)	13.	(a)	17.	(b)	21.	(c)	25.	(b)
2.	(c)	6.	(a)	10.	(c)	14.	(d)	18.	(b)	22.	(d)		
3.	(b)	7.	(c)	11.	(c)	15.	(b)	19.	(d)	23.	(b)		
4.	(c)	8.	(a)	12.	(c)	16.	(c)	20.	(b)	24.	(a)		

Chapter 12

1.	(b)	5	(c)	9.	(c)	13.	(d)	17.	(a)	21.	(c)	25.	(a)
2.	(c)	6.	(c)	10.	(c)	14.	(c)	18.	(c)	22.	(b)		
3.	(c)	7.	(b)	11.	(c)	15.	(c)	19.	(c)	23.	(d)		
4.	(c)	8.	(a)	12.	(c)	16.	(b)	20.	(c)	24.	(c)		

Chapter 13

1.	(c)	5	(c)	9.	(d)	13.	(a)	17.	(b)	21.	(c)	25.	(b)
2.	(b)	6.	(b)	10.	(c)	14.	(a)	18.	(c)	22.	(a)		
3.	(c)	7.	(b)	11.	(a)	15.	(a)	19.	(b)	23.	(b)		
4.	(b)	8.	(c)	12.	(b)	16.	(b)	20.	(a)	24.	(b)		

Index

E

F

G

I

J

L

M

N

O

P

Q

R

S

T

V

W

www.ingramcontent.com/pod-product-compliance
Lightning Source LLC
Chambersburg PA
CBHW071222230926
51849CB00001B/10
* 9 7 8 9 3 4 9 5 6 2 1 0 3 *